A·N·N·U·A·L E·D·I·T·I·O·N·S

Homeland Security *04/05*

First Edition

Y0-CAD-809

EDITOR
Thomas J. Badey
Randolph-Macon College

Thomas J. Badey is an assistant professor of political science at Randolph-Macon College in Ashland, Virginia. He received a B.S. degree in Sociology from the University of Maryland (University College) in 1986 and an M.A. degree in political science, with a focus on military and security studies, from the University of South Florida in 1987. In 1993 he received a Ph.D. in political science at the *Institut fuer Politische Wissenschaft* of the *Ruprecht-Karls Universitaet* in Heidelberg, Germany. He served as a security policeman in the United States Air Force from 1979 to 1988 and was stationed in the United States, Asia, and the Middle East. Dr. Badey has written a number of articles on terrorism.

McGraw-Hill/Dushkin
530 Old Whitfield Street, Guilford, Connecticut 06437

Visit us on the Internet
http://www.dushkin.com

Credits

1. **The Concept of Homeland Security**
   Unit photo—© 2004 by PhotoDisc, Inc.
2. **Organizing Homeland Security**
   Unit photo—ANSER Institute for Homeland Security, 2002.
3. **The Federal Government and Homeland Security**
   Unit photo—© 2004 by PhotoDisc, Inc.
4. **State and Local Governments and Homeland Security**
   Unit photo—© 2004 by PhotoDisc, Inc.
5. **First Responders**
   Unit photo—Courtesy of Charlie Vitelli.
6. **New Technologies in Homeland Security**
   Unit photo—© 2004 by PhotoDisc, Inc.
7. **Vulnerabilities and Threats**
   Unit photo—Reuters/Fabrizio Bensch/Archive Photo.
8. **Civil Liberties and Civil Rights**
   Unit photo—Courtesy of Library of Congress.
9. **Intelligence and Homeland Security**
   Unit photo—Courtesy of the Library of Congress.
10. **The Future of Homeland Security**
    Unit photo—© 2004 by Sweet By & By/Cindy Brown.

Copyright

Cataloging in Publication Data
Main entry under title: Annual Editions: Homeland Security. 2004/2005.
1. Internal security—United States. 2. Terrorism—United States—Prevention. 3. United States. Department of Homeland Security. I. Badey, Thomas J., *comp*. II. Title: Homeland Security.
ISBN 0–07–294955–4   363'.3   ISSN 1545-9047

First Edition

Cover image © 2004 PhotoDisc, Inc.
Printed in the United States of America   1234567890BAHBAH54   Printed on Recycled Paper

Editors/Advisory Board

Members of the Advisory Board are instrumental in the final selection of articles for each edition of ANNUAL EDITIONS. Their review of articles for content, level, currentness, and appropriateness provides critical direction to the editor and staff. We think that you will find their careful consideration well reflected in this volume.

To the Reader

In publishing ANNUAL EDITIONS we recognize the enormous role played by the magazines, newspapers, and journals of the public press in providing current, first-rate educational information in a broad spectrum of interest areas. Many of these articles are appropriate for students, researchers, and professionals seeking accurate, current material to help bridge the gap between principles and theories and the real world. These articles, however, become more useful for study when those of lasting value are carefully collected, organized, indexed, and reproduced in a low-cost format, which provides easy and permanent access when the material is needed. That is the role played by ANNUAL EDITIONS.

On November 25, 2002, 14 months after the terrorist attacks of September 11, 2001, President George Bush signed into law the Homeland Security Act of 2002. A new Department of Homeland Security was created combining 22 federal agencies with over 170,000 employees and a projected budget of over $40 billion into one department. With the appointment of Tom Ridge as its new secretary on January 24, 2003, the Department of Homeland Security began the monumental tasks of restructuring major elements of the federal government, while improving domestic security and preventing a repetition of the events that gave it birth. As the Department of Homeland Security struggles to reorganize 22 already existing agencies into 5 new directorates, the debate about the long-term implications of these efforts continues. Some, already before critical of the lack of cooperation between government agencies September 11, doubt that the creation of yet another mammoth government bureaucracy will make America safer. Others are convinced that only massive efforts at the federal level can prepare America for future biological, chemical, or radiological attacks from rogue states or international terrorist networks. This anthology attempts to highlight the complex challenges and the potential pitfalls of a developing homeland security policy.

The selections in *Annual Editions: Homeland Security* were chosen to reflect a diversity of viewpoints and perspectives. In the midst of the uncertainty surrounding the creation of a new government department and with new policy announcements issued almost every week, the selection of current articles on the topic of homeland security presented a particular challenge. Articles in this introductory reader were chosen from a variety of sources and thus reflect different writing styles. Elements such as the timeliness and readability of the articles were important criteria used in their selection.

This new anthology is divided into 10 units. Unit 1 provides an overview of a myriad of challenges faced by the U.S. government in developing its plans for an effective homeland defense. Articles in this unit highlight practical problems and political factors that the new agency must consider in its efforts to protect the United States from future attacks. Unit 2 focuses on some of the organizational questions facing the new Department of Homeland Security. It examines problems related to the proposed merger of different functions and tackles important issues such as funding, oversight, and information management. The role of federal agencies in homeland security is examined in unit 3. The role of agencies such as the Nuclear Regulatory Commission and the Transportation Security Agency and programs such as Total Information Awareness are discussed. Unit 4 offers some insight into the problems faced by state and local governments and the conflicts between the federal government and localities, particularly as they relate to distribution of federal funds for homeland security. Unit 5 focuses on homeland security first responders, while unit 6 examines the role that new technologies may play in improving security. Existing vulnerabilities and potential future threats are the subject of unit 7. Threats such as bioterrorism, nuclear terrorism, and cyberterrorism are discussed. Unit 8 weighs the potential impact of homeland security legislation, such as the U.S. Patriot Act, and programs such as Total Information Awareness on civil liberties. The Intelligence Community (IC) plays a vital role in protecting the United States from future threats. Unit 9 explores some of the problems that may have led to 9/11 and offers potential solutions that may help prevent future terrorist attacks. Finally, unit 10 examines the future of homeland security.

I would like to thank Ted Knight, managing editor at McGraw-Hill/Dushkin, for suggesting the creation of this new anthology and for the tremendous support that he and the editorial staff have provided in the completion of this project. I am also particularly grateful to two of my undergraduate students, Erin Attkisson and Eric Smith, at Randolph-Macon College who served as my research assistants on this project.

Annual Editions: Homeland Security provides a broad overview of the major issues associated with homeland defense. It is our hope that this anthology will provide students with an introduction to the topic of homeland security and serve as a stimulus for further in-depth exploration of this vital topic. Please take the time to fill out the *article rating form* in the back of this volume. We appreciate your thoughts and suggestions so we can improve future editions of this anthology.

Thomas J. Badey
Editor

Contents

UNIT 1
The Concept of Homeland Security

Four unit articles examine the challenges that the United States government face as it develops its plans for defending the homeland.

Unit Overview   xvi

Department of Homeland Security
Proposed Organization by Function

UNIT 2
Organizing Homeland Security

In this unit, four articles focus on efforts to organize the new Department of Homeland Security and to define its role in the war on terrorism.

Unit Overview   30

The concepts in bold italics are developed in the article. For further expansion, please refer to the Topic Guide and the Index.

UNIT 3
The Federal Government and Homeland Security

The role of various federal government agencies within the Homeland Security Department is examined in these three articles.

Unit Overview

UNIT 4
State and Local Governments and Homeland
Security

The five articles in this unit examine the challenges that state and local governments
face in their efforts to ensure homeland security.

Unit Overview

The concepts in bold italics are developed in the article. For further expansion, please refer to the Topic Guide and the Index.

UNIT 5
First Responders

In this section, five articles discuss the role of first responders to homeland security events.

Unit Overview   **92**

The concepts in bold italics are developed in the article. For further expansion, please refer to the Topic Guide and the Index.

UNIT 6
New Technologies in Homeland Security

The three articles in this section focus on new technologies that may improve our security against terrorists.

UNIT 7
Vulnerabilities and Threats

The four selections in this section consider potential future threats such as bioterrorism, nuclear terrorism, and cyberterrorism.

The concepts in bold italics are developed in the article. For further expansion, please refer to the Topic Guide and the Index.

UNIT 8
Civil Liberties and Civil Rights

In this unit, five selections consider the impact on civil rights and civil liberties by new legislation passed to enhance security.

Unit Overview   **146**

UNIT 9
Intelligence and Homeland Security

Three selections in this unit examine the role of the Intelligence Community within homeland security.

Unit Overview   **166**

The concepts in bold italics are developed in the article. For further expansion, please refer to the Topic Guide and the Index.

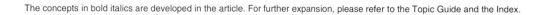

UNIT 10
The Future of Homeland Security

This final unit examines the future of homeland security in four articles.

The concepts in bold italics are developed in the article. For further expansion, please refer to the Topic Guide and the Index.

Topic Guide

This topic guide suggests how the selections in this book relate to the subjects covered in your course. You may want to use the topics listed on these pages to search the Web more easily.

On the following pages a number of Web sites have been gathered specifically for this book. They are arranged to reflect the units of this *Annual Edition.* You can link to these sites by going to the DUSHKIN ONLINE support site at *http://www.dushkin.com/online/.*

ALL THE ARTICLES THAT RELATE TO EACH TOPIC ARE LISTED BELOW THE BOLD-FACED TERM.

World Wide Web Sites

The following World Wide Web sites have been carefully researched and selected to support the articles found in this reader. The easiest way to access these selected sites is to go to our DUSHKIN ONLINE support site at *http://www.dushkin.com/online/*.

AE: Homeland Security 04/05

The following sites were available at the time of publication. Visit our Web site—we update DUSHKIN ONLINE regularly to reflect any changes.

General Sources

Anser Institute for Homeland Security
http://www.homelandsecurity.org

The Anser Institute puts out a Journal of Homeland Security as well as a weekly newsletter. Current news, upcoming events, state resources, and links about homeland security are available here.

Center for Strategic and International Studies (CSIS)
http://www.csis.org

The Center for Strategic and International Studies (CSIS), which is a nonpartisan organization, has been dedicated to providing world leaders with strategic insights on, and policy solutions to, current and emerging global issues for 40 years. Currently, CSIS has responded to global terrorism threats by developing a variety of well-defined projects and responses that are available at this Web site.

UNIT 1: The Concept of Homeland Security

Department of Homeland Security (DHS)
http://www.dhs.gov/dhspublic/

The Department of Homeland Security (DHS) Web presence offers news and other vital information about emergencies and disasters, travel and transportation, immigration and borders, research and technology, and threats and protection.

National Homeland Security Knowledgebase
http://www.twotigersonline.com/resources.html

This important nongovernmental information source offers homeland security quick links and sections on nuclear, radiological, biological, and chemical emergencies, as well as facts on hazardous devices, bombs, and explosive ordnance emergencies and natural disasters. This page links to a great number of important related sites, including quick links to federal and state security agencies and organizations.

Securing America's Borders Fact Sheet: Border Security
http://www.whitehouse.gov/news/releases/2002/01/20020125.html

Here, from the White House, is an action plan for creating a secure and smart border, an essential part of homeland security. The site offers facts about America's borders, describes the smart border of the future, explains border security initiatives in the 2003 budget, and tells how the U.S. Customs Service, the Immigration and Naturalization Service, and the United States Coast Guard will be enabled to help with homeland security.

U.S. Custom Service's Container Security Initiative
http://usinfo.state.gov/topical/pol/terror/02022505.htm

This Web site describes an initiative to safeguard the U.S. and global economies by securing an indispensable but vulnerable link in the chain of global trade: the oceangoing sea container. The plan as set forth will strengthen port and maritime security without interrupting trade flows.

UNIT 2: Organizing Homeland Security

Congress Must Reform Its Committee Structure to Meet Homeland Security Needs
http://www.heritage.org/Research/HomelandDefense/EM823.cfm

This article by Michael Scardaville may be found on this Heritage Foundation site. Scardaville explains what Congress must do to streamline the legislative process for homeland security.

Federal Emergency Management Agency (FEMA)
http://www.fema.gov

FEMA, whose presence was apparent at the site of the World Trade Center attack, reports on disasters of every sort and is part of the new homeland security organization. This home page of FEMA describes active disasters and emergencies, spotlights a guide for hurricane preparedness, the wildfire season, the federal response plan, and an "Are You Ready? Guide."

Mitretek Systems: Homeland Security & Counterterrorism
http://www.mitretek.org/home.nsf/BusinessAreas/HomelandSecurity

This Web site discusses Mitretek Systems' focus on America's vulnerability to terrorist attacks, developing solutions that enable federal, state, and local officials to detect suspicious activities, respond to crises, and help with investigations. The site discusses Mitretek's present role in homeland security and counterterrorism.

Keeping Tabs on Homeland Security
http://www.gao.gov/cghome/hs/homelandsecurity.html

This page is part of the U.S. General Accounting Office's Web site. Its table of contents links to information on all of the financial aspects of budgeting for homeland security, from finding funding to spending it.

UNIT 3: The Federal Government and Homeland Security

Container Security Institute (CSI)
http://www.csiinstitute.com/default.htm

At this Web site, you can learn about the Container Security Initiative, including relevant news articles, a list of related links, pertinent white papers, such as "Barcode Issues," which examines the role of updated barcodes in the CSI, and what impact they will have on businesses.

Customs & Border Protection
http://www.customs.ustreas.gov/xp/cgov/newsroom/press_releases/05052003.xml

This U.S. Treasury Department site offers an article that explains how Hong Kong is implementing the CSI and beginning to target and pre-screen cargo destined for the United States.

Transportation Security Administration (TSA)
http://www.tsa.dot.gov/public/index.jsp

This is the site of the government agency responsible for creating new initiatives for port security. The TSA site features a news release on the subject by Secretary of Homeland Security Tom Ridge.

UNIT 4: State and Local Governments and Homeland Security

Dark Winter

http://www.homelandsecurity.org/darkwinter/index.cfm

The Anser Institute was one of the participants in the Dark Winter study, a senior-level war game examining the national security, intergovernmental, and information challenges of a biological attack on the United States. Read all about the exercise at this page.

High Alert Status Costs Cities

http://www.fcw.com/fcw/articles/2003/0407/pol-cities-04-07-03.asp

Dibya Sarker wrote this article on the FCW.Com (Federal Computer Week) page. You'll also find many related links to the subject of the cost to cities for homeland security needs.

NGA Center for Best Practices

http://www.nga.org/center/divisions/1,1188,T_CEN_HS,00.html

This site of the National Governors Association Center for Best Practices is devoted to homeland security issues that affect states. The site's weekly newsletter reports on federal policies affecting states, offers links to respected research, as well as quick analyses on hot topics.

Security Clearance Process for State and Local Law Enforcement

http://www.fbi.gov/clearance/securityclearance.htm

The Securitiy Clearance Process for State and Local Law Enforcement is the new agency of the Federal Bureau of Investigation (FBI) for sharing with state and local law enforcement personnel pertinent information regarding terrorism, especially classified information, on a need-to-know basis. This site explains how it works.

UNIT 5: First Responders

CDC Radiation Emergencies

http://www.bt.cdc.gov/radiation/index.asp

The Centers for Disease Control and Prevention (CDC) offers the information on this page to help people prepare for a radiation emergency. It includes separate information for the public, clinicians, and first responders, and it describes CDC's role in a radiation emergency.

Community Policing Institute

http://www.umcpi.org/websites.html

This site contains a map featuring regional community policing institutes for the United States. The site contains links to the Office of Homeland Security, terrorism sites, related government agencies, and other relevant information.

FEMA: Are You Ready? A Guide to Citizen Preparedness

http://www.fema.gov/areyouready/

This guide, available at the FEMA Web site for downloading, brings together facts on disaster survival techniques, disaster-specific information, and how to prepare for and respond to both natural and man-made disasters.

Responding First to Bioterrorism

http://www.nap.edu/firstresponders/

This page from the National Academies includes expert-selected resources for first responders on bioterrorism and public safety, with a search engine of more than 3,000 related Web pages.Browse by subject area, audience, source, or type of content.

U.S. Fire Administration (USFA)

http://www.usfa.fema.gov/index.shtm

As an entity of the Department of Homeland Security and the Federal Emergency Management Agency, the mission of the USFA is to reduce life and economic losses due to fire and related emergencies through leadership, advocacy, coordination, and support.

UNIT 6: New Technologies in Homeland Security

Communications Interoperability and Information Sharing

http://www.ojp.usdoj.gov/nij/sciencetech/ciis.htm

The National Institute of Justice sponsors technology research, evaluation, and demonstration projects to address criminal justice and public safety agency communications and information-sharing needs. Read about the program at this site and also see current projects, related links, and contact information related to communications interoperability.

Defense Advanced Research Project Agency

http://www.fas.org/irp/agency/dod/poindexter.html

Dr. John Poindexter offers these remarks about the Information Awareness Office, in which he introduces new programs that are being developed with the help of information technology to deal with the asymmetric threats of terrorism to the United States. Called DARPA, the site has put forth several "way out" ideas that have been challenged by Congress.

TEN: The Enterprise Network

http://www.ten-net.org/homelandsecurity.html

Silicon Valley entrepreneurs have banded together to consider how they can apply technology to the problems of homeland security. The U.S. government has welcomed the program that TEN has presented. Find out all about this "marriage" at this site.

UNIT 7: Vulnerabilities and Threats

CDC Public Health Emergency Preparedness & Response Site

http://www.bt.cdc.gov

This site of the Centers for Disease Control and Prevention discusses biological agents and threats, tells whom to contact in an emergency, and offers resources and links as well as news. Selected agents discussed include smallpox, anthrax, botulism, plague, sarin nerve gas, ricin, and sulfur mustard.

Emergency Preparedness Information for Terrorism

http://www.tnema.org/EP/EP_DomPrep.htm

Find out about the Domestic Preparedness Program, a partnership of federal, state, and local agencies with the goal of ensuring that the nation is prepared to respond to any kind of terrorist attack. Find out more about this important program at this Web site.

The Myth of Cyberterrorism

http://www.washingtonmonthly.com/features/2001/0211.green.html

In this article, written after the September 11, 2001, terrorist attacks, Joshua Green says that there are many ways that terrorists can kill you, but that computers aren't one of them. This 10-page article makes interesting reading.

Nuclear Terrorism

http://www.nci.org/nuketerror.htm

How to prevent nuclear terrorism is the subject of this extremely thorough 29-page Web site. The site also features links to key documents.

www.dushkin.com/online/

UNIT 8: Civil Liberties and Civil Rights

EFF Analysis of USA Patriot Act

*http://www.eff.org/Privacy/Surveillance/Terrorism_militias/
20011031_eff_usa_patriot_analysis.html*

These 22 pages, presented by the Electronic Frontier Foundation,
analyze the provisions of the USA Patriot Act (USAPA) relating to
online and surveillance activities.

EPIC USA Patriot Act Page

http://www.epic.org/privacy/terrorism/usapatriot

The Electronic Privacy Information Center offers an in-depth
critique of the USA Patriot Act (USAPA) at this page. The site
includes news of several lawsuits brought by organizations under
the Freedom of Information Act seeking disclosure of information
concerning implementation of the controversial USA Patriot Act.

Human Rights Watch

http://www.hrwatch.org/press/2002/11/homeland1121.htm

Writing about the U.S. Homeland Security bill, Wendy Patten finds
that civil rights are vulnerable and immigrant children are not
protected. She calls for a bill with better safeguards for the civil
rights of individuals.

UNIT 9: Intelligence and Homeland Security

Domestic Security: The Homefront and the War on Terrorism

http://www.pbs.org/newshour/bb/terrorism/homeland/intelligence.html

Maureen Hoch reports on intelligence reform in the wake of
September 11, 2001—specifically the relationship between the
FBI and the CIA in gathering intelligence.

FAS Intelligence Resource Program

http://www.fas.org/irp/congress/2002_hr/index.html

This Web site provides material from the Joint House and Senate
Intelligence Committee hearings of 2002.

Statement of DCI Tenet on Homeland Security and Intelligence

http://www.fas.org/irp/congress/2002_hr/062702tenet.html

On June 27, 2002, George Tenet gave the testimony found at this
site before the Government Affairs Subcommittee. He describes
how the U.S. Intelligence Community plans to support the
Department of Homeland Security and all other policy agencies in
this vital area.

UNIT 10: The Future of Homeland Security

Homeland Security Act of 2002

*http://www.outsourcing-law.com/
homeland_security_critical_infrastructures.htm*

The role of private enterprise in antiterrorist operations is
described on this page with insights on effective IT outsourcing.

UNIT 1
The Concept of Homeland Security

Unit Selections

1. **America the Vulnerable**, Stephen E. Flynn
2. **The Experiment Begins**, *National Journal*
3. **A Watchful Eye**, Steven Brill
4. **The State of Our Defense**, Romesh Ratnesar

Key Points to Consider

- Is the regulation and strict policing of global transportation networks possible? Is it necessary? Why or why not?

- What are the major challenges that face the new Department of Homeland Security?

- Does the continued politicization of homeland security issues undermine national security? Defend your answer.

- Has the United States done enough to improve security since September 11, 2001? Explain.

 **Links: www.dushkin.com/online/**
These sites are annotated in the World Wide Web pages.

Department of Homeland Security (DHS)
http://www.dhs.gov/dhspublic/

National Homeland Security Knowledgebase
http://www.twotigersonline.com/resources.html

Securing America's Borders Fact Sheet: Border Security
http://www.whitehouse.gov/news/releases/2002/01/20020125.html

U.S. Custom Service's Container Security Initiative
http://usinfo.state.gov/topical/pol/terror/02022505.htm

The events of September 11, 2001, have left deep scars on the American psyche. It is almost inconceivable that the actions of so few men could change the lives of so many. Fourteen months after 9/11, on November 25, 2002, President George Bush signed into law the Homeland Security Act of 2002. In the most comprehensive reorganization of the nation's security apparatus since the passage of the National Security Act of 1947, a new Department of Homeland Security (DHS) was created. While the ultimate extent of the restructuring taking place is still unclear, most agree that this reorganization will encompass at least 22 existing federal agencies and may have an impact on as many as 180,000 employees. In its efforts to consolidate the nation's response capabilities to disasters and emergencies, natural or man-made, the Bush administration has created a new superbureaucracy that is eclipsed only by the existing Department of Defense.

As the primary legislative response to the attacks on September 11, the new DHS is in the unenviable position of having to be everything to everyone. At first glance, the mission of the DHS appears simple—to make Americans safer. Accomplishing this mission, however, will be difficult. The success or failure of the DHS depends not on its own ability to restructure bureaucracies but on the actions of others. In the long run, the new DHS is heavily dependent on support from the president, Congress, the Intelligence Community, and local law enforcement agencies to be successful.

In the wake of devastating attacks on the United States, President Bush championed the creation of the DHS. As the new kid on the block in the executive branch, however, it remains to be seen how well DHS will fare in inevitable interagency rivalries. As political leadership changes and as national priorities shift, continued executive support is critical for the long-term success of DHS. Congressional support is equally important. While the DHS was built on promises that it would cost no more than the operation of the already existing agencies, the reality is that even beyond so-called transitional costs the new department will require significant increases in future funding to be successful. A record national debt, increasing deficits, escalating defense costs, and an uncertain economic future will very quickly test congressional resolve in funding this new department.

Partly to allay the fears of the Intelligence Community that portions of its $30 billion budget could be usurped by the creation of a new department, DHS was left without its own intelligence collection capacity. In addition, DHS remains heavily dependent on the analytical capabilities and the resources of an Intelligence Community known for its reluctance to share information with others. While directors of the CIA and FBI appear to have pledged their support for the new department, it remains to be seen how bureaucratic hurdles, interagency rivalries, and future turf wars may affect this commitment. At the other end of the spectrum, DHS is also dependent on the cooperation of first responders and local law enforcement agencies. While many agree that local law enforcement agencies may be the key to the success of DHS, beyond promises of additional federal funds and some joint disaster exercises, there appears to be little effort to actively incorporate these agencies into the day-to-day activities of the DHS. Amidst rising criticism from state and local government officials of inadequate or inequitable distribution of federal counterterrorism funds, DHS faces an uphill battle as it tries to pacify the economic concerns of local law enforcement agencies and first responders, while eliciting their cooperation and support for national security priorities and policies.

As DHS begins to negotiate its new role in national security, the debate about what exactly that role should be continues. The articles in this first unit focus on the broad context in which this new role will be defined. The first article, while focusing primarily on international trade, highlights the difficulties and the complex systemic changes required to significantly reduce existing vulnerabilities. It becomes readily apparent that without significant national and international support, U.S. policies will not succeed. The second article offers an overview of some of the most important issues that face the new department, while the next article points out potential political pitfalls along the way as the DHS asserts itself in its new role. The final article in this unit, critical of administration efforts, pursues the important question of whether enough has been done to improve our national security.

America the Vulnerable

Stephen E. Flynn

THE UNGUARDED HOMELAND

It is painful to recall that, prior to September 11, Washington's singular preoccupation when it came to protecting the U.S. homeland was national missile defense. That urgency about guarding the United States from a potential missile attack now stands in stark contrast to the government's complacency about policing America's transportation networks and land and sea borders. On September 10, just over 300 U.S. Border Patrol agents supported by a single analyst were assigned the job of detecting and intercepting illegal border crossings along the entire vast 4,000-mile land and water border with Canada. Meanwhile, after a decade of budgetary neglect, the U.S. Coast Guard, tasked with maintaining port security and patrolling 95,000 miles of shoreline, was forced to reduce its ranks to the lowest level since 1964 and to cannibalize its decades-old cutters and aircraft for spare parts to keep others operational. While debates over the merits of new missile-intercept technologies made headlines, the fact that America's terrestrial and maritime front doors were wide open did not rate even a brief mention.

Until the World Trade Center towers were reduced to rubble and the Pentagon was slashed open, most Americans, along with their government, were clearly in denial about their exposure to a terrorist attack on their own soil. Oceans to the east and west and friendly continental neighbors to the north and south had always offered a healthy measure of protection. And Americans have generally disapproved of extensive efforts at domestic security. They were willing to staff and bankroll the defense and intelligence communities to contain the Soviet Union and to deal with conflicts "over there," but the quid pro quo was supposed to allow civilians at home to enjoy the full extent of their accustomed freedoms.

As Americans now contemplate the road ahead, they need to accept three unpleasant facts. First, there will continue to be anti-American terrorists with global reach for the foreseeable future. Second, these terrorists will have access to the means—including chemical and biological weapons—to carry out catastrophic attacks on U.S. soil. And third, the economic and societal disruption created by both the September 11 attacks and the subsequent anthrax mailings will provide grist for the terrorist mill. Future terrorists bent on challenging U.S. power will draw inspiration from the seeming ease with which the United States can be attacked, and they will be encouraged by the mounting costs to the U.S. economy and the public psyche exacted by the hasty, ham-handed efforts to restore security.

STOPPING THE PENDULUM

The campaign in Afghanistan has commanded the bulk of the waking moments of the senior leadership at the White House, the Pentagon, and the State Department. But at the end of the day, even if all goes well in this fight, only the terrorists of the moment will have been defeated. Places will always exist for terrorists to hide, especially before they have committed large-scale atrocities, and new adversaries will eventually arise to fill the shoes of those who have perished. As with the war on drugs, "going to the source" is seductive in principle but illusive in practice.

Governments around the world that share an interest in sustaining the free flow of people, goods, capital, and ideas must be encouraged to develop and enact common preventive and protective measures to facilitate legitimate cross-border movements while stopping illegitimate and dangerous ones.

Focusing exclusively on the current terrorist hunt, moreover, takes precious time and political capital away from confronting perhaps the most serious danger emanating from the September 11 attacks: the exposure of the soft underbelly of globalization. The very same system that fueled the glory days of the 1990s—the openness of the U.S. economy to the world, which helped spawn unparalleled growth—also increased America's vulnerability. For years U.S. policymakers, trade negotiators, and business leaders have operated on the naive assumption that there was no downside to building frictionless global networks of international trade and travel. "Facilitation" was the order of the day. Inspectors and agents with responsibility for policing the flows of people and goods passing through those networks were seen as nuisances at best—and at worst, as barriers to competitiveness who should be marginalized, privatized, or eliminated wherever possible.

By the afternoon of September 11, however, the pendulum had swung the other way. The attackers had hijacked four domestic airliners. Federal authorities nevertheless immediately ordered the closing of U.S. airspace to all flights, both foreign and domestic, shut down the nation's major seaports, and slowed truck, car, and pedestrian traffic across the land borders with Canada and Mexico to a trickle. This draconian response reflected an appropriate lack of confidence in the routine measures used for filtering the dangerous from the benign in the cross-border flows of people, cargo, and conveyances. Nineteen men wielding box-cutters ended up accomplishing what no adversary of the world's sole superpower could ever have aspired to: a successful blockade of the U.S. economy.

Luckily, an alternative exists between maintaining trade and travel lanes so open that they practically invite terrorists to do their worst, and turning off the global transportation spigot whenever a terrorist attack occurs or a credible threat of one arises. It is possible to keep global commerce flowing while still putting in place systems that reduce risk. But the first step has to be an acknowledgment that we have been sold a bill of goods by the purveyors of a "less-is-more" approach to managing globalization. Global integration will be sustainable, we now know, only if systems for regulating and policing it keep improving as well.

Governments around the world that share an interest in sustaining the free flow of people, goods, capital, and ideas must be encouraged to develop and enact common preventive and protective measures to facilitate legitimate cross-border movements while stopping illegitimate and dangerous ones. Washington has the leverage necessary to gain support for such a process, since all roads lead to and from U.S. markets. It must now put that leverage to good use. Most of the owners, operators, and users of the global transportation networks are in the private sector, however, and they must also be enlisted in any effort to enhance security and controls. The result will be an imperfect system but one that will do a much better job at controlling the risks and consequences of catastrophic terrorist attacks than do the arrangements prevailing now.

THE SHIPPING NEWS

THE WORLD was understandably shocked by the carnage and the audacity of the September 11 attacks. But the aftermath may have been almost as distressing. Americans who had felt invulnerable discovered that their government had been lax in detecting and intercepting terrorists alighting on U.S. shores. Queasiness about border control and transport-security measures quickly spread to include many of the systems that underpin the U.S. economy and daily life. Suddenly guards were being posted at water reservoirs, power plants, and bridges and tunnels. Maps of oil and gas lines were removed from the Internet. In Boston, a ship carrying liquefied natural gas, an important source of fuel for heating New England homes, was forbidden to enter the harbor because local fire officials feared that, if targeted by a terrorist, it would create a destructive bomb that could lay low much of the city's densely populated waterfront. An attack on a driver by a knife-wielding lunatic on a Florida-bound Greyhound bus led to the immediate cessation of the entire national bus service and the closing of the Port Authority Bus Terminal in New York City. Agricultural crop-dusting planes were grounded out of concern that they could be used to spread chemical or biological agents.

As Americans continue their ad hoc post–September 11 domestic security survey, they will likely be horrified by what they find. The competitiveness of the U.S. economy and the quality of life of the American people rest on critical infrastructure that has become increasingly more concentrated, more interconnected, and more sophisticated. Almost entirely privately owned and operated, the system has very little redundancy. But most of the physical plant, telecommunications, power, water supply, and transportation infrastructure on U.S. territory lies unprotected or is equipped with security sufficient to deter only amateur vandals, thieves, or hackers. For terrorists interested in causing mass disruption, these vulnerable networks present extremely attractive targets.

The U.S. economy rests on a virtually endless menu of attractive targets for terrorists.

The problem, however, is not just that the United States offers an almost limitless menu of enticing targets. It is that the existing border-management architecture provides no credible means for denying foreign terrorists and their weapons entry into the United States to get access to these targets. Given the limited staff and tools border inspectors have to accomplish their mission, they face horrific odds. In 2000 alone, 489 million people, 127 million passenger vehicles, 11.6 million maritime containers, 11.5 million trucks, 2.2 million railroad cars, 829,000 planes, and 211,000 vessels passed through U.S. border inspection systems. And the majority of this traffic was concentrated in just a handful of ports and border crossings. One-third of all the trucks that enter the United States annually, for example, traverse just four international bridges between the province of Ontario and the states of Michigan and New York.

The rule of thumb in the border-inspection business is that it takes five inspectors three hours to conduct a thorough physical inspection of a loaded 40-foot container or an 18-wheel truck. Even with the assistance of new high-tech sensors, inspectors have nowhere near the time, space, or personnel to inspect all the cargo arriving. A case in point is the Ambassador Bridge between Detroit, Michigan, and Windsor, Ontario. There, at the world's busiest commercial land-border crossing, nearly 5,000 trucks entered the United States each day in 2000. With only 8 primary inspection lanes and a parking lot that can hold just 90 tractor-trailers at a time for secondary or tertiary inspections, U.S. Customs officers must average no more than two minutes per truck. If they fall behind, the parking lot fills, trucks back up onto the bridge, and the resulting pileup virtually closes the border, generating roadway chaos throughout metropolitan Windsor and Detroit.

The loads these trucks carry are mostly low-risk shipments of auto parts and materials, but a substantial amount of the cross-border cargo with Canada originates overseas. One half of the one million containers arriving in the Port of Montréal each year, for instance, is destined for the northeastern or midwestern United States. In trying to figure out whether these containers might pose a risk, Canadian inspectors have little to go by. The cargo manifest provides only the sketchiest of details about a container's contents and in many cases includes no information about the original sender or the ultimate customer. To get more information, inspectors must engage in the labor-intensive and time-consuming act of tracking down shipping intermediaries, who are often difficult to reach.

Moreover, whether a container arrives in the United States through Canada or directly from Europe or Asia, it is unlikely to be examined when it first arrives on U.S. soil. The U.S. Customs Service inspection system is built around clearing cargo not at its arrival port but at its final destination (confusingly known as the "port of entry," referring to the point at which goods enter the U.S. economy). Chicago, for example, is the nation's fourth-largest port of entry. An importer operating there can count on Customs officers' never reviewing the cargo manifest until after a container has reached the city itself, even though the shipment may have actually entered the United States through Los Angeles, Miami, or the St. Lawrence Seaway. Furthermore, the importer has up to 30 days to transport cargo from its arrival port to its port of entry. At any given time, therefore, U.S. authorities are not in a position to verify the contents or senders of thousands of multi-ton containers traveling on trucks, trains, or barges on U.S. roads, rails, and waterways through America's heartland.

MALIGN NEGLECT

THE REMARKABLE ADVANCES in U.S. economic competitiveness over the last decade are rooted in the very openness and efficiency that have permitted people and commerce to flow so readily within and across U.S. borders. Modern businesses have capitalized on improvements in the timeliness and reliability of transport by constructing global assembly lines centered around outsourcing contracts. At the same time, managers have squeezed inventory stocks to reduce overhead costs. Traditionally, companies could ensure their ability to meet customers' demands by relying on internal production or well-stocked shelves. The advent of "just-in-time" delivery systems, however, has lowered the need to carry such insurance and has allowed corporations such as Wal-Mart to become enormously profitable.

Not surprisingly, many private-sector actors have not been fans of the administrative and inspection work of regulatory and enforcement officials charged with overseeing the people, conveyances, and cargo arriving at U.S. borders or moving through global transport networks. The pervasive view among many in the private sector has been that more inspectors mean more inspections, which translates into slower shipments. Accordingly, the growth in the volume and velocity of cross-border trade has generated little political support for a commensurate growth in the staffing, training, and equipping of the agencies responsible for providing security. Instead, those agencies have been starved of personnel, forced to work with obsolete data-management systems, and even, thanks to congressional pressure, subjected to performance sanctions if they disrupt the flow of commerce by making anything more than token random spot-checks.

Even as U.S. trade with Canada climbed from $116.3 billion in 1985 to $409.8 billion in 2000, for example, the number of Customs inspectors assigned to the northern border decreased by roughly one-quarter. Prior to September 11, half of the primary inspection booths at the border crossings in the states of Washington, Montana, North Dakota, Minnesota, Michigan, New York, Vermont, and Maine routinely remained closed because no one was there to staff them. And those inspectors working the booths that were open were evaluated in part by how well they met "facilitation" performance standards designed to reduce waiting times.

The only surprise is that the United States managed to dodge the terrorism bullet for so long.

The world may be well into the electronic age, but the U.S. Customs Service is still struggling with paper-based systems. For years its proposed Automated Commercial Environment and International Trade Data System projects have run aground on the twin shoals of flat federal budgets and industry disputes over the timing, format, and quantity of commercial data to provide to Customs in advance. It was only in April 2001 that the Customs Service received the seed money to get started on these projects, which it projects will take years to develop and implement. In the interim, inspectors will have to rely on only the bluntest of data-management tools.

If the data-management and data-mining situation is grim for Customs, it is even grimmer for other front-line agencies such as the Coast Guard, the Immigration and Naturalization Service (INS), and the Department of Agriculture, all of whose officers desperately need communication and decision-support tools to carry out their jobs. But even if these agencies did join the information age, they would still face bureaucratic and legal barriers that currently hinder them from talking with one another.

For example, consider the case of a ship with a shadowy record of serving in the darker corners of the maritime trade. Its shipping agent sends notice that it will be importing a type of cargo that does not square with its home port or its recent ports of call. Some of its crew are on an intelligence watch list because they are suspected of having links with radical Islamist organizations. And the ship is scheduled to arrive on the same day as a tanker carrying highly volatile fuel. The U.S. public might reasonably expect that with a shady past, suspect cargo, questionable crew, and clear target of opportunity, such a ship would be identified, stopped, and examined before it could enter U.S. waters. The odds of such an interdiction happening are slightly better now than prior to September 11, but there remain significant structural hurdles to anyone's being able to see all the red flags simultaneously.

The Coast Guard would be likely to know something about the ship itself and about the scheduled arrival of a tanker carrying hazardous cargo. The Customs Service might have some advance cargo manifest information (although if a ship is carrying bulk materials, this information is typically not collected until after the ship gets to its arrival port). The INS should know something about the crew, but its information is likely to arrive in a fax and must be manually entered into its computers by an agent. None of the front-line inspectors in these agencies, meanwhile, is likely to have access to intelligence from the FBI or the CIA. None of them, therefore, would see the whole picture or pass on his or her information to somebody who would. And in today's system, all of the agencies face far more potentially suspect people, cargoes, and ships than they can ever manage to inspect.

THE PRICE OF HOMELAND INSECURITY

GIVEN the disgraceful neglect of front-line regulatory and law enforcement agencies, the surprise is not that the attacks of September 11 took place; it is that the United States managed to dodge the catastrophic terrorism bullet for so long. Now that this sad precedent has been set, however, improving the capability to detect and intercept terrorists or the means of terrorism heading for U.S. shores is even more critical than before, for three reasons.

First, the absence of a credible capacity to filter illicit cross-border activity will carry a high price tag in a newly security-conscious world. The automotive industry offers a simple example. Just 36 hours after the September 11 attack, DaimlerChrysler announced that it would have to close one of its assembly plants because Canadian supplies were caught in an 18-hour traffic jam at the border. Ford then announced that five of its assembly plants would have to lie idle the following week. The cost of this loss in productivity? Each assembly plant produces on average $1 million worth of cars per hour.

A sense of defeatism about the possibility of stopping terrorism places a heavy burden on domestic policing and civil defense.

In the future, not only will the risk of another attack be higher but the number of threats and warnings that must be taken seriously will increase dramatically. U.S. policymakers may thus find themselves routinely compelled to order up a transportation quarantine as a preventive measure to protect the homeland. The costs are difficult to calculate, but they are sure to take a toll on international trade and U.S. competitiveness. Companies have made massive capital outlays in technology and infrastructure to leach as much uncertainty and friction as possible from the logistics and transportation networks. Now they may see the expected savings and efficiencies from their investments in just-in-time delivery systems go up in smoke.

The political and diplomatic costs of not getting border management right, meanwhile, will also be painfully high. If U.S. policymakers believe the chances of detecting and intercepting terrorist attacks are small, they may feel compelled to rush into foreign counterterrorist operations that are ill-advised or premature. The price of securing foreign cooperation in these efforts—often some form of diplomatic concession or averted eyes—could prove high in the long run. So restoring a sense that terrorist threats to the United States can be managed, thus giving Washington the breathing room to make considered choices about counterterrorism policy, is important.

Finally, a sense of defeatism about the possibility of stopping terrorism places a heavy burden on domestic policing and civil defense. If the assumption is that terrorists will always be able to slip through the border and set up shop on U.S. soil, then the argument for allowing law enforcement and intelligence agencies to conduct increasingly more intrusive domestic surveillance becomes compelling. Giving up on border management could also lead to the imposition of an extremely costly "security tax" on significant areas of national life.

FILTERING BAD FROM GOOD

INTERNATIONAL transportation networks are the arteries that feed global markets by moving commodities, cargo, business travelers, and tourists. Protecting that circulatory system from compromise by terrorists is an imperative unto itself, even if an adversary or a weapon of mass destruction could find an alternative way into U.S. territory. In fact, this task deserves top billing over other, competing defensive measures such as constructing a missile defense system. If a missile were fired at a U.S. city and it could not be intercepted, it could cause horrible destruction and mass casualties. But if a weapon of mass destruction were loaded on a boat, truck, train, or maritime container and set off in a congested seaport, on a bridge during rush hour, or downtown in a major urban center, the results would be even worse. In addition to the local destruction and casualties, such an attack would expose the lack of credible security within the country's transportation networks and bring them to a complete standstill. The first scenario would involve damage caused by the adversary; the second would include both the damage caused by the adversary and the costs associated with a self-applied tourniquet to our global transport lifelines.

Enhancing security for transportation networks, therefore, is partly about preventing terrorists from exploiting those networks and partly about sustaining the continued viability of international commerce. The authorities can accomplish this task by moving from ad hoc controls at the borders of individual countries toward point-of-origin controls, supported by a concentric series of checks at points of transshipment (transfer of the cargo from one conveyance to another) and at points of arrival. This more comprehensive system is particularly important for the United States, where trying to distinguish the illicit from the licit at the border or within ports is like trying to catch minnows at the base of Niagara Falls.

Moving upstream is not as difficult or futuristic a task as it might appear. As a start, the United States and its allies should capitalize on the enormous leverage over global transportation networks that just a few key jurisdictions exercise. The overwhelming majority of trade moves by sea, and at some point during its journey nearly all the ships that carry it must steam into or out of just a handful of global megaports such as Long Beach and Los Angeles, Hong Kong, Singapore, Hamburg, Antwerp, and Rotterdam. If the port authorities and governments responsible for just these seven ports could agree to common standards for security, reporting, and information-sharing for operators, conveyances, and cargo, those standards would become virtually universal overnight. Anyone who chose to not play by those rules would be effectively frozen out of competitive access to the world's major markets.

Megaports could require, for example, that anyone who wants to ship a container through them must have that container loaded in an approved, security-sanitized facility. These facilities would have loading docks secured from unauthorized entry and the loading process monitored by camera. In high-risk areas, the use of cargo and vehicle scanners might be required, with the images stored so that they could be cross-checked with images taken by inspectors at a transshipment or arrival destination.

After loading, containers would have to be fitted with a theft-resistant mechanical seal. The drivers of the trucks that deliver goods to the port would be subjected to mandatory background checks. Jacob Schwartz, a professor of mathematics and computer science at New York University, has suggested that the routes of trucks into ports could be monitored and even controlled by available technology. A microcomputer connected to a transponder and global positioning system (GPS) could be attached to the motor control system of the trucks involved, so that if they strayed out of licensed routes their engines would shut down and the authorities would be automatically notified. The transponder, like those used for the "E-Z Pass" toll-payment system across the northeastern United States, would give authorities the ability to monitor and control each vehicle's movements, and it would be programmed so that tampering with it would result in an automatic alert to the police.

GPS transponders and electronic tags could also be placed on shipping containers so that they could be tracked. A light or temperature sensor installed in the interior of the container could be programmed to set off an alarm if the container were opened illegally at some point during transit. Importers and shippers would be required to make this tracking information available upon request to regulatory or enforcement authorities within the jurisdictions through which their cargo would move or toward which it would be destined.

Manufacturers, importers, shipping companies, and commercial carriers, finally, could agree to provide authorities with advance notice of the details of their shipments, operators, and conveyances. This early notice would give inspectors time to assess the validity of the data, check it against any watch lists they may be maintaining, and provide support to a field inspector deciding what should be targeted for examination.

As with many safety or universal quality-control standards, private trade associations could hold much of the responsibility for monitoring compliance with these security measures. As a condition of joining and maintaining membership within an association, a company would be subjected to a preliminary review of its security measures and would agree to submit to periodic and random spot checks. Without membership, access to ships servicing the megaports, in turn, would be denied.

Many border-control agencies are still using nineteenth-century means for collecting and sorting data.

To confirm the legal identity and purpose of international travelers, off-the-shelf technologies could be readily embraced to move away from easily forgeable paper-based documents such as visas or passports. Governments could embrace universal biometric travel identification cards that would contain electronically scanned fingerprints or retina or iris information. These ATM-style cards would be issued by consulates and passport offices and presented at the originating and connecting points of an individual's international travel itinerary. Airports, rail stations, rental car agencies, and bus terminals could all be required to install and operate card readers for any customers moving across national jurisdictions. Once entered, electronic identity information would be forwarded in real time to the jurisdiction of the final destination. The objective would be to provide authorities with the opportunity to check the identity information against their watch lists. If no red flags appeared, it would not be necessary to conduct a time-consuming and intrusive search. For noncitizens, a country could also require the presentation of these cards for renting cars, flying on domestic flights, or using passenger rail service.

Mandating that data be provided is one thing; effectively managing and mining it so as to make a credible determination of risk is another. Front-line agencies must be brought out of their stovepiped, nineteenth-century record-keeping worlds. To reduce the potential for overload, some existing data collection requirements could be eliminated, consolidated, or accomplished by other methods, such as statistical sampling. The goal should be to create within each national jurisdiction one clearinghouse for receiving data about people, cargo, and conveyances. All government users of the data could then collect and analyze what they needed from that pool.

Inspectors and investigators assigned to border-control agencies will continue to play a critical role in the timely detection and interception of anomalies. To be effective, however, a serious effort must be made to improve their pay, staffing numbers, and training, and to push them beyond the border itself into common bilateral or multilateral international inspection zones. Megaports and regional transshipment ports should play host to these zones and allow agents from a number of countries to work side by side. Such an approach would take better advantage of information collected by law enforcement officials at the point of departure, allow transport-related intelligence to get into the security system sooner, and reduce the congestion caused by concentrating all inspections at the final destination. The bilateral inspection zones set up by French and British officials at both ends of the English Channel tunnel could serve as a model.

RETHINKING HOMELAND SECURITY

AS THE NINETEENTH-CENTURY Prussian military theorist Karl von Clausewitz famously noted, "war is not an independent phenomenon, but the continuation of politics by other means." At its heart, therefore, an appropriate response to the kind of asymmetric warfare that catastrophic terrorism represents must weaken its political value for an adversary. If an attack, even on the scale of those carried out on September 11, fails to translate into any tangible change in U.S. power or policies, then it becomes only a contemptible act of mass murder and high-end vandalism. Of course, a few evil people will still remain willing to commit such crimes. But a terrorist who concludes that the business of America will continue unabated despite an attack on U.S. soil will likely find little value in launching such an attack.

Reducing the risk and consequences of attacks directed against the United States cannot be accomplished simply by tweaking the role and capabilities of agencies whose writ runs only to the nation's shores.

Building a credible system for detecting and intercepting terrorists who seek to exploit or target international transport networks would go a long way toward containing the disruptive potential of a catastrophic terrorist act. A credible system would not necessarily have to be perfect, but it would need to be good enough so that when an attack does occur, the public deems it to be the result of a correctable fault in security rather than an absence of security.

Such a system, however, must extend beyond U.S. borders. Washington must move quickly beyond the Bush administration's initial steps in this area, which seem based on a mission of homeland security seen largely through the prism of civil defense. If America's future safety and prosperity were tied only to infrastructure located on U.S. soil, then a White House Office of Homeland Security dedicated to herding federal, state, and local bureaucratic officials might be appropriate. In fact, however, the United States depends on infrastructure that spans the globe.

Reducing the risk and consequences of attacks directed against the United States, therefore, cannot be accomplished simply by tweaking the roles and capabilities of agencies whose writ runs only to the nation's shores. Better preparedness and coordination of domestic agencies is important and necessary, but it is not sufficient. And the same is true for military and diplomatic campaigns overseas to root out international terrorism at its source. Manhunts carried out by U.S.-led international posses will continue to be an essential weapon in the counterterrorism arsenal. But the more daunting challenge will be to reduce the vulnerability of the systems of transport, energy, information, finance, and labor.

The massive post–September 11 outpouring of public and international support for combating terrorism will inevitably wane. This makes it all the more urgent to begin the painful process of fundamentally reforming border-management practices so that good and bad flows can be distinguished from one another and treated appropriately. Ultimately, getting homeland security right is not about constructing barricades to fend off terrorists. It is, or should be, about identifying and taking the steps necessary to allow the United States to remain an open, prosperous, free, and globally engaged society.

STEPHEN E. FLYNN is Senior Fellow in the National Security Studies Program at the Council on Foreign Relations and a Commander in the U.S. Coast Guard. This article is adapted from his chapter in *How Did This Happen? Terrorism and the New War*, published by PublicAffairs and *Foreign Affairs* with the support of the Council on Foreign Relations.

Homeland Security

The Experiment Begins

A NEW HOMELAND SECURITY DEPARTMENT FACES ENORMOUS CHALLENGES IF IT IS TO MAKE THE COUNTRY SAFER. *NATIONAL JOURNAL* WRITERS LOOK AT 15 SUCH CHALLENGES, FROM SIMPLE ENACTMENT TO FINDING ENOUGH MONEY AND STAFF.

No matter how you cut it, putting together a new Homeland Security Department will be a jigsaw puzzle of the most demanding kind. The pieces are supposed to come from eight major departments of government and dozens of smaller agencies. The parts touch on more than 80 congressional committees of oversight and funding. And the new conglomeration must fuse together 170,000 government employees who do everything from cleaning up oil spills to preventing germ warfare. Here are some key tests.

FROM THE HILL, 535 IDEAS

CONGRESS

Ask 10 lawmakers their thoughts on the best way to handle President Bush's proposal to create a Homeland Security Department, and you're likely to get 20 different answers. Most members of Congress generally agree that it is a worthy idea. And there is little doubt that Congress will ratify the creation of the department sometime later this year.

But crafting the actual legislation, and gaining support for it among 535 often-unruly members, will certainly be messy. Moreover, assuming that the department is created, larger long-term problems loom, as congressional leaders will have to decide which committees will oversee it and handle its appropriations. At bottom, Bush's proposal not only surprised Capitol Hill, it has also focused unwelcome attention on the internal problems and increasing dysfunction of the narrowly divided House and Senate.

As the White House has pointedly noted, some 88 congressional committees and subcommittees have jurisdiction over the various agencies that will make up the proposed department. Members of many of those panels can be expected to fight vigorously to protect their legislative turf. The face-offs "will probably resemble Afghani warlords dividing territory," said congressional expert Marshall Wittmann of the Hudson Institute.

"I was watching the President's speech the other night in the cloakroom," remarked Sen. Evan Bayh, D-Ind., in an interview, "and one of my colleagues sitting next to me said, 'Wonderful, another agency to have jurisdiction over.' My colleague wasn't joking. That will cross a lot of minds here. And that game has already begun. But, at the end of the day, the American people are going [to demand] that we accomplish this."

Nevertheless, passing the requisite legislation will pose severe strains on members as they prepare for the November election and struggle to move other essential bills. In the wake of the terrorist attacks last year, Congress was able to respond unusually rapidly to approve several urgent measures. Since then, however, more-routine legislation has fallen victim to partisanship and gridlock.

HILL LEADERSHIP: The lawmakers will have to add this massive reorganization to an already busy summer calendar.

"This has to be looked at seriously," said Rep. Sander M. Levin, D-Mich., of Bush's proposal. "But you can't do that if we [in the House] continue to meet only two days a week.... There will have to be a very different relationship between the White House and Congress, between the majority and the minority."

The White House has offered to send Congress specific legislation to assist in creating the new department, something this administration isn't in the habit of doing. But on June 11, White House Press Secretary Ari Fleischer said, "It will take a couple of weeks" to deliver. That would get the bill to Congress just as it leaves for its weeklong Fourth of July recess. After that, the House is scheduled to be in session for only three weeks, and the Senate for four weeks, before departing on their long summer recess until after Labor Day.

House Minority Leader Richard A. Gephardt, D-Mo., got a positive response on June 11 when he urged fellow congressional leaders to pass the legislation creating the new department by September 11, the one-year anniversary of the terrorist attacks. But a June 7 comment by a spokesman for House Speaker J. Dennis Hastert, R-Ill., may have been more realistic: "It will be a miracle if we don't have a lame-duck" session after the November election to finish the job, the aide said.

On the positive side for the proposal, Democrats cannot afford to appear to stall a popular president's priority in the war against terrorism. In the Senate, Majority Leader Thomas A. Daschle, D-S.D., has been advocating the creation of such a department for some time. The Governmental Affairs Committee, chaired by Sen. Joe Lieberman, D-Conn., last month approved a bill, on a party-line vote, to do just that, and the White House drew heavily from the committee's plan. To speed the process, Daschle will make Lieberman's panel the primary voice on the bill in the Senate.

In the House, deciding which panel should handle the bill is dicier. The chamber's rules give the Government Reform Committee authority over reorganization plans, but Chairman Dan Burton, R-Ind., is a fiery maverick with modest legislative skills. Republican leaders appeared inclined to create a select committee to work on the bill, a move that would allow them to more tightly control the process.

As the debate begins, many members are suggesting that Congress has its own restructuring to do in order to effectively oversee what would be the federal government's second-largest department. "It is hard to see how Congress could do a decent job of authorizing and overseeing what the new department does without a new Committee of Homeland Security," Lieberman said in an interview. "It's that big."

The start of the new Congress in January would be the ideal time for each chamber to make changes to its rules—primarily on committee jurisdiction—to respond to the new imperatives. Especially in the House, party leaders have additional leverage during the organizational period. The possibility of a change in party control in each chamber could add to that opportunity.

–Kirk Victor and Richard E. Cohen

THE SEARCH FOR A MAGICIAN

LEADERSHIP

WANTED: Drill sergeant, manager, cheerleader, politician, guerrilla fighter, tent preacher, juggler, comedian, school principal, arm-twister, and multitasker for thankless job. Expertise necessary in: national defense; management of a large government agency, state, or company; law enforcement; intelligence analysis; and domestic threat assessment. Familiarity with corporate or government mergers, large computer systems, natural disasters, immigration law, industry lobbying, environmental protection, maritime safety, drug interdiction, and animal diseases a plus. Candidates under retirement age preferred.

The universe of serious potential contenders for the yet-to-exist job of secretary of the yet-to-exist Department of Homeland Security is small. Ideally, the new secretary would be a larger-than-life figure, a friend of George W., and someone who would command instant respect and possess the managerial ability to get an organization comprised of bureaucratic orphans to all salute one new departmental flag.

"You want a combination of three or four different leaders: H. R. Haldeman, William Ruckelshaus, Donna Shalala, a little Don Rumsfeld. You want Joe Califano's independent streak. You want a little bit of John Foster Dulles—he was crazy but brilliant," offers Paul Light, vice president of governmental studies at the Brookings Institution. Still, Light warns, "it is a job made for failure."

So we are looking for a cross between President Nixon's sharp-elbowed chief of staff; the first administrator of the Environmental Protection Agency; a former tough-cookie secretary of Health and Human Services; a hawkish secretary of Defense; a former deputy secretary of Defense and secretary of Health, Education, and Welfare; and President Eisenhower's secretary of State.

The early, unofficial contenders for the dubious honor of becoming secretary of Homeland Security include Federal Emergency Management Agency Director Joe M. Allbaugh, a Bush confidante; Deputy Secretary of State Richard L. Armitage; former Lockheed Martin CEO Norman R. Augustine; former Secretary of State James A. Baker III; Sen. Bill Frist, R-Tenn., who is a surgeon; former Virginia Gov. James S. Gilmore III; former New York City Mayor Rudolph W.

Giuliani; Secretary of State Colin L. Powell; and, of course, Homeland Security Director Tom Ridge.

Other lesser-known, but perhaps equally qualified candidates could include New York Police Commissioner Raymond W. Kelly, a former commissioner of the Customs Service; former Coast Guard Commandant Adm. James M. Loy; Gen. Barry R. McCaffrey, the Clinton administration's drug czar; and John J. Hamre, president of the Center for Strategic and International Studies and former deputy secretary of Defense.

In an unscientific *National Journal* poll of homeland security experts, the top nominee by far was Powell. But if the president can't clone Powell and doesn't want to transfer him, the White House will have to weigh other options. Although Ridge is the leading candidate, he may not fit the bill. The new secretary "is going to have to have an iron fist and a velvet glove. He's got to reassure the public that he's making progress, but he's going to have to discipline this agency. I don't know if [Ridge has] got it," Light says. "I would go with a governor. I don't know whether Tom Ridge is the right governor." Columnist Robert Novak revved up the Washington rumor mill when he reported that some White House insiders don't want Ridge.

Having sponsored a bill to create a Homeland Security Department, Rep. Jane Harman, D-Calif., has put considerable thought into who should run it. "It should be someone with big vision and attention to the hard work of integrating very diverse cultures. I think the kind of challenge here is comparable to the challenges of a big corporate merger," she says. Plus, she adds, the secretary needs "an ability to play Washington politics" and "a thick skin."

Thick skin and sharp elbows. The first challenge a new secretary will face may be securing the new department's bureaucratic territory. This week, Attorney General John D. Ashcroft was homeland security's globetrotter-in-chief as he traveled from Moscow to Budapest to Bern, Switzerland. Would such duties fall to the Homeland Security secretary? "With this system in place, there will be a risk that there will be interagency competition," says Gilmore, who is heading an ongoing congressional commission on homeland security. "If that should emerge, this department head is no stronger than the attorney general or secretary of Defense or secretary of State. Sure, he will have to be assertive."

In Light's view, the new secretary will have to tell the president. "You need to muzzle John Ashcroft."

Unfortunately, none of the men now being mentioned for the new job seems to be the perfect candidate, so Bush needs to look for the best combination of leaders, according to homeland security expert Frank Hoffman. That strategy might put a former governor, such as Ridge or Gilmore; a known hard-hitter, such as Armitage; or a former CEO, such as Augustine, at the top of homeland security to work their political and managerial magic. And the No. 2 slot might go to someone, such as Kelly or

Loy, who knows the federal bureaucracy and who would be more likely to win the trust of the department's newly assembled troops.

Regardless of who gets tapped, the new secretary's level of success might be difficult to measure for a very long time. "A year from now, we'll be saying, 'What's different?'" Light predicts. But he cautions that an accurate assessment may not be possible for years.

–Siobhan Gorman

CREATING A NEW CULTURE

ESPRIT DE CORPS

Creating a unified "corporate culture" is sure to be one of the toughest challenges facing the proposed new Department of Homeland Security, which will be cobbled together from 22 different federal entities, each with its own historical role and professional expertise.

> **JOSEPH L. BOWER:** "The best person is an 'insider-outsider,' someone who's enough of an insider to know the business, but is also a maverick who isn't afraid to shake things up."

Experts point to private-sector mergers as an analog for understanding the challenge. Judging by the experience of business conglomerations, "the new department will face enormous problems," says Ralph Biggadike, a professor of management at Columbia University. "To think that a structural solution can bring about a major improvement in performance is a major mistake. Fixing the structure alone isn't enough to get at the culture."

Ironically, the plan for a new, multifaceted department emerges at a moment when the corporate world has begun to shy away from complicated conglomerations. Beginning in the 1970s, corporations considered it fashionable to buy up related—and unrelated—businesses and put them under one umbrella, hoping to hedge the parent company's financial bets or to promote "synergy" among similar types of enterprises.

The difficulty of creating a coherent corporate culture is one of the main reasons why management thinkers are now questioning these once-hot notions and advocating a return to "core competencies." The stock market's slide and the implosion of such mega-corporations as Enron and Tyco International have contributed to the skepticism.

One consistent problem with bringing together an array of entities under one roof, says Princeton University sociologist Frank Dobbin, is that it's hard to find leaders with experience in all the relevant operational areas. If a company or a Cabinet department is forced to hire a manager without hands-on experience in all fields, that manager will necessarily depend on subordinates to manage their own fiefdoms. And that is a recipe for "a holding company, not a department," says Dobbin, who has studied organizational behavior in both government and the corporate world.

"One of the problems is that employees often have existing loyalties to the old chain of command, and it's hard to get people to switch over," he says, adding that creating a truly integrated corporate culture "can take 10 to 15 years—enough time for a large portion of the workforce to turn over."

Many of the merged companies that have created a strong, unified culture—such as Cisco Systems following several targeted acquisitions, and Chase Manhattan after its 1996 merger with Chemical Bank—have worked extraordinarily hard at it, Biggadike says. These companies established post-merger committees to ensure that the newly acquired company became fully integrated into its new parent.

Strong leadership is also crucial, says Joseph L. Bower, a professor of business administration at Harvard Business School. According to Bower, "The best person is an 'inside-outsider,' someone who's enough of an insider to know the business, but is also a maverick who isn't afraid to shake things up." Using carrot-and-stick incentives with senior and midlevel managers is also important. "The companies that succeed provide payoffs for abandoning the old culture and administer penalties if [employees] don't," he says.

On the upside, a new Department of Homeland Security will have an important prerequisite for establishing a strong corporate culture—the clear and unassailable mission of preventing terrorist attacks on U.S. soil. On the downside, leaders won't have the luxury of time to forge a department-wide culture and assimilate the entities that come together from many existing departments and agencies.

There's also an irony: Creating a culture at the new department will mean minimizing or erasing the existing cultures of the entities that are being merged—even of those, such as the Coast Guard and the Customs Service, that work well now.

–Louis Jacobson

INFORMATION UP, PROTECTION DOWN

INFORMATION-SHARING

To build a good intelligence apparatus that gets critical information to top leaders, a new homeland security department must create "an environment that allows second- and third-tier managers to flourish [with] the right incentive systems," said Michael Bromwich, who served as inspector general at the Justice Department from 1994

until 1999. Creating such incentives, he said, "is a matter of tone, of example, of exhortation, [and] of strategic planning in assigning top priority to these matters." It is easier to create incentives for a new organization than to incorporate them into a long-established bureaucracy, he added.

COLEEN ROWLEY: The Minneapolis FBI agent said higher-ups thwarted good field investigations.

President Bush has recognized this information-flow challenge, not only by pushing for a centralized homeland security command but also by urging low-level intelligence experts to push back against risk-averse managers. "If you're a front-line worker for the FBI, the CIA, some other law enforcement or intelligence agency, and you see something that raises suspicions, I want you to report it immediately," Bush said on June 6. "I expect your supervisors to treat it with the seriousness it deserves."

A critical test, said Bromwich, will come when an intelligence official sparks a firestorm, perhaps by opening himself or herself to charges of racial profiling. "There will be a lot of media and congressional pressure to hang him out to dry," Bromwich predicted.

Lower-level officials must be protected if those higher up want the new organization to be willing to act on incomplete information and make potentially controversial decisions, such as shutting down an airport the day before Thanksgiving, say intelligence experts. "In the past, Congress and the press have excoriated CIA and FBI officers for alleged misdeeds.... From the point of view of the career officers, people were out there taking risks, and they got in trouble for it," said Jeffrey Smith, who was general counsel to the CIA in 1995 and 1996 and is now a partner at the law firm Arnold & Porter.

A new Homeland Security Department will help deal with managers' aversion to risk because the department head's only responsibility will be homeland defense, said Stewart Baker, who was the general counsel at the National Security Agency from 1992 until 1994. The chief "has got to get that job done, and so he is less likely to be deterred by things that are potentially painful—bad press—than would someone for whom it is one of six jobs," said Baker, now a partner at the law firm Steptoe & Johnson.

Moreover, once they are gathered in a focused organization, the lower-level intelligence experts and their midlevel managers should see a clear set of top-level customers for their work and also get constant guidance and support from the top, Baker said.

But Bill Arkin, an independent military analyst, argues that the government needs better intelligence analysts, not another bureaucracy. "Our problem from 1990 to the present is that we face a crisis of intelligence analysis… because who wants to have a high-level job in the U.S. government as an intelligence analyst?"

Getting the right analysts and other staffers for the proposed department won't be easy, said Bromwich. They have to be trained well, understand how their enemy thinks, and, preferably, speak his dialect. "It is a lot easier said than done," Bromwich said.

Technology can help, but only after the department mission is made clear and a supportive bureaucratic culture starts to grow, Baker said. "The culture comes first, not the technology," he said. But once culture and technology are in place and become complementary, each will foster the other, he predicted.

–Neil Munro

FBI AND CIA REMAIN UNTOUCHED

INTELLIGENCE-GATHERING

One of the ironies of Washington politics is that major reforms of the federal government often have only a tangential connection to the scandals that propel them. Case in point: Because the Bush administration's proposed Department of Homeland Security came amid congressional hearings into intelligence lapses leading up to last year's terrorist attacks, much commentary has cast the ambitious plan as an answer to intelligence failures. In fact, the proposed reorganization leaves the nation's vast intelligence apparatus—comprising mainly the CIA, the FBI, the National Security Agency, and the Defense Department—largely untouched.

JAMES STEINBERG: "Before and after September 11, the major problem we've had in counter-terrorism is a disconnect between intelligence-gatherers, policy makers, and field operators."

A Homeland Security Department, however, would undoubtedly add a significant new player to an already crowded national security arena, with uncertain effect. Its proposed 1,000-person Information Analysis and Infrastructure Protection Division, 80 percent of which would be staffed by the FBI's relocated National Infrastructure Protection Center, is supposed to act as an analytical "clearinghouse" fusing all relevant intelligence on threats to the American homeland gathered by the U.S. intelligence community. Lost in much of the coverage to date is the fact that Homeland Security would also have significant intelligence-gathering and law enforcement capability of its own that is currently embedded in agencies such as the U.S. Coast Guard, the Secret Service, the Customs Service, the Border Patrol, and the Immigration and Naturalization Service.

Some experts view a Homeland Security Department's greatest potential attribute as the direct connection it could establish between intelligence analysis and action. "Before and after September 11, the major problem we've had in counter-terrorism is a disconnect between intelligence-gatherers, policy makers, and field operators," said James Steinberg, a National Security Council official in the Clinton administration and now a senior fellow at the Brookings Institution. A Homeland Security Department, by putting all those players under one umbrella with a single overriding mission, "can create better linkages between intelligence on the threat, informed policy choices, and operators in the field who need improved intelligence to do their jobs better."

A new department would do little, however, to address persistent problems within U.S. intelligence agencies, which collectively have struggled to adjust to emerging post-Cold War threats. In particular, the CIA and FBI have failed to share information or coordinate their operations sufficiently to thwart transnational terrorists who are increasingly adept at exploiting the gaps in borders between nations, and between U.S. government departments. If Homeland Security becomes just another competing player in an already dysfunctional intelligence community, or if it inadvertently creates gaps in America's defenses during this vast restructuring, some experts fear the department could do more harm than good.

"Though the details remain vague, the idea that you are somehow going to solve our intelligence problems by creating a third, potentially competing, entity for intelligence analysis doesn't strike me as a promising solution," said Jeffrey Smith, a former general counsel of the CIA. "Creating a huge department so quickly will also inevitably create massive dislocations and disruptions in the affected agencies. I'm concerned the terrorists will see that as an opportunity to attack us while the government is distracted."

Though it is presently being eclipsed by the proposed Homeland Security Department, the major restructuring of the FBI that was announced in May is likely to have an even more profound impact on U.S. intelligence operations. The FBI, besides relaxing headquarters oversight of field offices and hiring hundreds of new analysts to bolster its feeble intelligence capability, has refocused its entire mission from fighting crime to preventing domestic terrorist attacks and disrupting terrorist organizations. Those reforms go a long way toward recasting the FBI as a domestic intelligence agency, a concept long rejected by an American public jealously protective of its civil liberties.

For the CIA, the most significant outstanding question is what kind of relationship it will establish with its new "customers" at a Homeland Security Department. If the CIA remains stingy in sharing its uncensored and unprocessed intelligence data—out of the understandable fear of compromising sacrosanct "sources and methods"—then it is unlikely that the proposed department will have sufficient dots to connect into a larger and coherent picture of the terrorism threat.

"If Homeland Security's analysis sector has unfettered access to intelligence data gathered by the FBI and CIA, then I think it will be able to create a highly focused overview of threats to the homeland," said retired Air Force Gen. Charles Boyd, the president of Business Executives for National Security and a former executive director of the Hart-Rudman commission, which in 2000 proposed establishing a homeland security department. "If the new department cannot get the raw data, then you simply haven't solved our intelligence problem."

–James Kitfield

A NEW INFORMATION CLEARINGHOUSE

INTELLIGENCE ANALYSIS

Assume, for one blissful moment, that intelligence flows like a living stream: Cultural barriers fall away, institutions open up, classified computer networks interconnect, and the FBI, CIA, DIA, NSA, and all their ilk share information freely with a Department of Homeland Security. Then what? What exactly does the department do with all this data, besides drown?

The administration has sold its proposed department as a central clearinghouse for terrorist threats, where each agency's leads are assembled like a giant jigsaw puzzle into a clear warning of the next attack. As the White House briefing book points out, the CIA collates data on threats to American interests abroad (or tries to: Remember the USS *Cole*, and the embassies in Nairobi and Dar es Salaam), but there is no one agency to piece together potential domestic threats. The planned department is to take up that task.

> JOHN GANNON: "No matter how many [technology] tools you have, when you're dealing with that volume of information, it's all the more important that you've got a person—a human being—who knows all the issues and can differentiate between what is good information and what is bad."

Rep. Curt Weldon, R-Pa., has been crusading for such a clearinghouse since 1997. He applauded the Bush proposal—but with one crucial caveat: An effective analysis center must actually be *central*. Weldon's original proposal called for a "National Operations and Analysis Hub" reporting directly to the president, independent of

any Cabinet department. A new Homeland Security Department could operate the new analysis system and be the funding channel, Weldon said, "but the actual oversight of that has to be with the national command authority": the president.

If the new analysis shop really does have the right connections—direct access both to the president and to the intelligence agencies' raw data—then Weldon and other experts agree that sorting through all the information is relatively simple. The private sector has already refined powerful software that combines different kinds of data for market research. The same techniques that match, say, sales of Polo shirts with ZIP codes to create a demographic database of consumers could be used to correlate visa records, spy reports, and FBI wiretaps to paint portraits of potential terrorists.

But technology is only a tool. "No matter how many tools you have," said John Gannon, a former deputy director for intelligence at the CIA now with the Washington consulting firm Intellibridge, "when you're dealing with that volume of information, it's all the more important that you've got a person—a human being—who knows all the issues and can differentiate between what is good information and what is bad."

But will Homeland Security have the right humans for the job? Not at the start. The president's proposal forms the new department's Information Analysis and Infrastructure Protection Division from five existing offices. All of them are concerned with "critical infrastructure": banking, gas pipelines, and above all, communications and computers. The FBI's National Infrastructure Protection Center—which would provide more than 80 percent of the proposed division personnel—is primarily concerned with catching cyber-hackers, although it is branching out.

So the proposed department would do much to bring together computer security experts who are now scattered across the government. But as skilled as these professionals are, they are not intelligence analysts. They are only a foundation—and a somewhat off-center foundation at that—for what will have to be a larger, longer-term effort to build a true analytical hub that pulls together intelligence on the full range of threats.

–Sydney J. Freedberg Jr.

ONE-STOP SHOPPING FOR THE LOCALS

STATE/LOCAL

While Washington debates the wisdom of a proposed Homeland Security Department, from beyond the Beltway the word is already in: "Finally."

As long ago as August 1998—three years before 9/11—a task force of fire chiefs and other local emergency officials, convened by the federal government, reported that there were simply too many programs designed to help lo-

What Each Department Loses

	FY 2003 Budget (IN MILLIONS)	Employees
Agriculture		
Animal and Plant Health Inspection Service	$1,137	8,620
Plum Island Animal Disease Center	25	124
Commerce		
Critical Infrastructure Assurance Office	27	65
Defense		
National Bilogical Warfare Denfense Analysis Center*	420	-
National Communications System	155	91
Energy		
Lawrence Livermore national Laboratory	1,188	324
Nuclear Incident Response	91	-
National Infrastructure Simulation and Analysis Center	20	2
Health and Human Services		
Chemical, Biological, Radiological, and Nuclear Response Assets	2,104	150
Civilian Biodefense Research Programs	1,993	150
Justice		
Immigration and Naturalization Service	6,416	39,459
Office of Domestic Preparedness**	-	-
National Infrastructure Protection Center (FBI)	151	795
National Domestic Preparedness Office (FBI)	2	15
Transportation		
Coast Guard	7,274	43,639
Transportation Security Agency***	4,800	41,300
Treasury		
Customs Service	3,796	21,743
Secret Service	1,248	6,111
FEMA	6,174	5,135
Government Services Administration		
Federal Protective Services	418	1,408
Federal Computer Incident Response Center	11	23
Total	**$37,450**	**169,154**

* A new program in the president's '03 budget originally planned for the Defense Dept.

** Already folded into FEMA's 2003 budget proposal.

*** Could rise to as many as 60,000 to 70,000 employees.

SOURCE: Office of Homeland Security

cal agencies prepare for terrorism. "It's very confusing for us to deal with the federal system," task force member John Eversole, a Chicago fire chief, told *National Journal* at the time. "We basically need one-stop shopping."

FIRST LINE OF DEFENSE: Local police and fire officials hope that a new department would provide a better flow of information.

But pre-September 11 attempts to establish a single clearinghouse instead created several competing "one-stop shops," the chief rivals being the Justice Department and the Federal Emergency Management Agency. "You have to figure out which is the appropriate agency, depending on what the question is," says Joseph Traylor, a retired Air Force chemical and biological defense expert who's now the fire chief in Crestview, Fla. "You could spend days calling different agencies, just asking the question and being shuffled from one to another."

If the planned Homeland Security Department would work as advertised, that would change, says Traylor, and one call would do it all. "We're looking for a single answer," agrees Matthew Bettenhausen, Illinois deputy governor for criminal justice and public safety. "It would represent a vast improvement."

As envisioned in President Bush's proposal, FEMA would become the core of the new department's Emergency Preparedness and Response Division. An agency much appreciated outside of Washington, FEMA has always kept its bureaucracy relatively small—4,000 staffers—and focused on supporting, rather than dominating, state and local agencies with funding and expertise.

"All response is local," says retired Army Col. John Brinkerhoff, who served as FEMA's director of civil defense during the Reagan administration. "The role of the federal government is to augment and reinforce."

Even before Bush's June 6 announcement on the new department, in fact, the administration's 2003 budget called for grant offices in the Justice Department to be folded into FEMA. "It's a good thing, because they were completely at odds with each other," says Clifford Ong, director of the Indiana Counter-Terrorism and Security Council.

But Ong adds a crucial caveat: "The vast majority of emergency response is *not* terrorism-related.... I certainly hope nothing gets shortchanged." Merging so many agencies would make life easier for him and other homeland security officials, Ong explains. But long-established ties between corresponding state and federal agencies—firefighters and FEMA, for example, or waterway safety agencies and the U.S. Coast Guard—could be strained as the merger buries the less-dramatic issues inside a huge counter-terrorism department. "Everyone's daunted by the size of this agency," says Ong.

A former governor himself, Homeland Security Director Tom Ridge has always emphasized the importance of state and local responders. Indeed, in an interview with *National Journal* just days before the new department was announced the state and local role was one of the few issues to rouse some passion in the otherwise cagey Ridge. "We must work with governors and mayors," he emphasized. "It cannot just be done by the federal government.... We can provide standards, we can provide resources, in some areas we provide the leadership; but this is a national effort."

Under the Bush proposal, the secretary of Homeland Security would have a special office devoted solely to state and local concerns. Yet reorganization at the federal level, as complicated as it is, would be only the first step toward achieving the "national effort" envisioned by Ridge.

"The roles are more clearly defined," says John Buckman, fire chief in Evansville, Ind., and president of the International Association of Fire Chiefs. But he's concerned that there's been more talk than action. "Since September 11 we've had a lot of posturing by officials in the federal government, but we've had very little delivery of direct assistance to local government," Buckman says.

Moreover, while the new department would have money, it could struggle to get access to another resource that is essential to state and local government: intelligence information. For example, though police departments currently get some warnings electronically from the FBI, there is no comparable system for other emergency responders. Concludes Florida fire chief Traylor: "Our best source of information right now, on the fire side, is CNN."

–Sydney J. Freedberg Jr.

UNANSWERED QUESTIONS ON ILLEGALS

IMMIGRATION

Controlling *legal* migration into the United States—a herculean task for the proposed Department of Homeland Security—is like trying to check everyone who's entering a giant party through the front door. And achieving that goal would solve only a fraction of the nation's internal security problems: Voices on many sides of the immigration debate warn that the government's failure to control *illegal* immigration leaves the back door swinging open.

"Any border that a Mexican busboy can sneak across is a border that an Al Qaeda terrorist can sneak across," says Mark Krikorian, executive director of the Center for Immigration Studies, which favors tougher restrictions on immigration. "Until we reassert control over our immigration process... there's no prospect of keeping out terrorists," he adds. The United States is now home to an estimated 8 million illegal immigrants.

Although consolidating border-control agencies might improve interagency communication, former Immigration and Naturalization Service General Counsel Paul Virtue predicts that, given the variety of tasks each agency is asked to do, the overall efficiencies will be small. And the new border policies enacted thus far, such as establishing an entry and exit system at legal points of entry, do nothing to stop someone from walking across an unpatrolled section of the border.

"Creating this [Homeland Security] Department won't make it any more likely" that we can prevent a determined terrorist from entering the country illegally, Virtue says. "I think there needs to be a clear immigration policy, … a clear statement on what is really necessary in order to develop an overall [border-security] strategy."

Conflicting messages from within the administration about how strenuously agents should enforce immigration laws have greatly hindered the agency's effectiveness, says former INS General Counsel David Martin. "If the INS message was clearly, 'We have a zero tolerance for illegal immigration,' they could be a lot more effective with the resources they have," Martin adds. Both the White House and Congress continue to discourage the INS from punishing employers who hire illegal immigrants.

Since September 11, illegal immigration has become a more difficult issue for President Bush. Days before the terrorist attacks, Bush was looking for a way to legalize much of the current population of illegal immigrants. Such a move would be wildly popular with a voting bloc that Bush has long wooed: Hispanics, especially Mexican-Americans. But since 9/11, the president has been reluctant to take a stand on illegal immigration. Any appearance of softening enforcement of immigration laws, whose lax enforcement is believed to have helped terrorists enter the United States undetected, would be politically dangerous and would risk alienating his core conservative supporters.

Politics aside, the correct policy response to the nation's wide-open borders is anything but obvious. Krikorian contends that the Bush administration should send a message that the nation will no longer tolerate illegal immigration. To drive that message home, federal officials would need to track down illegal immigrants, deport them (not just order them to leave), and enforce laws banning undocumented workers. In addition, he says, proof of U.S. citizenship or legal residency should be required for anyone obtaining a driver's license or opening a bank account.

But Demetrios G. Papademetriou, co-director of the Migration Policy Institute, counters that September 11 actually "shifts the envelope in favor of legalization." The fastest way to identify the unknown 8 million illegal immigrants is to offer them legal status in exchange for coming forward and submitting to a background check, he argues. INS Commissioner James W. Ziglar has made a similar argument.

To try to avoid any immediate political fallout, Papademetriou says, the Bush administration could delay taking any new positions on illegal immigration until after the November midterm elections. But if the administration continues to ignore illegal immigration, Papademetriou warns, "this is going to be an unresolved issue that is going to be hanging over this domestic security department and raising questions about whether it can do what it's paid to do."

–Siobhan Gorman

TRACKING DOWN TERRORISTS

LAW ENFORCEMENT

If the proposed Homeland Security Department eventually improves threat analysis to the point that federal officials know the identity of many of the would-be terrorists in this country, what's the next step? The Immigration and Naturalization Service, which would be transferred to the new department under the president's plan, has long been the lead agency charged with tracking down foreigners wanted by the federal government. Unfortunately, the INS has a poor track record and finds very few people. "I think that issue is always going to be there," says former INS counsel Paul Virtue.

The INS's current attempt to locate 314,000 foreigners who have fled deportation orders illustrates the scope of the agency's problem. Since November, only 676 of those people have been rounded up. Meanwhile, Attorney General John D. Ashcroft last week ordered the INS to register those male U.S. residents—mostly from the Middle East—whom he described as being of "high national security concern."

Virtue notes that with just 2,000 agents patrolling inside the nation's borders, the INS is spread incredibly thin. "If the Homeland Security Department is going to be serious about identifying, apprehending, and removing suspected dangerous people in the United States, then they're going to have to add resources," he contends. Yet the White House insists that the creation of a new department won't increase the size of the federal government.

Former INS General Counsel David Martin warns that the success of INS searches often depends more on luck than on skill. Right now, INS agents get more internal credit for starting deportation proceedings than for tracking down people who've already been ordered to leave. In Martin's view, a new department should create a new set of internal rewards for INS agents who apprehend potential terrorists.

But Frank Hoffman, a former aide to the Hart-Rudman commission on terrorism, says, "I don't necessarily want the INS chasing these kinds of people." The FBI should be the agency responsible for finding people deemed dangerous by the Homeland Security Department, he says.

But would the secretary of Homeland Security have the power to demand that the FBI, which would still be part of the Justice Department under the Bush administration's proposal, track down particular people—who might or might not be wanted by the FBI itself? Or would the secretary have to cajole the FBI into acting? "There's lots of room for different priorities to slip in there," Martin says.

For now, the White House says it doesn't anticipate communications problems between a new department and the FBI. Homeland Security Director Tom Ridge has said the president could be the arbiter if problems do occur.

–Siobhan Gorman

The Military Happily Stands Aside

PENTAGON

Of all the many agencies involved in the war on terror, perhaps the one least affected by the proposed Department of Homeland Security is that other department tasked with the national defense—the one headquartered at the Pentagon. Under the president's plan, the Defense Department loses very little, chiefly a secure communications network and a not-yet-built bio-defense center, which together total just 0.15 percent of its $379 billion budget.

And Defense's open secret is that it spent the 1990s trying to get *out* of the homeland security business—backing away from counterdrug border patrols and transferring a counter-terrorism training program for local firefighters and police to the Justice Department. In fact, ever since the withdrawal of federal occupation forces from the former Confederate states and the passage of the 1878 Posse Comitatus Act (barring military personnel from domestic law enforcement), the U.S. military has held a deep distaste for domestic entanglements of any kind. Furthermore, since 1917, when the United States intervened in Europe's First World War, the American military has been organized, trained, and equipped to fight "over there."

The Defense Department got into the war on drugs in the 1980s, and into fighting domestic terrorism in the 1990s, less out of a desire for empire-building than on orders from successive administrations and Congresses that could not find anyone else with the required expertise. With a new, civilian Department of Homeland Security, however, the nation's leadership would have someone else to pick on. Said Michele Flournoy, deputy assistant secretary of Defense for strategy in the Clinton administration, "My guess is that many in DOD are heaving a sigh of relief."

Even with a new security department, the military would always have a crucial supporting role domestically. No other agency can mobilize tens of thousands of trained personnel—from doctors to truck drivers to morticians—not to mention mounts of supplies, from tents to

water purifiers. The Pentagon is already creating a civilian staff and a uniformed "Northern Command" precisely to coordinate such support. But even in this area, the proposed department would make the old one's work easier. Instead of the wide array of civilian agencies the Pentagon must support at present, there would be one clear customer. That simplified system would let the military focus on the mission dearest to its heart: hunting America's enemies abroad.

–Sydney J. Freedberg, Jr.

Fragmentation Concerns

BIO-TERROR

So far, the government's efforts to combat bio-terrorism seem to have largely escaped the problems of over-lapping jurisdictions that have plagued other counter-terrorism functions. Perhaps that's because bio-terrorism is essentially the responsibility of one agency: the Department of Health and Human Services. After some initial missteps in dealing with anthrax, HHS Secretary Tommy G. Thompson has gotten good marks for marshaling department resources.

GERM ATTACK: This is a copy of one of the letters sent last year that tested positive for anthrax.

President Bush's proposed reorganization would end HHS's dominant role by transferring 300 employees and $4 billion from HHS to a new Department of Homeland Security—a move that Thompson says would allow bio-terrorism experts to benefit from other intelligence data. Some members of Congress, however, worry that the transfer could create a duplication of effort and uproot some public health specialists from their traditional home at HHS.

"I don't know a lot of the details [about the HHS transfers], but I'm very uneasy about it," said Sen. James M. Jeffords, I-Vt., who sits on the Health, Education, Labor and Pensions Committee, which has jurisdiction over public health. "It's strange to think it's going to be a wonderful thing."

Sen. Bill Frist, R-Tenn., said that important questions need answering. "I'll be concerned if they start to separate scientific research and begin fragmenting it to the point where it's losing the synergies of having one place," he said, adding he's starting to talk to "friends" at HHS to see whether the move "makes sense or not."

Currently, Thompson has a one-stop shop at HHS. He has authority over the Public Health Service, which includes the Centers for Disease Control and Prevention (the experts on infectious disease); the Food and Drug Administration (the regulator of vaccines, drugs, and food safety); and the National Institutes of Health (the premier medical research entity). Moreover, HHS is home to the Office of Emergency Preparedness, which seeks to ensure that hospitals and other bio-terrorism responders are ready to meet the challenge of an attack. In addition, Thompson has created the Office of Public Health Preparedness to coordinate the department's many efforts on bio-terrorism.

Kevin Keane, assistant secretary for public affairs at HHS, said he expects the national pharmaceutical stockpile, the Office of Emergency Preparedness, and the new Office of Public Health Preparedness to move. Keane also believes the proposed department would take control of most of the bio-terrorism grants that Thompson recently approved for states and cities to build up their public health systems.

But any division of labor could run into problems. Many NIH scientists working on bio-terrorism have other responsibilities as well. "If you're an infectious-disease specialist, you know smallpox, but you also know West Nile virus and influenza," said Keane. One possibility being considered, Keane said, is to leave CDC and NIH personnel where they are, but to have the new department contract with them for bio-terrorism-related work.

–**Marilyn Werber Serafini**

FLIGHT TEST

TRANSPORTATION

On paper, it's a bureaucratic no-brainer: Moving the fledgling Transportation Security Administration from the Transportation Department to a new Homeland Security Department provides a better way to gather all of the information about people coming into and leaving the United States. "We need an apparatus that allows intelligence to flow from Border Patrol to harbor patrol to the aviation system," said Kevin P. Mitchell, chairman of the Business Travel Coalition, a group that represents companies whose employees travel frequently. "Getting them into the same room makes a lot sense."

But whether this reorganization is good public policy—and makes our aviation system safer—is a much harder question to answer.

One potential shortcoming for airport security will be the quality of intelligence flow, since the nation's two most important intelligence-gathering organizations, the CIA and the FBI, won't be included in the new department. That's one reason why Mitchell thinks the Bush administration should re-examine its plan. "Prudence dictates that we seriously take a step back here," he said.

Another question is whether the proposed Homeland Security Department will have enough transportation knowledge and expertise to effectively manage the nation's aviation security system. During the debate over airport security legislation last fall, Congress decided to house the TSA inside the Transportation Department to tap that department's knowledge and expertise. Lawmakers also believed that Transportation would do the best job of balancing the competing demands of tightening airport security while still fostering a healthy economic environment for the airline industry and making sure that passengers get to their gates as quickly as possible.

But so far, the airline industry and other transportation observers haven't been too impressed with the TSA's operations under the Transportation Department. They have criticized the agency for not responding to the industry's economic concerns and for moving too slowly to meet important security deadlines. As a result, the airlines aren't that upset about the plan to move the TSA into the planned department. "They don't think it can get any worse than it is now," said one transportation lobbyist. "They are so frustrated with dealing with the TSA and [Transportation Secretary Norman] Mineta." Another lobbyist added: "The thinking has been, why not let somebody else take a crack at it?"

Indeed, many experts believe that the proposed department might be much more receptive to the industry's concerns. For example, TSA Director John W. Magaw recently opposed an industry-backed plan to create a "trusted traveler" card, which would help frequent fliers get through airport security faster. However, Tom Ridge—likely to top the list of potential nominees for secretary of Homeland Security—supports the idea.

But can the country realistically expect a new department to make up for the shortcomings of an agency that was created less than a year ago? Rep. David R. Obey, D-Wis., the ranking member of the House Appropriations Committee, doesn't think so. "If they've got this wired to go as badly as the Transportation Security Administration has been wired, God help us all," Obey told *The New York Times.*

–**Mark Murray**

A SIN OF OMISSION?

VISAS

While the expansive Department of Homeland Security, as proposed, would combine a host of agencies from existing departments, many experts are scratching their heads over what they see as a glaring omission: the State Department's Bureau of Consular Affairs. "If you want to say, 'We want to prevent the entry of the evildoers upstream,' you've got to include Consular Affairs," said Paul Light, vice president for governmental studies at the Brookings Institution. "What the new department is saying is, 'Our job begins at the border.' That may well be a mistake."

> **BIOMETRIC IDENTIFIER:** The Homeland Security Department would take responsibility for adding a biometric identifier—such as a fingerprint or iris scan—to U.S. Visas to ensure that the person entering this country is actually the one who was issued the visa.

The new department would envelop all the U.S. border-control officials stationed in this country but leave out the 800 or so Foreign Service officers responsible for deciding—at U.S. embassies and consulates around the world—whether to grant foreigners a visa. Since 9/11, many terrorism experts have questioned the wisdom of having the State Department's most junior diplomats handle what in many ways is a police function—determining which foreigners can safely be allowed into this country. Insiders say that the White House mulled shifting Consular Affairs before deciding to leave it in the State Department.

The proposed Homeland Security Department would take responsibility for adding a biometric identifier—such as a fingerprint or iris scan—to U.S. visas to ensure that the person entering this country is actually the one who was issued the visa. And the new department would keep track of who should not be issued visas.

The easiest way to prevent terrorism on American soil is to keep terrorists from reaching America. Consular officers are the first Americans to make decisions about whether someone should be allowed into this country, and they have the most time to reach a decision. (Theoretically, officers can take all the time they want on a given visa but are often asked to process hundreds of visa requests per day.) Inspectors at the Immigration and Naturalization Service have the power to turn foreigners away at the door, but they usually defer to consular decisions because they don't have the time or resources to assess everyone thoroughly.

Leaving Consular Affairs out of the Homeland Security Department, experts say, would make it difficult to achieve the seamless coordination among border officials that the White House is trying to foster, because the first line of border defense won't be under the same commander as the rest of the border agencies. The exclusion would also mean no improvement in the quality of visa decisions. Under the State Department, consular officers are inexperienced junior officers who often have their sights set on sipping cappuccino with fellow diplomats in a piazza in Rome, not sitting behind a plexiglass window interviewing visa applications.

Consular officials are trained with an eye toward serving foreigners quickly and fairly. They generally don't have the law enforcement mind-set necessary to see each visa applicant as a potential security risk, says former Foreign Service officer Wayne Merry. Plus, he says, the embassies reward consular officials not for rejecting potentially dangerous applicants, but for approving as many visas as possible. Left to its own devices, the State Department won't change anything, he warns, even though the 9/11 terrorists had entered this country legally. "I have yet to hear the Bureau of Consular Affairs share any responsibility for September 11," Merry said. "They don't recognize that they did anything wrong."

The rationale for leaving out Consular Affairs is that all embassy activities should fall under the purview of the State Department. But Merry calls that a "hollow argument," and says that when he was a consular officer in Moscow his embassy housed employees from at least 30 different agencies, including NASA.

Light said that it would make much more sense to include Consular Affairs, whose duties are almost entirely related to border security, than to include the Coast Guard. Only about 25 percent of the Coast Guard's duties involve border security. The rest involve environmental and maritime projects, such as rescuing sea turtles. "We've got the sea turtles and fruit flies covered. But, no, we can't do Consular Affairs," Light said. "If it wasn't political, I cannot see the rationale for not including Consular Affairs."

Congress will have the option of folding Consular Affairs into the new department. And the absence of Consular Affairs from the new Homeland Security Department could be a sizable chink in the nation's border-security armor. "I think it's a huge problem," Merry said. "We'll be vulnerable."

–Siobhan Gorman

GETTING RID OF FIEFDOMS

THE LAW

While the idea of shoving disparate agencies together into a new organizational chart now has credibility on Capitol Hill, nobody is sure how the bills creating a Homeland Security Department would be written to make all the pieces work together effectively. Will old boxes merely coexist on a new set of department stationery? Or would any Homeland Security Department have a free hand to consolidate or cancel redundant functions?

"That's one of the things we're trying to find out right now," said one Senate GOP source. "Making this a strong and effective department [means] giving it the authority it needs to make sure it is coherent."

It is challenging enough to move an agency with a comfortable perch in one department to someplace new in the government. It is especially daunting to rip up the legal authorities for many agencies and budgets and then sew them back together into a single body. The White House's proposal appears to favor the ripping-up approach: "The Secretary," it says, "should have broad reorganizational authority in order to enhance operational effectiveness, as needed."

That authority doesn't exist today. Under the Reorganization Act, most presidents from Harry Truman to Ronald Reagan could submit reorganization plans to Congress for approval. If neither house vetoed the plan, the plan was enacted. But the act expired in 1984 after the Supreme Court threw out the congressional veto process.

As a result, for the past 18 years, executive branch reorganizations have had to get a thorough vetting from Congress. Not surprisingly, few proposals survive intact. Norman Ornstein, resident scholar at the American Enterprise Institute, thinks the Bush administration wants "to allow the secretary, once he's got a new department, to rearrange the boxes and move authority and even move budget around without, in each instance, having to go back and get congressional approval. My guess is if this is what we're talking about, then Congress may look at it with a skeptical eye."

UNCERTAIN LEGALITIES: A new department may face civil-liberties issues, as the military did with Al Qaeda captives at Guantanamo Bay.

Giving the administration the power to reorganize could be crucial in creating a Homeland Security Department that will be organized by functions instead of by fiefdoms. Consider an example from the White House's proposal on the new department. Today, a ship coming into the United States falls under the jurisdiction of the Customs Service, the Immigration and Naturalization Service, the Coast Guard, and the Agriculture Department. Even if these groups are all moved into one department, a menacing ship could still face scrutiny from agents wearing four different uniforms.

Some government-watchers are doubtful about giving an executive department the sweeping power that would be needed to effectively combine the agencies. Gary Bass, the executive director of OMB Watch, says that such a move would undermine the Constitution's balance of powers. "If there was language that allowed the executive

branch to fundamentally alter the functions or responsibilities of individual departments without consultation to Congress," he says, "then that shifts the balance in favor of the executive branch."

Alan Dean, a fellow with the National Academy of Public Administration, argues that open-ended authority to reorganize isn't necessary. The secretary of Homeland Security would have all the power he or she needs to get the job done, Dean says, if the legislation creating the new department gets the organizational structure right and strips subagency heads of independent authority. "The real question is, do we want somebody to run this department or not?" Dean says. "If you want the secretary to run the department, you give him all the statutory authority."

Civil-rights groups, meanwhile, are also awaiting details on the new department's powers and how it will carry out its work. The ACLU has called for an independent watchdog within Homeland Security. Laura Murphy, the head of the ACLU's Washington office, says that the operations of any new department will "bear watching."

–Corine Hegland

ADDITION WITHOUT SUBTRACTION

BUDGET

When Congress eventually gets around to lamenting that Homeland Security, stitched together like a fancy quilt, is not, as President Bush promised, going to be "revenue-neutral," the White House will quickly tell lawmakers that the president "always said" such an important and complex mission was going to cost more than $37.5 billion. That's the fiscal 2003 estimate the White House distributed last week as part of its color-coded, multi-tabbed briefing booklet on reinventing government. And that will be true. The White House will have it both ways.

No one knows what a Department of Homeland Security—Bush's version or anyone else's—is really going to cost taxpayers. That's because no one is exactly sure what government functions will eventually go into the proposed department; or the number of employees it will require (169,154 is a White House estimate, but Senate Minority Leader Trent Lott, R-Miss., has suggested downsizing by 5,000 jobs); or the new technologies it will need. And no one has yet suggested getting rid of any office or any function now performed by Uncle Sam. Lots of addition, not a lot of subtraction.

"We're going to use the same dollars that we're spending right now," explained Office of Management and Budget Director Mitchell E. Daniels Jr. on June 9. Translation: The White House—wary of conservative charges that the era of Big Government has been reborn—reprised for Bush's proposed department a fiscal 2003 spending figure already presented to Congress. It was a number that Bush proudly declared in February represented an $18 billion increase over fiscal 2002 spending for homeland security.

"Budget-neutral," White House homeland security adviser Tom Ridge said, is a long-term goal, measured against budgets that have yet to be written. "I think, initially… transitional costs—there may be additional," admitted the former Pennsylvania governor on June 9. "But … we're working really hard to make sure that we keep… those transition costs to the minimum. In the long term, I think it should be… budget-neutral."

In the long term, Bush candidly admitted in his February budget submission to Congress, "the administration intends to provide whatever resources are necessary to secure the homeland, but is committed to ensuring that taxpayers' money is well spent." The president at the time said that the $38 billion he requested was not the "totality of the homeland security agenda." The full picture would be drawn in his fiscal 2004 budget blueprint, he promised. A new Cabinet flowchart is one thing; the price tag for homeland security policies is another. Because Bush is not expected to describe until fall the comprehensive policies a new department would embrace, the costs remain a mystery.

There were clear signs almost immediately last week that packing homeland security into the old $38 billion suitcase was an artful exercise. Take, for example, the Lawrence Livermore National Laboratory operated by the University of California. Under the president's plan, it would abandon its home in the Energy Department and

become part of the new department's division for countering terrorist weapons of mass destruction. How much of the lab's budget would go to the planned department? The White House said $1.2 billion, along with the equivalent of 324 full-time federal workers. The laboratory's entire fiscal 2002 budget was just over $1.5 billion (a new department would swallow the lab's fiscal 2003 budget), but there are only 160 federal employees among the lab's 7,500 workers, said spokeswoman Lynda Seaver. "We just don't know what those numbers mean," she added.

Another example is the Transportation Security Administration, hastily created by Congress on November 19, 2001. Struggling to fulfill congressional mandates, it is growing on a daily basis, even as the president proposes plucking it out of the Transportation Department to make it part of a new border and transportation division in a Homeland Security Department. The fiscal 2003 budget Bush sent lawmakers last winter asked for $4.8 billion for 41,300 TSA workers. So, those became the mothball figures the White House used to help estimate what a new agency might cost. Trouble is, the TSA now wants 67,000 employees and expects Congress any minute to approve bonus funding for fiscal 2002 in the neighborhood of $4.4 billion. Security may eventually be more efficient, but it isn't cheap.

—Alexis Simendinger

The authors of these stories can be reached by e-mail at addresses in this pattern: jdoe@nationaljournal.com.

A Watchful Eye

Politics is clouding the homeland-security picture. The reality and the rhetoric.

By Steven Brill

I F YOU LOCK THREE OF YOUR CAR'S four doors, is it three times safer than if you locked only one? Obviously not. If all four doors aren't secured, the car isn't safe. Then again, suppose a thief can't tell which of the doors are locked, and if he tries to open one that is locked he gets an electric shock that disables him and the police immediately show up to arrest him. In that case, having three locked doors is indeed three times better than one and infinitely better than if a thief knows that no doors are ever locked.

That, in a nutshell, describes what is going to become an increasingly partisan debate in advance of the 2004 elections over homeland security—a battle in which Sen. Hillary Clinton fired the first shot last month, when she called homeland security "a myth." As Orange Alert and pre-Iraq-war jitters intensify, it's a fight that's certain to continue to heat up, and likely to flare out of control when another terrorist attack occurs.

Here are five realities to keep in mind to help cut through the rhetoric:

Saying the country is not doing enough will always be true.

Senator Clinton was right. After all, in a country that has 7,500 miles of border, thousands of miles of natural-gas pipelines, tens of thousands of facilities storing or shipping dan-

gerous chemicals, infinite entrances to subways, trains or building lobbies and just as many points of vulnerability related to the food or water supply or office-building-ventilation systems, it is impossible to plug all the holes—or lock all the car doors.

Homeland security is a great issue for the Democrats.

It's a smart way for Democrats to sound tough and patriotic, and criticize Republicans for being soft. But the funding issue is more complicated than Democrats like Clinton have made it out to be; the Bush administration's new budget includes significant increases for homeland security at a time when most other domestic spending is being tightly controlled. Still, the Democrats have a good argument that the administration seems willing to spend much more on dividend tax cuts than on port security or equipment for local first-responders. Then again…

Spending more on homeland security is not synonymous with strengthening homeland security.

Clinton bashed Bush using a study that said most cities and counties in New York state had not yet received any aid from Washington to fight terrorism. But the delay in sending out aid has to do not only with the

fact that Congress is five months late in finishing the current-fiscal-year budget, but also with a dispute over who gets to decide how the money is spent. What Clinton was really arguing for was a system of unrestricted block grants for these local governments, whereas Bush and his new secretary of Homeland Security, Tom Ridge, want to provide the aid through the states so the states can vet the communities' homeland-security battle plans, and decide what deserves to be funded.

True, some cities, especially larger ones like New York, have sophisticated antiterrorism programs that merit their own grants from Washington. But unrestricted grants to every locality in the name of fighting terrorism could end up being something quite different. After all, state and local officials are facing their own budget crises, and will find it awfully tempting to keep some extra cops on the payroll by calling them terrorism fighters rather than invest the funds in real antiterrorism efforts, such as radiation detectors or bioterror evacuation drills.

Conversely, beefing up homeland security doesn't always require large amounts of new taxpayer money. For example, by refining its risk criteria for deciding which cargo containers need careful inspection, Customs inspectors at the ports have already boosted safety, even while they await additional research and funds for better sealing of cargo containers in transit. But on other fronts, the Bush administration is vulnerable in this regard. The chemical and nuclear-power industries need tougher regulation of their safety procedures, not federal funds. Yet except for a few senators, such as Jon Corzine of New Jersey and Clinton, the administration hasn't been given much grief for its unwillingness to clamp down. Similarly, one would think that a political party that puts so much stock in the ability of the private sector to solve problems would be aggressively jawboning insurance companies to set rates and offer discounts based on evaluations of the security precautions taken by all varieties of business clients—from office buildings to theaters. No sign of that yet.

The Pearl Harbor analogy is facile but not completely fair.

Senator Clinton and others have evoked the way FDR summoned the nation following Pearl Harbor as an example of what this president failed to do. It's true that President Bush did not ask us to sacrifice when he could have and probably should have, perhaps with a mandatory national-service program aimed at getting young people enlisted for a year or two in the various aspects of the homeland-security fight. Nonetheless, it must be remembered how different and how multifaceted this new threat is. It is one thing to enlist troops and retrofit factories to fight a conventional war against a visible, foreign enemy. It is quite another to protect the homeland against hidden terrorists. There's a tricky balance to be struck between galvanizing people and alarming them so much that

they are scared out of their way of life, which is the terrorists' goal.

We're never doing enough to fight terrorism, even if we're doing all we can

The Democrats' eagerness to get as many "I told you so's" on the record in advance of the next attack is understandable, indeed helpful in terms of pushing the government to act. Yet significant progress has been made on most fronts. To deny that, or to slough it off as "not enough," ignores what tens of thousands of dedicated people—from Customs inspectors at the ports, to the new federalized screeners at the airports, to their "bureaucrat" bosses in Washington—did in the year after September 11. They worked backbreaking hours and came up with all kinds of solutions on the fly worthy of the Pearl Harbor generation that preceded them.

The debate needs to be about tangible results coming from better management.

Casting blame after the next attack will be easy. So is claiming credit simply by spending money or establishing a new cabinet agency. But if either side wants the debate to be credible and useful, it should specify now in terms that everyone can understand what the goals should be for the next six and 12 months and then ask an independent agency, like Congress's General Accounting Office, to report on how the goals are

being met. For example, Ridge should define in unfudgeable specifics what he will have achieved by then with the Immigration and Naturalization Service's entry-exit system, which is designed to make sure foreigners entering the United States on visas leave when they are supposed to. The current system is a farce; let's see what putting it under Ridge in his new megadepartment has achieved in six months and a year.

Similarly, the opposition should tell us what they think Ridge should be able to achieve and how he should be able to achieve it—not in terms of checks written, but in terms of actually making the country safer. For example, the new Homeland Security Task Force, organized by Senate Democrats and chaired by New York Sen. Charles Schumer, could set a demonstrably realistic standard for improving the chances of Customs' finding radiation bombs in the ports (a pet issue of Schumer's). Then they could ask the GAO to measure progress by sending undercover teams in to try to smuggle that kind of material in.

A regular GAO report card on both sets of goals would be more useful than what is now shaping up as an argument where both sides have a good but empty claim. For when it comes to terrorism, we're never doing enough, even if we're doing all we can. The question is not how much either side cares or how much we're spending, but what we're achieving.

Contributing Editor STEVEN BRILL's book, "AFTER: How America Confronted the September 12 Era," will be published in early April.

THE STATE OF OUR
DEFENSE

The Bush Administration believes al-Qaeda is poised to strike the U.S. again,
but has it done enough to improve homeland security?

By ROMESH RATNESAR

WHEN TOP OFFICIALS AT THE FBI ARRIVED FOR WORK LAST week, they had reason to feel even more anxious than usual. Beginning each day before dawn, FBI Director Robert Mueller and his top aides huddled on the seventh floor of the J. Edgar Hoover Building, reviewing overnight intelligence reports gathered from human and electronic sources around the world. Taken together, the reports suggested what intelligence officials had suspected for weeks: al-Qaeda operatives, in the words of a senior U.S. official, "are in the execution phase of some of their operations." The intelligence sources couldn't pinpoint the kind of strikes in the works or the cells charged with executing them. But U.S. officials told Time that earlier this month Mueller and other top officials received credible intelligence that al-Qaeda had an attack—or multiple attacks—set to begin at some point last week, perhaps to coincide with the end of the hajj, the five-day Muslim pilgrimage to Mecca. Officials say the intelligence specifically mentioned that the likely targets were New York City and Washington.

Even though the feared attacks failed to materialize, the anxieties didn't subside. Inside the FBI, fears of a devastating attack are as high as they've been in months, in part because of the possibility that "other tools are in play"—meaning biological and chemical weapons. A senior Administration official says that telephone calls and e-mails exchanged between several suspected terrorists and intercepted by the U.S. and foreign intelligence agencies pointed to a plot inside the U.S. using nerve gas, poisons or radiological devices. "It wasn't just chatter," says Republican Senator Pat Roberts, chairman of the Senate Intelligence Committee. "It was a pattern."

Some of the plots are believed to be in the planning stages. A senior Administration official tells TIME that domestic law-enforcement agencies are investigating a report that Islamic extremists in this country are trying to acquire parts to build an unmanned aerial vehicle (UAV) abroad—the kind of machine that terrorism experts believe could be deployed to spray chemical agents over populated areas. The fear is that a UAV assembled overseas could be used against U.S. assets there.

Some alleged terrorist plans were very close to home. Counterterrorism officials say they received a phone tip that unnamed members of Congress could be the targets of assassination attempts. On Wednesday, U.S. Capitol Police chief Terry Gainer warned House members to be on alert for attempts on their lives. At a closed-door briefing Thursday a group of Senators grilled Secretary of Homeland Security Tom Ridge about whether they should clear their families out of the capital in anticipation of an attack. Ridge counseled them against it, but when pressed by the Senators for the odds of an attack on U.S. targets at home or abroad in the next several weeks, Ridge, according to one source familiar with the meeting, put the probability at "50% or greater." Ridge's spokesman denies that the Secretary gave that figure. Still, a congressional source says the White House is "definitely worried. They're not jacking this up for effect." In private, White House officials sounded almost resigned to the inevitability of catastrophe. "All we can do," Vice President

THE THREATS

WHAT TO LOOK FOR— AND WHAT TO DO

On 9/11, terrorists turned ordinary airliners into deadly missiles. Now experts fear the use of these three types of unconventional weapons

Dirty-Bomb Attack

WHAT IT IS
A crude method—using conventional explosives like dynamite—of scattering low-level radioactive materials, such as those found in X-ray machines or food-irradiation plants

WHAT COULD HAPPEN
If the bomb is large enough, the explosion would level a small building and subject hundreds of people to high levels of radiation. The target area would suffer long-term contamination

PROTECTING YOURSELF
Have enough food and water to stay indoors for a few days. Avoid the blast area, and stay upwind. If exposed, dispose of your clothes, wash thoroughly and seek medical care

Chemical Attack

WHAT IT IS
Poisonous compounds that can be mixed into food or water supplies or spread by a bomb or spray

WOULD COULD HAPPEN
Chemicals tend to dissipate rapidly, making large-scale attacks difficult. The most likely assault is an isolated one such as the 1995 sarin-gas attack in the Tokyo subway that killed 12 people

PROTECTING YOURSELF
Have emergency supplies of food and water in case public supply is disrupted or you are instructed to stay indoors. If you see signs of a chemical attack, such as people choking or tearing, move upwind from the area. If you must remain in place, seal vents, doors and windows

Biological Attack

WHAT IT IS
Bacteria, viruses and toxins spread through spraying or contamination of food or water. Some, like smallpox, are contagious

WHAT COULD HAPPEN
Biological agents are difficult to grow and disperse, but such an attack could kill thousands

PROTECTING YOURSELF
Listen to news reports and follow instructions for receiving care, vaccines or antibiotics. A surgical mask rated N95 can help protect against contagious diseases

Dick Cheney told a gathering of top Administration officials to discuss bioterrorism, "is ask ourselves, Have we done everything we can to prevent an attack? I want to be able to look all of you in the eye and (have you) tell me that we have done all that we can."

So have we? While the Administration demonstrated again last week its determination to remind Americans of the dangers of terrorism, it has done far less to prepare the country for actually defending against it. While the White House's suggestion that Americans defend themselves against chemical or biological attacks with duct tape and plastic sheeting was dismissed by many for its naivete, it laid bare a sobering truth: the U.S. still doesn't have a credible and comprehensive system in place to cope with such attacks. "We're not building the means to respond well," says Stephen Flynn, a homeland-security expert at the Council on Foreign Relations. "And when we have that next terrorist incident, there will be hell to pay, because the American people will be in disbelief about how little has been done."

Though President Bush pledged last January to send $3.5 billion to the state and local authorities who will bear the burden of responding to a terrorism emergency, the money was appropriated by Congress only last week. Interviews with dozens of homeland-security officials, from New York City to Long Beach, Calif., reveal that while local authorities around the country are more aware of the potential for terrorist strikes, they lack the resources to upgrade defenses against them. Hospitals say they can't train enough employees to effectively spot and treat victims of biological attacks; fire departments can't afford to buy the haz-mat suits needed to guard against deadly germs; sheriffs say they still learn about terrorist threats from CNN. The bottom line is that in many respects, the homeland is no more secure than it was on Sept. 10, 2001. "The biggest thing we've done," says William Harper, head of homeland security for the state of Arkansas, "is to avoid feeling comfortable."

The White House contends that every locality can't be sprinkled with money from the Federal Government. Early this month, Budget Director Mitchell Daniels said that "there is not enough money in the galaxy" to devise a homeland-security system strong enough to protect every American. The White House points out that the $41 billion the Administration's current budget devotes to homeland security is double the amount spent on domestic defense programs before Sept. 11. But because of the partisan bickering that delayed the creation of the Department of Homeland Security, almost none of it has actually been spent. Democrats are accusing the White House of neglecting homeland security while it slashes taxes and takes up fights with enemies abroad. "How is it," says Oregon Senator Ron Wyden, "that we're asking widows to put duct tape on their house, when police, firemen and medical personnel don't have adequate resources?"

Part of the answer rests in the new Homeland Security Department itself, the impetus behind the biggest reorganization of the Federal Government in a half-century. The new department, first proposed by the President last July, aims to bring 22 agencies and 175,000 employees, from border agents to biologists, under a single bureaucratic roof—and to do it before al-Qaeda tries to mount another attack. But the department is only beginning to pick up momentum. Since it opened its doors Jan. 24, only three out of a possible 23 appointees to the new department have received confirmation; most have not even been named.

Tale of the Tape

People are debating the usefulness of duct tape in a biochemical attack, but there's no doubting its efficacy in plenty of other situations:

- **HOLD THE AMMO** During WW II, the tape (then olive green) protected ammunition cases from moisture damage and covered aircraft gunports

- **WARTS AND ALL** A study in the *Archives of Pediatrics & Adolescent Medicine* found duct tape removed warts more effectively and less painfully than liquid nitrogen

- **GLUEY COUTURE** Duct-tape hats, belts, wallets, guitar straps and roses are sold at www.ducttapefashion.com

- **BREATH SAVING** Apollo 13 astronauts avoided carbon dioxide poisoning by rigging a filter with duct tape

- **LIFE SAVING** Bleeding is slowed if wounds are bound up with it, say fans

---

Given the challenge he faces in launching a new department in the midst of war and mushrooming deficits, Ridge has stayed upbeat. He has tried to shrug off the late-night barbs aimed at the department's color-coded alerts and duct-tape tutorials. A sheepish but good-humored Ridge finally said last week that "we do not want individuals or families to start sealing their doors or their windows," adding that "there may come a time" when authorities recommend that Americans do so. Undaunted by criticism that the White House may be needlessly frightening the public, Ridge plans to unveil this week yet another set of practical guidelines for how citizens should prepare for attacks.

Ridge insists that on the whole, the country is safer than it was on Sept. 11. "Let me count the ways," he says, rattling off improvements in aviation security—from the hiring of 45,000 new federal screeners to the hardening of cockpit doors. Ridge says the Administration has improved communication between the FBI and the CIA, struck agreements with Mexico and Canada to tighten border controls and upgraded the "push packs" of medicines that can be dispatched to cities hit by biological or chemical attacks.

THE TARGETS

...AND ARE WE REALLY ANY SAFER THAN BEFORE?

Safeguarding against terrorism is an endless task. The U.S. has beefed up security in the following areas, but the job is far from over.

AIRPORTS A newly federalized work force screens checked baggage for explosives, and armed guards fly on commercial flights. Soon cockpit doors will be bulletproof. We lack a passenger-profiling system, and bomb-detection devices often issue false alarms. **ASSESSMENT: Considerably safer**

BORDERS More agents guard the Canadian border, aided by new remote video surveillance technology. Additional aircraft patrol the Canadian and Mexican borders. The INS is stricter about immigrant background checks and has tightened customs inspections. **ASSESSMENT: Safer but still an uphill struggle**

SEAPORTS $148 million will be spent on port, bus and cargo security for safety assessments, strategies and training. So far, seaports have taken a backseat to airports in security. **ASSESSMENT: They're just starting**

NUCLEAR FACILITIES Power plants have upped security patrols and built physical barriers. Fewer aircraft now fly over the facilities. The Energy Department is studying the vulnerability of electricity, oil and natural-gas sectors. **ASSESSMENT Limited progress**

"SOFT TARGETS" High-rise buildings—offices, residences and hotels—have security departments that partner with law enforcement. The security chief safeguards the area, handles cybersecurity and investigates employees suspected of corruption, industrial espionage or collusion with criminals or terrorists. **ASSESSMENT: Little has been done; little can be done**

SPECIAL EVENTS Organizers of mass events like the Super Bowl or Olympics hire a large security force of retired FBI, Secret Service or other law-enforcement officials who secure the perimeter and employ biometric technology, like facial scanners. General-aviation flights are banned over some special events. **ASSESSMENT: Improved, but there are still many holes**

But bad guys may still be slipping in—or eluding detection. FBI officials told TIME the bureau has identified "less than a dozen" Islamic men residing in the U.S. who have been to al-Qaeda training camps and are currently in contact with al-Qaeda leaders. Law-enforcement agents are monitoring these men with wiretaps, physical surveillance and other covert means; a handful of known Iraqi intelligence agents and 20 to 40 suspected al-Qaeda associates are receiving similar scrutiny. Officials say there's no credible evidence that Saddam, on his own or in league with al-Qaeda, has managed to smuggle biological or chemical weapons into the U.S.

Still, so many targets on U.S. soil remain undefended or indefensible. Federal Homeland Security officials confided last week that the country's major subway systems are vulnerable to a toxic attack. The government has developed new sensors that can detect a toxic-chemical release and instantly alert emergency workers to where the substance is and how to fight it. So far, Washington has installed 100 sensors in its Metro stations; Boston has a small program in place, while New York City is still experimenting. That's it. The agency that regulates the country's 103 nuclear plants ordered security around sites tightened after Sept. 11. But watchdogs say those measures haven't been rigorously tested, and past test runs identified obvious security lapses like unlocked doors.

Federal Homeland Security officials say they are now focused on bolstering security at the country's commercial seaports, which counterterrorism experts believe would be the most likely point of entry for a nuclear or dirty bomb. Customs officials have invited port owners to apply for grants for increased video monitoring, strengthened security fences and patrol boats; U.S. agents have also been deployed to foreign ports to check out containers before they head Stateside. But U.S. ports are still porous. The Coast Guard says it needs $4.4 billion to make minimal improvements to physical security at the nation's 361 ports, but so far the government has authorized only $92 million. The Long Beach-Los Angeles port, which handles 43% of the nation's incoming seaborne cargo, has received just $5.8 million. "Right now," says Flynn, a former Coast Guard commander, "we have a port system running that practically invites terrorists to attempt to come after us."

So why are the holes so large? Put the question to just about anyone outside the Bush Administration, and you'll hear a familiar answer: money. It's a typical complaint, but experts of both parties agree that in this case increased funding would actually lead to more protection. A Brookings Institution study released last month estimates that the President's 2003 budget falls $7 billion below what's needed to fund basic security needs. Others want even bigger boosts. Last week Connecticut Senator Joseph Lieberman called for an additional $16 billion in homeland-security spending, to pay for thousands of additional border-patrol agents, bigger stockpiles of vaccines and antidotes and more aid to fire fighters and police departments.

Outside Washington, at least, there is consensus. In New York City, police commissioner Ray Kelly says the

WAR FEARS

How to Talk to Your Kids

Kids are absorbing anxiety from the news, snippets of adult conversation and those deepening worry lines on Mom's and Dad's brows. Three tips from TIME FOR KIDS managing editor Claudia Wallis on how to calm their fears:

1 Parents should keep their own worst fears out of the conversation. Answer their questions briefly, reassuringly and without excess detail. The amount of elaboration depends on the child's age and level of curiosity. If a 5-year-old asks, "Why are you buying that duct tape?" it may be enough to answer, "It's a handy thing to have around." A teenager who asks hard questions about biological weapons is looking for some facts and maybe a chance to express his fears.

2 More important than what you say is what you hear. "Don't push things on kids," says Chris Kaufman, lead psychologist for the Portland, Maine, school system. "Spend much more time listening and asking probing questions about what they know. Look for misinformation." Kaufman says it was upon close questioning that a frightened boy revealed his mistaken belief that there was a terrorist cell in every U.S. town. Boys, he says, are particularly prone to obsessive fantasies about war and weaponry, so parents should limit their exposure to the nuts and bolts of war preparations.

3 For young kids, parents need to convey a sense of safety at home. Tell them that if we fight a war in Iraq, it's far away and that our country has taken all sorts of measures to keep families protected. Even if you're holding yourself together with duct tape, your kids need to feel their world is intact.

city is still waiting for $900 million it has requested from the feds, some of which would go toward training police officers. "We are continuing to ask Washington for that money," he says. In Detroit, a critical node of homeland security, given its heavily trafficked border and large Arab-American population, city officials say they have spent $10 million on helicopters, protective suits and beefed-up border patrols. But other needs, including a communications system that would allow the city's emergency teams to talk with one another and their Canadian counterparts, have been shelved until federal help arrives. Detroit mayor Kwame Kilpatrick says he has pleaded for more money. "It's very frustrating," he says. Smaller cities have fared even worse, with many forced to spend money on basic equipment they expected the feds would pay for. Says Donald L. Plusquellic, mayor of Akron, Ohio: "If you had told me when we met with Bush that it would now be some 500-plus days since Sept. 11 and we would still not have this money, I wouldn't have believed you."

And yet in small and even heroic ways, officials across the country have thrown themselves into roles as the country's new defenders. Officials in rural Hardin County, Ohio, purchased a portable decontamination shower and are planning to simulate a terrorist-sponsored train derailment to test the danger posed to the area's local chemical facilities. In Iowa, state officials have held eight-hour seminars with farmers on the possibility of "agroterrorist" attacks on the food supply.

But do citizens in Akron and Hardin County have any real reason to believe they could be hit next? The Administration's duct-tape alert had the perhaps counterproductive effect of suggesting that every household should consider itself a target—even while prime targets went undefended. "These threats are real," says Brian Jenkins, a terrorism expert at the Rand Corp., "but the increased probability of a terrorist attack does not increase the risks to any single individual." At the same time, even strengthening our defenses won't deter terrorists forever. The truth is, we probably have no way of knowing whether the country is prepared for the next attack until after it occurs. —*Reported by Timothy J. Burger, James Carney, John F. Dickerson, Viveca Novak, Elaine Shannon and Michael Weisskopf/Washington, Maggie Sieger/Detroit, Leslie Whitaker/Chicago, Steve Barnes/Little Rock and Leslie Berestein/Los Angeles, with other bureaus*

UNIT 2
Organizing Homeland Security

Unit Selections

5. **Organizing the War on Terrorism**, William L. Waugh Jr. and Richard T. Sylves
6. **The Ultimate Turf War**, Richard E. Cohen, Siobhan Gorman, and Sydney J. Freedberg Jr.
7. **Requirements for a New Agency**, *Government Computer News*
8. **Homeland Security Funding Primer: Where We've Been, Where We're Headed**, *Center for Arms Control and Non-Proliferation*

Key Points to Consider

- How should the war on terrorism be organized?

- Why are congressional committees not likely to give up their right to oversee the new Department of Homeland Security?

- Why are effective internal and external communications vital to the success of the DHS?

 **Links: www.dushkin.com/online/**
These sites are annotated in the World Wide Web pages.

Congress Must Reform Its Committee Structure to Meet Homeland Security Needs
http://www.heritage.org/Research/HomelandDefense/EM823.cfm

Federal Emergency Management Agency (FEMA)
http://www.fema.gov

Mitretek Systems: Homeland Security & Counterterrorism
http://www.mitretek.org/home.nsf/BusinessAreas/HomelandSecurity

Keeping Tabs on Homeland Security
http://www.gao.gov/cghome/hs/homelandsecurity.html

One of the most difficult challenges facing the Bush administration is how to structure its domestic security efforts. As the military services, the Intelligence Community, federal law enforcement agencies, and state and local governments vie for funding and control of various aspects of the domestic security mission, the new Department of Homeland Security faces the problem of joining together 22 separate government bureaucracies into one cohesive, coordinated unit. Differing functions, management styles, corporate cultures, and potential internal rivalries notwithstanding, the DHS must find a way to effectively integrate the activities of various agencies in order to be successful. While some have criticized the lack of a "long-term strategic vision" in its organizational planning, the DHS announced that it will arrange the existing agencies into five broad areas of responsibility.

Organizational Overview

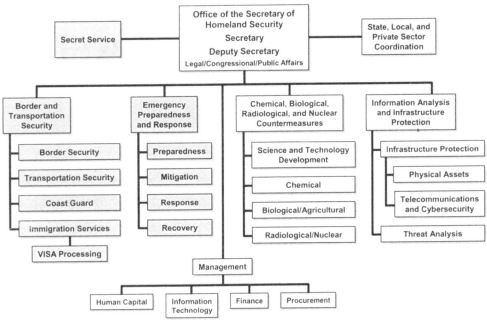

Department of Homeland Security
Proposed Organization by Function

According to the DHS, existing agencies will be organized by function into five major areas:

Border Transportation and Security (BTS), Emergency Preparedness and Response (EPR), Science and Technology (S&T), Information Analysis and Infrastructure Protection (IAIP), and Management. The largest of these five new divisions is the Directorate for Border and Transportation Security. Incorporating, among others, the more than 40,000 employees of the Transportation Security Administration, hastily created after 9/11, and the U.S. Customs Service, it will also include some of the functions of the agency formerly known as the Immigration and Naturalization Service. While the U.S. Coast Guard is slated to "maintain a separate identity," it is to "work closely" with the new head of the new BTS. The Directorate for Emergency Preparedness and Response will house the department's response capabilities to both natural and man-made disasters. Building on the work of the Federal Emergency Management Agency (FEMA), this directorate's task is to plan and organize DHS's crisis response capabilities.

The research and development functions of DHS will be housed in the Directorate for Science and Technology. In addition to identifying and developing new technologies that may help in the war on terrorism, this directorate will focus on research concerned with biological, chemical, radiological, and nuclear threats. The Directorate of Information Analysis and Infrastructure Protection represents the apparently limited intelligence function of the DHS. Focusing primarily on the analysis of data provided by others, the IAIP hopes to "bring under one roof" the assessment of intelligence "concerning threats to the homeland." Last, but, in the early stages of this massive reorganization probably most important, is the Directorate of Management. Charged with management and budgeting functions, it will oversee the complicated merger of the new department.

As the DHS embarks on this complicated merger of agencies and functions, questions concerning the scope of this merger continue to arise. The first article in this unit questions the potential compatibility of the emergency management and counterterrorism functions. It argues that the creation of DHS could undermine existing disaster response efforts. The next article focuses on the oversight problems created by the merger. It argues that under the present system as many as "88 congressional committees and subcommittees have jurisdiction of issues related to homeland security." The third article highlights the information technology challenges posed by the creation of the DHS. In a business in which communication and rapid exchange of information may save lives, the integration of existing and the development of new, more effective information technology systems is critical. The final article in this unit provides a quick overview of funding priorities and requests for homeland security.

Organizing the War on Terrorism

The network of public agencies, private firms, nonprofit organizations, ad hoc groups, and individual volunteers that deals with natural and technological hazards and disasters did a remarkable job of responding to and helping us recover from the September 11th attacks. That national emergency management network, along with the national security and law enforcement networks, provides a foundation for our war on terrorism, helps us mitigate the hazard of terrorism, and improves our preparedness for future violence. However, coordinating the efforts of the networks will be a real challenge for the director of homeland security and his or her state and local counterparts. Coordination will necessitate using legal authority to assure compliance, economic and other incentives to encourage compliance, formal partnerships to encourage collaboration, informal understandings to encourage cooperation, and personal encouragement to influence appropriate action. A top-down, command-and-control approach to the war on terrorism, such as the proposed Department of Homeland Security is intended to provide, may be counterproductive.

William L. Waugh, Jr.
Georgia State University

Richard T. Sylves
University of Delaware

The United States is now at war with terrorists and terrorism. It is, therefore, vital to inquire about whether the war effort is organized in a manner that will prove effective, and whether post–September 11 national investments in programs to reduce the hazard of terrorism are changing national, state, and local policy priorities for the better. Is the war organized to assure that we are prepared for the next attacks? Will the tidal wave of new federal laws and the mammoth increase in terrorism budget authority help federal, state, and local authorities address the threat of terrorism? Will the new emphasis on counterterrorism complement or undercut state and local governments' capacities to manage the many common hazards that are more likely to befall them?

The federal government is investing tens of billions of dollars in developing antiterrorism capabilities, based on the presumed potential for catastrophic terrorism rather than on measured risk. The identification of cities needing counterterrorism training, for example, was based on population and not

on their likelihood of becoming terrorist targets. Indeed, notwithstanding the events of September 11, the concern about nuclear, biological, and chemical terrorism has largely shaped the war effort. Such agents, including plutonium and other radioactive materials, were left in the rubble of the Soviet war machine and have been sold, lost, and temporarily misplaced. Nuclear, biological, and chemical agents also have been created by so-called "rogue states" and by independent terrorist organizations. Although delivery systems may still pose problems, terrorists do have the wherewithal to obtain such weapons and to carry out mass casualty attacks. Perhaps more important, some terrorist organizations have demonstrated their willingness to kill hundreds—if not thousands—of people in order to achieve their political goals.

We used to think, because many experts had surmised, that political terrorists "want a lot of people watching and not a lot of people dead." The attacks by Islamic fundamentalists on the World Trade Center in 1993, the Aum Shinryko sarin gas release in the Tokyo subway system in 1995, the attack perpetrated by Timothy McVeigh and Terry Nichols against the Alfred P. Murrah Federal Building in Oklahoma City in 1995, and the multiple attacks on the World Trade Center, the Pentagon, and the passengers of Flight 93 on September 11, 2001, manifestly demonstrate the willingness of terrorists to kill large numbers of people. The FBI and other agencies warned of possible incidents, and President Clinton signed Presidential Decision Directive 39 (PDD 39) in June 1995, which took on the threat of nuclear, biological, chemical, and radiological (that is, weapons of mass destruction) terrorism. In 1996, Congress passed and President Clinton signed the Nunn-Lugar-Domenici or Defense against Weapons of Mass Destruction Act, which further defined agency responsibilities and provided initial funding for the implementation of the national program to meet the threat of terrorism. Presidential Decision Directives 62 and 63 followed in 1998 to provide mechanisms for dealing with the threat of terrorism to America's critical infrastructure. Following the September 11 attacks, President Bush created the Office of Homeland Security and the Homeland Security Council by executive order, and a plethora of programs have been created to protect airports, seaports, public buildings, and other potential terrorist targets and to engage the American public in the war. Immigration policies are being reexamined as well. Political and administrative mechanisms to deal with the threat of terrorism are being designed, implemented, and refined.

Prior to September 11, the General Accounting Office reported some problems in priority setting and in how the Defense Department and other federal agencies were dealing with state and local agencies.

In essence, the "war on terrorism" creates a new set of organizational structures to address the threat of nuclear, biological, chemical, and radiological terrorism. The FBI houses the interagency program and coordinates its operations. The Department of Defense has a key role because of its expertise with nuclear, biological, and chemical warfare and with external threats, and the Department of Health and Human Services has a key role because of its expertise in dealing with public health hazards. The Federal Emergency Management Agency (FEMA) also has a key role in coordinating federal efforts and supporting state and local efforts. Washington basically directs the program such that federal agencies assume the lead in helping state and local governments improve their ability to respond to terrorist incidents involving weapons of mass destruction.

There has been some disagreement about the progress of the war. Some have opposed federal efforts because they discount the need to spend billions of dollars on programs to deal with the threat of weapons of mass destruction or because they do not

trust the Defense Department and federal law enforcement agencies. Because of September 11, some of this opposition has waned, but there is an increasing challenge to any new security measures that might infringe on civil liberties and affect political and administration prerogatives. Clearly, the September 11 event may mean for quite some time that any bill with the word "terrorism" in the title is assured congressional support. However, the design and implementation of the counterterrorism program, even before September 11, has been controversial.

For example, prior to September 11, the General Accounting Office reported some problems in priority setting and in how the Defense Department and other federal agencies were dealing with state and local agencies. Spending priorities sparked debate. Initially, there were concerns that the "Defense of the Homeland" was not integrated into the national emergency management system. The program was accused of dedicating too many resources to the threat of weapons of mass destruction and too little to the conventional weapons threat. Fertilizer bombs and other homemade devices are well within the capabilities of most domestic and international terrorists, while nuclear, biological, and chemical weapons are not; automatic rifles, plastic explosives, and other military weapons are readily available on the commercial and black markets. In short, while weapons of mass destruction may pose the greatest threat, less sophisticated attacks are more probable (see, for example, Smithson and Levy 2000).

Only days after the September attack, many were asking whether federal interagency competition and conflicts, combined with differences in organizational cultures and missions, would confound the homeland security initiative. The threat of terrorism elicits a military crisis-management response in terms of the potential scale and nature of attack. However, the American political system requires a law enforcement approach to domestic threats (unless the scale is so large that government function and national survival are threatened). September 11 has muddled this considerably. The military presence at airport security checkpoints is only one of the changes that has occurred. The U.S. mail is irradiated to counter anthrax contamination, and almost every facet of daily American life has been affected by the threat of terrorism. Americans do not know whether the next terror attack against the nation will transpire thousands of miles away from the homeland or simply down the block. Perhaps the most important lesson from the World Trade Center and Pentagon attacks is that terrorism cannot be prevented entirely. Some acts can be thwarted and some effects can be lessened, but there are too many potential targets to protect, and our open society affords opportunity for enemies to attack.

Fortunately, a national emergency management system has been in place to deal with catastrophic disasters of natural and unnatural origin for quite some time. When incidents at the state or local level exceed the capabilities of first responders, additional resources are brought to bear from adjacent jurisdictions and from the federal government. Emergency managers are well practiced in coordinating their work in multijurisdictional and multiorganizational operations. There are lessons to be learned from that system, and first among them is that emergency management is a bottom-up process. Capacity building has to begin at the level of the first responders who will be responsible for dealing with crises and their consequences until support arrives. The second lesson is in how multiorganizational, multisector, and intergovernmental operations are coordinated.

The increased professionalization of state and local emergency managers has encouraged movement away from the command-and-control approach that was common two or three decades ago, when civil defense against nuclear attack was the paramount concern. Coordination, rather than command and control, has become the more common approach (Waugh 1993, 1994, 2001a). Indeed, it is a concern of emergency management professionals that the response to September 11 will bring back that earlier era rather than produce a more consensually based and elegantly interlaced emergency management system—one that does not superimpose overbearing command systems riddled with secrecy requirements that complicate the collaboration and public involvement essential to dealing with hazards and disasters.

Will a post–September 11 emergency management system break down the networks of public, nonprofit, and private disaster organizations, or will it empower state and local governments and their partners to contribute to the counterterrorism effort in a reasonable way? If the war on terrorism inadvertently undercuts or distorts an emergency system designed to deal with so-called routine disasters, it may well weaken current capabilities to manage conventional hazards *and* the hazard posed by terrorism. FEMA's Office of National Preparedness may assure that the threat of natural and technological hazards is not forgotten in the rush to prepare for terrorist-sponsored catastrophes, but it is also important that the war on terrorism be understood in the context of all of the other major hazards that face America.

The War on Terrorism

In large measure, current U.S. counterterrorism policy is a direct reaction to the events of September 11. The war on terrorism was announced, and the U.S. government responded with air strikes against al-Qaeda and Taliban bases in Afghanistan and police raids on suspected terrorist cells in Europe and elsewhere. In essence, national policy became a multilevel operation to kill or apprehend those associated with Osama bin Laden and his organization. Historically, this has been the pattern of U.S. policy making. Crisis—whether precipitated by national security threat or natural disaster—gives the impetus for policy makers to act, and they, as a rule, define the policy problem narrowly. In the parlance of the military, policy makers always prepare to fight the last war. In this case, they are responding to the kind of terrorism experienced on September 11 without necessarily addressing the broader threat posed by terrorist violence. To be sure, we have had recent acts of domestic terrorism, evidently including the anthrax attacks, and there are other terrorist organizations operating in the world that pose threats to U.S. citizens at home and abroad. Not all terrorist groups have the same objectives, modus operandi, or capabilities as al-Qaeda, and, if our programs are to address future

threats, they should be focused broadly enough to accommodate at least the most serious known threats.

The question, then, is how to organize the war on terrorism to best meet the range of threats posed to the United States and its citizens by terrorists. In the March/April 2002 issue of *Public Administration Review,* Charles Wise examines the organizational issues surrounding the Office of Homeland Security and suggests the homeland security program might best be structured in a less hierarchical manner than many believe. At present, the coordinator of homeland security has little real authority over the myriad of departments, agencies, and offices that are involved in dealing with the terrorist threat. Governor Ridge has to rely on the cooperation and resources of others in order to design, implement, and maintain a coherent set of programs. Wise concludes that a network approach will be more appropriate and likely more effective.

Network management is an emerging art in public administration and is particularly appropriate—if not absolutely necessary—when officials lack the direct authority to pursue policy goals. The sheer number of actors involved makes coordination a serious problem, particularly when many view the task as a peripheral mission. Coordinating agencies might use direct authority when it is available, direct influence (such as financial incentives) when circumstances permit, indirect influence (such as technical assistance) when feasible, and less formal supports (such as expressions of personal support) when more formal and substantive support is not appropriate. Goals are pursued through some combination of regulatory relationships, contractual relationships, formal and informal partnerships, and personal relationships (see Waugh 2002). As Wise points out, direct command-and-control approaches may even be counterproductive (142). Control encourages resentment and resistance, while collaboration encourages commitment and cooperation.

So, again, how should the war on terrorism be organized? The discussion to follow will describe the current national emergency management system and how it deals with hazards such as terrorism, the new counterterrorism structures that are part of the "Defense of the Homeland" programs, and the poor fit between the new structures and the national emergency management system. It will conclude with an examination of the policy implications of the current war on terrorism.

Crisis Management before September 11

When three airliners struck the World Trade Center towers and the Pentagon on September 11 and a fourth crashed in Pennsylvania, the national emergency management system was activated. While military aircraft were positioned to protect New York City and the national capital from aerial attack, and security forces were positioned to protect the nation from land and sea attack, thousands of first responders were mobilized to deal with the immediate crisis and the consequences of the attacks. Tens of thousands of additional emergency responders followed to provide support for the rescue and recovery efforts. The emergency response included the agencies identified in the National Response Plan as having lead and supporting responsibilities, including the American Red Cross. It also included state and local government agencies, nongovernmental organizations, ad hoc groups that emerged to provide assistance and tens of thousands of unaffiliated volunteers who wished to assist. Medical volunteers and search and rescue teams came from all over the United States and even from outside. In most respects, the response was similar to what might be expected following a major natural disaster, such as an earthquake, although the scale and nature of the World Trade Center disaster likely increased the attraction of outside groups. The point is simply that a national emergency management system was already in existence and offered remarkable capacity to respond to the events on September 11. The system was able to deal with a terrorist disaster.

The National Emergency Management System

The national emergency management system has expanded and evolved over the past two decades. Throughout American history, when disasters have occurred, communities have relied on nongovernmental organizations, private firms, individual volunteers, and the ad hoc groups that emerge in response to need, as well as their public safety agencies. The disaster network is loosely structured, organizationally diverse, motivated by a broad range of interests, and, in part, ad hoc. It is also flexible and very capable. Most communities still rely on the American Red Cross, the Salvation Army, and a few other general-purpose relief agencies to take care of the victims of smaller disasters and to assist public agencies during larger disasters. In other words, FEMA and its state and local counterparts are only the tip of the proverbial iceberg.

Formal partnership arrangements, memoranda of understanding, contractual relationships, personal connections, and informal agreements to cooperate and share resources hold the network together.

The network is extensive. There are thousands of organizations, large and small, in the United States that are engaged in disaster-related activities. Nonprofit voluntary organizations range from large environmental groups to small faith-based groups. Some have highly specialized skills, such as search and rescue, amateur radio communications, and emergency feeding or shelter, and others are much broader in scope. The American Red Cross has a national network of offices, intensive training programs for volunteers, and capabilities to respond to many kinds of disaster. Smaller organizations may operate out of the basements of churches, synagogues, or mosques, or even out of members' garages, but they often provide critical services. Coordination and cooperation among nonprofit, voluntary groups has been increasing at the national and state levels. The National Volunteer Organizations in Action in Disaster was

formed to provide a vehicle to coordinate the planning of disaster responses and to minimize duplications of effort. State volunteer organizations fulfill similar regional and local roles. Members range from the American Red Cross and the Salvation Army to smaller organizations such as the Mennonite Disaster Services, the Phoenix Society for Burn Victims, Volunteers in Technical Assistance, and the Second Harvest National Network of Food Banks. State and local emergency management agencies are relying more on such groups to provide essential services that are unavailable through government offices.

Professional organizations are also involved. Some of the more prominent organizations are the National Emergency Management Association (representing state emergency management agencies and managers), the International Association of Emergency Managers (representing local emergency managers), the American Planning Association, the American Psychological Association's Disaster Response Network, the American Public Works Association's Council on Emergency Management, and the American Society for Public Administration's Section on Emergency and Crisis Management. The network also includes organizations representing engineers, architects, airline pilots, floodplain managers, funeral home directors, dam safety officials, local government officials, insurance companies, fire chiefs and firefighters, risk managers, and other professions with disaster skills and concerns. Many of these groups assisted in the World Trade Center and Pentagon response and recovery operation. Private-sector organizations provide a variety of services ranging from technical assistance to debris management, and associations from particular industries—for instance, the Chemical Manufacturers Association—provide resources. The threat of terrorism to business is being addressed through the training programs of the American Society for Industrial Security, for example.

Ad hoc or "emergent" groups of volunteers also form in the aftermath of disaster, as they did following the September 11 attacks. Some groups can be highly organized, and others may be amorphous groupings of volunteers. Such groups and individual volunteers can provide needed manpower for disaster operations if they are integrated into the existing emergency management system, but they may interfere with operations if they are not organized and used effectively. Coordinating the activities of volunteer and other nonprofit groups, for-profit organizations and individuals, and government agencies is a complex and difficult task. Emergency managers have to anticipate the emergence of such groups and individuals and find ways to utilize the financial, administrative, and political resources they bring to hazard reduction and disaster management. It is a complex network with fragmented authority. Formal partnership arrangements, memoranda of understanding, contractual relationships, personal connections, and informal agreements to cooperate and share resources hold the network together. While some agencies use command-and-control mechanisms (such as the incident command system) in their own operations, most are loosely structured, consensually oriented, and dependent on trust and commitment from professional and volunteer staff to maintain organizational purpose.

The Counterterrorism System

U.S. policy on terrorism has evolved over the past half-century. President Nixon and Secretary of State Henry Kissinger formally enunciated a "no negotiation, no compromise" policy in the early 1970s following an international terrorist incident in which two American diplomats were killed. The policy was also applied to domestic terrorist incidents. Nonetheless, there have been incidents in which negotiations were held and terrorist demands were met in order to secure the release of hostages (see Waugh 1982, 1990). In response to increased international terrorism, President Reagan signed National Security Directive 207 in 1986, assigning responsibility for coordinating the U.S. response to international terrorist incidents to an Interagency Working Group under the auspices of the National Security Council. The State Department was the designated lead agency for terrorist incidents outside the United States, and the FBI was the designated lead agency for incidents within the United States.

In June 1995, President Clinton signed Presidential Decision Directive (PDD) 39, reaffirming U.S. policy on terrorism and spelling out the strategy to "reduce vulnerabilities and prevent and deter terrorists acts before they occur; respond to terrorist acts that do occur, including managing crises and apprehending and punishing terrorist perpetrators; and manage the consequences of terrorist attacks" (GAO 1997, 2). The directive reaffirmed the lead responsibilities for the Department of State and the FBI for crisis management and assigned lead responsibility for domestic consequence management to FEMA.

As the lead agency for domestic terrorist incidents, the FBI can call upon virtually any federal agency that has needed expertise. The Bureau may also request the activation of a Domestic Emergency Support Team with representatives from agencies that can provide specialized expertise (GAO 1997, 43). Partial Domestic Emergency Support Teams have been deployed for major events, including the 1996 Olympics and the 1997 presidential inauguration, to involve agencies with expertise that might be needed in the event of a terrorist incident (GAO 1997, 45). The Department of Defense can provide assistance through a variety of facilities and units, including the Chemical, Biological Defense Command, the U.S. Army Explosive Ordnance Disposal group, the Defense Technical Response Group, and the U.S. Army Technical Escort Unit (GAO 1997, 45). The Defense Department also provides Civil Support Teams to support state and local first responders early in a crisis. Ten regional teams were created initially, each with 22 full-time National Guard personnel, to identify biological and chemical agents and to assess situations so that additional resources can be brought in. More teams have been added, and there is increasing pressure to expand the number even more—eventually, perhaps, to permit each state to create its own team. The Environmental Protection Agency has response teams and research laboratories to deal with chemical and radiological incidents, and the Department of Energy can use its radiological monitoring and response units (GAO 1997, 61). The Department of Energy also can activate a nuclear incident team, if needed.

If an incident exceeds FBI capabilities, the attorney general and the secretary of defense may agree that an exception to the Posse Comitatus Act is necessary and ask the president to sign an executive order and issue an emergency proclamation for the use of the military to enforce civilian law. Draft documents are held for the president's signature, should action be required on very short notice (GAO 1997, 47). The counterterrorism effort is largely top-down, with the lead agencies deciding what resources are needed and who should participate.

By contrast, dealing with the consequences of terrorist attacks more closely resembles the response to natural and technological disasters. FEMA coordinates the consequence management operation following the Federal Response Plan and its Terrorism Annex or, if it is a radiological incident, the Federal Radiological Emergency Response Plan. The Department of Health and Human Services can activate Disaster Medical Assistance Teams to provide emergency medical care. In cooperation with FEMA, the Departments of Defense, Veterans Administration, and Health and Human Services can activate the National Disaster Medical System to locate hospital beds for victims and Disaster Mortuary Teams to assist in processing deceased victims. The Defense Department's medical facilities and research institutes also may be called upon. The Health and Human Services Department's National Pharmaceutical Stockpile program provides necessary pharmaceutical supplies to local, state, and federal authorities in the event of a disaster, including incidents involving nuclear, biological, or chemical contamination.

Other federal agencies are tasked under the Federal Response Plan to provide emergency medical care, temporary shelter, search and rescue, and measures to restore critical lifelines, as well as providing traditional disaster assistance (for example, public assistance, small business loans, and individual assistance) to the victims. It is important to note that, as in other kinds of disasters, the federal government is not the lead government in managing the consequences of terrorist incidents. State and local governments have primary responsibility for disaster response and recovery from domestic terrorist incidents, and host nations have those responsibilities following international terrorist incidents. When the resources of state and local governments are overwhelmed, the governor can request assistance from the federal government. The Robert T. Stafford Disaster Relief and Emergency Assistance Act permits the president to issue a presidential disaster declaration or designate an incident as a "major emergency." The declaration or designation permits FEMA and other federal agencies to provide a range of disaster assistance to individuals, businesses, communities, and governments. Following the September 11 attacks, presidential disaster declarations were issued for affected counties in New York, New Jersey, Connecticut, Virginia, and Maryland, and for the District of Columbia.

To some extent, PDD-39 does recognize that crisis management and consequence management functions may be carried out at the same time. An Interagency Consequence Management Group is included in the Joint Operations Center to advise officials. The differentiation between crisis management and consequence management is an important one for a variety of reasons, not least of which is that it suggests a two-phase process. The comprehensive emergency management model currently used in dealing with natural and technological disasters was originally conceptualized as having four phases: mitigation (hazard reduction), preparedness, response, and recovery. Increasingly, however, it is recognized that the four functions are not separate or sequential. Mitigation should begin before there are consequences, so that officials can minimize loss of life and reduce property loss and, thereby, speed recovery. In the "Homeland Security" program, there is some consideration of consequences, but until the FBI decides the "crisis" is under control, consequence management may be a low priority. Fortunately, the creation of FEMA's National Preparedness Office seems to reflect an understanding of the need for mitigation before terrorist incidences.

More than 40 federal departments and other agencies were involved in combating terrorism prior to September 2001, and the number has increased since.

Congressional "Homeland Security" (or Domestic Preparedness) priorities were spelled out in the 1996 Nunn-Lugar-Domenici or Defense Against Weapons of Mass Destruction Act (an amendment to the National Defense Authorization Act for FY97, P.L. 104-201). Under the act, "weapons of mass destruction" are defined in Section 1403 as "any weapon or device that is intended, or has the capability, to cause death or serious bodily injury to a significant number of people through the release, dissemination, or impact of (1) toxic or poisonous chemicals or their precursors; (2) a disease organism; or (3) radiation or radioactivity." The act specifically cites the potential transfer of devices, materials, and information on nuclear, biological, and chemical weapons from the former Soviet states to terrorist organizations and hostile nations.

The act requires the secretary of defense to implement a program to train and provide technical assistance to local, state, and federal civilian personnel so they can respond to emergencies involving the use or threatened use of such an attack (see Section 1411a). The assistance to federal, state, and local agencies includes training to use equipment for the detection of chemical and biological agents or nuclear material; protecting emergency responders and the public; decontamination; establishing a "hot line" for information dissemination; using the National Guard and Reserves; and loaning equipment (Section 1412e).

The secretary of defense was designated the responsible official for implementing the program until October 1, 1998, when President Clinton assigned responsibility to the attorney general and a new FBI-led interagency office was created for the National Domestic Preparedness program. The act reaffirmed the legal restrictions on the use of military personnel and units in civilian law enforcement (that is, the Posse Comitatus Act) and the acceptability of using military personnel for the "immediate protection of human life" when law enforcement

officials are unable to do so (Section 1416d). The act goes on to mandate that the president assist in building the capacities of federal, state, and local agencies to deal with the use or threatened use of "weapons of mass destruction," and it provides additional funding to support efforts to interdict, control, and coordinate policies and measures designed to stop the proliferation of such weapons, as well as to support the cooperative threat-reduction program with the former Soviet states. It was unclear that funding would be more than one year, and the limited definition of weapons of mass destruction defined spending priorities.

The Department of Defense was also tasked with training local first responders to deal with terrorist incidents involving weapons of mass destruction. The Chemical Defense Training Facility at Fort McClellan, Alabama, was designated as the site for training, and training sessions began in October 1995. The Domestic Preparedness Program began in FY 1997, with the goal of training police, fire, and emergency medical services personnel in 120 designated U.S. cities by 2001. Under the program, each city received $300,000 in equipment from the Defense Department. FEMA also began providing grants to states for terrorism-preparedness activities, including consequence management planning, exercising, and training, and to state fire-training centers for first-responder terrorism training courses (NDPO 1999a, 2). The Department of Health and Human Services, through the Public Health Service, began setting up Metropolitan Medical Response Systems and providing equipment and pharmaceuticals (NDPO 1999b, 3–5).

On May 22, 1998, President Clinton signed PDD-62, establishing the Office of the National Coordinator for Security, Infrastructure Protection, and Counterterrorism to oversee counterterrorism, infrastructure protection, consequence management, and preparedness programs. The national coordinator works within the National Security Council, reports to the president through the assistant to the president for national security affairs, and makes recommendations on budgets and policies regarding terrorism (White House 1998a). On the same day, President Clinton also signed PDD-63 on protecting America's critical infrastructures to address the vulnerability of the nation's information system infrastructure. The National Infrastructure Protection Center was created by the FBI to deal with attacks, with a national coordinator to oversee efforts to reduce vulnerabilities (White House 1998b).

More than 40 federal departments and other agencies were involved in combating terrorism prior to September 2001, and the number has increased since. Now there is a homeland security chief, Governor Tom Ridge, and a Homeland Security Council with a rapidly expanding staff. There is also a Transportation Security Administration in the Department of Transportation to oversee efforts to protect the nation's transportation systems. The Defense Department has created a Northern Command to oversee military efforts to defend the nation and to coordinate those efforts with other agencies. FEMA has been given an enhanced role in the homeland security program as officials have come to appreciate the magnitude of the effort and the need to coordinate with state and local agencies. FEMA has developed a strong information technology system to support disaster operations (Lisagor 2002), and its new Office of National Preparedness will have a lead role in preparing first responders to deal with terrorism, coordinating federal programs, and supporting the development of the Citizen Corps (U.S. House 2002).

How Should We Organize the War on Terrorism?

Prior to September 2001, the General Accounting Office had identified a number of serious problems with the "Defense of the Homeland" programs, including the lack of a common definition of terrorism among the lead agencies (GAO 1997, 16); the selection of cities for first-responder training without appropriate attention to the existing emergency management networks that would be involved in any major incident (GAO 1998, 2); confusion about the "loan" of equipment by the Defense Department (even though the department considers the loans to be permanent) (GAO 1998, 2); and the lack of a systematic assessment of the risk of attack by terrorists using biological or chemical weapons and the vulnerability of potential targets (GAO 1999). Problems in the relationships among the Defense Department and other agencies and the complexity of the weapons of mass destruction program were also noted (GAO 1998, 2–3). The TOPOFF ("top official") exercise in 2000 revealed many of the same coordination problems. Turf battles, communication problems, and differences in how the threat was defined raised serious questions about the nation's capability to respond to catastrophic terrorist incidents. Another TOPOFF exercise is planned.

The 120 cities designated for first-responder training were selected based on population (all over 144,000 based on the 1995 census estimate) and represented 22 percent of the U.S. population, 38 states and Washington, D.C., and one-quarter of the cities in California and Texas. No threat or vulnerability analyses were conducted to choose the cities. In fact, the General Accounting Office concluded that training in fewer cities and including the local emergency management networks responsible for dealing with disasters would speed the process and be more effective (GAO 1998, 6–8). Some of the problems identified by the General Accounting Office have already been addressed, such as the need to broaden the training to include metropolitan response networks. However, threat assessments are still needed. Using worst-case scenarios to set training priorities and allocate funding is not good policy.

PDD-39 and the Nunn-Lugar-Domenici Act of 1996, as well as PDD-62 and 63, created a national-security-focused counter-terrorism structure that was, in effect, layered over the national emergency management system, with little attempt to integrate the two. For minor incidents of terrorism, the system will likely work as intended. For major incidents of terrorism involving mass casualties and/or large areas of contamination or destruction (whether caused by the use of nuclear, biological, or chemical weapons or the use of more conventional weapons), the system will be much less effective than it might be. As Charles Wise suggests, coordinating such diverse elements will require considerable political and administrative skill. The principal reasons for concern are the shifting of decision-making responsibilities from agencies with strong working relationships with their state and local counterparts to agencies (such as the Defense Department and, perhaps to a lesser extent, the Department of Justice) that do not have strong records of cooperation with state and local government agencies, nongovernmental organizations, private firms, volunteers, and victims. The focus on crisis management will not encourage attention to preparedness and mitigation measures and, even with a consequence management team participating in the response, to recovery needs. If a catastrophic terrorist event occurs, consequence management may well be the immediate priority, with law enforcement concerns being secondary.

Homeland security suffers from the variety of perspectives on terrorism that its constituent agencies bring to the table. The focus on weapons of mass destruction is problematic because the definition permits the inclusion of agents that pose threats to only a very small number of people. Poison-dipped bullets and small quantities of biological agents with little or no potential for wide dispersal have been termed weapons of mass destruction, for example. Radiological material might conceivably contaminate large numbers of people if dispersed widely, such as in a "dirty bomb" incident, or concentrated in large-enough quantities in a heavily populated area, but the imprecise definition deems virtually all radiological material as weapons of mass destruction. After the Oklahoma City bombing, explosive devices were added to the list, although analysts all too frequently revert to the old nuclear, biological, and chemical definition. While the terminology, in and of itself, may facilitate legal action, it also may lessen the likelihood that such threats will be taken seriously by responders and potential victims.

The focus on weapons of mass destruction is also distracting state and local emergency management agencies from their responsibility to address more common hazards. Terrorism is a serious hazard that should be addressed, but emergency managers in California have to concentrate their efforts on the earthquakes that are certain to occur, emergency managers in Florida have to concentrate on the next Force 5 hurricane, and emergency managers in Texas, Pennsylvania, and elsewhere have to concentrate on their next floods, tornadoes, and other hazards. To justify the attention that homeland security requires, state and local emergency managers need to build capacities to deal with the more common and certain hazards and to expand their networks and resource bases. They need to integrate essential emergency response elements into their networks and provide mechanisms to facilitate a collaborative effort. The definition of "consequence" is vague and certainly makes it unclear whether such efforts should include the kinds of hazard management activities that would be used in dealing with natural and technological hazards. Homeland security needs to be based on a broad perspective on the phenomena of terrorism and integrate a broad range of mitigation and preparedness programs into the antiterrorism effort.

There is a decided tendency to define the terrorist threat in law enforcement and military terms only. That is the nature of war, perhaps. However, if we are dealing with a hazard that will remain with us well after the al-Qaeda network and its sponsors are subdued, we should be prepared for whatever form the next round of violence takes. History has, in fact, demonstrated that terrorism is relatively common, and there is no reason to think it will disappear. Therefore, we should be prepared to manage the hazard in the long term (Waugh 2001a). The war effort should include law enforcement and military options to prevent acts of terrorism against the United States and its citizens, and against others in the world, but it should also include those actions that may facilitate security. For example, the principles of Crime Prevention through Environmental Design can be used to reduce the threat to public buildings by controlling access and facilitating security. We can be protected from terrorists, disgruntled employees, abusive spouses, and other criminals at the same time (Waugh 20001b).

However the war on terrorism is organized, will it be open, building upon decades of investment in community capacity-building, or will it be yet another classical closed bureaucracy, preparing to respond for rather than with communities?

Lastly, any weapon that can cause mass casualties or large-scale economic or social loss is a weapon of mass destruction. A computer virus that shuts down critical services can be a weapon of mass destruction. A ship aimed at port facilities or dams can be a weapon of mass destruction. The World Trade Center disaster involved airplane crashes, high-rise fires, and structural collapses. In many respects, the disaster response was similar to what has occurred during major earthquakes. The threat of chemical weapons has often been described as similar to a hazardous materials accident, and in many respects that is probably true. The difference, however, is in the number of potential casualties. The threat of bioterrorism is usually defined in terms similar to a major pandemic, such as the Spanish flu outbreak of 1918; again, in many respects, the analogy may be well chosen. We have capabilities to respond to hazardous materials spills and even pandemics.

The real issue may be the scale of the disaster. A serious chemical attack could cause mass casualties and require a much larger response than fire departments and hazmat specialists generally understand. In short, the attack and its consequences may be much more than a large hazmat incident. Trying to extrapolate from our familiar disasters to far larger catastrophes may be a serious problem. Focusing on large events such as the World Trade Center tower collapses, which required resources far beyond those of New York City, from federal and state assets to small community groups and unaffiliated volunteers, may be the key. A national system to deal with the threat of terrorism should include those who are responsible for the less obvious mitigation, preparedness, response, and recovery efforts.

Many lessons can be drawn from our experience with natural and technological hazards, if we are willing to broaden our view of the terrorism hazard (Sylves 2002).

The proposed Department of Homeland Security is intended to assure coordination of the counterterrorism effort. However, the new bureaucracy is already excluding those without security clearances in hand and legally defined roles in homeland security. Law enforcement and national security agencies are not noted for their openness to public participation, their willingness and abilities to work with communities and to integrate volunteers into operations, and their sensitivity to the plights of victims. Notwithstanding the call for a Citizen's Corps of volunteers, there has been little indication that the homeland security apparatus knows how to integrate civilians into its operations. Whether the department will be open to those with expertise and resources when a catastrophic disaster occurs, be it terrorist-spawned or a natural disaster, is also a serious question. Many of the organizations that assisted in the September 11th rescue and recovery operation are already out of the loop. Whether the commitment to disaster mitigation, preventing or reducing the effects of disaster, will continue is also a serious question. Efforts to encourage communities to become more disaster resistant and resilient have been based upon formal and informal partnerships. The imposition of federal or state authority would be fatal to many of those relationships. Lastly, the American public has come to expect a great deal of transparency and sensitivity when dealing with FEMA and other disaster agencies. However the war on terrorism is organized, will it be open, building upon decades of investment in community capacity-building, or will it be yet another classical closed bureaucracy, preparing to respond for rather than with communities?

References

General Accounting Office (GAO). 1997. *Combating Terrorism: Federal Agencies' Efforts to Implement National Policy and Strategy.* Washington, DC: Government Printing Office, GAO, GAO/NSAID-97-254.

_____. 1998. *Combating Terrorism: Opportunities to Improve Domestic Preparedness Program Focus and Efficiency.* Washington, DC: Government Printing Office. GAO, GAO/NSIAD-99-3.

_____. 1999. *Combating Terrorism: Observations on Biological Terrorism and Public Health Initiatives.* Washington, DC: Government Printing Office. GAO/T-NSIAD-99-112.

Lee, Deborah. 1998. Integration of Reserve Components Responds to New Threat. *Defense Viewpoint* 13(29). Available at *http://www.defenselink.mil/speeches/1998/s19980s07-Lee.html. Accessed June 14, 2002.*

Lisagor, Megan. 2002. Reinventing FEMA. *Federal Computer Week,* March 25. Available at *http://www.fcw.com. Accessed June 14, 2002.*

National Domestic Preparedness Office (NDPO). 1999a. FEMA Terrorism-Related Grants. *The Beacon,* January 22, 2. Available at *http://www.ndpo.gov/beacon/1999/jan99.pdf. Accessed June 14, 2002.*

_____. 1999b. Department of Health and Human Services Role at the NDPO. *The Beacon,* June 15, 1–5. Available at *http://www.ndpo.gov/beacon/1999/jun99.pdf. Accessed June 14, 2002.*

Smithson, Amy, and Leslie-Anne Levy. 2000. *Ataxia: The Chemical and Biological Terrorism Threat and the U.S. Response.* Report no. 35. Washington, DC: Henry L. Stimson Center.

Sylves, Richard T. 2002. Comments on "Countering Terrorism: Lessons Learned from Natural and Technological Disasters." National Academy of Sciences Natural Disasters Roundtable, February 28–March 1.

U.S. Congress. 1996. Defense Against Weapons of Mass Destruction Act of 1996. *National Defense Authorization Act for Fiscal Year 1997, Conference Report,* 104th Cong., 2d Sess., July 30, 303–21.

U.S. House Committee on Transportation and Infrastructure. 2002. New Office Will Better Coordinate Domestic Terrorism Response, According to Government Officials. Press Release, April 11.

Waugh, William L., Jr. 1982. *International Terrorism: How Nations Respond to Terrorists.* Salisbury, NC: Documentary Publications.

_____. 1990. *Terrorism and Emergency Management.* New York: Marcel Dekker.

_____. 1993. Co-ordination or Control: Organizational Design and the Emergency Management Function. *International Journal of Disaster Prevention and Management* 2(2): 17–31.

_____. 1994. Regionalizing Emergency Management: Counties as State and Local Government. *Public Administration Review* 54(3): 253–58.

_____. 2001a. Managing Terrorism as an Environmental Hazard. In *Handbook of Crisis and Emergency Management,* edited by Ali Farazmand, 659–76. New York: Marcel Dekker.

_____. 2001b. *Terrorism and Emergency Management.* Emmitsburg, MD: FEMA, Emergency Management Institute. Available at *http://training.fema.gov/emiweb/edu/Terrorism.zip.* Accessed June 14, 2002.

_____. 2002. *Leveraging Networks to Meet National Goals: FEMA and the Safe Construction Networks.* Washington, DC: PricewaterhouseCoopers Endowment for the Business of Government.

White House, Office of the Press Secretary. 1998a. *Fact Sheet: Combating Terrorism: Presidential Decision Directive 62,* May 22. Available at *http://www.fas.org/irp/offdocs/pdd/index.html.* Accessed June 14, 2002.

_____. 1998b. *Fact Sheet: Protecting America's Critical Infrastructures: Presidential Decision Directive 63,* May 22. Available at *http://www.fas.org/irp/offdocs/pdd/index.html.* Accessed June 14, 2002.

_____. 1998c. *White Paper: The Clinton Administration's Policy on Critical Infrastructure Protection: Presidential Decision Directive 63,* May 22. Available at *http://www.fas.org/irp/offdocs/pdd/index.html.* Accessed June 14, 2002.

Wise, Charles R. 2002. Organizing for Homeland Security. *Public Administration Review* 62(2): 131–44.

William L. Waugh, Jr., *teaches public administration in the Andrew Young School of Policy Studies at Georgia State University. His research focuses on the design of disaster policies and hazard-reduction programs and on the coordination of multiorganizational and intergovernmental operations. His publications include* Living with Hazards, Dealing with Disasters *(2000),* Terrorism and Emergency Management *(1990), and* International Terrorism *(1982).* **Email: padwlw@wfw@langate.gsu.edu.**

Richard T. Sylves *teaches environmental, energy, and disaster policy and public budgeting in the Department of Political Science and International Relations at the University of Delaware. His recent research has focused on the politics and economics of presidential disaster declarations. He has authored and coauthored many publications, including two books,* Disaster Management in the U.S. and Canada *(1996) and* Cities and Disaster *(1990).* **Email: sylves@udel.edu.**

The Ultimate Turf War

THE ALREADY-DIFFICULT JOB OF THE NEW HOMELAND SECURITY DEPARTMENT IS GREATLY COMPLICATED BY THE FACT THAT MULTIPLE CONGRESSIONAL COMMITTEES ARE VYING FOR OVERSIGHT RIGHTS.

BY RICHARD E. COHEN, SIOBHAN GORMAN, AND SYDNEY J. FREEDBERG JR.

Last June, President Bush called congressional leaders to the White House to lay out the challenge they faced in creating the massive new Homeland Security Department he had just proposed. "There's going to be a lot of turf protection in the Congress," Bush pointedly warned some of the potential culprits seated around the table in the Cabinet Room. Then, raising the stakes, the president added, "I'm convinced that by working together, we can do what's right for America." It took Congress almost six months of often-bitter debate to get the job done.

Now, Homeland Security Secretary-Designate Tom Ridge must assemble a functioning team for his new department out of 170,000 employees as diverse as Coast Guard captains, Federal Emergency Management Agency relief workers, ex-FBI computer experts, and Agriculture Department scientists. Meanwhile, he must rely heavily on other still-independent agencies to handle key parts of the homeland security job; the CIA is in charge of intelligence, for example, and the Energy Department manages high-tech research.

Coordinating all of that may be a piece of cake, however, compared with another challenge facing the Bush administration. When asked to name the chief obstacle, one pessimistic yet well-informed official said, "What's going to sink the Department of Homeland Security is the fact that there's no single oversight or Appropriations subcommittee."

That is a stark assessment and, at first, it seems a bewildering one. With all the other problems confronting the new department, how can the biggest one be the seemingly arcane issue of congressional committee organization?

Well, by the White House's count last June, a total of 88 congressional committees and subcommittees have jurisdiction over issues related to homeland security, and now the new department will handle many of those issues. (*See chart, Congressional Committees with Homeland Security Jurisdiction.*") That gives the Homeland Security Department a lot of congressional bosses to work with—and answer to—in its drive to make America safer. In fact, at the end of the 107th Congress, the membership of those 88 committees and subcommittees with homeland security jurisdiction included all 100 senators and all but 20 of the 432 House members. These House and Senate panels are chaired by lawmakers who value their gavels highly, and who did not get where they are by stifling their ambition or competitive drive.

LET THE GAMES BEGIN: President Bush's signing of legislation creating a Homeland Security Department in late November set off a congressional power struggle.

In a worst-cast scenario, rival chairmen are "going to try to get Ridge involved in their own committee fights" over who has jurisdiction over the new department, predicted a former Pentagon lawyer who advised members of Congress on homeland security legislation. He added that chairmen may schedule competing hearings and tell Ridge, "'Come to me first, I've got your priority. Yeah, I know this other committee has asked you to testify, but that's *our* jurisdiction.' Depending on how nasty it gets, subpoenas start flying," the lawyer speculated. "It'll be chaos, and if the congressional leadership isn't willing to step up, it'll fall on Ridge to honor this committee and not that committee."

Members of Congress from time to time bemoan their byzantine committee structures, which have been shaped far more by parochial influence and historical accident than by rational policy making. But members have rarely been willing to modify their committees, because in many cases, they can manipulate the complexities to their advantage. The House and Senate have broad discretion to organize themselves whatever way they wish, giving lawmakers enormous power to meddle.

AT ODDS:
A proposal by Rep. Curt Weldon to consolidate authority over the new department has committee chairmen such as Rep. Don Young grumbling.

Nevertheless, a small number of members have been crusading to reorganize the committees in order to oversee the Homeland Security Department more effectively. A week after the November election, the House Republican Conference quietly passed a nonbinding resolution, sponsored by Rep. Curt Weldon, R-Pa., "to consolidate the authorization and appropriations processes" for the new department. Weldon and other reformers argue that a single new committee in each chamber should oversee and authorize all homeland security programs, and that a single Appropriations subcommittee should fund them.

Such an overhaul would take authority away from dozens of chairmen who hold jurisdiction now, many of whom are reluctant to give up that influence. Take House Transportation and Infrastructure Committee Chairman Don Young, R-Alaska, whose panel claims responsibility for two of the biggest agencies and half of the federal employees being folded into the new department. Young is adamantly defending his turf. Since 9/11, his committee has written the aviation security bill and a maritime safety bill. He's working on rail safety, bridge and dam security, and Coast Guard security issues.

"Creating a new committee with members and staff who have little or no experience in dealing with these issues and the agencies themselves would be a huge setback for Congress in trying to have oversight over the workings of the agency," said Young spokesman Steven Hansen. "Most people don't think it's a good idea—talk to probably every chairman and every subcommittee chairman."

But many experts say that sharply paring down the number of committees with jurisdiction is the only way to ensure the success of the Homeland Security Department. "If they don't create a separate oversight committee in the House and the Senate, there's never going to be a functioning department," said John Hamre, a former deputy Defense secretary and the current president of the Center for Strategic and International Studies. "You can't create a new department if all the elements of the new department keep going back to their old bosses."

Former House Speaker Newt Gingrich, R-Ga., agreed, calling it "a big mistake" to retain the current committee setup. "It is absurd how many places a secretary of Homeland Security has to report to.… It's just the wrong way to handle it," he said. "How do you get a coherent policy, and how do you get a coherent budget?… There's no place where homeland security is the No. 1 topic." Gingrich contended that Congress should create a single authorizing committee and a separate Appropriations subcommittee for homeland security, but, he conceded, "They probably won't do it."

Gingrich may be right. But during private meetings the week before Christmas, Speaker J. Dennis Hastert, R-Ill., and a handful of other top House Republicans decided to take a first step toward a committee reorganization, according to a senior Republican source. When the 108th Congress convenes on January 7, they will ask the House to create a select committee to serve for the next two years coordinating the activities of the various committees with jurisdiction over the Homeland Security Department.

Interestingly, House Republican leaders plan to put forth their proposal for a select committee in a separate resolution rather than including it in the usual opening-day House rules package, which typically is approved by a party-line vote. That may be a signal that GOP leaders are worried about potential opposition from turf-conscious Republicans. The leaders decided at their December 17 meeting to keep their plans secret until they brief the House Republican Conference on the evening of January 6, according to Republicans familiar with the closed-door discussions.

While details regarding the select committee are subject to further negotiation, it probably will have less authority than did the select committee that Hastert created last year to coordinate the House legislation creating the new department. That panel was chaired by then-Majority Leader Dick Armey, R-Texas, who has retired. With that coordinating committee dissolved, the absence of a clear front-runner to take over its role may make House members open to a new committee of some form. The transitional approach of creating a select committee is designed to give the House time to adjust to the new department. But the delay could entrench bad legislative habits and could jeopardize Bush's managerial goals.

"The Congress loves to shine the light on others.… We make demands on everyone else to streamline and be effective. Congress needs to do the same thing," said Rep. Steve Buyer, R-Ind., an Army reservist who is active on national security issues. "Probably, we'll do it slowly.

It's painful for me to say that. I would love for us to see a realignment of the committee structure, [but] what you have are some very powerful committee chairman.... Not a lot of people in this town give up power."

In the Senate, meanwhile, no changes to the committee structure are imminent. It is unlikely that incoming Senate Majority Leader Bill Frist, R-Tenn., would want to tackle the issue early in his tenure. For now, the Governmental Affairs Committee, which handled the Senate legislation creating the Homeland Security Department, may be the most aggressive in the power grab over jurisdiction.

WHY CONGRESSIONAL OVERSIGHT MATTERS

Congress has four broad areas of responsibility related to the Homeland Security Department: nominations, budget, oversight, and future legislation. The Senate this month is expected to begin confirming Bush's nominees for top department posts, including Ridge and 24 others. Early on, Congress will also be monitoring how the department spends its money, identifying persistent gaps in internal communication, offering legislative fixes as unintended consequences materialize, and assessing the department's performance in the event of another attack. Down the line, Congress will have to make important calls on budget priorities and oversee new management and technology. Experts worry that without centralized oversight, the likelihood that Congress will address any of those responsibilities effectively is nearly nonexistent.

Ivo Daalder, a national security expert at the Brookings Institution and a former aide to the National Security Council, sees myriad problems arising from the current committee structure. First, he said, lawmakers will disagree about who is in charge of different parts of the department, making it difficult, if not impossible, to demand account-

ability. Second, because of the scattered jurisdiction, Congress will have minimal ability to guide homeland security policy as a whole. Third, the committees will nibble the department to death. "You're likely to make a mess of it, because everybody is competing for a piece of the pie, rather than the whole thing," Daalder said.

A CAUTIONARY TALE:
Since the Energy Department's creation in 1977, its leaders have had to answer to too many congressional bosses, says former Rep. Phil Sharp.

Homeland security expert Frank Hoffman worries that, without focused congressional oversight, no one will be paying attention to either civil liberties or fiscal responsibility at the new department. Hoffman was a top aide to the commission chaired by former Sens. Gary Hart, D-Colo., and Warren Rudman, R-N.H., whose report on U.S. national security policy provided the foundation for what became the Homeland Security Department. Hoffman said that components such as the Transportation Security Administration and the Immigration and Naturalization Service are already broken and will need significant parenting by lawmakers who are aware of what is going on elsewhere in the department.

"The mess we're in is in large part an outgrowth of completely dysfunctional oversight of these agencies," said Stephen Flynn, a senior fellow at the Council on Foreign Relations and another former National Security Council aide. Without congressional coherence, he added, members of committees with homeland security jurisdiction will be more likely to push for projects that have immediate payoff in their states or districts, such as highway-building, rather than otherwise invisible

investments such as monitoring the management of the TSA.

Flynn recently directed a task force, sponsored by the Council on Foreign Relations, that followed up on the Hart-Rudman Commission's initial findings. The task force's report, issued in October, found minimal evidence of progress since September 11 in securing the country against terrorist threats. In a "relatively flat budget environment" (the administration maintains that the Homeland Security Department won't cost any additional money), Flynn said, a department with multiple congressional masters is likely to see some of its components better funded than others—a political reality that will pit agencies against each other at the very time cooperation is most critical.

The creation of the Energy Department in 1977 was the last time Congress consolidated disparate agencies into a new Cabinet department to coordinate the response to a pressing national problem. (In that case, it was the nation's dependence on foreign oil.) But even today, the Energy Department still struggles to mesh its various components effectively. A quarter-century of highly visible scandals—over toxic spills, Chinese spying, missing hard drives, credit card fraud, and so forth—hints at broad institutional incoherence within the department. And this dysfunction is mirrored and magnified by the numerous congressional panels with jurisdiction over Energy, an oversight structure that was never significantly reorganized to dovetail with the merged department. DOE answers to some 17 committees and subcommittees on Capitol Hill.

Former Rep. Philip R. Sharp, D-Ind., who helped to oversee the department as a member of the House Energy and Commerce Committee from 1975 to 1995, called the situation unworkable. "We had so many different committees in Congress that the leaders of the department were pulled in so many different directions that they couldn't provide the necessary leadership," said Sharp, who is currently a fellow at Harvard University's John F. Kennedy School of Government and a senior adviser to the Van Ness Feldman law firm in Washington.

The tangled chain of command created when the Energy Department was put together is "a model for how *not* to make a department," said DOE's elder statesman, scientist Sidney Drell. It's also a model for how not to oversee a department. "You're spending a lot of time trying to explain what you're doing to a lot of committees," Drell said. "There's a lot of duplication, [and] the people running the department were torn between the different interests of the different committees."

Adm. James Watkins, the retired chief of naval operations who headed DOE throughout the first President Bush's administration, said the oversight by multiple committees "wasn't crippling, but it was a huge problem, because we had to go before two primary committees in the House, for example, that didn't speak to each other." He said he once was impolitic enough to mention one panel's priorities while testifying before another. "I said, 'I'm covering that issue under the jurisdiction of another committee,'" Watkins recalled, "and I was severely chastised."

AN UPHILL BATTLE:
Reps. Ellen Tauscher and Mac Thornberry are among those advocating committee reform.

Current members of Congress who want to streamline the committees with homeland security jurisdiction point to the Energy Department example as a cautionary tale. Rep. Mac Thornberry, R-Texas, who chaired a special panel formed in 1999 to reorganize DOE's national security functions, and who championed a Homeland Security Department long before 9/11, lamented

that Congress "never really bit the bullet of having clear lines of authority" over Energy.

"We never wanted to face that, because it affects people's jurisdictions and it makes winners and losers," Thornberry said. "No congressional committee had a clear responsibility for making sure things ran properly. And that is what we must avoid with Homeland Security."

Rep. Ellen Tauscher, D-Calif., who co-chaired the special panel on Energy reform with Thornberry, agreed. "It's too many chefs in the kitchen, but nobody accountable," she said. "You can cross your hands over your chest and point your hands to the left and the right at the same time and say, 'They went thataway. It's not that *I* didn't do it. The *other* committee didn't do it.'"

REFORM EFFORTS OF THE PAST

The current committee structure on Capitol Hill dates back to a comprehensive congressional reorganization in 1946. In that shuffle, the House reduced its committees from 48 to 19, and the Senate cut it panels down from 33 to 15. In addition, committee jurisdictions were written into the rules for the first time. The reorganization consolidated military oversight under the House and Senate Armed Services Committees, which proved fortunate the following year, when Congress passed the National Security Act merging all of the armed services under the Defense Department.

The Legislative Reorganization Act of 1946 came at a time when government clearly needed modernization after the Great Depression and World War II, and when Congress itself was relatively weak. And many older members who might have objected to such reforms were retiring after hanging on through the war. "You had, for all practical purposes, a fresh start," Hamre said.

Committee reform again became a hot topic in Congress during the 1970s, both before and after the Energy Department was born. The

most serious effort came from a bipartisan House select committee chaired by former Rep. Richard Bolling, D-Mo., who in 1974 championed a comprehensive overhaul that would have rationalized the committee structure and consolidated jurisdiction along subject lines. A key piece of the select committee's package was a new Energy and Environment Committee, which would have superseded the work of five other House committees. But the sweeping proposal fueled intense opposition from a cross section of committee barons. The House Democratic Caucus instead developed a far more limited plan that largely kept the existing structure intact.

During the remainder of the Democrats' 40-year reign over the House, committee reorganization efforts were "fruitless," Sharp said. "Reform must be a leadership issue," he said. "If they don't take it on at the outset, it becomes more difficult to do when committee leaders are more certain of their influence" on an issue.

SUSAN COLLINS:
The incoming Senate committee chairwoman is staking her claim over the Homeland Security Department.

When the Republicans captured House control in 1994, Speaker Gingrich centralized authority in the leadership and required committee chairmen to follow his broad agenda. But the new GOP majority made only modest changes in the encrusted committee structure that House Democrats had built. Republicans eliminated just three minor committees—District of Columbia, Merchant Marine and Fisheries, and Post Office and Civil Service—that served mostly Democratic constituencies, although they did significantly reduce the number of committee staff across the board.

"We changed a few small things, but not many," Gingrich conceded. "People go in and they pick a committee to spend their career on.... You're now coming in with what is a very personal request—you're asking them to change their career, their power, their importance," he said. "The human reaction is to say no."

DON'T TREAD ON ME

The best bet for wholesale committee reform now would be a lightning strike by the leadership. In theory, leaders in both chambers could quickly clip the existing committees' wings before chairmen got too comfortable in their homeland security prerogatives—especially in the Senate, where the Republican takeover changes the leadership of every committee. But such a plan does not appear to be in the offing.

Instead, House leaders are poised to take an interim step by proposing the new select committee to coordinate the various committees with jurisdiction over the Homeland Security Department, and Senate leaders plan to do nothing for now. The leaders' reluctance to go further is not all that surprising, given that chairmen are already sending strong signals of "don't tread on me."

One such message is coming from Sen. Susan Collins, R-Maine, who is taking over as chairwoman of the Senate Governmental Affairs Committee. Collins has been arguing that because her committee handled the bill establishing the new department, the panel should be responsible for seeing the job through.

Incoming Senate Finance Committee Chairman Charles E. Grassley, R-Iowa, is also protecting his turf. "We made it clear during statements in the record that we intended to keep jurisdiction over Customs," Grassley said. "We would not have jurisdiction over [confirmation] hearings on the secretary of Homeland Security. Presumably, that's Governmental Affairs. But we

would still have jurisdiction over this stuff. And maybe it would end up being joint jurisdiction." And Grassley, who also sits on the Senate Judiciary Immigration Subcommittee, added, "I would hope that Immigration [jurisdiction over the Immigration and the Naturalization Service] would still be within Judiciary."

In the House, Hastert's plan for a new select committee will be a hard sell to notoriously hard-driving chairmen of such key committees as Judiciary, Transportation and Infrastructure, and Ways and Means. Judiciary Committee Chairman F. James Sensenbrenner Jr., R-Wis., said that while he's "not a knee-jerk opponent" of consolidating jurisdiction over homeland security, proponents have the burden of proof "to show that it can be done in a way to provide more-effective oversight." Sensenbrenner noted, for example, that if oversight of the INS is handed to a new committee with no experience in immigration law, it won't have the expertise to monitor the agency effectively.

Even members with relatively small stakes have sworn resistance to change. For instance, jurisdiction over a disease-research facility on tiny Plum Island, off Long Island, N.Y., is slated to move from the Agriculture Department to the Homeland Security Department. But outgoing Senate Agriculture, Nutrition, and Forestry Committee Chairman Tom Harkin, D-Iowa, "is going to fight and definitely work to make sure that Plum Island would stay under the jurisdiction, at least for oversight, of the Agriculture Committee," said spokesman Seth Boffeli. "The research they do is critical for agricultural safety and farming."

The impending Battle of Plum Island underlines the biggest obstacle to change: Because the challenge of homeland security cuts across so many different issues—from public health to disaster relief to intelligence—every part of the new department is important to more than one lawmaker for more than one rea-

son. The Coast Guard, for example, not only provides security along the shores but also protects the environment and maintains navigation buoys. And so, many members contend that they have a legitimate interest in retaining their jurisdiction.

"There are many members who have very specific expertise built up over the years" regarding one agency or another, said a House Appropriations Committee Democratic staffer. "We wouldn't want [them] to be summarily cut out. I very much hope the Republican leadership does not insert itself into the process at the micro level in terms of reorganizing committees," the staff said. "It would be a mistake for the Republican leaders to say, 'This is how it's going to be, and that's it.'"

POTENTIAL PATHS FOR CONGRESS

In the face of such resistance, even some strong advocates of committee reform are calling for cautious change. "There are arguments for just bearing down and doing it, and there are arguments for phasing it in," Tauscher said. "Wild gyrations of organizations, even when they're well intended, have serious deleterious effects, so maybe we need to figure out how to do this in a bite-size way. But we need to be moving forward," she said. "I don't think any of us are interested in leading the American people to believe that we are more interested in protecting turf than we are in protecting them."

But assembling even a select coordinating committee without treading on too many toes would take some time. And larger questions loom about the authority of a new committee—even a temporary one—in one, or both, chambers.

The Hart-Rudman Commission tried to achieve a balance between coherent organization and turf sensitivities by calling for a select oversight committee in each chamber, composed of members of the committees currently involved in homeland security. But such a committee

Congressional Committees with Homeland Security Jurisdiction

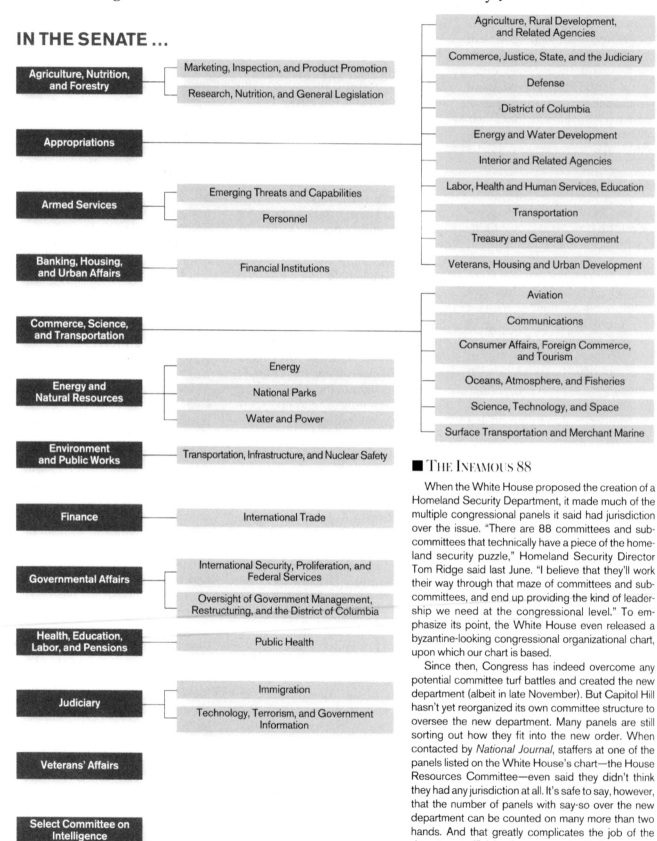

IN THE SENATE ...

Agriculture, Nutrition, and Forestry
- Marketing, Inspection, and Product Promotion
- Research, Nutrition, and General Legislation

Appropriations
- Agriculture, Rural Development, and Related Agencies
- Commerce, Justice, State, and the Judiciary
- Defense
- District of Columbia
- Energy and Water Development
- Interior and Related Agencies
- Labor, Health and Human Services, Education
- Transportation
- Treasury and General Government
- Veterans, Housing and Urban Development

Armed Services
- Emerging Threats and Capabilities
- Personnel

Banking, Housing, and Urban Affairs
- Financial Institutions

Commerce, Science, and Transportation
- Aviation
- Communications
- Consumer Affairs, Foreign Commerce, and Tourism
- Oceans, Atmosphere, and Fisheries
- Science, Technology, and Space
- Surface Transportation and Merchant Marine

Energy and Natural Resources
- Energy
- National Parks
- Water and Power

Environment and Public Works
- Transportation, Infrastructure, and Nuclear Safety

Finance
- International Trade

Governmental Affairs
- International Security, Proliferation, and Federal Services
- Oversight of Government Management, Restructuring, and the District of Columbia

Health, Education, Labor, and Pensions
- Public Health

Judiciary
- Immigration
- Technology, Terrorism, and Government Information

Veterans' Affairs

Select Committee on Intelligence

■ THE INFAMOUS 88

When the White House proposed the creation of a Homeland Security Department, it made much of the multiple congressional panels it said had jurisdiction over the issue. "There are 88 committees and subcommittees that technically have a piece of the homeland security puzzle," Homeland Security Director Tom Ridge said last June. "I believe that they'll work their way through that maze of committees and subcommittees, and end up providing the kind of leadership we need at the congressional level." To emphasize its point, the White House even released a byzantine-looking congressional organizational chart, upon which our chart is based.

Since then, Congress has indeed overcome any potential committee turf battles and created the new department (albeit in late November). But Capitol Hill hasn't yet reorganized its own committee structure to oversee the new department. Many panels are still sorting out how they fit into the new order. When contacted by *National Journal*, staffers at one of the panels listed on the White House's chart—the House Resources Committee—even said they didn't think they had any jurisdiction at all. It's safe to say, however, that the number of panels with say-so over the new department can be counted on many more than two hands. And that greatly complicates the job of the department officials who must work with Congress.

IN THE HOUSE ...

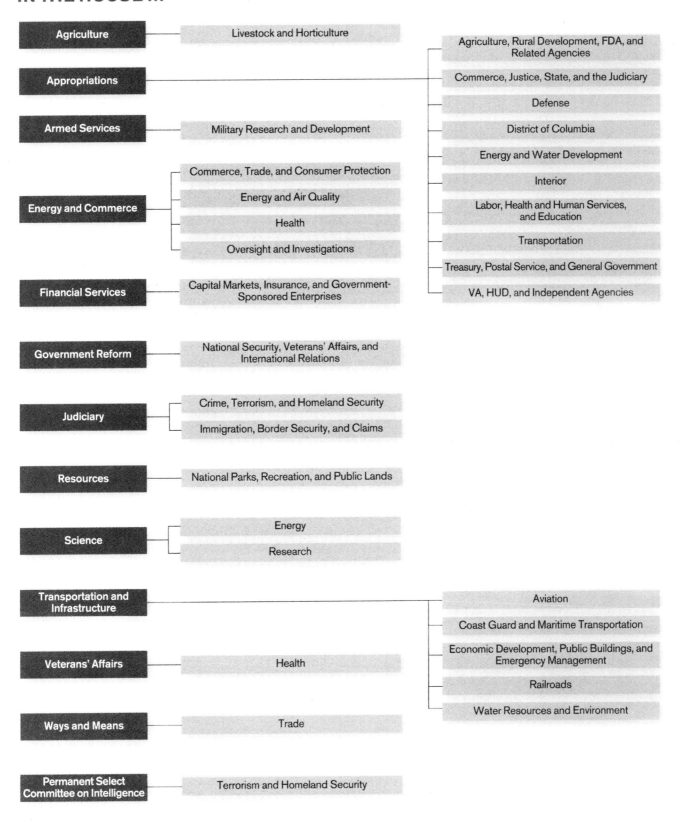

would have no powers of appropriation or authorization, according to the Hart-Rudman model. Gingrich and former House International Relations Committee Chairmen Lee Hamilton, D-Ind., helped to craft that proposal. "We did not win any debates about moving committees," said former commission aide Hoffman. "We had to make sure that when the music stopped, everybody had a chair and had something to do."

Since then, some well-placed Republicans have developed variations on that theme. After reading the Hart-Rudman report and its predecessors and holding hearings on the threat of terrorism, Sens. Pat Roberts, R-Kan., and Robert Bennett, R-Utah, put together a proposal in the spring of 2001 to establish a Senate select committee on homeland security. The committee would have two ex officio chairs, the majority and minority leaders, plus two "worker-bee chairmen," one from each party, Roberts said. Then, as security issues arose, the committee could pull in a handful of chairmen from other committees and subcommittees to address problems quickly. "It would be a facilitator, a grand central station, a belly-button kind of thing," he said.

Robert's proposal was later overtaken by other post-9/11 priorities. He pushed to include a chapter on congressional reform in the Select Intelligence Committee's report on 9/11 that was released last month, but he lost. Roberts is now taking over as Intelligence Committee chairman, and he vows, "I'm not giving up."

Rep. Porter Goss, R-Fla., who chairs the House Permanent Select Committee on Intelligence, established a Terrorism and Homeland Security working group in early 2001 at the leadership's request. After 9/11, it became an Intelligence subcommittee. Now, Goss says, the House needs a more formalized entity to handle the new Homeland Security Department. "I don't care what they call it," he said. It should involve "regularly interested" members on homeland security and should be flexible enough to pull in relevant committee chairmen, depending on the topic du jour. "We've used [that model], and it's worked," Goss said.

GARY HART AND WARREN RUDMAN: Their commission proposed a select committee in each chamber to oversee the new department.

But the Homeland Security Department wasn't born of the easy-does-it approach. Daalder and other experts say Congress needs to step up and create a new standing committee on homeland security, plus an Appropriations subcommittee. The longer Congress drags out its disconnected oversight, these experts argue, the less likely it is that change will come and the more likely that chaos will reign at the new department.

Likewise, Thornberry warned that with agencies on a tight schedule to move to the new department, "we can't have a six-month dispute over who gives up jurisdiction. If we're going to play our role, Congress needs to hit the ground running in January," he said. "These early months of a new department are going to be critical—not only in setting it up for decades to come, but while you're setting it up, not losing any ground in day-to-day missions."

The White House, while clearly an interested party, is letting Congress decide how to oversee the Homeland Security Department. "We think that if they undertook some reorganization with regard to how they look at this new department and deal with this new department, it might streamline some of the processes," said Homeland Security spokesman Gordon Johndroe. "But beyond that, their reorganization is up to them."

Surely the president won't want his newly ensconced Secretary Ridge spending all his time running around Capitol Hill to testify before 88 panels of one interest or another. If Bush wants Congress to realign itself with the executive branch, he may have to expend some political capital. And don't forget that congressional Republicans are still euphoric over the gains they made in the November election with the help of their popular president.

"If there is any reluctance among Republicans [to reorganize the committees], that would melt away if there were a signal from the White House," said a top aide to a House chairman. "No one will stand in the way if the president says an action is important for homeland security."

Well, that may be stretching it. But if Bush could convince veteran committee chairmen that it's in their interests to relinquish their turf, that indeed would be the strongest indication yet of his power.

Staff Correspondent Marilyn Werber Serafini contributed to this article. The authors can be reached at rcohen@nationaljournal.com, sgorman@nationaljournal.com, and sfreedberg@nationaljournal.com.

Security

Requirements For a New Agency

The integration of 22 formerly disparate departments around the Homeland Security mission will be a critical event in American IT history.

On the eve of the largest federal re-organization since the Defense Department was formed, Homeland Security secretary Tom Ridge spelled out what DHS is all about in no uncertain terms:

"We face a hate-filled, remorseless enemy that takes many forms, has many places to hide, is often invisible, and does not distinguish between innocent civilians and military combatants," Ridge told a Senate committee. "Terrorism directly threatens the foundations of our nation, people, freedom, and our economic prosperity."

If we imagine a 22-sided fort we only begin to get a sense of the requirements its connecting beams and support elements must meet.

Indeed. This re-organization would not be fathomable but for the threat which compels it. Looking only at how information technology evolved as a plethora of disparate stovepipe systems within just one agency over decades is sobering for those who construct today's Enterprise Architectures and e-government systems. But 22 different agencies…?

If we imagine a 22-sided fort we only begin to get a sense of the requirements its connecting beams and support elements must meet. Select any two "sections" of the wall and you are sure to have two sets of systems that evolved of entirely disparate interests, along entirely disparate lines.

The sheer scope of just one requirement can seem imposing. The U.S. Customs Department must oversee the arrival of 16 million fully packed cargo containers entering the U.S. each year. The Immigration and Naturalization Service, and the Border Patrol, deal with visitors in double the numbers. The Transportation Security Agency monitors as many as 5,000 commercial air flights boarding passengers per day. And on it goes.

Depth can be as staggering to contemplate as scope. The U.S. Secret Service, for instance, must quick-study every incremental change in technology for everything from elevators to emergency lighting as it seeks to keep up with the systems that might be exploited by would-be assassins and other blackhats. So, even if Secret Service does not intend to use pcAnywhere tech itself, it must understand its innards all the same, noted Thomas Galligan a special assistant in the Secret Service's financial crimes division.

Sometimes the very opposite of "scope" frames the requirement. On a globe of oceans and waterways and thousands of shipping platforms, roughly thirteen freighters are rumored to be owned and operated by Osama bin Laden's al Qaeda organization. The 24/7/365 duty the U.S. Coast Guard performs comes now with an "exacting" requirement unlike any other. To monitor our massive coastal waters, it will often require a microscope.

Where systems differ dispute is often inevitable. The Federal Emergency Management Agency will occupy a challenging point position in the funding and standardization of emerging wireless technologies for first-responders, a horizon that merely begins with police, fire and medical personnel working in thousands of departments across the 50 states.

How tough will FEMA's job be? You do not even have to leave the District of Columbia to confront your first "competing standards/inoperable systems" debate.

THE D.C. SNIPERS CASE

One place where every sector of DHS will knit up fast, we think, is the effort to engage the American public in the mission. The arrest of the D.C. snipers was a bellwether homeland security operation in part for the assembly of multiple agencies and jurisdictions under a single command structure.

But, and more importantly, the snipers were only caught when the task force was able to provide the American public with specific descriptions of the car, its license plate, the weapon and the suspects themselves. In a matter of minutes, the release of such information cold-stopped what had seemed an endless spree of tragic shootings.

The homeland security mission has no better resource than the American people. Every PC user is a potential observant truck driver at a rest stop, where information illuminates the dark of night.

DHS's IT pioneers have given the mission its first tactile dimensions with a national cyber security strategy. The strategy engages the PC-using public as well as critical industries and infrastructures, government, and even America's electronic global partners.

DHS's founding strategies observe the practicality that "eighty-five percent of the critical infrastructure is owned and operated by the private sector," noted Howard Schmidt, vice chair of the president's Critical Infrastructure Protection Board, which produced the strategy.

The White House and DHS want the breadth of the commercial and citizen sector, including the IT industry, to "begin seeing security from our perspective-meaning as part of national security, public safety and economic prosperity," Schmidt said.

IT'S COMPUTER V. COMPUTER

Repelling attack is as much an IT requirement for DHS as it is for war-planners in the Pentagon.

Al Qaeda began using the Internet for recruiting and communicating at about the same time Amazon began selling books online. Terrorist acts in Yemen were commanded in real-time by satellite phone in London as long ago as 1992. The first WTC bomber Ramzi Yousef was a devotee of his laptop and the programs he ran to support his bomb making and plotting missions.

On Day One of its existence DHS absorbed a vast and exacting set of mission-critical IT requirements in part because it confronts a technologically skilled threat.

At least one American al Qaeda sympathizer is already on trial for his "contractor" relationship to terror, having allegedly built web sites for terrorist recruiters and delivered laptops to Afghanistan terror training bases during the Taliban/al Qaeda rule. The recently raided Finsbury Park mosque in North London is thought to have operated as a C41 base for al Qaeda, according to American and British law enforcement officials.

Investigators in the U.S., Britain, France, Spain, Canada, Germany, Australia, Pakistan, Israel, Italy, India, the Philippines, Egypt and elsewhere are continuing to identify and arrest, almost on a weekly basis, terrorist IT experts and wannabe's who operate consumer scanners and COTS software for the creation of fake transnational Ids—just as one of the D.C. snipers also allegedly did.

A sophisticated prototype "honeynet" system built here has already been used to identify and apprehend malicious hackers of military systems as far away as Pakistan, when cyber terrorists attempted to penetrate and disrupt India's defense systems.

On Day One of its existence DHS absorbed a vast and exacting set of mission-critical IT requirements in part because it confronts a technologically skilled threat. Which is to say, there are at least 22 panels forming the adversary's structure too—with no requirement to contend with civil liberties or privacy complaints as new, more diabolical attacks are launched.

The Homeland Security department will attempt to make American history as it transforms disparate elements of government into a reliable strategic and tactical force. The agency's IT experts and advocates will also attempt to make history by providing point-specific solutions to each task DHS faces while also unifying the whole of it.

DHS will only be as effective as its Information Technology allows it to be.

Homeland Security Funding Primer:
Where We've Been, Where We're Headed

"The U.S. government has no more important mission
than protecting the homeland from future terrorist attacks."
—President George W. Bush, July 16, 2002

Highlights

• The fiscal year (FY) 2004 $41.3 billion homeland security budget request is a $3.2 billion increase over $38.1 billion in FY 2003 homeland security spending, excluding $3.9 billion allocated to the Department of Homeland Security (DHS) in a FY 2003 Supplemental.[1] In FY 2002, homeland security spending totaled $32.8 billion.[2] Administration projections suggest that in the next five years homeland security funding increases will be modest.

• There are over 100 agencies in 12 federal Departments outside of the DHS that contribute to homeland security. Of the $41.3 billion FY 2004 budget request for homeland security, $23.8 billion, or 57.7%, is for the Department of Homeland Security's homeland security programs. The Department of Defense would receive the second largest portion of FY 2004 federal homeland security funds, $6.7 billion.

• In FY 2004, one-third of the Department of Homeland Security's $36.1 billion budget request, or $12.2 billion, is designated for non-homeland security missions. Therefore, the DHS budget request for homeland security activities is $23.8 billion, a $4.7 billion increase from the $19.1 billion the DHS is spending on homeland security activities in FY 2003.

• In percentage terms, the largest increases in homeland security spending since 9/11 have been in the areas of emergency preparedness and response, and technological development. Between FY 2002 and FY 2004, the Emergency Preparedness and Response Directorate has seen its budget increase 1,095.5%. The Science and Technology Directorate's homeland security budget has increased 927.9%. However, the latter received no additional funding in the FY 2003 Supplemental.

• Federal spending for homeland security has more than doubled since FY 2002, yet the U.S. still has glaring vulnerabilities:

Port Security: A December 2002 Coast Guard report estimates costs for vessel, facility, and port security to be $1.3 billion in FY 2003, and $6.0 billion through FY 2012.[3] This does not include additional costs incurred because of elevated threat levels. In FY 2002, Congress appropriated $250 million for port security grants, and in FY 2003, $150 million in regular appropriations, and $20 million in the Supplemental. To date, the Transportation Security Administration has issued port security grants for $93 million and has been encouraged by Congress to issue these grants more quickly. The FY 2004 budget request includes no funds for port security grants.

First Responders: An elevation of the national threat level requires states to increase their security measures, e.g. at water and food supplies, airports and critical infrastructure. The FY 2003 Supplemental includes $2.2 billion for these additional needs. A recent survey by the U.S. Conference of Mayors estimates that cities nationwide are spending nearly $70 million/week in additional homeland security costs due to the elevated national threat level.[4]

FY 2004 Government-wide Homeland Security Budget Request

Overview

The FY 2004 federal budget request for all federal homeland security spending is $41.3 billion, a $3.2 billion, or 8.5%, increase over $38.1 billion enacted for homeland security in FY 2003. The FY 2003 Supplemental Appropriations Act will add $3.9 billion for the DHS. In FY 2002, regular appropriations of $20.6 billion for homeland security were augmented with $12.2 billion through two supplementals. The FY 2004 request is a $8.4 billion, or 25.7%, increase over spending on homeland security activities in FY 2002.

Table 1

Top 5 Departments Receiving FY 2004 Homeland Security Funding

($ in millions)

Department	Request	% of Total Request
Homeland Security	$23,890	57.78%
Defense	$6,714	16.24%
Health & Human Services	$3,776	9.13%
Justice	$2,290	5.54%
Energy	$1,361	3.29%
Other	$3,316	8.02%
Total FY04 HS Request	$41,347	100%

Source: OMB, Budget of the United States Government, Fiscal Year 2004, Summary Tables, Table S-5.

According to the Office of Management and Budget (OMB), over 30 federal agencies receive funding specifically for homeland security which is embedded in their larger, department-wide budget requests. However, over 90% of federal homeland security spending is concentrated in the Departments of Homeland Security, Defense, Health and Human Services, Justice, and Energy.

While OMB budget documents detail which federal departments receive funds for homeland security, it is not always entirely clear what agencies within these departments receive funds, and which homeland security missions they support. To remedy this lack of transparency, the Homeland Security Act of 2002, the legislation that created the Department of Homeland Security, requires that beginning with the budget submissions for FY 2005, the OMB submit, "a detailed, separate analysis, by budget function, by agency, and by initiative area... identifying the amounts... that contribute to homeland security...". For FY 2004, the OMB has identified the departments in Table 1 as recipients of homeland security funds.

Homeland Security Dispersed Across the Government

According to an analysis by the House Appropriations Committee minority staff, there were 133 federal agencies and offices in 12 federal departments involved in homeland security prior to the creation of the DHS. The Homeland Security Act consolidated 31 of these agencies in the Department of Homeland Security, while over one hundred, such as the Department of Treasury's Financial Crimes Enforcement Network, remain outside the DHS.

The lack of a clearly accepted definition of homeland security and the many entities involved require an immense level of coordination and cooperation in both the executive and legislative branches of government. One component of homeland security, combating terrorism, has long been treated as a multi-departmental, inter-agency mission. Since 1998, Congress has required the OMB to provide an annual report that details federal funding for counter-terrorism precisely because of that mission's interagency character. However, in its latest 'Combating Terrorism' report, the OMB concedes that, "Collecting data... is difficult because agencies usually do not have distinct funding lines for these activities. Instead, funding is embedded in larger, 'host' programs in agency budget requests. The Congressional budget process, as well, does not usually make explicit appropriations for combating terrorism. Instead, agencies often make specific allocations for these activities after appropriations are enacted, based on overall funding for the 'host' programs."[5] These difficulties are exponentially larger when budgeting for homeland security, because homeland security covers a wide-ranging spectrum of missions from prevention to protection to consequence management.

FY 2004 Department of Homeland Security Budget Request

Overview

The FY 2004 budget request for the Department of Homeland Security (DHS) is $36.1 billion. This is a $2.4 billion, or 7.4%, increase over $33.6 billion appropriated in FY 2003 for the agencies that are now part of the DHS. The FY 2003 Supplemental provided $3.9 billion for the DHS. In FY 2002, agencies that are now in the Department received $22.1 billion through regular appropriations, and an additional $5.9 billion through the supplementals.

The DHS is organized into five major Directorates:

- Border and Transportation Security
- Information Analysis and Infrastructure Protection
- Science and Technology
- Emergency Preparedness and Response
- Departmental Management

Table 2

Government-wide Homeland Security Funding by Agency/Department

($ in millions)

	FY 2002 Enacted	FY 2002 Supp.	FY 2003 Enacted	FY 2003 Supp.	FY 2004 Request
Agriculture	$230	$322	$385	—	$390
Commerce	$99	$19	$110	—	$153
Defense	$4,423	$733	$8,860	—	$6,714
Energy	$1,067	$153	$1,266	—	$1,361
HHS	$433	$1,480	$3,962	—	$3,776
Homeland Security	$11,398	$5,982	$19,136	$3,910	$23,890
Justice	$1,019	$1,125	$1,921	$387	$2,290
State	$438	$39	$658	—	$811
Treasury	$84	$32	$80	—	$91
Transportation	$635	$785	$380	—	$284
Veterans Affairs	$47	$2	$132	—	$145
Corps of Engineers—Civil Works	—	$139	$36	—	$104
EPA	$13	$174	$107	—	$124
SSA	$113	$8	$132	—	$147
NASA	$114	$109	$163	—	$170
Natl. Science Foundation	$240	$19	$259	—	$307
USPS	—	$587	—	—	—
Other Agencies	$267	$556	$533	—	$590
TOTAL	**$20,620**	**$12,264**	**$38,120**	**$4,297**	**$41,347**

Source: OMB, Budget of the United States Government, Fiscal Year 2004, Summary Tables, Table S-5.

Table 3

Department of Homeland Security Budget FY 2002-2004

($ in millions)

Directorate	FY 2002 Enacted	FY 2002 Supp.	FY 2003 Estimate	FY 2003 Supp.	FY 2004 Request
Border Security & Transportation	$9,096	$4,150	$18,335	$3,400	$18,051
Emergency Preparedness & Response	$4,556	$1,145	$5,125	$99.75	$5,963
Science and Technology	$90	$77	$561	—	$803
Information Analysis & Infrastructure Protection	$117	$36	$177	—	$829
Coast Guard	$5,179	$464	$6,174	$228	$6,789
Secret Service	$1,117	$73	$1,207	$30	$1,324
Other	$1,966	$37	$2,106	$153	$2,419
DHS TOTAL	**$22,121**	**$5,982**	**$33,685**	**$3,910.75**	**$36,178**

Source: Department of Homeland Security, Budget in Brief, February 2003.

Additionally, the Coast Guard and the Secret Service moved into the Department as entities that are not included in any Directorate, but report directly to the Secretary.

Border and Transportation Security Directorate

The FY 2004 budget request for the Border and Transportation Security Directorate is $18.051 billion, a $284 million, or 1.55%, decrease from FY 2003 funds. The FY 2003 Supplemental included $3.4 billion for this Directorate. The regular FY 2002 budget was $9.0 billion, and the FY 2002 Supplemental provided an additional $4.1 billion for border and transportation security. The Directorate is charged with ensuring the safety of the nation's 7,500 miles of land borders and 95,000 miles of shoreline and navigable rivers, as well as administering U.S. immigration and customs laws.

The Directorate consists of: The Immigration and Customs Enforcement Bureau, which merged Immigration and Naturalization Service and Customs Enforcement functions and Federal Protective Services; the Customs and Border Protection Bureau, which merged Agriculture Quarantine Functions, INS Border Patrol, border-related functions of Customs; the Transportation Security Administration (TSA); the Federal Law Enforcement Training Center (FLETC); and the Office of Domestic Preparedness, which merged the Office of Domestic Preparedness from the Justice Department and the Office of National Preparedness from Federal Emergency Management Agency.

Major Initiatives

- *Container Security Initiative (CSI)*
  The administration requested $61.75 million for CSI in FY 2004, a $50 million increase from the $12 million provided in FY 2003. The FY 2003 Supplemental includes $35 million for CSI.

  Through CSI, the Directorate stations inspectors at foreign ports to identify high-risk containers bound for the U.S. The Initiative consists of four elements: use of automated information to target high-risk containers; pre-screening of identified high-risk containers before arrival in the U.S.; use of non-invasive detection technology in screening; and continued development of smarter, tamper-proof containers. As of March 12, 2003, 18 of the world's 20 largest ports, which account for nearly 70% of all cargo containers arriving in the U.S., are now participating in CSI.

- *Customs Trade Partnership Against Terrorism (C-TPAT)*
  The administration requested $16 million for C-TPAT in FY 2004, a $12.1 million increase from $3.9 million enacted in FY 2003.

  C-TPAT is a joint government-industry initiative that protects the entire supply chain against terrorists or their weapons. Companies agree to conduct comprehensive self-assessments of their supply chain security and can count on expedited processing times in

return. As of January, 2003, 300 companies are certified members of C-TPAT.

- *TSA Land Security Activities*
  In FY 2004, the administration requested $85 million to develop and implement security standards in non-aviation transportation security areas, and an additional $65 million to develop better screening technology and methods of detecting chemical and biological threats endangering aircraft and passengers.

Emergency Preparedness and Response Directorate

The FY 2004 request for the Emergency Preparedness and Response Directorate is $5.9 billion, an $838 million, or 16.3% increase over $5.1 billion provided in FY 2003. The FY 2003 Supplemental provided $99.7 million. In FY 2002, the Directorate's programs received $4.5 billion through regular appropriations, and $1.1 billion in the supplemental. In FY 2004, over three-quarters of the Directorate's budget is for non-homeland security missions. This Directorate is designed to prepare for, mitigate the effects of, respond to, and recover from both major domestic natural and manmade disasters, including terrorism, by focusing on both the human and infrastructure costs of such disasters.

The Emergency Preparedness and Response Directorate includes the FIRESAT, formerly known as the Integrated Hazard Information System of the National Oceanic and Atmospheric Administration in the Department of Commerce, interagency Nuclear Incident Response Teams, the Office of Emergency Preparedness from the Department of Health and Human Services, The Strategic National Stockpile, FEMA, interagency Domestic Emergency Support Teams, and the National Domestic Preparedness Office.[6]

Major Initiatives

- *Strategic National Stockpile*
  The administration is requesting $400 million to maintain the stockpile that contains drugs, vaccines and other medical supplies that can be delivered to any place in the country within 12 hours of a request for assistance.

Science and Technology Directorate

The FY 2004 request for the Science and Technology Directorate is $803 million, a $242 million, or 43.1%, increase over $529 million provided in FY 2003. No funds were provided in the FY 2003 Supplemental. In FY 2002, the Directorate received $75 million through regular appropriations, and $77 million in the Supplemental. The Directorate is charged with providing new capabilities to the operational units of the Department, such as technologies for countering chemical, biological, radiological and nuclear threats, and for information sharing and analysis.

The Science and Technology Directorate includes: Plum Island Animal Disease Center, National Bioweapons De-

Table 4
DHS Border and Transportation Security Directorate Budget Request
($ in millions)

	FY 2002 Actual	FY 2003 Estimate	FY 2004 Request
Customs & Border Protection Bureau	$4,063	$5,466	$5,649
Immigration & Customs Enforcement Bureau	$2,127	$2,375	$2,488
Transportation Security Administration	$1,242	$5,338	$4,812
Federal Law Enforcement Training Center	$137	$143	$146
Office of Domestic Preparedness	$260	$3,564	$3,558
Mandatory Spending	$1,267	$1,449	$1,398
Total	**$9,096**	**$18,335**	**$18,051**

Source: OMB, DHS
Note: The Directorate received supplemental appropriations of $4,150 million in fiscal year 2002 and $3,400 million in fiscal year 2003.

fense Analysis Center, and several research and development capabilities from the Department of Energy.

Major Initiatives

- *Development of Biological Countermeasures*
  $365 million
- *Development of Radiological/Nuclear Countermeasures*
  $137 million
- *Chemical/High Explosives Countermeasures*
  $65 million to protect civilians from chemical weapon attacks, and enhance TSA's explosives detection capabilities
- *Academic Community*
  $62 million for supporting research

Information Analysis and Infrastructure Protection Directorate

The FY 2004 request for the Information Analysis and Infrastructure Protection Directorate is $829 million, an increase of $652 million, or 368.36%, over the $177 million its programs received in FY 2003. No funds were provided in FY 2003 Supplemental. In FY 2002, the Directorate's programs received $177 million through the regular budget process, as well as $36 million in the Supplemental. The Directorate is designed to integrate terrorist threat information, produce a comprehensive analysis of threats to the U.S., assess vulnerabilities and implement an action plan to reduce threats and vulnerabilities.

The Information Analysis and Infrastructure Directorate includes the Critical Infrastructure Assurance Office, the National Communications System, Energy Security and Assurance Programs, the National Infrastructure Simulation and Analysis Center, the Federal Computer Incident Response Center, and the FBI's National Infrastructure Protection Center.

In the January 28, 2003 State of the Union Address, President Bush called for the development of a Terrorist Threat Integration Center (TTIC) to merge and analyze all threat information in a single location. According to the White House, the TTIC, which includes the CIA's Counterterrorism Center and the FBI's Counterterrorism Division, will begin its work on May 1, 2003. Once fully operational, it will consist of 250–300 staff and serve as the *'government hub for all terrorist threat-related analytic work.'*[7] The DHS, through its Information Analysis and Infrastructure Protection Directorate, is expected to fully participate in the TTIC, by—after receipt of terrorism-related information from the Intelligence Community—mapping the threats against U.S. vulnerabilities; taking and facilitating action to protect against identified threats; and setting national priorities for infrastructure protection. In turn, the TTIC will provide the Department with a full and comprehensive picture of the terrorist threat that will inform the actions of the Department. Additionally, the DHS, working hand-in-hand with the FBI, will be responsible for ensuring that threat information, including information produced by the TTIC, is disseminated quickly to the public, private industry, and state and local governments as appropriate.

Major Initiatives

FY 2004 requested funds for the Information Analysis and Infrastructure Protection Directorate fall into two broad categories:
- *Infrastructure Analysis: ~ $500 million*
  Includes $200 million to develop a database of the nation's critical infrastructure and $299 million to work with states and private industry to mitigate the risks of identified targets by providing sufficient protection to defeat these threats;
- *Communication Capabilities: ~ $300 million*
  Includes $30 million for the development of a 24/7 Intelligence and Warning capability, $155 million for

Table 5

Non-Homeland Security Spending in the Department of Homeland Security Fiscal Years 2002-2004

($ in millions)

	FY 2002 Enacted	FY 2003 Estimate	FY 2004 Request
DHS TOTAL	$22,121	$33,685	$36,178
Homeland Security Spending	$11,458	$22,035	$23,890
Non-Homeland Security Spending	$10,663	$11,655	$12,246
Non-HS Spending % of Total DHS	**48.2%**	**34.6%**	**33.85%**

Source: OMB, Fiscal Year 2004 Budget, `Homeland Security Funding—By Agency and Bureau'

National Security and Emergency Preparedness communications, and $60 million to develop state and local partnerships for the purposes of enhancing communications capabilities.

Other Entities: Coast Guard and Secret Service

The Homeland Security Act moved the Coast Guard and the Secret Service into the DHS as separate entities that report directly to the Secretary.

The Coast Guard is the nation's lead federal agency for maritime homeland security. However, its considerable non-homeland security missions account for approximately 50% of its budget. The Coast Guard's overall budget request is $5.6 billion in FY 2004, a $485 million or 9.4% increase over $5.1 billion appropriated in FY 2003. The homeland security portion of its budget request increased by $296 million, or 11%, from $2.6 billion in FY 2003 to $2.9 billion in FY 2004. The FY 2003 Supplemental provided $228 million for the Coast Guard's homeland security programs, and $400 million for expenses related to Operation Iraqi Freedom. In FY 2002, the Coast Guard's total budget was $5.1 billion, yet only $2.1 billion, or 41.9%, was designated for homeland security missions. In the FY 2002 Supplemental, the Coast Guard received $464 million.

Major Initiatives

- *Deepwater Fleet*
  The administration requested $500 million in FY 2004 for further upgrades to replace or modernize obsolete assets. At full implementation, the interoperable Deepwater Fleet will comprise of three classes of new cutters and their associated small boats, a new fixed-wing manned aircraft fleet, a combination of new and upgraded helicopters, and both cutter-based and land-based unmanned air vehicles (UAVs).
- *Maritime Domain Awareness*

The administration requested $34 million to enhance the Coast Guard's analytical and intelligence capabilities.

The Secret Service is primarily dedicated to securing the safety of the President and other senior dignitaries. As a component of the DHS, it will draw upon DHS intelligence and analysis to perform this mission. Additionally, the Secret Service has responsibility to protect the U.S. from counterfeiting and thwarting the financing of terrorist activities. The FY 2003 Supplemental provides $30 million for the Secret Service.

Non-Homeland Security Spending in the Department of Homeland Security

Because many agencies that were moved into the Department have long-standing non-homeland security missions in addition to their homeland security missions, one-third of the requested DHS budget for FY 2004, or $12.246 billion, funds non-homeland security missions. This reduces the Department's spending on homeland security to $23.932 billion, 66.15% of its total $36.178 billion budget.

The Homeland Security Act explicitly states that non-homeland security missions are not to be diminished or neglected within the Department. However, a recent GAO study shows that the Coast Guard's performance in non-homeland security missions has declined, even though over 50% of its budget is for non-homeland security efforts.[8] On April 11, 2003, Sen. Akaka (D-HI) introduced legislation, S. 910, to ensure the continuation of non-homeland security functions in the DHS. The bill requires the undersecretaries to report to Congress on the Department's non-homeland security missions, including the number of personnel and budgets dedicated to these efforts, as well as the directorates' organizational structure. Akaka's legislation would further require regular evaluations from the General Accounting Office on the effectiveness of the Department in executing its non-homeland security missions. Non-homeland security funds support functions such as FEMA's responsibility for natural disasters, the Coast Guard's search and rescue functions, immigration services, and the Secret Service's protection of the President and other dignitaries.

Notes

1. Unless otherwise noted, all figures are budget authority.
2. Fiscal Year 2002 funds come from three different appropriations bills: the regular FY 2002 appropriations legislation, the FY 2002 Department of Defense and Emergency Supplemental Appropriations legislation, and the FY 2002 supplemental legislation passed in August 2002. Funds from the latter two are combined under the column FY 2002 Supp.
3. Cost analysis report for vessel, facility, and port security, Standards Evaluation and Analysis Division, U.S. Coast Guard Headquarters, December 20, 2002, USCG-2002-14069-6.

Table 6

FY 2004 Non-Homeland Security Spending in the Department of Homeland Security

($ in millions)

Directorate	Total Request	Non-HS Spending	Non-HS In %
Border & Transportation Security	$18,051	$2,786	15.43%
Emergency Preparedness & Response	$5,963	$4,624	77.54%
Science and Technology	$803	$32	3.99%
Information Analysis & Infrastructure Protection	$829	$0	0%
Coast Guard	$6,789	$2,645	38.96%
Secret Service	$1,324	$342	25.83%
Other	$2,419	$1,817	75.11%
DHS TOTAL	**$36,178**	**$12,246**	**33.85%**

Source: OMB, Fiscal Year 2004 Budget, `Homeland Security Funding–By Agency and Bureau'

4. Additional City Homeland Security Spending Due to War/High Alert, U.S. Conference of Mayors, March 27, 2003.
5. Office of Management and Budget, Annual Report to Congress on Combating Terrorism, June 2002, p. 5.
6. With the exception of the Border and Transportation Security Directorate, the FY 2004 budget request does not break down the Directorates' funding request by agency. The latest budget information available for agencies that were moved to the DHS is in the FY 2003 budget request.

7. Department of State, International Information Programs, *Fact Sheet: New Terrorist Threat Integration Center Will Open May 1,* February 14, 2003.
8. Comprehensive Blueprint Needed to Balance and Monitor Resource Use and Measure Performance for All Missions, Statement of JayEtta Z. Hecker, Director Physical Infrastructure, before the Senate Subcommittee on Oceans, Atmosphere and Fisheries, Committee on Commerce, Science, and Transportation, March 12, 2003, GAO-03-544T.

From *Center for Arms Control and Non-Proliferation*, May 1, 2003, pp. 1-8.

UNIT 3

The Federal Government and Homeland Security

Unit Selections

Key Points to Consider

- Is current security at U.S. nuclear power plants sufficient? What could be done to improve security?

- What are the most important challenges for the new Transportation Security Agency?

- Does the Total Information Awareness program undermine constitutional protections? Defend your answer.

 **Links: www.dushkin.com/online/**
These sites are annotated in the World Wide Web pages.

Container Security Institute (CSI)
http://www.csiinstitute.com/default.htm

Customs & Border Protection
http://www.customs.ustreas.gov/xp/cgov/newsroom/press_releases/05052003.xml

Transportation Security Administration (TSA)
http://www.tsa.dot.gov/public/index.jsp

Department of Homeland Security

Despite ongoing efforts to consolidate existing functions into the new Department of Homeland Security, individual federal agencies continue to play a critical role in our domestic security. The criticisms of the agencies involved in various aspects of homeland security mirror those of other parts of the federal government. Supporters of a federalist approach to problem solving would argue that only the federal government has sufficient economic, bureaucratic, and legislative resources to effectively address threats to our security. Skeptics point to unbridled growth, massive bureaucracies, and inefficiency in spending. As students of American history and politics will quickly recognize, this debate is not a new one. It has become an integral part of American political culture to question government, particularly the federal government.

The success of the federal government and the new DHS is heavily dependent on the ability of individual federal agencies to contribute to this mission. The three articles in this unit focus on three key agencies with four seemingly impossible tasks. The first article examines the Nuclear Regulatory Commission. Highly critical of the lack of reform in the nuclear industry, the author argues that security at nuclear power plants in the United States has been and continues to be "inadequate." He leads to the conclusion that the NRC is not only unable, but also unwilling to reform. The second article focuses on the formidable task fac-

ing the Transportation Security Administration, which was hastily assembled in November of 2001. The TSA has been asked to do the impossible in record time. Aided by massive infusions of federal funds, yet constrained by strict legislative mandates, the TSA has struggled to accomplish its goals. Whether this "knee-jerk" approach to policy making fosters efficient government bureaucracies or effective long-term policy, however, remains to be seen.

The final article in this unit focuses on a program developed by the Defense Advanced Research Projects Agency (DARPA). The Total Information Awareness Program (TIA) is spearheaded by former Admiral John Poindexter, known for his involvement in the Iran-Contra affair during the Reagan administration. The program, which is described as "one of the most ambitious government surveillance programs ever," gathers and analyzes personal information from computer databases in its effort to identify potential terrorists. The program, developed "without congressional oversight," clearly signals the potential for abuse inherent in the rush toward homeland security. While the program itself may have some merit, a rogue program led by rogue government officials with a history of deceiving Congress and the American public does little to inspire confidence in the actions of federal agencies tasked with this important mission.

THE NRC:
WHAT me worry?

by Daniel Hirsch

The question immediately arose on September 11 and has persisted: As horrific as the terrorist attacks were, what might have happened if the terrorists who seized jumbo jets and used them as weapons against the World Trade Center and the Pentagon had aimed them at nuclear power plants instead? And if more attacks are likely, as government officials have said, are nuclear facilities on the terrorist target list?

The *Sunday Times* of London reported in October that some intelligence assessments suggest that the intended target of the fourth plane, the one downed in Pennsylvania, was a nuclear power reactor. The plane had descended much too soon for Washington to be its intended destination, these assessments indicate, suggesting that the true target may have been one of several nuclear plants in its flight path, with the single still-operating unit at Three Mile Island seeming the most likely. This assessment cannot be confirmed, of course. But if it is correct, we owe even more to those brave passengers who succeeded, at the cost of their own lives, in bringing the plane down before it reached its intended target.

Misleading statements

Immediately after the September 11 attacks, the U.S. Nuclear Regulatory Commission (NRC) and the nuclear industry issued statements asserting that U.S. reactor containments were designed to withstand the crash of a fully loaded jumbo jet. Within days, both had to recant and admit that the opposite was the case. Just hours after the terrorist attacks, NRC spokesperson Breck Henderson said U.S. nuclear plants were safe because "containment structures are designed to withstand the impact of a 747."

The Nuclear Regulatory Commission requires nuclear power plants to protect against only three intruders. An attack by four outsiders, it says, just isn't credible.

Ten days later he admitted that "the initial cut we had on that was misleading." In a formal statement, the agency conceded that it "did not specifically contemplate attacks by aircraft such as Boeing 757s and 767s, and nuclear power plants were not designed to withstand such crashes." A similar pattern of assurance followed by retraction characterized the behavior of public relations personnel for a number of specific nuclear sites.

Early on, however, David Kyd, spokesperson for the International Atomic Energy Agency (IAEA), was quoted as saying that most nuclear plants, built during the 1960s and 1970s, were designed to withstand only accidental, glancing impacts from the smaller aircraft used at the time. "If you postulate the risk of a jumbo jet full of fuel, it is clear that their design was not conceived to withstand such an impact," he said. In reporting Kyd's comments, the Associated Press quoted an unnamed U.S. government official to the effect that a direct hit at high speed by a modern jumbo jet "could create a Chernobyl situation."

The press has focused on the vulnerability of reactor containment buildings to airborne attack. But there are also "soft targets" outside containment, and their protection is critical to preventing radioactive release. Excessive emphasis on the risk of air attack obscures the far larger and more frightening possibility of ground assault or the threat from insiders. Security at the nation's nuclear plants has been grossly inadequate for decades, and the nuclear industry and its captive regulatory agency, the NRC, have refused to do anything about it—both before and after September 11.

1,000 times more

A typical nuclear power plant contains within its core about 1,000 times the long-lived radioactivity released by the Hiroshima bomb. The spent fuel pools at nuclear power plants typically contain some multiple of that—several Chernobyls' worth.

Any analogy with the dropping of a bomb is imperfect, of course, because much of the destruction caused by an atomic bomb comes from blast effects, and the damage caused by a terrorist attack on a nuclear plant would stem almost exclusively from the release of radioactivity. However, the potential casualties from an atomic attack and those resulting from using conventional explosives to produce a radiological release from a nuclear facility would be surprisingly similar. For example, the NRC estimated years ago that a meltdown at one of the San Onofre reactors in Southern California could produce 130,000 "prompt" fatalities, 300,000 latent cancers, and 600,000 genetic defects. Analyses for other reactors performed by Sandia National Laboratories for the NRC estimated damages up to $314 billion in 1980 dollars (the equivalent of about $700 billion today).

Because there is an immense amount of radioactivity at a reactor, and because the fuel must be constantly cooled to prevent it from melting and releasing that radioactivity, it is not difficult to understand why nuclear facilities might be a tempting target. As Bennett Ramberg pointed out in 1984 in his seminal book on the subject, *Nuclear Power Plants as Weapons for the Enemy: An Unrecognized Military Peril*, any country that possesses nuclear energy facilities gives its adversaries a quasi-nuclear capability to use against it. Conventional explosives—a truck bomb, for example—could cause a massive radiological release, with terrorists turning their adversaries' own technology against them. And just as simple box-cutters were used to convert U.S. jumbo jets into guided missiles, conventional means could turn U.S. nuclear plants into radiological weapons. The need to protect nuclear facilities against terrorist attack should be obvious.

Minimal protection

Yet for decades, NRC regulations have required only minimal security. Fifteen years ago in the March 1986 *Bulletin* ("Protecting Reactors from Terrorists"), two colleagues and I warned even then that terrorist trends were rendering the NRC security rules inadequate. But with only a single, partial exception, the agency's primary security regulations are unchanged from a quarter century ago. And despite September 11—when the NRC's assumptions crumbled at the moment the Twin

Towers fell—both the industry and the agency that regulates it continue to resist making any significant improvement to dismally inadequate and outmoded security regulations.

We reported in 1986—and it is still the case today—that NRC regulations require nuclear reactor operators to protect against no more than a single insider and/or three external attackers, acting as a single team, wielding no more than hand-held automatic weapons.

Security personnel at power reactors are not required to be prepared for:

- more than three intruders;
- more than one team of attackers using coordinated tactics;
- more than one insider;
- weapons greater than hand-held automatic weapons;
- attack by boat or plane; or
- any attack by "enemies of the United States," whether governments or individuals.

For years, reactor sites were not even required to provide protection against truck bombs. But after a decade of efforts by the Committee to Bridge the Gap and the Nuclear Control Institute to get the agency to strengthen security and repeated refusals by the NRC to require greater protection, the 1993 World Trade Center bombing and an intrusion event at Three Mile Island finally propelled the agency to amend the rules. But the truck bomb rule is still a concern because of the limited size of the explosion that operators must protect against. It apparently requires protection against truck bombs of roughly the size used at the World Trade Center in 1993, but not the larger quantities of explosives that have been used in similar attacks since then. The NRC is behind the curve, "fighting the last war" rather than protecting against threats that can materialize without warning.

To deal with the limited threat that the NRC does recognize—called the "design basis threat" (DBT)—the agency requires a nuclear power plant to be guarded by a total of five individuals. It may seem incomprehensible in today's world that targets capable of producing tens or hundreds of thousands of casualties and hundreds of billions of dollars of damage are protected by a mere five guards, but that is the minimum the NRC mandates.

The events of September 11 demonstrated the inadequacy of the agency's quarter-century-old security rules. There were 19 terrorists on the planes, and possi-

bly additional participants in the conspiracy—far in excess of the three external attackers the NRC envisages. They acted as four coordinated teams, but the NRC rule requires the nuclear industry to guard against only a single team. They used jumbo jets filled with jet fuel as their weapons, far more lethal than the hand-carried automatic weapons and explosives contemplated in the regulation. They were very sophisticated, training for months to fly big jets, and willing to die—a level of motivation and capability far beyond that upon which the NRC rules are predicated.

None of the details of the agency's DBT are secret. With a single exception discussed below, they can all be found in the Code of Federal Regulations, available in most libraries and on the Internet. Any potential adversary can immediately learn that the required security arrangements that protect these high-value targets are inadequate.

Three external attackers...

The only aspect of the DBT that is not explicitly stated in the Code is the famous number "three"—the maximum number of external attackers against which reactor owners must provide protection. The Code indicates that reactors must be protected against an attack by "several" intruders, and that "several" is less than the number required to operate as more than one team. This is enough to give a pretty clear indication of exactly how small the DBT is, but other publicly available documents make it clear that "several" means three.

The number was publicly revealed as a consequence of the licensing hearings for the Diablo Canyon nuclear plant in California in the early 1980s. The Governor of California was a party in the hearings, in which the adequacy of security at the plant was a key issue. The state's security experts testified that a dozen attackers was a credible number to safeguard against. But the utility, Pacific Gas & Electric (PG&E), and the NRC staff argued that irrespective of any threat that might exist, NRC requirements were far more modest. The precise number in the DBT became a key issue in the hearings.

The NRC's Atomic Safety and Licensing Appeal Board decided in favor of PG&E and the NRC staff, expressly ruling on how many attackers a reactor operator is required to protect against. The ruling was not immediately published on the theory that it contained sensitive information. The specific number for the DBT, according to the Diablo decision, was withdrawn at the last minute from the published regulations and replaced with "several," not for any security reason, but because the commission thought it would have trouble explaining to the public why it was requiring a lesser level of protection against sabotage for reactors than against theft at non-reactor sites. This remains the case today—NRC nervousness about public discussion of the DBT of three external attackers is not motivated by a security concern, but by fear of embarrassment were it widely known that it only required reactors be capable of protecting against no more than a trivial terrorist challenge.

The Governor of California, however, asked that an expurgated version of the decision be published, and the agency agreed. When the "sanitized" Appeal Board decision was released, the actual number had been deleted. But ironically, the remaining text explained what "several" meant, and other underlying documents cited in the text—which had been publicly released—gave away the actual number.

The Appeal Board ruling cited a number of NRC documents it relied on in concluding that the DBT should be limited to three attackers. And although the ruling was redacted, all of the underlying documents were available in the NRC's public reading room. Those documents, the "SECY Memoranda," are the agency's actual decision documents on adopting the rule. Over and over again the SECY Memoranda state that the DBT in the rule is "an external threat of one to three persons armed with pistols, shotguns, or rifles (including automatic weapons), and who may be assisted by an insider (employee or unescorted person)." This is the so-called "three-and-one" threat described in publicly available NRC documents.

The Appeal Board decision discloses some of the rationale for settling on three external attackers. First, the board states, power plants by rule are not required to protect against more than one team of attackers—only fuel-cycle facilities with weapons-grade material must do that. Because the minimum number of attackers who could operate as more than one team is obviously four, three is the maximum number of attackers who cannot act as more than one team.

...and five guards

Second, and perhaps most astonishingly, the Appeal Board discloses how the regu-

lation's minimum force of five guards was derived:

"A response force ratio (i.e., ratio of guards to attackers) must be equal to 1 [1 to 1] to protect power reactors. The report [the NRC staff report that formed the basis for the numerical determination for the design basis threat] then states: 'Given the above response force ratio *modified by a measure of conservatism*, the minimum number of guards available for response to an assault may be determined. Therefore, for the presently specified threat, the minimum number of guards available for response at a nuclear power plant is judged to be 5'" (emphasis added).

The Appeal Board decision went on to indicate that the "presently specified threat" referred to was the external threat (of three) along with a single insider capable of participating in a violent attack. This three-and-one threat created a maximum total of four attackers. A 1:1 ratio of guards to attackers would require only four guards. But modifying the ratio "by a measure of conservatism" (giving the guards a one-person advantage) resulted in the regulations requiring a minimum of five guards.

(The actual regulation mentions a "nominal" number of 10 guards, with a minimum of five. But the Diablo decision and underlying documents indicate that this "nominal" number was employed to "camouflag[e] the exact threat.")

Thus, the NRC security regulations, unchanged except to require protection against small-sized truck bombs, require operators to protect against an attack by three outsiders, perhaps aided by one insider, with no team-maneuvering tactics, no attack by boat or air, and minimal hand-held weapons.

This rule made little sense when it was first adopted, and it makes even less today. The September 11 attacks—with at least 19 attackers, four times as many teams, and a level of sophistication far beyond that contemplated by the agency—blew away the NRC's security regulations. Yet those regulations remain unchanged.

Seventeen years of trying

For 17 years, my group, the Committee to Bridge the Gap, joined by the Nuclear Control Institute, has worked quietly behind the scenes in a largely futile effort to convince the NRC to upgrade its security requirements. With one partial exception, the truck bomb rule, we have failed.

In 1984, in the wake of truck bombings in the Middle East, the NRC staff decided to consider requiring protection against truck bombs at U.S. power reactors. It commissioned Sandia National Laboratories to study the vulnerability of plants to truck bomb attacks. The results were frightening—small truck bombs could cause "unacceptable damage to vital reactor systems," and larger truck bombs could have the same effect, even if detonated off site, because the exclusion zone surrounding many facilities is small. Inexplicably, after the study was conducted, the agency dropped the idea of a truck bomb rule.

In 1985, the Committee to Bridge the Gap testified before the Safeguards and Security Subcommittee of the NRC Advisory Committee on Reactor Safeguards, pointing to data showing increasing terrorist capabilities and actions, urging the agency to upgrade the regulations to deal with larger attacking forces and with truck bombs. The response was unenthusiastic, with many subcommittee members indicating that there were so many ways to destroy a reactor that, if you protected against truck bombs, you'd have to protect against all those other vulnerabilities as well.

Over the next few years, both the Committee to Bridge the Gap and the Nuclear Control Institute continued to push the NRC to upgrade security regulations, to no avail. In 1991, at the time of the war with Iraq and the prospect of terrorist attacks against U.S. targets, we formally petitioned the NRC to upgrade its regulations. In addition to urging protection against truck bombs, the petition called for a new DBT with 20 external attackers (ironic in light of the 19 terrorists on the planes on September 11) capable of operating as two or more teams, with weapons and explosives more significant than hand-held rifles. The NRC denied the petition, ruling that "there has been no change in the domestic threat since the design basis threat was adopted that would justify a change."

Finally, after the truck bomb attack on the World Trade Center in 1993 and an event at Three Mile Island in which an intruder drove a station wagon through the perimeter and into the turbine building, where he stayed for hours while security tried to figure out if he had a bomb, the NRC adopted a new rule requiring some measure of protection against truck bombs. However, the rule may not be sufficient to protect against truck bombs of the size that have been used since 1993.

The rest of the DBT remains unaltered, despite the NRC's promises in 1994 that in a second phase it would consider upgrading the rest of the security regulations.

In fact, a number of actions have weakened security. For example, in 1996 the NRC issued Generic Letter 96-02, "Reconsideration of Nuclear Power Plant Security Requirements Associated with an Internal Threat." It permitted "reductions in unnecessary or marginally effective security measures," granting licensees the option, for instance, to keep "doors to vital areas… unlocked."

One counterterrorism program, killed

In late 1998, I received a plain manila envelope in the mail. Inside were documents indicating that the NRC had recently terminated its only counterterrorism program, called the Operational Safeguards Response Evaluation program, (OSRE). The program evaluated nuclear plant security by undertaking mock terrorist attacks—"black hat" force-on-force exercises. The documents contained astonishing information: Given six months advance warning, including the date on which the security test would occur, plants prepared by increasing their guard force by as much as 80 percent. Even so, security failed the tests. In nearly half of the tests conducted at the the country's reactors, mock terrorists penetrated security and reached at least one "target set" that, had the intruders been actual terrorists, could have resulted in a meltdown and massive radioactivity release.

This failure rate is extraordinary. No terrorist group is going to give notice six months in advance of when and where it intends to attack. And these tests were against the existing DBT—against only three intruders.

Other publicly available NRC documents from the early 1990s indicate that in an OSRE test at the Peach Bottom reactor, it took only 17 seconds for the mock terrorists to penetrate the perimeter fence and breach the access control barrier. It took intruders 18 seconds at San Onofre, 30 seconds at Duane Arnold, and 45 seconds at Maine Yankee.

And what was the response to this dismal failure rate? The NRC killed the program—there could be no more failures if there were no more tests.

My organization passed the OSRE documents along to the *Los Angeles Times*, which ran a major story about the program's termination. The agency was sufficiently embarrassed that a couple of days

later Shirley Jackson, then NRC chair, reinstated the program. Since then, however, the industry and the agency have worked together to gut the tests. Earlier this year, the NRC approved the industry's proposed self-evaluation program that would replace NRC-run force-on-force tests. Companies failing the independent tests are now able to test themselves! The problems inherent in self-regulation should be obvious.

After September 11

Our two organizations have persisted in so-far-fruitless attempts to get the DBT upgraded. Last year, we met with NRC Chairman Richard Meserve, trying once again to get the NRC to fix gaping security problems. Nothing came of the meeting. As we were leaving, Meserve said we should feel free to see him again, adding something to the effect that he meets with industry "all the time," and there is no reason he can't meet with public groups from time to time as well. (And indeed, as we left we saw a number of industry lobbyists sitting outside his office waiting to go in.)

After September 11, we wrote to Chairman Meserve, urging him to recommend that the National Guard be called out to protect all the nation's reactors, that air defenses be deployed to protect them, and that employees and contractor personnel be thoroughly re-vetted.

After September 11, Cong. Ed Markey introduced legislation to beef up security at nuclear power plants with a federal guard service. His bill was gutted, but four senators have introduced a new bill. The NRC has joined the industry in opposing the bill, arguing security does not need strengthening.

We also asked the NRC to upgrade its security regulations immediately to protect against attacks involving greater numbers, operating as multiple teams, with more than one insider; require a strong two-person rule and other enhanced measures to protect against insiders; require protection against a truck bomb as big as a large truck can carry; require protections against boat and airplane attacks; require full security protection of spent fuel storage pools and dry cask storage, including after reactor

closure; and that the Operational Safeguards Response Evaluation program be reinstated and expanded.

The NRC response was business as usual. The agency is continually reviewing the DBT, we were told, just as we have been told for the last 17 years.

But no improvements were promised and none has been made. Both the Committee to Bridge the Gap and the Nuclear Control Institute have decided that after years of quiet work it is time to go public about these problems. It is clear that the United States has sophisticated adversaries out there and everything we know is available to them as well. The only people not taking the danger seriously are the ones who should be required to do something about it—the nuclear industry and the agency that is supposed to regulate it.

All the NRC has done in the wake of the attacks on the World Trade Center and the Pentagon is to recommend—not even require—that licensees go to a higher state of alert within their existing security system and within the existing DBT. A no-fly-zone excluded small planes from flying near power reactors, but after a week that restriction was lifted. The federal government has failed to call out the National Guard—although in the absence of federal action, some governors have taken that step on their own. The NRC and the industry strongly oppose legislation introduced by Sens. Harry Reid, Hillary Clinton, Jim Jeffords, Joe Lieberman, and Cong. Ed Markey that would have required the agency to upgrade security regulations.

In 1981, the NRC and industry argued against the Governor of California's contention in the Diablo case that there should be protection against up to a dozen terrorists, saying such an attack wasn't credible. In 1991, the NRC and industry argued against our rulemaking petition that the DBT be increased from three to 20 external attackers operating as several teams, against asserting that there was no evidence there could ever be an attack of more than three as a single team. Protections against attacks by boats, large truck bombs, or from the air remain beyond the design threat. On September 11, 19 attackers in four teams using planes caused the worst terrorist event in U.S. history. Yet the NRC and industry refuse to upgrade the DBT regulations to a level consistent with the now-evident threat.

The industry's response is shocking. Rather than conceding the vulnerability of its facilities and the need to upgrade security, at a press conference on September 25 a spokesman for the Nuclear Energy Institute took the extraordinary stand that greater security isn't required because Chernobyl wasn't that bad.

Why does the industry continue to ignore the need to protect its facilities? First, more security means more expense, and its every instinct is to avoid current expenses. Second, if it admits its reactors are vulnerable, the industry's dream of a nuclear renaissance is diminished.

Having received a big boost from the Cheney energy plan, the industry had been hoping to build new reactors, supposedly of the new pebble-bed design. In order to save money, these "passively safe" reactors would be built without a containment structure. In addition, they are made of graphite, which burns readily, as evidenced by Chernobyl and the earlier Windscale accident in Britain. As poorly resistant to terrorism as today's reactors are, pebble-bed reactors would be far worse. Furthermore, the industry-Cheney proposals involve a revival of the idea of reprocessing spent fuel to separate plutonium, which would then be used in civil reactors, creating a massive additional risk that terrorists might acquire nuclear weapons materials from poorly guarded civilian power plants. The nuclear industry hopes that its post–September 11 problems will go away, without having to upgrade security.

And why has the NRC not imposed upgraded security requirements? Put bluntly, the NRC is arguably the most captured regulatory agency in the federal government, a creature of the industry it is intended to regulate. Efforts to separate its promotional and regulatory functions, which led to the breakup of the Atomic Energy Commission in the mid-1970s, have failed utterly. The NRC's principal interest is in assisting the industry, keeping regulatory burdens and expenses to a bare minimum, and helping to jumpstart the nuclear enterprise.

But the risk of terrorist attack at one or more nuclear plants is simply too great to allow this failed agency and the industry it allegedly regulates to continue to ignore the need to provide reasonable protection. The industry's short-term economic or political concerns pale in comparison to the damage that would occur if attackers turn the nation's reactors into radiological weapons.

Daniel Hirsch is president of the Committee to Bridge the Gap, a Los Angeles-based nuclear policy organization.

From *Bulletin of the Atomic Scientists*, January/February 2002, pp. 39-44. © 2002 by Bulletin of the Atomic Scientists.

Transportation Security Administration Faces Huge Challenges

Steve Dunham, Editor—ANSER

As John W. Magaw takes the reins of the new Transportation Security Administration within the federal Department of Transportation, he faces the challenge of overseeing all transportation security matters. The most pressing concern is airline security, evidenced by the name of the legislation that created his agency: the Aviation and Transportation Security Act, signed by President Bush on 19 November 2001. Virtually all of the act's 21,000-plus words deal with increasing airline security, but the law charges Magaw, as Under Secretary for Transportation Security, with "(1) ... civil aviation security, and related research and development activities; and (2) security responsibilities over other modes of transportation that are exercised by the Department of Transportation."

That covers virtually all transportation in the United States, because the federal Department of Transportation includes the Federal Aviation Administration, the Federal Highway Administration, the Federal Railroad Administration, the Federal Transit Administration, and the Coast Guard—just to mention some of its major components. Magaw himself reports to an oversight board that includes Transportation Secretary Norman Mineta, the attorney general, and a representative of the Office of Homeland Security.

However, Magaw's initial task will be to remedy the security deficiencies in air travel in the United States. His responsibility is enormous.

Mandates for the Transportation Security Administration

The Under Secretary for Transportation Security will "be responsible for day-to-day Federal security screening operations for passenger air transportation and intrastate air transportation" and will develop standards for hiring, retaining, training, and testing airport security screening personnel.

On 18 January 2002, the Transportation Security Administration and Federal Aviation Administration published plans for training security screeners and guidance for training flight crews to deal with threats, meeting a deadline in the Aviation and Transportation Security Act.

Within three months of the law's enactment—that is, by 19 February 2002—Magaw must "assume civil aviation security functions and responsibilities" and "implement an aviation security program for charter air carriers."

Within one year—that is, by 19 November 2002—he must establish a program for screening "passengers and property" at airports, "carried out by the screening personnel of a qualified private screening company." At every screening location, he "shall order the deployment of law enforcement personnel authorized to carry firearms."

Also within one year, he must deploy "a sufficient number of Federal screeners, Federal Security Managers, Federal security personnel, and Federal law enforcement officers to conduct the screening of all passengers and property" at commercial airports.

Magaw has authority to "provide for deployment of Federal air marshals on every passenger flight"; he must make sure that marshals are deployed on every high-risk flight, as determined by the Secretary of Transportation, and he is responsible for the marshals' "training, supervision, and equipment."

The law required screening of "all checked baggage at all airports in the United States" by 19 January 2002. On 16 January 2002, Secretary of Transportation Norman Y. Mineta announced the implementation of this requirement: "Every available [explosives-detection system] machine will be used to its maximum capacity. Where we do not yet have [explosives-detection system] resources in place, we will use other options outlined in the law. On originating flights, baggage will be matched to its passenger. Computers will screen passengers, and passengers will be screened for weapons—often multiple times."

"In addition, more bags will also be subject to sniffing by trained dogs, to more comprehensive screening by both explosive-detection and explosive trace detection

Transportation Security Administration Major Dates

19 November 2001:

Transportation Security Administration (TSA) created

19 January 2002:

TSA deadline to "develop detailed guidance" for flight and cabin crew training, have a system "in operation to screen all checked baggage at all airports in the United States," develop a plan for training "security screening personnel," and "require alternative means for screening any piece of checked baggage that is not screened by an explosive detection system."

19 February 2002:

TSA deadline to "assume civil aviation security functions and responsibilities" and "implement an aviation security program for charter air carriers."

19 May 2002:

TSA deadline to review the effectiveness of biometrics and other security access systems and recommend "commercially available measures or procedures to prevent access to secure airport areas by unauthorized persons."

19 November 2002:

TSA deadline to establish a program for screening "passengers and property" at airports, "carried out by the screening personnel of a qualified private screening company." At every screening location, the Under Secretary for Transportation Security "shall order the deployment of law enforcement personnel authorized to carry firearms" and must deploy "a sufficient number of Federal screeners, Federal Security Managers, Federal security personnel, and Federal law enforcement officers to conduct the screening of all passengers and property" at commercial airports.

31 December 2002:

All large airports must "have sufficient explosive detection systems to screen all checked baggage." TSA must ensure that the screening systems are fully used and that "if explosive detection equipment at an airport is unavailable, all checked baggage is screened by an alternative means."

devices, to manual searches, or to a combination of those techniques. We will continuously upgrade our screening capability, ultimately meeting the requirement that each checked bag be screened by an explosive detection system by the end of this year." By 31 December 2002, all large airports must "have sufficient explosive detection systems to screen all checked baggage." The Transportation Security Administration must ensure that the screening systems are fully used and that "if explosive detection equipment at an airport is unavailable, all checked baggage is screened by an alternative means."

A system for checking air freight must be implemented too, "as soon as practicable."

By 19 May 2002, Magaw must recommend to airport operators "commercially available measures or procedures to prevent access to secure airport areas by unauthorized persons. As part of the 6-month assessment," he must "(A) review the effectiveness of biometrics systems currently in use at several United States airports, including San Francisco International; (B) review the effectiveness of increased surveillance at access points; (C) review the effectiveness of card- or keypad-based access systems; (D) review the effectiveness of airport emergency exit systems and determine whether those that lead to secure areas of the airport should be monitored or how breaches can be swiftly responded to; and (E) specifically target the elimination of the 'piggy-backing' phenomenon, where another person follows an authorized person through the access point. The 6-month assessment shall include a 12-month deployment strategy for currently available technology."

The Transportation Security Administration's other responsibilities including guarding airport perimeters where necessary and defining security standards for airport ground operations such as baggage handling, catering, and vendors.

Authority

Magaw has broad authority. He may

- "Require effective 911 emergency call capability for telephones serving passenger aircraft and passenger trains."
- Establish a uniform system of identifying state and local law enforcement personnel who are authorized to carry weapons in aircraft cabins and to gain access to secured areas of airports.
- Establish requirements for "trusted passenger" programs and use available technologies to expedite the security screening of trusted passengers.
- Develop, with the Commissioner of the Food and Drug Administration, alternative security procedures for transporting medical products that might be damaged by inspection.
- Provide for the use of wireless, wire line data, and other technologies for private and secure communication of threats to aid in screening anyone on airport property who is on a state or federal watch list.

- "In consultation with the Administrator of the Federal Aviation Administration, consider whether to require all pilot licenses to incorporate a photograph of the license holder and appropriate biometric imprints."
- "Provide for the use of voice stress analysis, biometric, or other technologies to prevent a person who might pose a danger to air safety or security from boarding."
- "Provide for the use of technology that will permit enhanced instant communications and information between airborne passenger aircraft and appropriate individuals or facilities on the ground."

Research and Development

The Under Secretary for Transportation Security has authority to use the research and development facilities of the Federal Aviation Administration and has authority to "develop and implement methods":

1. to use video monitors or other devices to alert pilots in the flight deck to activity in the cabin…
2. to ensure continuous operation of an aircraft transponder in the event of an emergency…
3. to revise the procedures by which cabin crews of aircraft can notify flight deck crews of security breaches and other emergencies.

Funding

The House-Senate appropriations conference committee provides $1.25 billion for Transportation Security Administration civil aviation security services.

In the Aviation and Transportation Security Act, Congress appropriated $500 million for fiscal year 2002 for Transportation Department grants to air carriers to fortify cockpit doors, provide video monitors for the cockpit crew to view the passenger cabin, ensure continuous operation of aircraft transponders in an emergency, and to provide "other innovative technologies to enhance aircraft security." (On 11 January 2002, the Federal Aviation Administration published new standards to protect cockpits from intrusion and small arms fire or fragmentation devices, such as grenades.)

Congress authorized, in the same act, $1.5 billion for fiscal years 2002 and 2003 "to reimburse airport operators, on-airport parking lots, and vendors of on-airfield direct services to air carriers for direct costs incurred by such operators to comply with new, additional, or revised security requirements imposed on such operators by the Federal Aviation Administration or Transportation Security Administration on or after September 11, 2001."

Congress also authorized an additional $50 million a year for fiscal years 2002 through 2006 for Transportation Security Administration research, development, testing, and evaluation of explosives detection technology for checked baggage; new screening technology for carry-on items; threat screening technology for cargo, catering, and duty-free items; evaluation of threats carried on persons boarding aircraft or entering secure areas; evaluation of integrated systems of airport security enhancement; expansion of the existing program for improved methods of education, training, and testing of key airport security personnel; and acceleration of research, development, testing, and evaluation of aircraft-hardening materials and techniques to reduce the vulnerability of aircraft to terrorist attack.

Intelligence

The Under Secretary for Transportation Security will also be the central point of intelligence on threats to transportation. Magaw will

- Receive, assess, and distribute intelligence related to transportation security
- Assess threats to transportation
- Develop policies, strategies, and plans for dealing with threats to transportation security
- Coordinate countermeasures with appropriate government "departments, agencies, and instrumentalities"
- Serve as the primary liaison for transportation security to the intelligence and law enforcement communities
- Work with the Federal Aviation Administration with respect to any actions or activities that may affect aviation safety or air carrier operations
- Work with the International Civil Aviation Organization and appropriate aeronautic authorities of foreign governments to address security concerns on passenger flights by foreign air carriers

During a national emergency, Magaw will "coordinate domestic transportation, including aviation, rail, and other surface transportation, and maritime transportation (including port security)"; "coordinate and oversee the transportation-related responsibilities of other departments and agencies" other than the military departments; "coordinate and provide notice to other departments and agencies of the Federal Government, and appropriate agencies of State and local governments, including departments and agencies for transportation, law enforcement, and border control, about threats to transportation."

The law also directs Magaw to enter memoranda of understanding with other agencies to share or cross-check "data on individuals identified on Federal agency databases who may pose a risk to transportation or national security"; "establish procedures for notifying the Administrator of the Federal Aviation Administration, appropriate State and local law enforcement officials, and airport or airline security officers of the identity of individuals known to pose, or suspected of posing, a risk of air piracy or terrorism or a threat to airline or passenger safety"; "establish policies and procedures requiring air carriers… to use information from government agencies to identify individuals on passenger lists who may be a threat to civil aviation or national security" and, "if such an individual is identified, notify appropriate law enforcement agencies, prevent the individual from boarding an aircraft, or take other appropriate action with respect to that individual"; and "consider requiring passenger air carriers to share passenger lists with appropriate Federal agencies for the purpose of identifying individuals who may pose a threat to aviation safety or national security."

Interagency Coordination

The specter of further skyjackings has created a Herculean agenda for the first year of the Transportation Security Administration. A further challenge will be to integrate the individual transportation security efforts inside and outside the Department of Transportation. Some examples:

- The Federal Motor Carrier Safety Administration, for example, plans to have its field officials "visit most of the nation's hazardous materials carriers in the coming months" to increase the carriers' awareness of hazardous materials in relation to terrorist threats.
- The Federal Transit Administration is arranging to have professional security experts conduct security assessments of the 100 largest transit systems and has compiled a Safety and Security Tool Kit.
- The Coast Guard's missions of maritime security, safety, mobility, law enforcement, and protection of natural resources are a big part of homeland security; the Coast Guard notes that it is at a "heightened state of alert" as it protects more than 361 ports and 95,000 miles of coastline, "America's longest border."
- Amtrak, the national intercity rail passenger operator, announced on 5 October 2001 that passengers at any station on the Washington, DC-Boston corridor (where virtually all stations have ticket agents) would be required to have a ticket prior to boarding a train. Photo identification is now necessary to purchase tickets on board trains or in stations or when checking baggage. Amtrak also proposed $3.2 billion in accelerated federal funding for increased security, safety and capacity measures, including bomb-detection technology, surveillance enhancements and the addition of 150 police officers to Amtrak's national accredited police force.
- The American Public Transportation Association has published a briefing titled "Terrorism and Public Transportation" and on its website provides links to information on threat assessment and countermeasures.
- The Volpe National Transportation Systems Center has published a Transit Security Handbook.
- The Transportation Research Board's 81st annual meeting, in January 2002, was devoted to transportation security.
- The Washington (DC) Metropolitan Area Transit Authority has requested $190 million in federal money "to fund additional security enhancements as well as the expansion of an existing chemical-biological sensor detection program."

On paper, at least, Magaw may have some responsibility for the success or failure of all these efforts, but the Transportation Security Administration will probably have its hands full for the first year trying to meet all the aviation security actions mandated in its establishing legislation. However, one role the law assigns to the Under Secretary for Transportation Security is to receive, assess, and distribute intelligence related to transportation security. This is one job that no one else appears to be doing yet, and it may be more important than the other work that Magaw must do once he has time and resources to devote to modes of transportation other than air travel.

Beyond the intelligence function, the training, security, and personnel now being provided to the air travel system could be done for the other modes of transportation as well.

A Plan

On 6 September 2000, the U.S. Department of Transportation released a new strategic plan. Under its National Security Strategic Goal, "Ensure the security of the transportation system for the movement of people and goods, and support the National Security Strategy," it specified seven desired outcomes, quoted from the strategy:

1. Reduce the vulnerability of the transportation system and its users to crime and terrorism
2. Increase the capability of the transportation system to meet national defense needs
3. Reduce the flow of illegal drugs entering the United States
4. Reduce the flow of migrants illegally entering the United States

5. Reduce illegal incursions into our sovereign territory

6. Increase support for United States interests in promoting regional stability

7. Reduce transportation-related dependence on foreign fuel supplies

The plan recognized the needs to "identify and reduce the vulnerabilities of all modes of transportation to security threats" and to "detect and counter threats to the security of the transportation system." It also acknowledged the need for increased airline security, stating:

Following the recommendations of the White House Commission on Aviation Safety and Security, [the Federal Aviation Administration] will expand its research to develop better technology and procedures to prevent weapons and explosive devices from being taken aboard commercial aircraft. Working with airlines and airports, [the Federal Aviation Administration] will continue to purchase and deploy advanced aviation security equipment, monitor its use, and test and assess performance of security programs including access control and cargo. The planned certification of screening companies is expected to increase levels of screener professionalism.

Having predated the 11 September 2001 terrorist attacks by more than a year, the Department of Transportation's strategic plan has the advantage of taking a broader view of transportation security and not reacting to the air system vulnerability identified by the 11 September attacks. Another round of terrorism could expose other vulnerabilities. If the Aum Shinrikyo gas attack in the Tokyo subway system were duplicated in New York, it could provide another reactive assault on transportation security deficiencies. However, the U.S. Department of Transportation has a strategic plan already, and though its implementation was neither thorough enough nor swift enough to prevent a catastrophic breach of transportation security, it may still be a solid outline for establishing transportation security in the future.

Steve Dunham has been an editor at ANSER since 1997. He has worked as a writer and editor for more than 20 years, and writes "Commuter Crossroads," a column for the Fredericksburg, VA, Free Lance-Star. He has been involved in public transit advocacy for a like amount of time; he was a founding member and treasurer of the Massachusetts Association of Railroad Passengers and is now chairman of the board for the Virginia Association of Railway Patrons. He also serves on an advisory committee to Virginia Railway Express.

From the *Journal of Homeland Security*, February 2002. © 2002 by Analytic Services. Reprinted by permission.

Total Information Awareness: Down, but not out

Congress may have put the brakes on the most
ambitious government surveillance program ever.
But for citizens worried about their privacy, TIA still means trouble.

By Farhad Manjoo

The first congressional consideration of Total Information Awareness, President Bush's superpowered spy initiative, was remarkably brief and uncomplicated. Indeed, it wasn't even a debate.

On Jan. 23, the Senate unanimously passed a measure requiring the government to produce a detailed report on the TIA system's goals, costs and consequences. The senator sponsoring the amendment, Ron Wyden, D-Ore., said he was worried that TIA—a Defense Department research project that aims to identify terrorists by analyzing personal data collected in computer databases—was being developed without congressional oversight; his plan, he said, would cause the program to be "respectful of constitutional protections and safeguards, while still ensuring that our nation can continue to fight terrorism."

But while Congress asks for reports, TIA is already steaming forward. According to people with knowledge of the program, TIA has now advanced to the point where it's much more than a mere "research project." There is a working prototype of the system, and federal agencies outside the Defense Department have expressed interest in it.

Most alarmingly, an examination of the research that has been conducted so far into TIA reveals that even while the project has been charging ahead, only token attention has been paid to perhaps its most critical aspect—privacy and civil liberties protection. The Defense Advanced Research Projects Agency (DARPA), which is taking the lead on TIA, has stymied the efforts of outside groups to find out more about TIA's protections.

Critics of TIA applauded the Senate's move as putting the kibosh on what they see as the most frightening example of government Big Brother-ism yet invented. But even if Wyden's amendment does become law, that doesn't mean that TIA opponents can relax. The federal government is unlikely to stop doing research into how to glean information from credit card databases, driver's license registrations and every other point at which human lives meet the computer.

Sept. 11, 2001, led many Americans to expect some loss of individual liberties in the interest of improved security. But how far is too far? TIA is the most ambitious government attempt ever to gather information on ordinary citizens, and, if realized, it will be a tool that could easily be abused by those who have (or can steal) the keys to use it.

"It's hard to come up up with an appropriate analogy for this," says Marc Rotenberg, executive director of Electronic Privacy Information Center, a Washington-based advocacy group. "We're talking about the most massive surveillance program ever tried by the federal government, and you ask them what they're doing for privacy and you get one 26-page paper. I mean, let's get serious."

TIA's lack of attention to privacy has politicians across the political spectrum riled up. The fact that TIA is headed by John Poindexter, the former Reagan administration official who was closely involved in the Iran-Contra affair, also hasn't helped the program's public image.

What is the Defense Department doing to make TIA safe? Not very much. It is on the verge of granting $1 million for the development of what DARPA calls a "privacy appliance" to be used in the system. But participants in a recent study DARPA commissioned to look into the security of databases containing private information—a study that Poindexter has often said proves his office is serious about privacy—don't believe the agency is looking closely enough at protections. Some of them say that TIA will never be safe. "I was stunned," said one participant, describing her reaction to a TIA briefing from Poindexter. "I'm too stunned to say anything."

During the past year, many people working on TIA, including Poindexter, have made a number of briefings to prominent engineers and other VIPs. (Poindexter has given only a few interviews to the press and did not respond to an e-mail interview request from Salon.) DARPA officials also presented their scheme at DARPA Tech, the agency's technology conference, held in Anaheim, Calif., in August. The briefings were not classified; people who attended them—including experts from privacy groups—are free to talk about what was said, and slides from the DARPA Tech presentations are available online.

The 18th slide out of 20 in Poindexter's standard presentation is titled "Privacy." A subtitle says, "Taking several actions to address." And the first bulleted item on his list is "ISAT summer study."

ISAT is the Information Systems Advanced Technology (ISAT) panel, a group within DARPA. Last year, ISAT commissioned a study of technological methods to protect private data in information systems. The study was not meant to focus on TIA; the participants, several of whom were willing to speak on the condition they were not quoted, took a more general look at methods to protect individual data contained in commercial and government databases. But TIA was discussed at the group's meetings, and not often in the most flattering of terms.

The ISAT group held five meetings during the spring and summer of 2002; those were attended by computer scientists, privacy experts, government officials and computer industry executives—sometimes as many as 30 to 40 people discussing privacy. The panel talked about technological issues, not matters of policy; in its final report, the group outlined a few areas of research for DARPA to look into further.

One way to make sure that private information in a database is kept safe, the panel suggested, is "selective revelation"—or the idea that when an analyst searches the databases, the computer should respond in a need-to-know fashion, giving out information only if the analyst has obtained certain legal clearances. "For example," the ISAT report says, "an analyst might issue a query asking whether there is any individual who has recently bought unusual quantities of certain chemicals, and has rented a large truck. The algorithm could respond by saying yes or no, rather than revealing the identity of an individual. The analyst might then take that information to a judge or other appropriate body, seeking permission to learn the individual's name, or other information about the individual. By revealing information iteratively, we prevent the disclosure of private information except when a sufficient showing has been made to justify that revelation."

The ISAT group also proposed that DARPA consider building databases that keep track of what has been asked of them, allowing for later inspection of possible abuses. If such a system has been used nefariously—if an analyst has leveraged other people's personal information for his own gain, for example—investigators could always find an "audit trail" of the bad deeds. "We need to 'watch the watchers,'" the group says in its report—though it concedes that building such audit mechanisms is technologically very complex, and they raise problems of their own: What if a foreign government got hold of a list of queries U.S. authorities were asking?

The group's report was intended to outline broad areas of study; the technology required to enable those areas requires money and time to produce, the group said. The report was also meant to be confidential. But last November, the Electronic Privacy Information Center filed a request under the Freedom of Information Act—or FOIA—asking the Defense Department for all information on the privacy implications of TIA; in December, the agency released only the ISAT study in its response to that request.

EPIC was not satisfied by this response. It had asked for all documents relating to Total Information Awareness, and the ISAT report explicitly states that it is "not a review of Total Information Awareness." Rotenberg, who directs the privacy group, says that while he believes some of the ideas in the ISAT report are "interesting," the report "doesn't begin to answer the larger issues. I think it's important to know that we're operating in an area that needs legal, technological and policy dimensions." On Jan. 16, EPIC won a lawsuit against the Pentagon regarding its FOIA requests; it now expects more information from DARPA.

Nor were participants in the ISAT study happy that DARPA released only their report in its response to EPIC. "I thought it was appropriate for them to turn this over," said one member of the study, "because if you look at the language of the request it's fairly broad. But it seems unlikely that this is the only document they had which relates to the topic of the request."

Barbara Simons, a computer scientist who is the co-chair of the U.S. Public Policy Committee of the Association for Computing Machinery, a worldwide computer science group, and who attended all the ISAT study meetings, is more critical. "It's really astounding that our study was the only thing they gave in response to the EPIC FOIA," she says. "If that's all they have on the issue of privacy, then all those people who are saying, 'Don't worry about TIA,' they're wrong. We should be worrying."

Simons first heard of TIA last May, when the ISAT group was briefed by Poindexter. "And I just couldn't believe what he was saying," she says. "Because he was talking about catching terrorists before they strike—and I just didn't think that was possible."

In a follow-up e-mail, she added: "I'm just not convinced that the TIA will give us tools for catching terrorists that we don't already have or that could be developed with far less expensive and less intrusive systems."

"Even if one were able to construct a system which did protect privacy in some sense, we certainly have not been very successful with building humongous databases that are secure," says Simon. "And think about all the people who have access to this thing. How many people are going to be authorized? What was the name of the guy in the CIA?" She was referring to Aldrich Ames, the CIA official who was convicted of spying for the Soviet Union. "What about someone like that? This takes huge amounts of data—tremendous amounts of data about people are being stored. You run the risk of rogue agents, of bribery, of blackmail." She said she did not believe that the privacy technologies included in the ISAT report would do much to solve such problems.

Does DARPA's response to EPIC mean that the only thing the agency has done on privacy in Total Information Awareness is hold five meetings and produce one 26-page report?

All public information seems to point in that dismal direction. "If you look at some of the presentations that the TIA program managers have made, you've seen they've all referenced privacy safeguards," says Lee Tien, an attorney at the Electronic Frontier Foundation. "But my recollection is that there isn't anything they talked about that wasn't bulleted out in the ISAT study. So if I'm a TIA project manager, I can say what I said after I read the ISAT study and look like I'm doing something good on privacy. And at this point the jury's out about whether they've actually done any more than that."

TIA has not unveiled any actual technology it's created with the specific aim of protecting private information collected by TIA. But in February, the agency is expected to approve its first grant for such technology; the contract has been promised to Teresa Lunt, a computer scientist at the Palo Alto Research Center, who is a veteran in the world of computer security.

Lunt will work on the privacy system for Genisys, the part of TIA that will actually access personal data. Genisys gets its information from third-party databases, such as the computer at your credit card company or driver's license agency. "We envisioned that these companies would want to have some serious control over how the government accessed that data," Lunt says, "so we proposed this idea of a privacy control—a 'privacy appliance,' is what the government calls it. The appliance is a physically separate box that could be inspected by third parties for accuracy and strength."

The privacy appliance would perform the "selective revelation" functions suggested in the ISAT study. The technology would not reveal any identifying data to analysts doing a search at the lowest level of authorization. It would block out names, credit card numbers, Social Security numbers—"any unique or close-to-unique data field would be withheld. We start out with the assumption that it is withheld," Lunt says.

But the systems would go beyond that by blocking out any of the remaining fields that could be used together to "infer" a personal identity. For example, a clever investigator who has determined enough information about you—how much money you make, how many cars you have registered to you, whether you like to pay off your credit cards each month or prefer to keep a balance—could search through all this information for those characteristics, and possibly ferret out more information.

Lunt's "inference analysis" tools are designed to prevent that sort of misbehavior.

Many computer scientists said that although they thought Lunt's ideas would be difficult to pull off, they're fundamentally sound. Still, some people in the computer security community, who declined to comment on the record, were nevertheless dismayed that Lunt looks like the only recipient of a privacy technology award from DARPA—and some wondered whether part of the reason she might have received that award was the fact that she once worked for the agency.

Lunt brushed off the suggestion that DARPA picked her for any reason other than her technology. "I don't see any connection between the two," said Lunt, "except the security research field is a very small field. There's maybe a community of a few hundred doing work in this kind of security. And how many are doing database security?"

She also said that DARPA was in fact taking a risk in going with her project, because nobody knew if such a system would actually work. "It may not allow the data to be useful," Lunt said. "If you start withholding a lot of this stuff it might make it hard for the analysts to see the relationships between people."

Experts involved in the ISAT study are dismayed at the size of Lunt's grant—$1 million a year, for three years. This is small compared to the entire TIA program, estimated to cost tens of millions. (Any dollar figures more specific than that are in dispute.) Lunt agrees that the grant is small; she wishes DARPA would put more money toward privacy research. The million dollars, she said, is "enough for us to succeed on our project, and I think our project goes a long way toward getting them there. DARPA sometimes funds research areas that are leading to some strategic thing—but they could have a research program on privacy which doesn't have a specific application in mind, one that is just designed to improve privacy tools."

Experts involved in the ISAT study echoed these thoughts. Wouldn't it be nice if, in addition to spending millions on security tools, the federal government made a large outlay toward privacy research? Something huge, dramatic, on the order of TIA itself?

But that's not happening. The sad fact about TIA is that, Lunt's research notwithstanding, the privacy schemes in it appear to be tangential, token ideas, added on to the system as a political afterthought.

Bob Barr, the former Republican congressman from Georgia, is among TIA's harshest critics. Barr, who lost his seat last year after redistricting in Georgia, was known as one of the House's most conservative members: He is famous for having introduced a resolution to impeach Bill Clinton in 1997, a few months before anyone had ever heard of Monica Lewinsky.

Barr calls TIA "one of the worst invasions of privacy I've ever seen," and he says that the only thing he regrets about the Senate's action is that it did not kill TIA entirely. On his Web site, Barr congratulates Russ Feingold, one of the Senate's most liberal members, who has proposed legislation that would stop the TIA program. Nothing short of that would satisfy him, Barr says, because "I suspect that based on my experience with the executive branch they will keep pushing and pushing and pushing, hoping Congress will not pay attention. And I think we'll see this program resurrected in other avenues."

Barr's stance proves that privacy is not a left-right issue; everyone should fight for strong privacy protections, he says, and he believes many members of Congress have been hearing that from their constituents. "And I think the hue and cry against these invasions of privacy will be heard much more in this Congress."

Last year, Barr sponsored a bill that would have required the federal government to produce a "privacy impact statement" each time it launches programs that could threaten civil liberties. The bill enjoyed broad support; both the ACLU and the NRA thought it was a good idea. In October, the bill passed the House, but it didn't get very far in the Senate. "Last year," Barr says, "it was so difficult to get members to focus on doing anything that would appear to be not giving the government anything it wanted to do as far as terrorism was concerned. The most we thought we could do was get it through the House."

Barr's idea is good policy; currently, federal agencies are not required to consider how their ideas affect civil liberties. After they tell a fearful public that a certain program is necessary to prevent our annihilation, officials seem to have a free pass to build programs like TIA, promising nothing on privacy other than "Taking actions to address." Thankfully, Wyden's proposal will prompt a cost-benefit calculation for TIA, but other security programs could also do with such an analysis—the Transportation Security Administration's Computer Assisted Passenger Prescreening System II, which profiles airline passengers, or the USA PATRIOT act, passed without much deliberation a few weeks after 9/11.

Recently, Ralph Nader and tech activist Jamie Love have taken up the cause to promote privacy impact statements. On Jan. 7, the two met for the second time with Mitch Daniels, the White House budget director, in an effort to persuade the administration to embrace the idea of putting a "value" on "privacy and dignity."

"Benefits to national security are measured and assigned monetary values [in the budget process]," Love says. "So we're asking to assign values on privacy and dignity—that's something people care about, and there's benefit in that." Love added that he didn't think the Bush administration was averse to the idea of preparing such impact studies; the White House has always said that it believes in a "strong regulatory review," relying heavily on cost-benefit analyses to determine the value of government projects.

And a cost-benefit analysis of privacy, Love says, one in which some "nonzero" value is assigned to the loss of privacy that comes from such programs as TIA, would lead to better government, and a more efficient fight on terrorism—government money would only go to projects that really worked.

A spokesman for the Office of Management and Budget said that no specific decisions had come of Daniels' meeting with Nader and Love, but that the White House was interested in "smart regulation," which it believes comes from a rigorous analysis of costs and benefits of government programs.

Ever since TIA was unmasked, the media's main source for information about it has been the program's Web site, which contained a lode of documents on the system's scope and design, as well as information about the people working on it. Much of what the public knows about TIA comes from the site, which was adorned with a notoriously creepy logo—the eye atop the masonic pyramid, familiar from the dollar bill, looking out over the world—and a Latin slogan, "*Sciencia est Potentia*": Knowledge is power. During the last couple of months, however, perhaps in response to public opinion, DARPA has quietly removed some Web documents. The logo and the slogan are gone. So are the short biographies of the personnel involved.

One hopes that with the Senate action, Congress will convince TIA to get more responsive than that. "I hope the Congress engages in some serious oversight," Barr says, "to make sure the executive branch doesn't resurrect this thing. I think that chances are overwhelming that they will—they always do."

Farhad Manjoo is a staff writer for Salon Technology & Business.

UNIT 4

State and Local Governments and Homeland Security

Unit Selections

Key Points to Consider

- What are the basic conclusions that former Governor Frank Keating draws from his experiences?

- What are the most important issues that states face in the aftermath of major catastrophic events?

- What role should the federal government play in funding local costs for homeland security?

- Why do local officials feel that their interests may be abandoned in the pursuit of foreign policy objectives?

 **Links: www.dushkin.com/online/**
These sites are annotated in the World Wide Web pages.

Dark Winter
   http://www.homelandsecurity.org/darkwinter/index.cfm
High Alert Status Costs Cities
   http://www.fcw.com/fcw/articles/2003/0407/pol-cities-04-07-03.asp
NGA Center for Best Practices
   http://www.nga.org/center/divisions/1,1188,T_CEN_HS,00.html
Security Clearance Process for State and Local Law Enforcement
   http://www.fbi.gov/clearance/securityclearance.htm

Major disasters, by definition, tend to very quickly overwhelm the resources and capabilities of local governments. When challenged beyond their means, cities and localities have come to rely on state governments for assistance. The involvement of state governments in disaster response is nothing new. Most states have had significant experience in disaster response and emergency management. Through years of trial and error, exposure to natural disasters such as earthquakes, floods, wildfires, tornadoes, hurricanes, and snowstorms, and man-made disasters such as plane crashes, train crashes, and chemical spills, states have managed to develop effective emergency management and disaster response capabilities.

States have developed significant infrastructure to assist in such responses. Command and control facilities, specialized equipment, and designated emergency personnel that includes, when needed, National Guard units, are important components of the disaster response plans of most states. While existing infrastructure may vary from state to state, based on threat perception and the availability of resources, it is an illusion to think that the federal government is more capable at planning for and organizing local disaster response than those who know the area and have been doing it for years.

The federal government can nevertheless play an important role. To effectively expand their response repertoire to include potential threats to homeland security, the two most important things that states need from the federal government are information and funding.

Information is probably the most important thing the federal government can contribute to state and local efforts. While a number of federal agencies are working on more effective ways to exploit data collected by local and state police departments, little has been done to eliminate the barriers that prevent the distribution of intelligence to these departments. The lack of information and lack of feedback from the federal government continue to be a source of frustration for state and local authorities. State and local police forces cannot become effective "eyes and ears" for federal homeland security efforts if they aren't told specifically who and what to look for. In addition to timely intelligence and accurate threat assessments, states need improved access to specialized knowledge and training that will allow them to prepare themselves for this new type of threat.

One of the biggest sources of contention between state and local governments and the Bush administration in regard to homeland security is funding. While most states and municipalities support the desire for improved security, few have sufficient economic resources to sustain this effort. In a time of deficits and budget cuts, preparing for future threats while responding to heightened terrorist "alert-levels" has become a near impossible task. Federal money to acquire new specialized equipment, conduct training, and field additional security forces is needed. As the Bush administration has increasingly shifted its attention to problems overseas, federal spending on state and local efforts has slowed, and states and municipalities have become critical of the lack of federal support.

The articles in this unit focus on the challenges that state and local governments face in their homeland security efforts. In the first article, former Oklahoma governor Frank Keating draws upon his experiences with the Oklahoma City bombing and his role in federal disaster exercises to develop five basic guidelines for interaction among state and federal authorities. In the second article, Maryland Governor Parris Glendening discusses some of the organizational, legislative, and economic challenges faced by states in the aftermath of September 11. The third and fourth articles attempt to capture the increasing dissatisfaction with the distribution of federal funds for homeland security, experienced by states and localities. Finally, the last article charges that the Bush administration's preoccupation with Afghanistan and Iraq has led to a "… near universal fear among state and local officials" that they may be abandoned in the administration's efforts to federalize homeland security.

Catastrophic Terrorism— Local Response to a National Threat

Frank Keating
25th Governor of Oklahoma

Governor Frank Keating is the second chief executive in Oklahoma history—and the first Republican—to win election to two consecutive terms. First elected in 1994 and re-elected by a landslide in 1998, Keating has been one of Oklahoma's most reform-minded and active governors. Under his leadership, Oklahoma has become a true two-party state and made significant progress in education reform, tax relief, roadbuilding, environmental protection, economic development and public safety. Beyond Oklahoma's borders, Frank Keating is widely recognized as one of America's most articulate and able political leaders.

The first Keating term was marked by significant achievement—and by an overwhelming tragedy. On April 19, 1995, a terror bomb exploded in downtown Oklahoma City, and Keating led a state response that drew worldwide admiration. The Governor and First Lady Cathy Keating were instrumental in organizing rescue and recovery operations and in assuring that those affected by the bombing received prompt assistance. They also took the lead in creating a $6 million fund that will provide college scholarships for children who were injured or who lost parents in the bombing. The Keatings were honored by the Salvation Army with the prestigious William Booth Award as recognition for their outstanding contributions to the recovery effort.

In June of 2001, I had the honor of taking the role of a state governor in an exercise that simulated the intentional release of the deadly virus smallpox in three US cities. During the simulated thirteen days of the game, titled *Dark Winter*, the disease spread to 25 states and 15 other countries. Fourteen participants playing roles of the President, the National Security Council, and myself (representing the likely actions of a seated Governor), and 60 observers witnessed terrorism/warfare in slow motion. Discussions, debates, and decisions focused on the public health response, lack of an adequate supply of smallpox vaccine, roles and missions of federal and state governments, civil liberties associated with quarantine and isolation, the role of the Department of Defense, and potential military responses to the anonymous attack. The scenario of that exercise was different from the real-life crisis we faced in Oklahoma on April 19, 1995, but the fundamental principles were the same. In both instances, our tasks as leaders of local, state and federal agencies were to respond to a terrorist assault in ways that protected and preserved lives and property, assured accountability and justice for those who were responsible for the attack and protected the national security. I was honored to share my own experiences from Oklahoma City with the group, and I am equally honored to share my perspective with the American public.

In that respect, I want to review very briefly what happened in Oklahoma City in 1995, and then relate the lessons we learned there to the experiences we shared at the *Dark Winter* exercise, and to the issues surrounding an incident of this magnitude.

You will recall that a massive terror bomb was detonated at 9:02 a.m. on April 19, 1995, in front of the Murrah Federal Office Building in the heart of our community. It killed 168 people, injured hundreds more and severely damaged many dozens of buildings. The rescue and recovery efforts that followed, and the criminal investigation, were both the most massive of their kind in American history. These efforts threw together, literally overnight, more separate agencies from the local, state and federal governments than had ever worked cooperatively on a single task. The outcome could have been chaotic—it has been before when far fewer agencies tried to coordinate their efforts on much more discrete and manageable tasks. But the outcome in Oklahoma City was not chaos. Later, observers would coin the label "The Oklahoma Standard" to refer to the way our city, state and nation came together in response to this despicable act.

I think what happened in Oklahoma City in 1995 served as a model for the *Dark Winter* participants, and I believe it should also help guide the deliberations on a national policy for responding to catastrophic events on the American homeland. Simply put, we did it right in 1995. The principles behind The Oklahoma Standard can help govern our nation's future course in responding to the terrorist threat.

On April 19, 1995, every injured person was cared for promptly and with great skill and compassion—in fact, at the closest hospital to the blast site, every arriving ambulance was met by an individual physician assigned to a specific victim. Of several dozen victims deemed critically injured on that day, only one who made it to the hospital alive subsequently died.

Every deceased victim was recovered, and all remains were restored to the families for burial, promptly and with great sensitivity.

Key evidence that would lead to the apprehension, conviction and eventual execution of the primary perpetrator of the crime was in law enforcement hands within minutes after the explosion. A local deputy sheriff found and recorded the serial number from the bomber's vehicle at almost the same moment that a state trooper was arresting the suspect some miles away. The criminal case built over the next few weeks was simply overwhelming. It assured our victims, and our society, of justice.

Finally, our national security was protected. Local and federal authorities in the months and years after the Oklahoma City bombing directed new attention to potentially dangerous domestic insurgent groups, defusing a number of similar terrorist plots before anyone was hurt. Congress also passed stronger anti-terrorism legislation.

The *Dark Winter* scenario involved a foreign source of terrorism, not one of our own citizens. In *Dark Winter*, the weapon was bacterial rather than explosive. But in virtually every other respect, these two scenarios shared these key goals and principles:

- **To protect, preserve and save lives and property;**
- **To hold accountable those responsible for terrorism;**
- **To protect and advance America's interests and security.**

Those are the three fundamental challenges presented by any terrorist attack, from a bomb to biological assault to the nightmare of a clandestine nuclear confrontation. I think it is instructive to compare how we pursued those goals in Oklahoma City with the outcomes of the *Dark Winter* scenario, and to look at how that comparison might reflect on future policy.

The conclusions drawn by a series of after-action analyses from Oklahoma City are remarkably similar. I will consolidate those conclusions into five basic findings, compare them to what we did (or did not do) at *Dark Winter*, and suggest resulting policy implications:

1. Recognize that in virtually every possible terrorism scenario, first responders will be local.

In Oklahoma City, the true heavy lifting of the initial rescue and recovery operations, as well as the key evidence collection that led to a successful criminal prosecution, was the task of local fire, police and emergency medical personnel. In fact, the real first responders were not even public employees; they were bystanders and co-workers of the trapped and injured, who often shrugged off their own injuries and got up out of the rubble to help others. The first Federal Emergency Management Agency (FEMA) Urban Search and Rescue Task Force did not reach Oklahoma City until late on the night of April 19—several hours after the last living victim had been extracted from the wrecked building. That task force, and the ten that followed it, were absolutely essential to the conduct of the successful recovery operations that followed, but it is important to note that even those FEMA Urban Search and Rescue Task Forces are drawn from local police and fire departments.

As an example, many of those task forces brought structural engineers to Oklahoma. They were able to work closely in planning the search and recovery operation with the local architect who had designed and built the Murrah Building in the 1970s. Who was better prepared and qualified for this crucial task? Neither party was; it was a true cooperative effort, blending federal and local resources to achieve outstanding results that allowed many hundreds of rescue workers to labor around the clock in a devastated and unstable structure without serious injury to any of those involved.

In the *Dark Winter* scenario, as in virtually any real-world terrorist assault, the first responders will also be local. The federal government does not maintain rapid response teams in any area of expertise close enough to any potential terrorist target, save perhaps the White House, to allow them to be first on the scene. In *Dark Winter*, local private physicians and public health officials were the first to detect cases of smallpox. Local government and law enforcement agencies were the ones with the power to impose and enforce quarantines, curfews and states of martial law, to disseminate information through local media and to collate and forward epidemiological data to federal agencies such as the Centers for Disease Control in Atlanta. Local law enforcement would be the ones to discover, preserve and secure any available crime scenes or evidence. As in Oklahoma City, the preponderance of personnel, vehicles, equipment and even the volunteer force of blood donors, Salvation Army canteen operators and the people who showed up to do laundry for the FEMA Urban Search and Rescue Task Force members will necessarily be drawn from local resources.

2. Insist that teamwork is not just desirable— it is possible.

The after action reports from Oklahoma City noted that agencies from various levels and jurisdictions which had not traditionally worked closely in the past did so to a remarkable extent at the Murrah Building site, and in the ensuing criminal investigation. They even did so in overcoming what was a huge potential initial hurdle— the conflicting purposes of those who were working through the rubble to extract the dead and those who saw the same rubble pile as a vast crime scene to be processed for evidence.

This is not to say that there were no conflicts. There were, but they were resolved, in virtually every case, to the mutual satisfaction of all of those concerned. We have seen too many cases in the past where an investigative agency or a rescue unit squabbled in private (and sometimes in public) over "my crime scene" or "our rescue mission." That this natural source of conflict did not overwhelm or dissipate the Oklahoma City effort is a tribute to the good sense and reason of those involved.

The one central problem which emerged in Oklahoma City was that of communications. From the initial first response effort through the final body recovery, it was noted that the many different radio frequencies and institutional policies in play all too often left many participants in the effort in the dark concerning vital decisions that should have been shared universally. This was remedied in part—but only in part—by the creation of a unified command center which invited key representatives from all of the agencies involved to frequent information briefings and discussions on tactics.

Ironically, local agencies were in some ways better equipped to overcome this communications gap than their federal counterparts, thanks to a quirk of geography. Because central Oklahoma is located dead-center in what is called "tornado alley," our public safety and emergency medical agencies had planned and even drilled for a large mass casualty incident in the past. They had on hand mobile command posts with some (though not all) interlocking radio capabilities. They also had the distinct advantages of familiarity with each other's basic operating procedures, local geography, even what local companies might be able to bring a large crane to the site on that first night to begin the search for buried victims. Time after time, I saw federal officials turn to local fire and police personnel and ask for assistance that only they could give.

I want to encourage the readers of this journal, and the general public, to visit the Oklahoma City National Memorial Institute for the Prevention of Terrorism, which was a direct outgrowth of our experiences in Oklahoma City and a co-sponsor of the *Dark Winter* exercise. No one has more information drawn directly from field experience of how to blend the many levels of responders together in an seamless a way as possible to react to a terrorist attack.

3. The rapid and accurate flow of information— both internally among government agencies and externally to the public—is absolutely essential.

Because the Murrah Building was located in downtown Oklahoma City, for all to see, we immediately stumbled into the right answer to the eternal question, How much do we tell the public? That answer is simple—We tell them everything that does not need to be safeguarded for valid reasons of security.

I know you will all recall the steady, 24-hour broadcasts and news dispatches that came from Oklahoma City in the first days after the 1995 bombing. Our policy was to conduct regular media briefings on everything from body counts to alerts involving the composite drawings of the principal suspects in the bombing, and the results were in virtually all cases positive. Certainly many aspects of the criminal investigation were not disclosed in those early days. The Oklahoma City Fire Department and the Office of the Chief Medical Examiner carefully controlled release of information concerning the dead to assure that families were fully notified before victim identities were made public. We did not allow open media access to the interior site itself for reasons of safety and efficiency. But in almost every other instance, our decision was in favor of openness and candor, and the results are very clear. I continue to receive letters, more than six years later, from Americans who have a permanently positive impression of how the bombing was handled.

In the *Dark Winter* exercise, many decisions concerning the release of information went in a different direction. From my own service in Washington, I know there exists an instinct for secrecy, and urge to classify, that often bears little relation to the realities of the moment. This happened in *Dark Winter* too. I believe that was, and is, a mistake, especially in a situation where bioterrorism was involved. Americans expect and deserve to be told the truth by government at all levels when their safety is at stake. Certainly I do not counsel revealing matters that would endanger national security or ongoing criminal investigations, but when the question is one between candor and secrecy in a matter of enormous public interest, and absent a clear and compelling reason for secrecy, candor should be the chosen option.

Our *Dark Winter* participants too often opted to conceal or obscure where openness would have done no harm—and where it would have increased public confidence. To cite a clear and compelling example of why this is true, contrast the high public approval of the FBI's successful identification and prosecution of Timothy McVeigh in the Oklahoma City bombing with the Bureau's present image problems related, in large part, to inept handling of documentation in that case. Simply put, the FBI was remarkably open—and praised—as it identified, caught and prosecuted McVeigh; it was closed, and justifiably mistrusted, when it misplaced the files.

Government at all levels earns the trust of those it serves every day. It does not merit that trust if it is overly secretive.

4. Experts are called experts for a reason—rely on them.

In Oklahoma City, the agency best equipped to handle the removal, identification and processing of the 168 people killed in the bombing was the Office of the Chief Medical Examiner, which did an outstanding job. I recall at least one federal official with some experience in mass-casualty incidents assuring the staff from the medical examiner's office that they would "never" be able to identify all of the victims. In fact they did so, with vast cooperation from local funeral directors, dentists, physicians and many others who worked countless hours at a most heartrending and often distasteful task. They were the experts, and they did their job well.

That was also true of the crane operators who helped remove the rubble, the federal agents who identified the explosive components, and many others. People work for many years to acquire skills; agencies involved in responding to a terrorist attack should let them do their jobs.

In *Dark Winter*, the obvious agency with the expertise to isolate and identify the smallpox microorganism was the Centers for Disease Control in Atlanta. The experts in potential delivery systems were chemists and physicists. Those best equipped to identify Iraqi origins for the terrorist act were from the intelligence field.

Conversely, those best qualified to assess what (and how) information is to be publicly released are the communications professionals. When a building is badly damaged by a bomb, engineers and architects play a central role; when germs are released on the public, doctors must be involved. In responding to any terrorist attack, supervising agencies should rely on the experts in their respective fields, and not seek to concentrate decision making powers above and removed from the level where those experts can be heard.

5. Resist the urge to federalize everything.

Perhaps the strongest lesson from Oklahoma City—and perhaps the most worrisome outcome from the *Dark Winter* exercise—concerns the almost instinctive urge common to officials of federal agencies and the military to open the federal umbrella over any and all functions or activities. Simply put, the federal government all too often acts like the 500 pound gorilla.

In *Dark Winter*, we encountered this tendency as soon as state National Guard units were activated in response to the bioterrorist attack. The function of those units—imposing curfews and quarantines and keeping public peace—were exclusively local in nature. Still, many of the participants sought to call the Guard into federal service immediately. I want to thank Senator Nunn, who played the role of the President in the exercise, for resisting this temptation and deciding not to federalize the Guard.

Federalizing makes sense when the mission is largely federal in nature—for example, a combat environment or an overseas deployment—but not when the mission remains largely local. I noted that I failed to see how a National Guard company, led by a local captain and staffed by local residents who had assembled at the local armory for duty, would perform in any different manner if it were formally inducted into federal service. My experience following the Oklahoma City bombing was that members of the Oklahoma Army and Air National Guards called to service did an excellent job under state control. In fact, the very first makeshift memorial to the dead was created near the Murrah Building site, along a security fence line, by Air Guard personnel who were mourning the deaths of their neighbors. The Guard blended well with other agencies, both local and federal. Its members took special pride in serving their Oklahoma neighbors as members of the *Oklahoma* Guard.

Certainly if a Guard formation cannot perform well, or if it requires specialized training or equipment to discharge its role in response to a terrorist incident, it should be promptly federalized. Equally surely, many components of the national response to an attack like that proposed in *Dark Winter* must be largely federal in nature—from the gathering of intelligence that pointed to an Iraqi connection to the formulation for diplomatic and military responses. But that does not mean that every part of the broad response must or should originate at the federal level, or that federal officials should assume supremacy in every aspect of the response, or that the military response should trump the humanitarian response. It was a deputy sheriff who jotted down the number from a mangled truck axle that, ultimately, brought McVeigh to justice. It was a surgeon from a state hospital who crawled into the Murrah rubble to amputate a trapped victim's leg as local police officers and firefighters held lights and moved obstacles. Oklahomans carried the first injured out of the building on April 19, and three weeks later they recovered the last of the dead. They continue to staff mental health and counseling services—funded in part by federal sources—to help with the healing.

My experiences in Oklahoma City in 1995, and my participation in *Dark Winter* this year, both taught me some valuable lessons.

- **Train and equip your first responders, for they are the front line in meeting the terrorist threat.**

- **Search for ways to support teamwork *before* an incident, and emphasize that teamwork after.**

- **Tell the truth, and be candid with the people we are working to protect and serve.**

- **Trust the experts to do what they know best.**

And remember that the response to terrorism does not begin and end in Washington. Trust local governments, local agencies and local citizens to do the right thing, because in the end, they are the real targets of terrorism, whether it's a bomb in front of a building filled with ordinary Americans or a germ unleashed on their neighbors.

From the *Journal of Homeland Security*, August 2001. © 2001 by Journal of Homeland Security.

Governing after September 11th: A New Normalcy

Parris N. Glendening
Governor, State of Maryland

A generation ago, one traumatic incident provided a common frame of reference for most Americans: "Where were you when President John F. Kennedy was shot?" Today, the question has become, "Where were you on September 11th?" That day, I was on my way to Baltimore for a routine meeting with business leaders to discuss education. A friend called me on my cell phone to tell me about the plane crashing into the World Trade Center. A short time later, a member of my executive protection staff interrupted my meeting to tell me about the additional plane crashes. America was under attack. We had a major emergency on our hands.

The nation's governors have responded in a number of ways to the terrorist attacks, both short- and long-term. As immediate past president of the National Governors Association and current president of the Council of State Governments, I immediately spoke to many of my peers on the morning of September 11th, and we have met frequently since then to address the challenges presented by the new level of threat exposed that day. The events demanded that government leaders reevaluate all emergency plans and ensure they are updated, coordinated, and effective. In Maryland, we have responded in a number of ways. In addition to activating Maryland's emergency response plan, we have reorganized government, reassessed priorities, and enacted new laws to better position the state to ensure the safety of all our citizens.

Among the most critical roles that government serves are emergency preparedness and management. As the state's chief executive, the governor is responsible for the public's safety and welfare. When a disaster occurs, the governor must be ready to calm and reassure the affected communities and ensure that help reaches those in need. Before the events of September 11, 2001, Maryland, like every state, had extensive emergency response plans in place. Yet no amount of preparation could have prepared any of us for the devastation that occurred that day. The unprecedented terrorism left an indelible mark on people around the world—and on Americans in particular as the targets of those outrageous acts.

After being advised that hijacked airplanes had slammed into the World Trade Center in New York and the Pentagon in Washington, Maryland's emergency response plan was activated. Less than two hours after the attack, I exercised the authority conferred upon me as governor by the state's constitution and laws and declared a state of public emergency in Maryland. Once an emergency is declared, the governor is authorized to take a number of actions to respond to the crisis, including issuing orders and suspending the provisions of any law or regulation. The declaration of an emergency also sets into motion state and local emergency response plans. Additional executive orders were issued to allow state agencies to render assistance to New York, Virginia, and the District of Columbia.

As a precaution, we closed state government operations and schools and put extra security around other potential targets of destruction such as the World Trade Center in Baltimore and Calvert Cliffs, a nuclear facility in Southern Maryland. To comprehensively manage the state's response to the attack, I traveled to the Camp Fretterd Military Installation, Maryland's emergency operations center, with my lieutenant governor, agency heads, and key staff members. From this center, we gathered the latest information and coordinated agency response to make sure that key personnel, infrastructure, and other resources were deployed where they were needed. As important, my public communications team was on hand to provide the public assurance that the state was responding. Communication from the governor's office was vital to get the public prompt and accurate information and to quell false rumors.

Fortunately, the terrorists did not make any attacks on Maryland soil. Nonetheless, the tragedy directly affected numerous Marylanders. Many Marylanders died or lost loved ones on September 11th. Maryland surrounds two-thirds of the District of Columbia. Many of our citizens work in the Pentagon. Fire and rescue personnel from Montgomery County, Maryland, were among the first responders to the plane crash into the Pentagon. Our National Guard units were some of the first called up by the president.

In addition, one of the planes used in the attacks originated from Dulles International Airport in neighboring Virginia, and the plane crash in Pennsylvania occurred near the Maryland border. We were alerted that a location in Maryland was likely the next terrorist target. Maryland is home to many important federal installations, including Camp David, the National Security Agency, Fort Meade, Aberdeen Proving Grounds, the Patuxent River Naval Air Station, the United States Naval Academy, and several federal laboratory research institutions, such as the National Institutes of Health.

Maryland's approach has been to move forward simultaneously on two fronts: making sure our citizens remain safe and secure while keeping our economy strong and prosperous. To ensure safety, we have increased security at our airports, public buildings, major events, bridges, and tunnels—anywhere that terrorists might look to further spread fear, violence, and death. At the request of the president, I activated the state's national guard to provide security at Baltimore-Washington International Airport. Guard members remained on duty until the new federal airport security force, created by Congress in response to the terrorist attacks, was deployed. I also put together an Emergency Response Assessment Workgroup to review and update our emergency response plans. I charged the group with conducting an in-depth review of each emergency plan to elevate the coordination across state agencies and with other levels of government.

Following the workgroup's assessment, we created rapid-response teams to make sure any threat or action is dealt with immediately and effectively. The teams are made up of pre-designated, pre-trained men and women with expertise in key areas who live in different regions of the state and can assemble quickly to respond to and assess major emergencies. Each team consists of seven members: a group leader, an engineer, a medical specialist, a chemical expert, a logistics person, a public-safety representative, and a public information officer. The teams will not be the first responders to emergency situations, but will be the second wave and will have on-site authority to coordinate and deploy state resources once the immediate needs have been met. The teams will coordinate the state, local, and federal response.

We also created a second workgroup, together with legislative leaders to propose antiterrorism legislative initiatives. We feared an overreaction to the terrorist attacks and did not want extreme measures. Therefore, we undertook a collaborative effort that reflected commonsense steps to protect our citizens yet preserve civil liberties. A series of legislation was recently enacted from the group's proposals. The new laws clarify the governor's emergency powers, including the authority to declare a public health catastrophe and take measures in the event of a bioterrorism event; create a 15-member Maryland Security Council; shield sensitive security documents from disclosure; and enhance law enforcement's ability to fight terrorism with additional tools such as roving wiretaps.

Maintaining a strong economy was a different challenge. Maryland has one of the strongest economies in the United States: Job growth is well above the national average; unemployment is well below the national average; we have one of the highest family income levels in the nation and the lowest poverty rate in the nation; and many independent economists see Maryland as well positioned to continue to prosper in the new economy.

Nonetheless, we faced unanticipated costs for heightened security measures and a major slowdown in the economy. Important sectors of our economy, such as tourism and travel, were severely affected. The state's revenues were down because of the reduction in taxes collected on capital gains. To ensure that Maryland's economy remains steady and the budget sustainable, we had to take careful and prudent actions. We instituted a hiring freeze throughout state government, except for critical security personnel; cut 1.5 percent in operation costs of every state agency; and delayed capital projects. These measures will result in a savings of more than $205 million.

To further pay for added security measures, Maryland sought and received federal assistance. In recognition of the integral role that state and local governments have in guarding against and responding to security threats, the federal government has already provided funds to pay for protective equipment, bioterrorism prevention efforts, and other security costs. But much more is needed. State and local government organizations such as the National Governors Association, the Council of State Governments, and the National Association of Counties are lobbying the White House and Congress to ensure we are at the table for decisions concerning homeland security. The National Governors Association explained that this is a national concern, not merely a federal one. The ongoing dialogue between the different levels of government addresses funding, planning, and coordination, particularly in communications. It is vital that state and local governments have adequate resources as well as timely and accurate information to respond to any threat.

The above actions address issues of government organization, laws, and budgets to prepare for, prevent, and respond to emerging threats exemplified by the terrorist attacks of September 11th. After the attacks of September 11th, we needed also to reestablish confidence in our economy, build momentum, and reengage. That is why we worked to get this simple yet important message out: If we allow the events of September 11th to break our spirits, make us withdraw, and hurt our economy, then bin Laden prevails.

To spread this message, one symbolic step we took was to organize a tour for a group of governors in late September to New York City and Washington, D.C. Joining me on the trip were Governors Paul E. Patton of Kentucky, Don Sundquist of Tennessee, Mike Huckabee of Arkansas, Ronnie Musgrove of Mississippi, and Mayor Anthony Williams of the District of Columbia. We traveled by commercial airlines to New York City. While there, we shopped, dined, and took in a Broadway show. Then we went to Washington and visited the Pentagon and the National Museum of History. The trip was well covered in the national media and heralded the public's return to many of our country's treasures such as Broadway and the Smithsonian museums.

We must face other long-term issues found in the attacks and their aftermath. While the leaders behind these terrorist attacks are driven by fanaticism and hatred, seeing the destruction of the United States as their religious duty, the many that follow them are driven by poverty, misery, and desperation. This is also our challenge.

Today we see the world mobilized in a justified military action against terrorism. When the battles are over and the military victory is secured, we must then find the political will to wage a second campaign. This must be a campaign aimed at defeating the conditions of poverty that enable hatred and violence to thrive. This must be a campaign based on the belief that real peace will come only when the world community protects the aspirations for freedom in people everywhere. This must be a campaign that understands that hope and freedom can be the only true victors over terrorism and fanaticism. We must find the will to undertake this monumentally important effort.

I had the great honor of speaking with Nelson Mandela when he visited Maryland in late 2001. We discussed that the United States has the ability to mobilize the world. We saw it a decade ago with the Gulf War. We see it today with the war on terrorism. Even traditional enemies are uniting for this cause. We must use this ability for other causes that are just as worthy and just as important. We must unite behind an effort to fight the poverty that gives rise to terrorism. We also must come together in an effort to protect the environment and fight global warming. And we must join together in an effort to fight AIDS in Africa and around the world.

America must take leadership in addressing these global crises, or we will be fighting wars constantly. As a result, our money and resources will be spent on instruments of destruction rather than invested in areas that can truly make a difference in people's lives—areas such as education, the environment, and health care. What I have experienced during my tenure as governor is that although public security and emergency preparedness are indispensable aspects of government, no amount of planning can ever predict every event. The challenge of leadership is facing public crisis with the confidence that it can be handled, the ability to devise solutions, the courage to be honest with the public, and the resolve to move on to a broader focus.

After receiving his doctorate in political science from Florida State University in 1967, **Parris N. Glendening** *became an associate professor of government and politics at the University of Maryland–College Park, where he taught until his election as governor of Maryland in 1995. Prior to becoming governor, he served on the Prince George's County Council and as Prince George's county executive. He has held the leadership positions of president, National Council of Elected County Executives; chair, Southern Regional Education Board; and chair, National Governors Association. He is currently the president of the Council of State Governments and chairman of the Democratic Governor's Association.* **Email: governor@gov.state.md.us.**

Bush meets with N.Y. mayor and promises more aid for cities

By John Machacek, Gannett News Service

WASHINGTON—After meeting with New York Mayor Michael Bloomberg, President Bush promised Wednesday to ask Congress for an immediate boost in homeland security aid for localities and give a bigger share to budget-strapped New York City and other high-risk metropolitan areas.

Bloomberg, the Republicans' star big-city mayor, said no specific dollar amounts were discussed during a half-hour meeting with Bush and Homeland Security Secretary Tom Ridge in the Oval Office. But he has said New York needs $900 million this year.

But Bush's pledge to change a government spending formula so that homeland security aid can be based on need and risk would help New York City pay for its new heightened security plan put in place Monday, expected to cost more than $5 million a week. The Bush administration raised the nation's terror alert level to orange or "high risk" on Monday.

"When you give out monies for military items, you do it based on need," Bloomberg told reporters after the session. "And we think that the homeland security (department) should gets its money from Congress and be able to distribute it based on what the governor perceives the risk would be. ... There is a two-front war here. One is in our streets and one is overseas."

Currently, homeland security aid is distributed under a population-driven formula that also sets minimum amounts to be received by each state. That minimum requirement reduces the amount of money that New York state and city would get under the per capita side of the formula, Bloomberg said.

Ridge, who was at Bloomberg's side at the news conference, announced that Bush would add homeland security assistance to a 2003 emergency spending bill the president will soon submit to Congress for covering the costs of war against Iraq. Ridge indicated that Bloomberg's specific ideas about addressing the security needs of New York City and other large communities will be reflected in Bush's emergency funding request.

Administration officials had previously said Bush would request between $90 billion and $110 billion for war costs alone. But some lawmakers, led by New York Democratic Sens. Charles Schumer and Hillary Rodham Clinton, urged Bush on Tuesday to include homeland security costs incurred by localities as a result of the higher security alert imposed Monday.

Ridge praised New York City's efforts to strengthen security since the Sept. 11, 2001, attacks on the World Trade Center.

"A lot of the public discussion and debate is often about (federal aid) for first responders," Ridge said. "But the number one mission for everyone engaged in homeland security is to prevent the attack from happening in the first place."

Clinton said Ridge's announcement is "good news" but added that the New York congressional delegation and other New York leaders need to make sure that the amount received by the state and city is sufficient. Many states are facing budget shortfalls while Bloomberg is working to close a budget gap of more than $3 billion.

"We are trying to pin down a number... so that we can hold everybody accountable," Clinton said Wednesday. "I want to know exactly what the commitment is.... Then we could hold the administration accountable month after month to actually make good on that."

Schumer, chairman of the Senate Democratic Task Force on Homeland Security, agreed, saying that the administration's stronger focus on homeland security is "something we have been asking for a long time."

"But how much money will they put in? Will it be adequate to reimburse our first responders who have been stretched thin and will be it be fair to New York state which has greater needs than other places," he said. "We're not ready to celebrate until we see the details."

Schumer said Bush needs to request $8 billion to $9 billion for homeland security aid in the emergency spending bill to cover needs nationwide for the remainder of the 2003 fiscal year, which ends Sept. 30.

Schumer and Clinton also will try to add money for homeland security to the 2004 federal budget blueprint that the Senate is currently debating. Schumer will offer the main Democratic amendment that proposes $88 billion over 10 years for homeland security. Clinton will seek approval for $7 billion for a "domestic defense fund" that would help pay for first responder costs and extra money for high threat states.

The budget resolution is nonbinding but is usually followed by committees empowered to authorize spending.

From *USA Today Newspaper,* March 19, 2003. © 2003 by USA Today Newspaper. Reprinted by permission.

States, cities step up security and squabble over costs

By The Associated Press

The war abroad has made defense at home an even more urgent priority, but the rising cost of security is sparking squabbles at all levels of government.

States and cities are faced with the burden of stronger homeland defense at a time when their finances are in the worst shape of the last half-century.

State troopers in Connecticut keep watch from the sky 24 hours a day, guarding reservoirs, bridges and more; National Guard troops in Arizona patrol the biggest U.S. nuclear power plant; safety worries shut Philadelphia's Independence Hall most of last week.

No overall, national figure for the cost of such measures to both cities and states is available, though partial estimates reach well into the tens of millions of dollars per week.

"Everybody's budget is hurting," said Baltimore Mayor Martin O'Malley. "This just whacks the heck out of it."

Security officials pledge that, come what may, they will redirect resources to keep the country safe. But the strain is obvious.

New York Gov. George Pataki sparred publicly with New York City Mayor Mike Bloomberg over how they'll share a still-evolving infusion of federal funds for security.

Elsewhere, governors are telling Congress they should get control of federal security funds, while mayors argue they are closest to first-responders—the police, fire and emergency crews that would deal most directly with terrorist activity.

Congress is working on a war budget that would add more than $4 billion for homeland security, including upward of $600 million for urban areas considered higher threats. And Homeland Security Director Tom Ridge has emphasized that state and local authorities are crucial.

"This war is being fought on two fronts," Ridge said in Florida as Week 2 of the Iraq campaign began. "There is a theater over there and a theater right here."

That was driven home when Iraqi leaders called for jihad and warned of suicide bombers that would "follow the enemy into its land."

Two days before the first bombs fell on Baghdad, the U.S. security alert went to orange, or high. Immediate changes followed.

National Guard troops were called up to patrol in many states, performing tasks such as watching state ports on the Gulf of Mexico and the Mississippi River, and protecting water supplies in Minnesota.

Black Hawk helicopters patrol above New York City, metal detectors check visitors at Rhode Island's statehouse, and Kansas Gov. Bob Holden has plans for a system to track bioterrorism and disease outbreaks in his state.

Los Angeles Police Chief William Bratton asked his city council for $4.5 million for biohazard suits and equipment, arguing that they couldn't wait for federal help.

"There's a lack of confidence that the federal money is coming anytime soon," Bratton said. "By the time it gets down to the states, then to the county and then to the city, we could be into the next war."

In several states, homeland security officials are keeping track of their spending in hopes that the federal government will pay them back later.

"There may be dollars that come back to relieve their pain," said Wisconsin's emergency management director, Ed Gleason, "and there will be pain."

The cost of all these efforts is tough to pin down.

Nationwide, some $21.4 million was being spent each week by 145 of the largest cities, towns and counties, according to a survey by the U.S. Conference of Mayors. But they estimate the total cost for cities could be $70 million a week.

No similar tally of state costs has yet been made.

Ridge maintains that the states will get upward of $8 billion when everything is accounted for in President Bush's several spending requests since Sept. 11.

Others say that falls far short. Cities have yet to be reimbursed for $3 billion in expenses; water system vulnerability assessments are estimated to cost $900 million; and much of the $3.5 billion in last year's federal budget was just a reallocation of previously designated funds, according to Federal Funds Information for States, a Washington data clearinghouse.

The fight over money will continue, even as homeland defenders adapt to their new tasks.

"America's different. The America that you and I knew pre-Sept. 11 is different," said Sheriff Joe Oxley in New Jersey's Monmouth County. "We're going to have to adapt and be fluid."

A Burnt-Orange Nation

DESPITE THE BUSH ADMINISTRATION'S DENIALS, STATE AND LOCAL HOMELAND-SECURITY OFFICIALS SEE WAR WITH IRAQ AS INTENSIFYING THE TERROR THREAT AT HOME. ORDINARY EXPLOSIVES WORRY THEM THE MOST.

BY SIOBHAN GORMAN AND SYDNEY J. FREEDBERG JR.

As war with Iraq grows ever more likely, Americans might need to get used to having everyday life tinged with a level of danger that is, quite literally, off the chart—off the federal government's color-coded terrorism threat advisory scale, that is.

OPEN INVITATION?

Cities and states have ranked their most-likely terror targets, such as the Golden Gate Bridge, and have put them under the closest watch they can afford.

Call the unofficial, nerve-racking threat level "burnt orange." That in-between shade symbolizes that the nation is in greater peril than the highest official threat level invoked so far, "heightened-alert orange," would suggest. It also symbolizes that, in the absence of government knowledge of a very specific threat, the nation won't escalate to the highest threat level, red. "Burnt orange" also represents a state of mind. For the public, it reflects higher anxiety, even by post-9/11 standards. And for the White House, burnt orange is perhaps the color of denial.

After a week of duct-tape guidance, ominous reports, and an audiotape in which Qaeda chieftain Osama bin Laden publicly allied his terror network with Iraq, Homeland Security Secretary Tom Ridge steadfastly maintained that going to war with Iraq would not put the nation in graver danger. "Al Qaeda will operate when they deem themselves ready to move," he told reporters on February 14. "They didn't need us to be engaged militarily in another part of the world on September 11." Then, on February 27, Attorney General John D. Ashcroft and Ridge lowered the official threat level to yellow, or "elevated."

Well, tell that to homeland-security chiefs in New York City, where law enforcement officials have been working for weeks on contingency plans for wartime. Or, tell it to the Richmond, Va., chapter of the Red Cross. With the prospect of war in Iraq looming large, Richmond Red Cross members spent a recent meeting mapping out plans for coping with possible evacuations of Washington, D.C., or Norfolk, Va., one of the Navy's biggest ports. The Richmond Red Cross estimates that, by relying on school gymnasiums and homeless shelters, the city could absorb 35,000 evacuees.

"Most states are very concerned," says Maj. Gen. Tim Lowenberg, Washington state's homeland security adviser. "That concern translates into substantially increased planning and preparation, on the assumption that [in wartime] the threat level will increase beyond what it is now."

'ORANGE' ACTION:

With the latest jump to the second-highest alert on the five-color federal terror threat chart, airports began random vehicle checks.

What terror dangers do state and local authorities most worry would jump higher because of war with Iraq? Conventional explosives, perhaps triggered by suicide bombers, top their lists, according to an informal survey by *National Journal*. That worry is followed by bioterrorism; opportunistic, homegrown terrorism; the extra vulnerability created by the loss of security forces who have been called to military duty overseas; and too little state and local money to adequately respond to an actual terror attack.

As recently as October, the Hart-Rudman Commission, which had warned of the nation's vulnerability to terrorism seven months before 9/11, declared, "America remains dangerously unprepared to prevent and respond to a catastrophic attack on U.S. soil."

Gary Hart, the commission's co-chairman and a former Democratic senator from Colorado, warns: "We should not go to war with Iraq until the country is better prepared to respond" to an attack at home. "We are not prepared to respond. It's a two-front war, and [President Bush] is only fighting it on one front.... We are kicking open a hornet's nest."

The Bush White House has gotten itself into a complicated homeland-security bind. It wants to bolster public support for war with Iraq by persuading the nation that there is a strong link between Saddam Hussein's regime and the terrorists responsible for the 9/11 attacks. It argues that forcing a regime change in Iraq would eliminate a major terror threat. Yet the administration would risk undermining public support for war with Iraq if it stated what many outside observers have concluded—that hitting Iraq would significantly increase the likelihood that America will itself be hit again soon.

"There is substantial political risk with the course they've undertaken," said Stephen E. Flynn, a homeland-security analyst with the Council on Foreign Relations. "They leave themselves exposed to the notion that you've generated the very threat you're supposed to be protecting us from."

Despite what recent news reports have implied, the federal government is still mum on a connection between the war and threats at home. The FBI last week sent state and local law enforcement officials a classified warning that "lone extremists...represent an ongoing terrorist threat in the United States." The bulletin said nothing about Iraq or the prospect of war, according to recipients. "I didn't think it was anything new," said Joe Huden, a Washington state homeland-security official.

ONE IF BY LAND...
Miami officials must be
concerned for the safety of
cruise ship passengers
in their port, as well
as of landlubbers.

For obvious strategic reasons, the administration doesn't want to share its timetable for going to war. But by being tight-lipped, the Bush team makes it especially difficult for state and local officials to prepare for whatever heightened risks war could bring.

On the other hand, officials beyond the Beltway don't need Uncle Sam to tell them that this is a particularly dangerous time. Sitting just 45 miles outside Washington, Baltimore Mayor Martin O'Malley believes war would "absolutely" increase the risk of a terror attack on his city. "I think for any mayor to think otherwise would be irresponsible," he says. In Indianapolis, Clifford Ong, who has been overseeing Indiana's homeland-security efforts since October 2001, contends, "It would be naive to think otherwise."

The worries of state and local homeland-security officials are echoed on Capitol Hill. "The potential war in Iraq may be an opportunity for terrorist groups like Al Qaeda to strike at a time when they think the nation's attention is diverted," said Senate Governmental Affairs Committee Chairwoman Susan Collins, R-Maine, whose panel oversees the Department of Homeland Security.

Brian Jenkins, a terrorism analyst with Rand for 31 years, ticks off several reasons to expect that war would intensify the threat of terrorism on U.S. soil. He starts by recalling that worldwide terrorist activity went up in 1991, when the United States fought Iraq in the Persian Gulf War. And with the United States now winding up to deliver what he calls one of "the most telegraphed military punches in history," terrorists have been given ample time to prepare for retaliation. Meanwhile, anti-war activists could choose to make a statement through anti-American violence. And Al Qaeda is very practiced at playing on Muslim fears that a U.S. invasion of Iraq would be a prelude to a crusade against Islam.

A U.S. attack on Iraq could also be a boon to Al Qaeda's recruitment efforts, worries Frank Hoffman, a former top aide to the Hart-Rudman Commission. And such U.S. aggression, he said, could push other radical groups over the brink into terrorism on American soil. Iraqi sympathizers might seek to launch terrorist attacks in the United States to try to undermine American support for the war. With that possibility in mind, the FBI has been attempting to locate and interview 50,000 Iraqi immigrants, 3,000 of them illegal.

Despite the rampant fear among outside analysts and officials that war with Iraq equals more danger for American civilians, the new Department of Homeland Security hasn't even mentioned the possibility of war to state homeland-security officials. Asked whether Homeland Security has wartime contingency plans, spokesman Brian Roehrkasse said his department prefers to look at "the whole picture" of potential terror threats rather than to single out one, even one as big as a war with a Middle Eastern country.

RANKING THE DANGERS

In the absence of federal guidance, state and local homeland-security officials are on their own in trying to prepare for and avert the once-unthinkable by calculating which terror threats to take most seriously in time of war. Wary of tipping off terrorists to specific vulnerabilities, these officials hesitate to go into great detail about their particular worries, such as, say, a nearby nuclear reactor or a high-profile corporate target. However, notably missing from their top concerns are nuclear warheads, radioactive "dirty bombs" powered by conventional explosives, and chemical weapons. What they see as bigger threats are conventional explosives, bioterrorism, and domestic terrorism. The state and local leaders also worry that the Pentagon's call-up of reservists has depleted the ranks of first responders—emergency personnel trained to react to crises—and that many of the remaining personnel are not adequately trained or equipped, because state and local governments are strapped for cash.

• **Conventional explosives:** Easiest to acquire and detonate, conventional explosives are the favorite weapon of terrorists worldwide. All of the state and local officials surveyed listed such arms as their top wartime worry. And ordinary bombs or guns have been the weapon of choice in every notable terror attack since 9/11, from Bali to Los Angeles International Airport.

Suicide bombers could quickly take a huge psychological toll on the American public by making ordinary trips to shopping malls or restaurants feel like combat duty. "It would be a shock level we haven't yet experienced," Hoffman predicts. "From a terrorist's perspective, if they did it in a crowded place where they would get some good pictures, it would be logistically and tactically simple, and it would be very effective."

Suicide bombers are difficult—but not always impossible—to stop. Israel has had significant success by training police officers to watch for telltale behaviors. In this country, employees at Boston's Logan Airport are trained to spot aberrant behavior. And Miami officials are making it a priority to keep tabs on rock quarries and other enterprises that keep explosives on hand.

• **Bioterrorism:** The weapons of bioterrorism are far more difficult to obtain and to use than ordinary explosives. However, they remain high on officials' worry list because, as of 2001, Saddam admitted having 2,200 gallons of anthrax. Iraq might also have stockpiles of smallpox. The consequences of a large-scale attack with a biological agent "could be devastating, and [the Iraqis] have got it," notes Col. Tim Daniel, Missouri's director of homeland security. Daniel worries that Saddam could hand off bioweapons to a willing third party and that early-detection technology isn't sophisticated enough to avert enormous casualties.

"Perhaps the most serious threat we face is a bioweapon attack," Sen. Collins remarked on her way back from a briefing on Vice President Cheney's new Project BioShield, which directs the Food and Drug Administration to approve and stockpile vaccines against bioterrorism agents.

SUSAN COLLINS:

"The potential war in Iraq may be an opportunity for terrorist groups like Al Qaeda to strike at a time when the nation's attention is diverted."

A few cities, including New York and Baltimore, have made strides toward monitoring changes in public health reports that could signal a bioterror attack. New York keeps tabs on sales of over-the-counter drugs. A spike in purchases of Pepto-Bismol, for example, might prompt public health officials to contact local doctors and hospitals to investigate whether something unusual is going on. The Environmental Protection Agency has begun monitoring the air in selected locations around the country to check for signs of a biological attack. And biosurveillance equipment would be near the top of many local emergency officials' shopping lists, they say, if only they could afford it.

• **Homegrown terrorism:** The lethal anthrax attacks that disrupted Congress and the U.S. mail soon after 9/11 are widely thought to be the work of a still-unknown American eager to jolt an already-frightened nation. Homegrown terrorists might try to similarly exploit public apprehension about war with Iraq. Chuck Lanza, director of the Office of Emergency Management for Miami-Dade County, said he suspects the biggest increase will be in hoaxes—not in actual attacks—but that one or more crazies might actually carry out an attack, using anything from germs to a truck bomb to a sniper rifle.

• **Depleted resources:** JoAnne Moreau's biggest wartime worry is that she won't have enough emergency workers to summon. "There will be manpower issues. A lot of our people are in the Reserve forces," said Moreau, director of emergency preparedness for Baton Rouge, La. "They're being called up." Her complaint is echoed by her counterparts all across the country.

About 75 percent of fire departments include reservists, and an estimated 44 percent of law enforcement agencies have already lost employees to call-ups. Col. Alan Smith, the ombudsman for the Employer Support of the Guard and Reserve, says that smaller first-responder agencies could lose 30 percent of their people to the Reserves. Meanwhile, the Coast Guard has sent one-fourth of its patrol-boat fleet from the mid-Atlantic and New England to the Gulf. "We're raising the threat of a likely attack. And we're taking the resources that are likely to be called upon at home and shipping them over to a war zone," observes Flynn of the Council on Foreign Relations. "There's a trade-off conversation that needs to happen, that isn't happening."

• **Empty coffers:** Tight on money, state and local homeland officials worry that they are having to skimp too much on preparedness. And Washington state's Lowenberg expects already-weak links to be further strained if the United States goes to war. Among the weaknesses he sees are communication systems that don't allow police officers, firefighters, and emergency personnel to talk with each other; a shortage of protective gear for chemical or biological attacks; and the lack of equipment and procedures to detect bioterror agents. In Lowenberg's view, "There's no way to address those problems, except through federal funding."

What happened in Tamaroa, a small town in southern Illinois, in early February was telling: A train loaded with toxic chemicals derailed, forcing a thousand residents to evacuate their homes. The derailment was an accident—

but just the sort of disaster that terrorists could easily replicate in dozens of places nationwide.

Tamaroa's volunteer firefighters responded first, followed by the county sheriff, and then the state police. "None of those people has the proper protective equipment," said Michael Chamness, director of Illinois's emergency management agency. The nearest hazardous-materials team was 30 miles away.

Illinois had hoped to buy $25 million worth of protective gear for agencies statewide; the state expected to receive $100 million in homeland-security grants from the federal government. But the final 2003 appropriations bill that Congress passed in February—nearly halfway through the fiscal year—cut Illinois's $100 million by about two-thirds.

PREPARING THE HOME FRONT

While the Pentagon focuses on positioning troops near Iraq, state and local officials on the front lines of the war on terrorism are hurriedly bracing for the heightened domestic dangers they expect to accompany an actual U.S. invasion of Iraq.

Washington state has been ramping up for wartime security for months. "It's not something you can do at the last minute," Lowenberg said. The state is hardening key potential targets, filling in for called-up reservists, and mapping out evacuation plans. In New York City, Police Commissioner Raymond W. Kelly has asked each of his divisions to assess how their responsibilities should change in the event of war. And in Virginia, "We are doing a government-wide planning activity," said George Foresman, a homeland-security specialist in the governor's office. "Many of our local governments are also doing this as well."

Foresman said he doesn't assume the federal government will automatically raise the threat level if war breaks out, but he adds, "We're not completely dependent on the federal family to guide our threat level in Virginia."

Likewise, in Missouri, Daniel doesn't expect the federal threat level to rise all the way to red if the United States goes to war. But, he said, "without going to Code Red, we need to be very concerned and go ahead and increase security for the first 48 to 72 hours and then make judgments on how the war is going and the information from the intelligence agencies." That translates into visibly tightening security at what the state considers terrorists' top potential targets and, perhaps, setting up traffic checkpoints.

Yet, in Indiana, Ong wonders what more his state can do to get ready for wartime dangers. Absent a specific threat, "I don't know that I necessarily would change anything," he said.

In many places, the level of precautions being taken at any given time is geared to the federal government's five-color threat-assessment chart. Illinois and Washington state have spelled out exactly what a host of local agencies are expected to do, depending on whether the nation is on, say, a yellow alert or an orange one. Many other states, as well as Washington, D.C., are still in the process of translating the colors of the federal alert into precise local responses. At least one locale, the Charlotte-Mecklenburg area of North Carolina, has adopted the federal government's color scheme but also uses its own judgment in determining how serious the terror threat is at any given time. While the federal level was orange, Winters Mabry, director of the homeland-security office for Mecklenburg County, said, "We are currently staying at yellow—but I would say a strengthened yellow."

Yet whether they consider their jurisdictions at Code Orange, Code Yellow, or on the brink of Code Red, many state and local officials are doing essentially the same things. They've gone through the painful process of figuring out their jurisdiction's most-likely terror targets and then put them under the closest watch they can afford. In Florida, that means paying special attention to protecting its Jewish population. In Illinois, that means tightly guarding its 11 nuclear reactors. And in Washington, D.C., it means trying to safeguard national landmarks.

Baltimore Mayor O'Malley said his police department "is putting additional eyes on more places in the city than they would have. We've done a vulnerability assessment of our critical infrastructure. And those things now have officers either on them or watching them." He added, "This is something we're trying to struggle to do in a flexible way, knowing we could be [on alert] for a long time."

One recurring theme among state and local officials is the importance of making security visible: It's the domestic version of deterrence. Studies of past Qaeda operations indicate that "they spend a lot of time on reconnaissance," scoping out potential targets, noted Missouri's Daniel. "If they see police doing a roadblock in some place they've never seen before, it's very disruptive to their plans."

Some jurisdictions want their security efforts to be variable as well as visible: a roadblock here one day, a cop on patrol over there the next—all intended to make terrorist attacks more difficult to plan or carry out.

MARTIN O'MALLEY:

"You cannot fund an adequate level of homeland security on local property taxes and the proceeds of firehouse bingo."

With the country seemingly headed toward war, most states have beefed up the staffing at their emergency response centers to give themselves a head start if an attack does come. Many specialized response teams—ones for hazardous materials, urban search-and-rescue, or general disasters, for example—are now on standby. These efforts amount to "shortening the leash a bit," said Glen Woodbury, director of emergency management for Washington state and president of the National Emergency Management Association.

Many of these back-office measures haven't cost much—yet. "The people that we activate are not people who get paid overtime," said Illinois's Chamness.

But a heightened level of alertness—especially with extra cops on the beat and on overtime—could become crushingly expensive. Already, many agencies are borrowing from tomorrow to pay for today. "It's not quite painful yet, but it could get painful, depending on how long we're at this stage," said Washington state's Woodbury.

The problem with stopgap measures, of course, is that the short term eats the long term's lunch. And a war with Iraq would likely have a voracious security appetite on the home front. Every hour spent scrambling on today's problem is another hour not spent planning for tomorrow's. Every cop watching a nuclear power plant, every firefighter responding to a bomb threat, every emergency manager pulling extra shifts is another person and another dollar unavailable for other, more-traditional priorities.

As fears of suicide bombings and bioterrorism climb along with expectations of war, many state and local officials fault the federal government for not doing more to help them cope. "You cannot fund an adequate level of homeland security on local property taxes and the proceeds of firehouse bingo," fumed Mayor O'Malley. "That's why we have a clause in the Constitution about providing for the common defense. It's the fundamental reason we have a union."

Already such grumbling has reached Washington, as has the suggestion that any new legislation to jack up military spending should include homeland-security aid for states and localities. As Washington state's Lowenberg sees it, "We need to recognize that a substantial part of the field of engagement won't just be in the Middle East." That, at least, is the nearly universal fear among the state and local officials charged with protecting the home front.

The authors can be reached at sgorman@nationaljournal.com and sfreedberg@nationaljournal.com.

UNIT 5
First Responders

Unit Selections

Key Points to Consider

- Do public service announcements and home emergency kits help to inspire confidence in the new Department of Homeland Security? Defend your answer.

- What role should individuals play in homeland security?

- How can programs like community policing help combat the threat of terrorism?

- Is the public health system in the United States prepared to cope with bioterrorist attacks? Explain.

- What are the main components of a "unified concept of operations"? How can such a concept help in the management of the response to terrorist incidents?

 **Links: www.dushkin.com/online/**
These sites are annotated in the World Wide Web pages.

CDC Radiation Emergencies
http://www.bt.cdc.gov/radiation/index.asp

Community Policing Institute
http://www.umcpi.org/websites.html

FEMA: Are You Ready? A Guide to Citizen Preparedness
http://www.fema.gov/areyouready/

Responding First to Bioterrorism
http://www.nap.edu/firstresponders/

U.S. Fire Administration (USFA)
http://www.usfa.fema.gov/index.shtm

First responders play a critical role in any disaster response. The heroic efforts of firefighters, police officers, and emergency medical personnel in New York City and Washington D.C. on September 11, and the sacrifices that they made are eternalized in the lives that they helped save. As the United States prepares for future attacks, the role of first responders clearly merits closer examination. The term "first responder," however, does not only apply to local emergency personnel. It includes people at various levels that may be directly affected by the actions of terrorists.

While the battle over increased federal funding and training for police and fire departments continues, most have come to realize the importance of individuals in homeland security. As the actions of the passengers on United Airlines flight 93, which crashed outside of Pittsburgh, Pennsylvania, on September 11 indicate, once people understand the nature of threat, they are willing to become involved and, when necessary, even a give their lives to save others. Realizing the plans of the terrorists, the passengers of flight 93 decided that they would rather take their chances fighting the hijackers than be used in a terrorist plot to harm others. The selfless actions of these passengers may have done more to prevent another attack using passenger aircraft than billions of dollars spent on airport security.

Beyond response to major disasters, local law enforcement, fire prevention, and medical personnel play an important role in homeland security. They provide a first point of contact for citizens and are in a unique position to help detect, report, and prevent terrorist activity. Respect for people and good policing build trust in and support for police officers in local communities. Information from these communities may help in the early detection of potential terrorist attacks. Fire departments play a critical role in the early identification of potential vulnerabilities and the planning of emergency responses and evacuations. Their contacts with local businesses and industry put them in a position to conduct emergency response training and help

in emergency planning. Local medical personnel are the first points of contact for potential threats to public health. Specialized training and access to appropriate equipment and resources can help in the early detection and containment of public health threats.

Managing the interactions among the first responders from various levels of government continues to be a challenge. Lack of planning and coordination can lead to conflicts, confusion, and a duplication of efforts. As federal emergency management exercises such as Dark Winter and Topoff 2 provide opportunities to practice these interactions, a lack of interoperability, communications problems, mistrust, and jurisdictional disputes continue to undermine effective cooperation.

The five articles in this unit attempt to speak to some of these issues. The first selection, an interview with Secretary Tom Ridge, is part of a public information campaign of the Homeland Security Department. Ridge urges Americans to prepare emergency survival kits to help them cope with future terrorist attacks. In the second article, Brian Jenkins suggests that the ultimate responsibility for security rests squarely on the shoulders of the individual. He argues that in the end, America's "… most important defense will not be duct tape, but Americans' determination, wisdom and courage." The next article argues that interactions between law enforcement officers and the public, through programs like community policing, may not only yield important information but also reduce fear during an attack. The fourth article underlines the importance of good communication between federal officials and first responders. Mistrust and the lack of specific information from the federal government have led some health-care workers to refuse voluntary smallpox vaccinations for first responders. The final article offers some insight into the complexities of disaster response management. It recommends the development of "a unified concept of operations" to manage multilevel, multijurisdictional disaster response.

Man with a Plan

What's in Homeland Security Secretary Tom Ridge's emergency kit?
Hint: It's not just water and duct tape

Tom Ridge wants you to know he sleeps well at night. "I'm not authorized to be stressed," says the Secretary of the new Department of Homeland Security, part of whose job is to prepare America for a potential terrorist strike. "It's not in the job description."

It's an example the former Pennsylvania governor hopes the public will follow. Starting this month, Ridge, 57, appears in public-service ads urging Americans to take precautions in case of an attack. He and wife Michele, 56, a former librarian, have already packed away three days' worth of supplies to protect themselves, their children Lesley, 16, and Tommy, 15, and their three Labrador retrievers should the worst happen. The Ridges let PEOPLE's *Macon Morehouse poke around their safe room and Rubbermaid containers full of tuna, dog chow and water.*

"The President says this is the first war of the 21st century," says Ridge.

When did you put together your family's emergency kit?

MICHELE: I started last September, when the country went on Orange Alert. The children and I had just moved to the Washington, D.C., area from Pennsylvania. We were in unfamiliar territory, and I felt I wouldn't be able to find things quickly in an emergency. I already had duct tape around for things like getting dog hair off. I stockpiled foods that you can eat without heating them. And I made sure I had granola bars. My kids love them.

Do your kids tease you about stockpiling supplies?

RIDGE: They're pretty cool about it. They were the first ones to remind us to set aside stuff for our pets.

Are there any luxury items that you have to have in your kit?

MICHELE: Dental floss!

RIDGE: We'll be in our basement rec room, and the kids have their keyboard and guitar down there. The standard luxuries would be cards and some games. Unfortunately, I'll probably be somewhere else if something happens.

Do you also travel with a kit?

RIDGE: On official trips the Secret Service takes care of my safety. For the family, we have a gym bag for emergencies with first-aid supplies, crackers, tuna, peanut butter and water.

What about your kids?

RIDGE: Lesley has a cell phone—she's 16 and thinks it's an entitlement—but Tom doesn't. If our kids are away from home, we have given them the names of people we want them to call and a place to meet. Not knowing where they are is the greatest fear.

The Ridges packed separate food bags for labs Allie, Molly and Gus.

Does all this scare them?

RIDGE: They haven't expressed that to me. They know what Dad is doing is important, because the President asked him to do it. They get it.

Do you think moving your family to Washington puts them at special risk?

RIDGE: There's nothing in our intelligence that suggests terrorism is just a problem for New York City and Washington, D.C. I was talking to a journalist a couple of months ago who asked if I'd left my family in Pennsylvania. When she found out I hadn't, she said, 'Really, I'm comforted by that.' I said, 'I hoped you would be.'

They're Prepared: The Ridges Stock Up

FOOD
- raisins
- canned green beans
- canned tuna
- canned soup
- apple-cinnamon granola bars
- crackers
- peanut butter
- honey
- 12 gallons of bottled water

TOOLS
- Swiss Army knife
- manual can opener
- scissors
- screwdriver

GENERAL SUPPLIES
- duct tape
- flashlights
- battery-operated clock radio

GENERAL SUPPLIES (cont.)
- garbage bags
- plastic sheeting
- paper towels
- wet wipes
- toilet paper
- antibacterial soap
- toothbrushes, toothpaste, floss
- plastic dishes, cups and utensils
- extra batteries

MEDICINE
- prescription medications
- Excedrin
- Benadryl
- first-aid kit

PETS
- first-aid kit for dogs
- dog food
- dog bowls
- dog toys

What are the chances that there will be another terrorist attack?

RIDGE: Do I think it will happen? Yes, I think there will be another incident. When? Can't tell you. What form? Don't know.

What has happened if we go to Code Red? Has a bomb been dropped?

RIDGE: We would likely go Code Red before an imminent attack. You really button up the entire country if you go Code Red. I know Americans are frustrated with the vagueness of these warnings, but it's hard to be specific about terrorist threats.

How involved is the President?

RIDGE: We meet every morning, early—the President, the Vice President, Dr. Rice, the Chief of Staff, the FBI director, CIA director, myself and a few others—and we review the intelligence received in the previous 24 hours. The President knows the terrorists names, places and connections.

What did you think when, thanks to the latest Orange Alert, store shelves were cleared of duct tape?

RIDGE: For the longest time I wondered if people were paying attention. Now I think they are.

All citizens now first responders

By Brian Michael Jenkins

Americans are wondering whether the war in Iraq will spark new terrorist attacks here. What, indeed, does the new orange alert on the five-color Homeland Security Advisory System really mean?

Most people don't realize that the color-alert system is mainly a way to consolidate all available intelligence and then communicate a judgment to those who have security responsibilities.

The primary targets of these warnings aren't individual Americans, but federal agencies, state and local governments, the country's approximately 18,000 police jurisdictions and those in the private sector with security responsibilities. They all have contingency plans to put into effect based on the specific alert level. Police departments, for example, might increase the number of uniformed officers on the streets. Corporations might tighten access control.

But what are individual Americans supposed to do?

After decades of being persuaded to behave as litigious victims, it's time the public became more realistic and accepted individual risk. Americans have to learn to take care of themselves, to be mentally tough and self-reliant. Those who expect the government to protect them from everything are in for a lot of disappointments.

If homeland security is to succeed, it needs to involve Americans in the defense of their communities, neighborhoods and families. In countries dealing with on-going terrorist campaigns, such as Israel and the United Kingdom, the authorities depend on public vigilance. With proper instruction, the entire United States can be turned into a vast neighborhood watch—a difficult environment for terrorists.

Look to each other, not authorities

First, Americans need to accept the fact that police and fire-fighters, no matter how brave or skilled, cannot protect them all at all times. There are just not enough of them, and there never will be. In most cases, the first people at the scene of an attack are the people who were there before the attack—employees, students, customers and anyone else unfortunate enough to be in the wrong place at the wrong time. So more Americans need to learn how to save and protect each other before the professionals arrive.

More "news you can use" stories in newspapers and on TV newscasts can give Americans information about the dangers they may face in a terrorist attack and what they can do to protect themselves. Schools, employers and private organizations can give practical instruction on what the real threats are and how to prepare and cope with them.

More individuals can sign up for CPR and first-aid courses or learn how they can volunteer with law enforcement organizations. Two federal Web sites—www.ready.gov and www.ed.gov/emergencyplan—contain advice, the first for individual citizens and the second for schools.

Tools exist; use them

America has about 2 million people involved in the private-security industry, the equivalent of the entire U.S. armed forces in the 1980s during the Cold War. Special training could be mandated for these security workers so they can become an even stronger backup force for police and firefighters.

The country used to have air-raid wardens. Office buildings have fire wardens. Why not neighborhood-security wardens—trained volunteers armed with communications equipment so they can offer immediate guidance in emergency situations?

Americans are not helpless victims doomed to spend their lives hiding under kitchen tables. They are strong and brave people living in a strong and brave nation. Further terrorist attacks must be presumed, but they will not bring this country down.

Ultimately, the United States will prevail. Its most important defense will not be duct tape, but Americans' determination, wisdom and courage.

Brian Michael Jenkins, who has studied terrorism for more than 30 years, is a special adviser at the non-profit Rand Corp.

Community Policing and Terrorism

Matthew C. Scheider and Robert Chapman

A great deal of the responsibility for preparing for and responding to terrorist events rests with local police departments. Community policing presents an overarching philosophical orientation that agencies can use to better deal with the threat of terrorist events and the fear that they may create. The community policing philosophy can be roughly divided into three interrelated elements: organizational change, problem solving, and external partnerships. Each element applies to the issues of terrorism prevention and response, as well as to fear.

Since 11 September, the federal government has greatly increased terrorism prevention and response efforts. However, a large degree of responsibility for dealing with these threats and for alleviating citizen fear rests at the local level. To some degree, the majority of local police departments in the United States have worked to reduce the fear of future terrorist attacks and to prevent and plan for attacks. Law enforcement officials are strategically rethinking public security procedures and practices to maximize the potential of their resources.

The philosophy of community policing is important for police in preparing for possible terrorist acts and in responding to the fear they may create. Community policing involves broadening the nature and number of police functions compared to traditional policing models. It emphasizes organizational change, active problem solving, and external partnerships to address issues that concern both the police and citizens. In recent years, the philosophy of community policing appears to have been adopted to differing degrees by a large number of law enforcement entities in the United States. For example, a 2001 U.S. Department of Justice report indicates that from 1997 to 1999, departments employing personnel designated as community police rose from 34% to 64%.[1] In addition, the absolute number of community policing officers rose from 21,000 to 113,000. However, traumatic events can cause organizations to revert to more traditional modes of operation. The events of 11 September may have been no exception for U.S. law enforcement. Some police departments may have been quick to dismiss community policing efforts and programs for seemingly more immediate and pressing security concerns. However, the community policing philosophy is well positioned to play a central role in local law enforcement responses to terrorism.

Community policing shifts the focus of police by placing equal emphasis on crime control, order maintenance, and service provision.[2,3] In addition, it asks police to work with citizens and with other government agencies in efforts to increase overall quality of life. Thus, the model moves away from police-dominated crime control through reactive responses to calls for service. Community policing models move toward active problem solving centered on the underlying conditions that give rise to crime and disorder and on fostering partnerships between the police and the community.[4,5,6]

There is no one commonly recognized definition of community policing. Here we offer one possible definition that we will then apply to preventing and responding to terrorist events. Community policing can be defined as a philosophy that, through the delivery of police services, focuses on crime and social disorder; the philosophy includes aspects of traditional law enforcement as well as prevention, problem-solving tactics, and partnerships. As a fundamental shift from traditional, reactive policing, community policing stresses the prevention of crime. Community policing requires police and citizens to join as partners in identifying and effectively addressing the underlying conditions that give rise to crime and disorder. Community policing can be roughly divided into three inter-related elements: organizational change, problem solving, and external partnerships.

The Community Policing Philosophy

Organizational Change

Ideally, community policing should be adopted organization-wide and be reflected through department participation at all levels as well as through the organization's mission, goals, objectives, performance evaluations, hiring and promotion practices, training, and all other systems that define organizational culture and activities. One of the most important specific aspects of organizational change relevant to community policing is a flattened organizational structure. Community policing departments are often less hierarchical, supporting management's dispersion of decision-making authority to the lowest organizational level and holding those individuals accountable for the outcomes. A second important element of organizational change is fixed geographic responsibility. Officers or deputies are assigned to fixed geographic areas for extended periods, based on social and cultural considerations and on the assumption that this fosters better communication with residents; increases the police officers' ability to understand, prevent, and respond to community problems; and enhances accountability to the citizens in that area.

Problem Solving

Community policing departments also actively address the underlying conditions that give rise to or facilitate crime or disorder in an effort to prevent future problems by identifying and analyzing problems and by developing tailored strategies that may include traditional and nontraditional responses that focus on deterring offenders, protecting likely victims, and making locations less conducive to crime and disorder. Departments should use a wide array of relevant traditional and nontraditional data sources to better understand and evaluate the nature of problems and work in conjunction with the community and other organizations to develop effective long-term solutions. Problem solving often manifests itself in the "scanning, analysis, response and assessment" problem-solving model.[7, 8] Departments first identify relevant or perceived crime problems (scanning), determine the nature and underlying conditions that give rise to those problems (analysis), craft and implement interventions that are linked to that analysis (response), and evaluate its effectiveness (assessment). The process is understood as continually involving feedback among the components. For instance, through in-depth analysis, agencies may come to define problems differently, effectively returning to the scanning phase. Likewise, an assessment may determine that a response was ineffective and that the problem requires additional analysis.

External Partnerships

Under a community policing philosophy, departments partner with other government, social service, and community agencies in attempts to identify and address persistent problems in the community. They form external partnerships in recognition of other agencies' unique strengths, tools, and expertise that can be leveraged when addressing community problems. The police are only one of a host of local government agencies responsible for responding to community problems. Under community policing, coordination with other government agencies in developing comprehensive and effective solutions is essential. In addition, the police are encouraged to develop working partnerships with civic and community groups to accurately survey community needs and priorities and to use the public as a resource in problem solving and in developing and implementing interventions.

Community Policing and Terrorism Prevention and Response

Organizational Change

A flat organizational structure may ensure more effective terrorist prevention and response. It has been demonstrated that local law enforcement officers are likely to come into contact with those who may be directly or indirectly involved in terrorist activities and most certainly will be among the first responders to any future terrorist attack. Empowering officers at lower levels with decision-making authority and familiarizing them with making (and taking responsibility for) important decisions could be of value in any crisis.

In a terrorist event, there may be little time for decisions to move up the chain of command. Officers who are accustomed to making decisions and retaining authority may be better prepared to respond quickly and decisively to any event. In addition, in terms of prevention, developing a flat organizational structure can help lower-level officers feel free to pursue leads or suspected terrorist activity. In addition, having fixed geographic responsibility may assist officers in identifying possible terrorist threats. Officers who work in a community or neighborhood for an extended time can develop specific intelligence concerning resident and community activities. This street-level knowledge is a vital part of counter-intelligence efforts.

Problem Solving

Problem-solving models are well suited to preventing and responding to terrorist activity. Departments can use many existing data sources ahead of time to develop detailed risk management and crisis plans. Identifying potential terrorist targets in local jurisdictions is an important first step. Police can determine what in their jurisdictions (dams, electric grids, chemical warehouses, large-scale public gatherings) are potential terrorist targets. Community policing encourages agencies to conduct complex analyses of the possible threats and of their relative likelihood of occurring. Finally, agencies in conjunction with other government, social, and community entities can develop detailed crisis prevention and response plans. Finally, the community policing model encourages continual refinement of these plans to suit changing conditions and threat levels.

External Partnerships

The threat of terrorism provides a unique opportunity to create partnerships with citizens, other government organizations, and other law enforcement agencies. Prior apathy toward these partnerships that may have existed is often reduced by the presence of terrorist targets and threats. Recent terrorist events and associated concerns may have created a sense of uneasiness and urgency in many communities. The specter of additional terrorist activity has created an opportunity to galvanize local police to work with their communities, other law enforcement agencies, and local, state, and federal entities.

The community policing model encourages the development of such ongoing and effective partnerships, which can be invaluable in preventing terrorist activity because of increased opportunities for intelligence gathering and sharing. They can also be central to developing coordinated responses to any actual terrorist events.

Community policing encourages agencies to establish and expand upon existing partnerships with a goal of developing model crisis plans and processes to deal with the aftermath of terrorist incidents. These plans and processes would consider the needs and concerns of all community stakeholders. Law enforcement and local government can come together with community partners to develop a plan on how to prepare for such a crisis, what to do in the event of such a crisis, and how to cope with its aftermath.

Community Policing and Fear of Terrorism

By definition, the primary goal of terrorism is to create fear and an atmosphere of uncertainty. This fear can greatly affect the quality of life of many individuals, extending far beyond those who are directly affected by a terrorist event. In the United States the police have in-

creasingly been asked to address the fear of crime generally. The expansion of their role to include quality of life and partnerships with citizens, as emphasized by the community policing philosophy, has increasingly brought fear of crime under the purview of police professionals. As A. Steven Dietz stated in "Evaluating Community Policing," "Reduction of fear of crime has been associated with community policing programs since their inception."[9] It is clear that reducing fear of crime has become an essential element and an often explicitly articulated goal of community policing.[10] Thus, community policing finds itself well positioned to deal with issues of fear that can arise as a direct result of terrorist activity. In addition, dealing directly with citizen fear of crime is important, as unchecked fear of terrorism (or feelings of revenge) can manifest itself in hate crimes and illegal bigotry targeted particularly at people who are Muslim and of Middle Eastern descent. These are important social problems that law enforcement should be prepared to respond to and prevent.

Organizational Change

Adoption of the community policing philosophy partly involves reengineering department processes and resources away from randomness and reactivity and toward information- and service-driven community-based approaches. Police officers are often assigned to specific geographic areas to foster communication with residents and are accountable to those residents and their superiors for the safety and well-being of that area. Other aspects of the agency are realigned to support the most fundamental focus of all activities, the beat.

As a result of this emphasis, police officers should be more attuned to rising levels of community concern and fear and, by virtue of the relationships they have established within the community, be in a position to respond effectively to those needs and concerns. Community policing has been found to engender trust and increased satisfaction among residents for the police,[11] which in periods of heightened unrest can be parlayed into dealing more effectively with community fear that can be based on both rational and irrational concerns.

Problem Solving

Community policing encourages a deeper understanding of the fear that may result from terrorist events. The first step is to determine whether fear is a problem in the community and to determine the extent of the problem. Police can conduct citizen interviews, surveys, and face-to-face interactions to determine levels of citizen fear. Then they can analyze the underlying conditions that give rise to or encourage fear. Perhaps it is a result of a specific terrorist-related fear such as living near what is perceived to be a potential terrorist target, or the fear may involve fear for loved ones who reside in high-threat areas. Finally, perhaps the fear is a more general fear of terrorism. In any event, law enforcement should work to understand the extent and nature of fear in their community if they want to develop effective responses.

Law enforcement should then work in partnership with other community groups to develop responses aimed at decreasing levels of fear if they are negatively affecting quality of life and are determined to be highly exaggerated. Community policing efforts to deal with citizen fear of crime have included foot and vehicle patrols in high-crime neighborhoods, as well as community meetings, citizen patrols, neighborhood cleanup programs, opening neighborhood substations, and citizen awareness campaigns.[12] Clearly, citizen fear of terrorist events is somewhat different than fear of crime generally. However, some of the same techniques may also be useful for reducing this type of fear. For example, citizen awareness campaigns can inform citizens about what the local police and city government are doing to prevent and prepare for possible terrorist events. Crisis response plans can be discussed in addition to general prevention activities. Citizens can be informed about what they themselves can do—such as preparing emergency survival kits for their own homes—to prepare for possible terrorist events and can be informed of evacuation routes to use in the event of a large-scale disaster. Finally, law enforcement agencies should assess the effectiveness of any fear-reduction efforts and modify their responses accordingly.

External Partnerships

The emphasis on building strong community partnerships encouraged by a community policing philosophy may also help reduce citizen fear of terrorist events. These partnerships may be able to directly reduce fear by increasing citizen feelings of efficacy, increasing the bond among neighbors themselves, and involving citizens in prevention and preparedness activities. Encouraging citizen involvement in neighborhood watch, youth education, and cleanup programs can increase social cohesion among citizens and has been found to result in decreased fear of crime.[13] It is likely that these increasing feelings of efficacy in response to terrorist events may have similar effects. Citizens can be involved to differing degrees in prevention and preparedness discussions.

Conclusion

Immediately following 11 September 2001, local law enforcement agencies in the United States responded to disasters, lost officers, were placed on various levels of alert, provided a visible security presence at public events, partnered with federal intelligence agencies, and investigated hate crimes at greatly increased rates and

with a new urgency. Community policing offers law enforcement agencies an overarching orientation from which to conduct this myriad of tasks. Since its inception, the success of community policing has been based on the relationships built between law enforcement and community members. These relationships, often expressed as collaborative partnerships, have served functions as diverse as the communities that maintain them: solving traffic problems, shutting down drug houses, keeping children safe in school and after school, referring offenders to drug courts, and cleaning up abandoned properties. Addressing these quality-of-life issues has helped give citizens a voice in the public safety of their community and an active way to address crime and their fear of crime. For the past 20 years, community policing has encouraged community members to partner with law enforcement to identify potential threats and create a climate of safety. The community policing philosophy is well positioned to take a major role in preventing and responding to terrorism and in efforts to reduce citizen fear. Instead of de-emphasizing community policing efforts, police departments should realize that community policing may be more important than ever in dealing with terrorism in their communities.

Bibliography

Trevor Bennett, "Confidence in the Police as a Mediating Factor in the Fear of Crime," *International Review of Victimology*, vol. 3, 1994, pp. 179–194.

Lee P. Brown and Mary Ann Wycoff, "Policing Houston: Reducing Fear and Improving Service," *Crime and Delinquency*, vol. 33, no. 1, 1987, pp. 71–89.

Gary W. Cordner, "Community Policing: Elements and Effects," in Roger G. Dunham and Geoffrey P. Alpert (eds.), *Critical Issues in Policing* (Prospect Heights, IL: Waveland Press, 1997), pp. 451–468.

A. Steven Dietz, "Evaluating Community Policing: Quality Police Service and Fear of Crime," *Policing: An International Journal of Police Strategies and Management*, vol. 20, no. 1, 1997, pp. 83–100.

Herman Goldstein, *Problem-Oriented Policing* (New York: McGraw-Hill, 1990).

Matthew J. Hickman and Brian A. Reaves, "Community Policing in Local Police Departments, 1997 and 1999," Bureau of Justice Statistics Special Report (Washington, DC: Office of Justice Programs, U.S. Department of Justice, 2001).

Michael S. Scott, *Problem-Oriented Policing: Reflections on the First 20 Years* (Washington, DC: U.S. Department of Justice, Office of Community-Oriented Policing Services, 2000).

Quint Thurman, Jihong Zhao, and Andrew Giacomazzi, *Community Policing in a Community Era* (Los Angeles: Roxbury Publishing, 2000).

Robert Trojanowicz and Bonnie Bucqueroux, *Community Policing: A Contemporary Perspective* (Cincinnati, OH: Anderson Publishing, 1990).

James Q. Wilson, *Varieties of Police Behavior* (Cambridge, MA: Harvard University Press, 1968).

James Q. Wilson and George L. Kelling, "Broken Windows: The Police and Neighborhood Safety," *Atlantic Monthly*, volume 249, no. 3, March 1982, pp. 29–38.

References

1. Matthew J. Hickman and Brian A. Reaves, "Community Policing in Local Police Departments, 1997 and 1999," Bureau of Justice Statistics Special Report (Washington, DC: Office of Justice Programs, U.S. Department of Justice, 2001).
2. Robert Trojanowicz and Bonnie Bucqueroux, *Community Policing: A Contemporary Perspective* (Cincinnati, OH: Anderson Publishing, 1990).
3. James Q. Wilson, *Varieties of Police Behavior* (Cambridge, MA: Harvard University Press, 1968).
4. Herman Goldstein, *Problem-Oriented Policing* (New York: McGraw-Hill, 1990).
5. Michael S. Scott, *Problem-Oriented Policing: Reflections on the First 20 Years* (Washington, DC: U.S. Department of Justice, Office of Community-Oriented Policing Services, 2000).
6. James Q. Wilson and George L. Kelling, "Broken Windows: The Police and Neighborhood Safety," *Atlantic Monthly*, volume 249, no. 3, March 1982, pp. 29–38.
7. Herman Goldstein.
8. Michael S. Scott.
9. A. Steven Dietz, "Evaluating Community Policing: Quality Police Service and Fear of Crime," *Policing: An International Journal of Police Strategies and Management*, vol. 20, no. 1, 1997, pp. 83–100.
10. Quint Thurman, Jihong Zhao, and Andrew Giacomazzi, *Community Policing in a Community Era* (Los Angeles: Roxbury Publishing, 2000).
11. Trevor Bennett, "Confidence in the Police as a Mediating Factor in the Fear of Crime," *International Review of Victimology*, vol. 3, 1994, pp. 179–194.
12. Lee P. Brown and Mary Ann Wycoff, "Policing Houston: Reducing Fear and Improving Service," *Crime and Delinquency*, vol. 33, no. 1, 1987, pp. 71–89.
13. Gary W. Cordner, "Community Policing: Elements and Effects," in Roger G. Dunham and Geoffrey P. Alpert (eds.), *Critical Issues in Policing* (Prospect Heights, IL: Waveland Press, 1997), pp. 451–468.

Matthew C. Scheider is a senior social science analyst with the U.S. Department of Justice, Office of Community Oriented Policing Services, in Washington, DC. He is involved in developing, managing, and evaluating federal government programs designed to enhance the community policing capabilities of local law enforcement agencies. He holds a Ph.D. in sociology from Washington State University.

Robert Chapman is a senior social science analyst with the U.S. Department of Justice, Office of Community Oriented Policing Services, where he is responsible for conducting and managing policy analysis, program development, and evaluation activities. He is enrolled in the graduate program at the Johns Hopkins University School of Government. He previously served as the Deputy Director for Legislative Affairs for the Police Executive Research Forum, a membership organization of police executives from the largest city, county, and state law enforcement agencies.

From the *Journal of Homeland Security*, April 2003. © 2003 by the Journal of Homeland Security.

Smallpox, big worries

Preparing medical-response teams is easier said than done,
according to healthcare providers across the nation

Julie Piotrowski

Hospital officials nationwide contend that the steps being taken to prepare healthcare workers to respond to a smallpox attack pose tough administrative, financial and logistical challenges that must be addressed in just a few short weeks.

By Jan. 24, when the Homeland Security Act takes effect, a carefully chosen corps of up to 500,000 nurses, physicians, technicians and other healthcare workers is expected to begin voluntarily receiving the smallpox vaccine as the first phase of the national smallpox strategy announced last month by President Bush.

This mobilization—unprecedented as a response to the threat of a bioterrorism attack, as opposed to a confirmed outbreak of a communicable disease—will commence even as the questions about the practical effects of the plan pile up.

On top of implementation challenges is the ethical question of whether to inject healthy patients with a potentially dangerous vaccine for a disease that was eradicated in the 1970s. Physicians who lead the medical staffs at some hospitals are refusing to expose their co-workers to the vaccine's risks, which include one or two deaths for every 1 million inoculations, unless and until there is more credible evidence that terrorists or rogue states have the means to turn smallpox into a weapon.

Virginia Commonwealth University Health System, Richmond, has no plans to inoculate any of its 1,000 physicians or 5,000 other healthcare workers, said Richard Wenzel, M.D., chairman of the department of internal medicine for the university.

"Our reasons were purely medical," Wenzel said. "We worry not only about the risk of the people who would get the vaccine, but also the risk to any of their potential contacts."

While the risks of serious complications are presented as being low, the federal data about adverse reactions to the vaccine are based on two studies conducted in 1968. Wenzel said rates of complication from the vaccine could be higher today because more people are immune-suppressed because of illness or have skin conditions that pose a greater risk for experiencing side effects.

"This is a medical issue, and we don't want it framed as an issue related to patriotism," Wenzel said, adding that VCU officials are willing to reconsider their decision. "If weapons inspectors in Iraq find a vial of smallpox, obviously that will change our thinking on this."

For hospital administrators, that medical dilemma comes with another raft of economic and legal questions related to compensation, implementation, liability and timing.

Support despite questions

Even as the start of inoculations looms less than three weeks away, "there are a lot of unanswered questions about this program," Roslyne Schulman, senior associate director of policy development at the American Hospital Association, told *Modern Healthcare* in an interview.

Still, the AHA; the Federation of American Hospitals, which represents investor-owned hospitals; and the American Medical Association, the largest physicians' group in the country, said they support the program.

"The nation's hospitals are committed to taking all necessary steps to prepare for the previously unthinkable possibility of a terrorist attack using a biological weapon such as smallpox," Schulman testified last month before an Institute of Medicine committee examining the policy. "Our members tell us that they want to be a part of this program for that very reason—because their job is to protect their communities."

Federation President Chip Kahn said in a written statement that initially offering essential healthcare workers the vaccine is a necessary effort to ensure homeland security.

"Hospital workers serve on the front lines in the domestic effort in the war against terrorism," Kahn said. "It is imperative that they and their families are protected against the possibility of a smallpox outbreak."

But as states prepare their health departments and public-safety agencies to securely receive the vaccine from the Centers for Disease Control and Prevention and transport it to local health departments and hospitals to administer the shots, healthcare officials are asking for more information. They view the Bush plan largely as an unfunded mandate and fret over a series of important questions. Should employees receive leave time after receiving the vaccine, to keep them from possibly infecting patients and co-workers who have not been inoculated? Should workers be paid if they are granted leaves? Will their hospitals be reimbursed by the state or federal governments for that pay? If workers become sick from the vaccine, will their health plans cover the costs of treatments? Will workers' compensation policies cover the expenses? Would hospitals be liable if patients become sick or die as a result of a secondary infection from an inoculated hospital worker?

AHA officials said last week they continue to hold discussions with the White House and HHS about these concerns.

How the plan will work

In the wake of the president's announcement, the Atlanta-based CDC, which is spearheading the process, said nearly 3,600 hospitals are eligible to form smallpox-response teams. Only four hospitals thus far have said they won't participate, but that number could grow. Participating hospitals each will gather lists of volunteers, screen them for conditions that heighten the risk for vaccine side effects and select from 50 to 100 healthy workers to receive the shot, primarily at public health clinics. The timeline for the prescreening process depends largely on how hospitals and public health departments divide the responsibility, but HHS has directed health departments to conduct secondary, in-depth screenings for volunteers who exhibit signs of conditions that complicate the use of the vaccine. These initial 500,000 inoculations form the first phase of the smallpox plan.

The specially designated smallpox-response teams would be mobilized only during a national emergency to vaccinate the public at large. Phase two of the federal plan calls for up to 10 million additional healthcare workers and first responders such as fire, police and other emergency management officials to be inoculated this summer.

To complete phases one and two of the national smallpox strategy, the government will rely upon undiluted smallpox vaccine that has been preserved since the 1970s, when it was last used for the public. A bifurcated needle is used to inject the vaccine.

The Bush administration currently is not recommending vaccination for the public. Under phase three of the plan, however, HHS will establish "an orderly process to make unlicensed vaccine available to those adult members of the general public without medical contraindications who insist on being vaccinated either in 2003, with an unlicensed vaccine, or in 2004, with a licensed vaccine," department officials said.

To complete phases one and two of the plan, the government will rely upon undiluted smallpox vaccine that has been preserved since the 1970s, when it was last used for the public. It was later used during the 1980s to vaccinate military personnel with no fatalities. President Bush directed up to 500,000 members of the military to receive vaccinations under the new plan, and he received the shot himself last month with no reported complications.

In March, HHS said it would purchase an estimated 75 million to 90 million additional doses of smallpox vaccine produced by Aventis Pasteur that had been stored in a secure location since 1972. Department officials said the nation's current vaccine stockpiles and contracts to produce new vaccine resulted in enough doses, 286 million, to vaccinate the public in the event of a national emergency. HHS will not disclose how much it is paying for the vaccine.

Nathaniel Hupert, M.D., a physician and assistant professor of public health and medicine at Weill Medical College of Cornell University, New York, said the healthcare community has carried out successful mass vaccinations for smallpox before. In 1947, after an immigrant infected 12 individuals, and two died, New York vaccinated 6 million people in a month, he said.

"Five million were vaccinated in a two-week period at 179 city clinics and hundreds of doctors offices," Hupert said. "If New York at that point could do it, I'm sure we could do it again."

Imperfect immunity

The AHA's Schulman said in an interview that the foremost concern is the extent to which hospitals and healthcare workers volunteering to participate will be protected from potential legal liability related to the federal program. So far, it appears that not all parties are free from liability, she said.

The Homeland Security Act includes a provision offering liability protection for manufacturers of the vaccine, those hospitals and healthcare workers administering the vaccine and for individuals receiving the shot. But Schulman said a document posted on the CDC's Web site appears to indicate that hospitals that do not serve as vaccination clinics would not be protected legally even if they are providing employee volunteers for the program. The CDC has charged all participating hospitals with not only screening, selecting and educating healthcare workers to receive the vaccine but also monitoring employees for adverse reactions and providing treatment when necessary.

This quirk in the liability provisions of the law is troublesome because many states are planning to vaccinate hospital workers at non-hospital sites, primarily public health clinics, Schulman said. For instance, the Seattle and King County Department of Public Health will vaccinate 1,800 public health and hospital workers, all of them off-site, "because we thought that would be logistically easier for (the hospitals)," Alonzo Plough, the department's director, said.

"Many hospital administrators have been prepared to volunteer their personnel and organizations for the program," Schulman testified before the IOM's smallpox committee. "However, we have received numerous reports that unless (the liability) matter is resolved, hospital attorneys have advised against participating."

Gerberding says the CDC has received plans from all 50 states.

In a letter to the Illinois Department of Public Health, Michael Zia, M.D., vice president of quality systems and medical affairs at 346-bed Decatur (Ill.) Memorial Hospital, said the hospital will not offer the vaccine to its employees, citing the liability issue. Another Illinois hospital, 421-bed Carle Foundation Hospital, Urbana, also has declined to participate in phase one, according to the state health department's spokesman, Tom Schaefer. Carle officials declined to comment.

"From our standpoint, that's fine," said Schaefer, adding that Carle's decision to hold off would not affect the state's ability to respond. "We'll move forward and maybe the hospital will be part of the second phase." Zia said Decatur Memorial continues to work on its smallpox response plan because hospital officials believe a 72-hour window for vaccination after exposure is sufficient to prepare hospital employees.

The CDC required state health departments, in cooperation with hospitals, to submit initial estimates last month for the number of healthcare workers and hospitals planning to participate in phase one. In a recent conference call with reporters, CDC Director Julie Gerberding, M.D., said the agency has received plans from all 50 states and the cities of Chicago, Los Angeles, New York and Washington, providing roughly 440,000 healthcare and public health workers to serve on smallpox-response teams. She said the CDC "fully expected" some hospitals would decide not to participate and planned around the likelihood when determining the amount of vaccine that would be allocated nationwide.

"This is a voluntary program, and we know from our long experience in working with the public health system that im-

plementation varies from jurisdiction to jurisdiction," Gerberding said. "What is important is that we have 3,600 hospitals that have been asked to consider participation, and know we're going to be far more prepared with the response teams that are being asked to step up to the plate than we are today. So we're very optimistic and confident that we'll be able to get the job done right."

Who picks up the tab?

Several state public health and hospital officials told *Modern Healthcare* the burden of carrying out the federal program poses both financial and administrative hurdles in terms of what costs will accrue to states and what costs hospitals will shoulder. Officials also are asking for clarification on how prevaccination education and post-vaccination monitoring responsibilities must be shared between local health departments and providers.

"Hospitals acting as vaccination clinics will have certain costs, but even those that aren't will have to educate workers and do the screening, adverse-event evaluation and treatment, and daily vaccine site management," Schulman said.

Dennis Douglas, director of the Pima County Health Department in Tucson, Ariz., and interim administrator at 114-bed Kino Community Hospital, the county's public facility, said providers in Tucson were advised by the state to pay for the new smallpox preparations with federal funding appropriated in fiscal 2002 after the Sept. 11, 2001, terrorist attacks. Congress has not yet designed or released federal bioterrorism funding for 2003.

"All of the vaccination program costs will have to be borne by our bioterrorism grant money or at the local level, and at the local level, our budgets are not prepared for that," Douglas said. Of the $16 million Arizona received from HHS and $1.2 million the Health Resources and Services Administration granted to Arizona hospitals as part of HHS' initial public health preparedness campaign, Pima County received a bit more than $1 million to prepare its nine hospitals, he said. The money now will have to be stretched to cover smallpox measures.

Johnese Spisso, chief operating officer of Seattle's Harborview Medical Center, said the hospital has been absorbing vaccination program costs as part of its overall operations, but that administrators were working on obtaining additional grants that would allow the hospital to purchase more equipment and expand its Web site. Those efforts represent the main costs right now, Spisso said, "but one of the concerns we have when we go to a broader vaccination (program) is potential lost work time and the replacement workers."

The CDC estimates that 30% of those receiving the smallpox vaccine will be unable to work for a period of time because of reactions. According to data from HHS and the CDC, between 14 and 52 individuals out of every 1 million vaccinated for the first time experience life-threatening skin reactions or brain inflammation, and one to two people out of every 1 million vaccinated may die from those reactions. It is estimated, in addition, that roughly 1,000 people for every 1 million vaccinated will experience nonlife-threatening adverse reactions, such as a toxic or allergic rash requiring medical attention. Citing the absence of a single confirmed case of smallpox, Atlanta's public hospital, Grady Memorial Hospital, has joined the two Illinois hospitals and Virginia Commonwealth University Health System in publicly declaring it will not participate.

"We're not walking out of the negotiation," said Carlos Del Rio, M.D., chief of medicine at Grady Memorial. "We're simply saying that for the time being we're not comfortable vaccinating our healthcare workers based on the information available."

Convincing employees

"One of the things we're really emphasizing about this program is that it's voluntary," Harborview's Spisso said. "Although our goal is to have a team of vaccinated staff available should we have an event, we really want each staff person to make that decision based on their own personal health, family issues and concerns."

The hospital is distributing regular newsletters with vaccination information for employees and holding regular lunch programs led by infectious-disease specialists to answer staff questions. Harborview employees also can set up a one-on-one meeting with an infection-control nurse or physician to discuss concerns about the vaccine.

AHA officials said federal officials need to clarify the necessity of prevaccination tests to screen out at-risk healthcare workers, including those who are pregnant or may have HIV, and whether workers should be placed on administrative leave after being vaccinated to prevent secondary transmission of infections. A CDC committee recommended against both mandatory screening prior to vaccination and routine administrative leave for vaccinated workers, but HHS has not formally adopted these recommendations, the AHA's Schulman said.

Workers' complications

Officials at the American Nurses Association are particularly concerned about complications of the vaccine associated with skin diseases because, according to ANA figures, 8% to 12% of healthcare workers have skin that is sensitive to latex, which often leads to dermatitis. "The potential for dermatological reactions must be taken into account both in discussing the overall vaccination policy and when developing the screening questionnaire and interview process," ANA President Barbara Blakeney said. The ANA contends that time off associated with the vaccination process, including administrative leave, should be paid leaves that are not charged to healthcare workers' sick or vacation time, Blakeney said.

Because the Homeland Security Act does not provide for the creation of a compensation fund for healthcare workers injured by the vaccine, another question is whether any such injuries would be covered by workers' compensation programs. Since the vaccine is voluntary and not a "condition of employment," it's "not clear whether state workers' compensation funds would cover those hospital employees who become ill," Schulman said.

She said the AHA supports the creation of a federal compensation fund similar to the federal Vaccine Injury Compensation Fund, a "no-fault" alternative to the traditional tort system for resolving vaccine injury claims, regardless of whether the vaccine is administered by the public or private sector. Gerberding acknowledged the CDC understands workers' compensation mechanisms vary from state to state and that HHS officials are working to address many unanswered questions about the scope of coverage.

Pima County's Douglas said, "We're going to do everything we can to take care of the members of our hospital and public health department but we're only going to be able to do so much. The liability exposure and workers' compensation problem simply has to be dealt with by the federal government."

From *Modern Healthcare*, January 6, 2003, pp. 6-7, 12-13. © 2003 by Modern Healthcare.

Managing the Response to a Major Terrorist Event

Creating a Network of Capabilities—Managing their Mobilization, Deployment and Utilization

By John R. Powers
For Homeland Defense Journal

A response to a major terrorist event would require the rapid assemblage of diverse capabilities, some from distant areas that have little operational familiarity with the others. This would occur in the midst of confounding uncertainties, conflicting priorities and potentially tragic misdirection. Many responders, lacking clear guidance, would simply react.

Excellent work is being done today to address these problems and most are building on the incident command system. Yet, without a unifying concept of operations, resources would be wasted, lives lost and the response hampered.

The starting point to avoid that is the recognition that a tightly managed response might be impossible, but a management concept could allow considerable independent action within centrally coordinated guidelines. This could be accomplished through a coherent "network of networks."

The Strategic Problem

The first objective of the National Strategy for Homeland Security is to "prevent terrorist attacks within the United States."

Despite best efforts, however, a determined and well-financed adversary would be able to access materials, fabricate weapons, move freely about the country, and employ a weapon with near impunity. Therefore, significant energy must be directed toward other objectives, namely reducing America's vulnerability to terrorism while minimizing the damage and recovering from attacks that do occur.

The Tactical Problem

To minimize the damage, decisive coordinated action would be required early and often. The confusion following the World Trade Center and Pentagon attacks was an ominous indication of the difficulties that would be encountered during a major attack. These difficulties need to be resolved to efficiently utilize the capabilities of large numbers of unrelated organizations with little operational familiarity.

Fiscal constraints would make it virtually impossible for jurisdictions to have all capabilities needed to respond to a major event, forcing them to draw on capabilities from many different locations. The mobilization, deployment and utilization of these capabilities would rival the management challenges of reinforcing Europe during the cold war. In this cold war, however, all of the needed capabilities were owned by a single entity—the Department of Defense. Here, they are dispersed throughout the public and private sectors of the country.

In addition, response managers would confront a number of problems:

- No jurisdiction would be fully prepared in its planning, training, information systems and working relationships for all possible scenarios.
- Many responses would be ad hoc, despite the best efforts to constrain such actions.
- Major uncertainties would abound regarding unknown agents and their effects, public reactions, other response activities and availability of supporting resources.
- Conflicting priorities, competition for resources and misdirection would pervade the response community.
- Tight command and control would be impossible during the initial moments following the attack, even if the incident commander had perfect communications support. In the first three to six hours much too much would be happening for the command element of the ICS to gather all of the necessary information and issue all of the necessary orders.

While there would be an incident commander and emergency operating centers coming on line across the region, the pace of activity and number of players would preclude centralized control. Under such circumstances, there would need to be a unified concept of operations to guide the responses until the pace slows to a manageable level.

There are single-service concepts of operations today that are very effective, such as those developed by the fire services.

A paramedic recalled, "As an old paramedic, we responded to each call with standing orders for everything from trauma to a heart attack. While we always worked under a MD's direction, time would not allow contact with the medical control before treatment. So our medical directors gave us a set of standing orders to begin treatment. Every hospital knew what we would be doing as well as other arriving EMS units, based on the situation."

Such standing orders could enable seamless operations across many jurisdictional lines and should be expanded and linked into a unified concept to pull all of the sectors together across jurisdictional boundaries.

Unified Concept of Operations

The objective of a unified concept of operations is to mobilize, deploy and utilize all essential capabilities in the absence of tight command and control. The first step in developing such a concept is to identify all of the priority actions that would be needed in response to a terrorist attack. However, this varies dramatically depending upon the nature of the attack.

The following is a suggested way of categorizing the attacks:

- enhanced conventional with mass casualties, including 100 to 10,000 or more injured
- chemical, radiological or noncontagious biological
- contagious biological
- fission

There is significant overlap. The all-hazard approach would continue to be relevant for some aspects of these different scenarios such as mass care, shelter and evacuation management. For example, planning for a catastrophic earthquake has many of the same features as preparing for an enhanced conventional attack with mass casualties. The other categories, however, would create distinct problems for the responders. Also there are important differences within each of these categories based on agents, magnitude, location and targets that would drive the response. In fact, the categories might need further refinement.

Assuming that agreement would be possible on a set of generic contingencies, priority actions would need to be specified. For an enhanced conventional attack with mass casualties, the priority actions would include stabilization and triage, transport to care centers and health-care delivery. That would include other supporting actions, such as maintaining a constant update of the available beds in each of the medical centers.

Most of these actions or functions have an inherent network of providers that could be readily identified. The collection of providers, such as EMS, are often referred to as "sectors." For example, casualty transport would involve the fire service and independent emergency medical service vehicles and independent ambulance companies. During a major event, that would be expanded to include military and civilian helicopter units that would be as critical as local health-care capacity is filled.

After identifying the priority actions needed in each of the contingencies, the next step would be building a concept of operations. This would include:

- **Creating networks for each of the essential functions.**

Using the generic response sectors, a network of responders could be identified for each. It is possible that the "emergency support functions (ESFs)" identified in the Federal Response Plan could serve as a framework for such an effort. At the federal level—and in some states—there is a network of players and some response structures.

- **Building from the bottom up.**

The grouping of the providers must make sense to the first responders and local jurisdictions. These are the basic building blocks of the network of networks and the providers would have to function semi-independently until the dust clears. Many—if not most—services and jurisdictions have their own ways of doing business with imbedded protocols and priorities. These would need to be harmonized to be consistent with area-wide operating practices.

- **Creating a network to link the functional networks (sectors) together; a network of networks.**

This is an analytic task that would eventually become the basis of a "grand systems model." The pieces are: functions, players, roles of the individual players, transactions among them, and protocols to guide the transactions.

- **Developing the information and communication support architecture needed to support the individual networks.**

If the network of networks is designed well, the supporting architecture should evolve naturally.

- **Divining a network management concept.**

This would be the most difficult step in the process. It is assumed that top down (hierarchical) management would be either ineffective or marginally effective in the hours immediately following a major event. If this is true—and provision should be made for it being true—some form of decentralized management must be developed, standardized and adopted. The specifics of this should be debated, but it must be loose and flexible allowing a fair degree of autonomy to the functional networks that would be responding.

It is here that the notion of "self-directed work teams" should be fully exploited. If this is possible, then the central management problem is reduced to the more tractable task of ensuring the devolution of accurate information and managing the interaction of the networks.

- **Establishing a common operational picture.**

This military concept is applicable to decentralized management. Its purpose is to provide a broadcast summary of what has happened, what is needed, the hidden dangers, and the response concept. The amount of detail needed by the responders on the ground and the emergency operation centers would vary widely depending upon specific functions.

- **Preparing quick response plans.**

Quick response plans are short, three- to five-page summaries of the key elements of the response: problems to be solved, players involved, their roles, processes to be followed including special conditions and alternate courses of action, authorities, and the concept of operations.

In many respects, the plans are simply an extrapolation of the "standing orders" used by many of the services today and should be prepared by jurisdictions using common language and procedures, coordinated with the political leadership and implemented by watch standers. Their main intent is to make sure that the core group of responders is "working off the same page" and to enable the immediate implementation by watch standers of the initial life saving and life protecting actions without need for further approvals once they are certain of the nature of the attack. This is predicated on considerable pre-coordination among the stakeholders and buy-in from the political leadership.

In order for this to be effective, unprecedented levels of collaboration and clear delegations of authority would be needed.

With respect to collaboration, while most services and jurisdictions do a great job working across boundaries when interests are in common, few do a very good job when interests are in conflict. This has been well documented in the WTC after-action reports and it goes well beyond traditional turf problems.

With respect to delegations, not only would watch standers need clear authorization to implement the necessary actions locally, but key figures in each of the networks would need the authority to summon and direct capabilities from adjacent jurisdictions, as well as from the states and federal government. The foundation for such delegations could be found in the mutual aid compacts accepted across most state boundaries and being negotiated within many states. These, however, might need to be reviewed to determine if the delegations are such that the response times would be equal to needs generated by the varied effects of a major terrorist event.

Recommendations

The aftermath of a major attack would be characterized by a huge amount of disorder and the most pressing need would be for a unified concept of operations that would reduce that disorder among the responding elements. Since it is assumed that central management would be overwhelmed in the first few hours, a concept is needed to enable the first responders and their supporting networks to function somewhat independently without a lot of direct guidance. In many respects, this concept builds upon the standing orders already used among many first responders.

The purpose of a unified concept of operations is to define and link each of the individual networks. EMS personnel would represent one network, transport would be another, corresponding to the ESF's in the Federal Response Plan.

The concept would provide each network with enough guidance to take information in the common operational picture and manage their part of the operation. For example, the urgent care centers would set up an information clearinghouse to match casualty demand with bed supply, and do so continuously.

Each network would have to provide information links to its corresponding networks. The hospitals would provide capacity information to the transport network; the on-scene casualty stabilization and triage network would provide casualty information (numbers, types and locations) to the transport network, and the transport network would generate its own transport missions—all in very short order.

Because of its seeming complexity, such a concept of operation would need the enthusiastic support of all of the major stakeholders in all major metropolitan areas and states plus the key nongovernmental organizations and federal agencies. All, or most, entities recognize the problem and have been working on aspects of the solution; all certainly have insights that would contribute to an effective unified concept. The most immediate need is to create a process that would pull together the insights of all of these key stakeholders into a unified concept of operations.

This might not be as difficult as it might seem. One option is to develop one or more local regional concepts of operations. This could be done in select major cities that are advanced in thinking about the problems associated with a major event and have already interacted with surrounding counties, states and the private sector.

This is consistent with the need to "build from the bottom up." Such a process would provide concrete prototypical concepts that could then be harmonized into a unified national concept—the first step in developing a national capability to respond effectively to a major terrorist event.

UNIT 6

New Technologies in Homeland Security

Unit Selections

22. **Guarding Against Missiles**, Fred Bayles
23. **Modernizing Homeland Security**, John D. Cohen and John A. Hurson
24. **Aerospace Giants Repackage Military Technology for Home**, John Croft

Key Points to Consider

- Should the U.S. government spend $8 billion to install antimissile systems on U.S. commercial aircraft? Why or why not?

- How can better communication and increased information sharing improve homeland security?

- Why are major defense contractors such as Raytheon and Northrop Grumman interested in developing products for homeland security? What do they have to offer?

 **Links: www.dushkin.com/online/**
These sites are annotated in the World Wide Web pages.

Communications Interoperability and Information Sharing
http://www.ojp.usdoj.gov/nij/sciencetech/ciis.htm
Defense Advanced Research Project Agency
http://www.fas.org/irp/agency/dod/poindexter.html
TEN: The Enterprise Network
http://www.ten-net.org/homelandsecurity.html

New technologies have had a tremendous impact on U.S. security. Surveillance cameras, metal detectors, and explosive detection equipment have become commonplace at U.S. airports. Yet, despite the existence of these precautionary measures, the September 11 hijackers managed to board and take over four U.S. aircraft. While some choose to blame the Intelligence Community for the security failures of 9/11, there has been little or no discussion of the failure of technology. Billions of dollars spent on new security measures and millions spent on new explosive detection equipment, installed at major U.S. airports on the recommendations of the Gore Commission after the crash of TWA Flight 800, did not prevent the attacks of 9/11. As we become increasingly dependent on technology in day-to-day security, we must recognize the limits of technology in homeland security. Technological solutions are expensive. They offer limited solutions to specific problems. Once in place, they are vulnerable to countermeasures.

One of the major drawbacks of technology solutions to security issues is cost. Since the first attack on the World Trade Center in 1993, counterterrorism funding has increased significantly. U.S. government spending on counterterrorism has risen from less than $1 billion in 1995 to well over $40 billion in 2003. As the federal budget deficits increase and counterterrorism spending reaches its limits, increased attention must be paid to the nature of investments in technology and the associated trade-offs.

Technological solutions often focus on very narrow problems. Metal detectors may detect firearms but are not likely to detect plastic explosives. Databases that maintain information on potential terrorists are only useful if they capture all possible suspects and if they can be easily accessed by those who need them. Systems designed to protect aircraft against heat-seeking missiles (see "Guarding Against Missiles") do not protect against other types of shoulder-fired weapons or prevent attacks against targets on the ground. The selection of one technology over another thus automatically determines the limitations of the security system.

Once a new technology is in use, it becomes susceptible to countermeasures. Terrorists have proven themselves extremely adept at circumventing existing security. Billions spent on technology for airport security were circumvented by 99¢ box-cutters. Systems that monitor the international transfer of funds have been rendered ineffective by traditional barter and exchange systems. Technology designed to intercept and monitor cell-phone calls has led to the development and use of alternate means of communication. Profiling of terrorists has led to the increased recruitment of individuals who don't meet the profile.

While technology alone cannot solve the complex problems posed by homeland security, the use of technology can significantly improve and enhance existing security. With this caveat, the articles in this unit examine the potential role of technology in homeland security. The first article focuses on an $8 billion congressional proposal to deploy antimissile defense systems on commercial U.S. airliners. The next article points out the importance of improved communications in homeland security. It recommends improved information sharing between local, state, and federal governments and argues for the increased integration of existing databases. The final article in this unit addresses the need for increased communications interoperability. Several major defense contractors are currently at work on projects that may help improve homeland security.

Guarding against missiles

By Fred Bayles, USA TODAY

Police and, in some instances, the National Guard are patrolling the perimeters and flight approaches of airports in Los Angeles, Chicago, Orlando and other major cities in an effort to stop terrorists from shooting down passenger jets with shoulder-fired missiles.

In San Francisco, New York and Washington, Coast Guard boats keep watch near waterfront runways. Boston Harbor clam diggers use cell phones to report suspicious activity near Logan International.

The increased surveillance is the first step in federal efforts to protect airliners that take off and land an average of 170,000 times a day.

Federal officials won't talk about pending strategies to prevent terrorists from launching heat-seeking missiles at passenger planes. But an unreleased FAA study lists the use of airborne patrols, ground checkpoints, observation posts and high-intensity lights in areas adjacent to airports.

Although there has never been an attack in the USA and federal officials discount the immediacy of the threat, some members of Congress have proposed putting antimissile systems on airliners within the next year.

One sponsor, Sen. Charles Schumer, D-N.Y., says that with thousands of the missiles on the black market and previous attacks on jets overseas, the risk to the flying public and the airline industry is too great to not take action.

"The damage a terrorist attack could do would be devastating," Schumer says. "Do you think anyone would fly for three to six months after an attack?"

Homeland Security Secretary Tom Ridge also sees the possible use of anti-missile systems on airliners in the future, but only after more study.

"I think the first public dollars we ought to expend should be to take a look at the technology itself to see if adaptation can be made," he told a gathering of reporters recently.

Security experts agree there is no fast or easy fix. They say airport surveillance is limited against a weapon that can be launched from a pickup, boat or rooftop. Many shoulder-launched missiles can hit a jet 4 miles away at altitudes of more than 10,000 feet. According to the FAA report, that would give terrorists a 150-square-mile area around an airport in which to hide and fire at aircraft that are taking off or circling to land.

Congress' hopes for a quick technological solution may be optimistic, too, they say. Adding a complex system of countermeasures to jets could take years to do safely.

"There is no silver bullet," says James Loy, head of the Transportation Security Agency (TSA), which is responsible for air travel safety.

Some federal officials also caution that the threat of shoulder-launched missiles may be overstated. So far, they have a poor record against passenger jets; only one has been downed in six attacks.

"These weapons pose a threat, but there is no specific credible evidence that they are in the hands of terrorists in the United States or that they plan to use them to shoot down airliners," says Brian Roehrkasse, a spokesman for the Department of Homeland Security.

The missiles, called Man Portable Air Defense Systems, or MANPADS, weigh about 35 pounds and can be fired with little training. Honing in on the heat from aircraft engines, the missiles travel at more than 600 mph, three times the takeoff or landing speed of an airliner.

The U.S. version, the Stinger, contributed to the defeat of the Soviet army in the 1980s in Afghanistan, where rebels used them to shoot down assault helicopters and jet fighters.

About 700,000 MANPADS have been produced worldwide since the 1970s. The most common is the 30-year-old Russian SA-7 Strela. The British, French and Chinese also produce them. Intelligence agencies say Al-Qaeda and 26 known terrorist groups have dozens of the weapons.

MANPADS have been used in 35 attacks against civilian airplanes in Africa, Asia, Afghanistan and Central America; 24 were shot down, killing more than 500 people. All but one of the planes shot down were propeller planes. The only jet, a Congo Airlines Boeing 727, was shot down by rebels in 1998.

In May, Al-Qaeda terrorists fired an SA-7 at a U.S. military jet taking off in Saudi Arabia. In November, terror-

Increasing runway security

Steps to improve security on airport grounds include:

- Area checkpoints.
- Perimeter and area observation posts.
- More ground patrols.
- Random ground patrols.
- High-intensity portable lighting directed outward in areas of woods, open waterways or uninhabited areas.
- Airborne patrols, observations using night-vision and heat-vision equipment if available.
- Special surveillance areas beyond the fence line in sectors parallel to the active runways.

Source: Unpublished 1996 FAA document

ists launched two SA-7s at an Israeli charter jet leaving Mombasa, Kenya. Both attempts failed.

The day after the Mombasa attack, the White House formed a group to study the threat. In December, the TSA surveyed about 80 major airports to identify vulnerabilities. Two months ago, after London's Heathrow Airport was nearly shut down by concerns of a possible missile attack, the TSA and FBI visited 22 of the largest airports to develop security plans.

Officials decline to identify the airports or talk about specific tactics. But an FAA study, initiated in 1996, points to possible countermeasures. They include:

- **Denying terrorists access to areas around the airport.** While the report considered this the most practical solution, it noted efforts would require manpower from federal, state and local agencies. It is also far from certain. Capt. Steve Luckey, chairman of the Air Line Pilots Associ-

ation's security committee, says neighborhoods around urban airports such as Los Angeles International and San Diego offer too many hiding places.

"I don't know how you can defend an airport surrounded by miles of rooftops," he says.

- **Changing flight operations.** Pilots could take off in faster, steeper climbs and descend in spiraling turns over the airport to reduce time spent at lower altitudes. Such changes would be difficult.

"It isn't something that can easily be accomplished given the fixed navigational aids used by the airplanes," says Ian Redhead of Airports Council International, an airport trade association.

- **Installing countermeasures on airliners.** Congress is considering a $30 million appropriation to test a system of lasers and other devices to throw heat-seeking missiles off target. Military aircraft already use flares and lasers to divert missiles. Air Force One and El Al airliners are believed to use similar devices.

"The technology already exists," says Schumer, who favors a bill that would require the system to be installed in 5,000 airliners at an estimated cost of $8 billion.

But aviation safety experts say the use of flares and other incendiary devices creates safety issues in the air and on the ground. They also worry about putting new technology into the already complex systems of a jetliner.

"It would take five to 10 years to do the engineering work to add these systems to a fleet of different aircraft," says Kevin Darcy, a former accident investigator for Boeing.

Modernizing Homeland Security

High-tech data links and inter-agency coordination could stop terrorists from slipping through our fingers again.

by **John D. Cohen** *and* **John A. Hurson**

Last year's terrorist attacks uncovered a deadly lack of integration among America's domestic defenses. Several of the future hijackers were briefly involved with police or other government agencies, which entered their names into government data systems. At least two of the men were sought by the FBI; the names of others were in other intelligence databases. But because the data systems were not linked, the dots were never connected, and the men went on their way. The chance to prevent terrorism was lost.

> We know that the nation's law enforcement and **emergency response** systems do not function cohesively because they are largely tied to geographical jurisdictions or **exclusive functions.**

Although we'll never know whether better data sharing would have thwarted the horrible attacks, we do know that terrorists often use traditional crime, such as drug trafficking to support their objectives.

We also know that the nation's law enforcement and emergency response systems do not function cohesively because they are largely tied to geographical jurisdictions or exclusive functions. When police and fire departments from Virginia, Maryland, and Washington, D.C. responded to the Pentagon attack, they were unable to radio one another because, like most public safety entities, each department had its own radio frequencies.

To prevent and respond to terrorism, we must change our approach to security.

First, we must redefine our concept of national security to include the pivotal role of states and localities. In the event of new terrorist attacks, some of the first people on the scene will be police officers, followed by local firefighters and health-care providers. Federal help will be hours and maybe even days away. One way or another, responsibility for homeland defense rests with state and local governments.

Second, our approach to domestic defense must be made national and seamless. In addition to coordinating federal agencies, the Office of Homeland Security must set clear national priorities to guide action for states and localities. And to help state and local governments build a seamless domestic defense, Congress must provide block grants with accountability provisions.

> "We must **build** on existing state and local partnerships and information sharing, **resisting the temptation** to create stand-alone agencies mobilized only in a **crisis.**"

Third, we must make domestic defense a top priority in the everyday work of government, not just in emergencies. We must build on existing state and local partnerships and information sharing, resisting the temptation

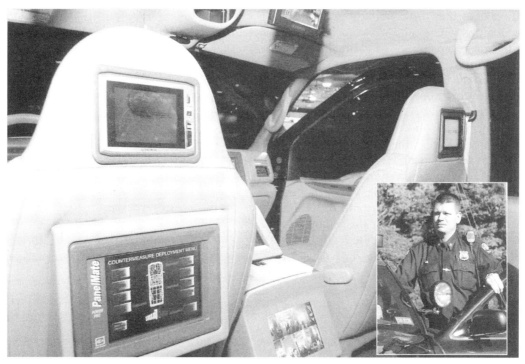

A SMART START: Upgraded anti-terrorist technology, like the U.S. Army's new SmarTruck, can help first responders, like patrolman Robert Berry (inset), of Byram, Connecticut.

to create stand-alone agencies mobilized only in a crisis. Information and communication technology and operational strategies used for emergencies should also support efforts to provide delivery of services by government agencies each day. With this infrastructure, state and local officials will not only have the foundation for efforts to prevent and respond to crises—everyday government will work better, too.

We should begin institutionalizing this new approach by immediately taking several steps. The first involves connecting the dots with the data. To link the information from various arms of the criminal justice system about the people who commit crime and the places where crime occurs, we must launch "integrated justice" information systems.

Just as search engines on the Web allow instantaneous access to vast sources of information, we must create a system in which secure facilities (such as airports) can access resources like the terrorist "watch list" in the National Crime Information Center at the FBI. Public safety information and communication systems should also be interlinked with those of other critical government systems that support transportation, social services, and public utilities. Efforts to "connect the dots with data" in 38 states and the District of Columbia must be accelerated and made universal.

In addition, we must integrate emergency response communications systems. This would enable first responders from different agencies and jurisdictions to talk to each other. Efforts to address such deficiencies have

been energized following the events of Sept. 11. For example, Maryland launched a project to patch disparate radio systems into an integrated network that offers a model for others.

At the same time, we need to bolster defenses against biological and chemical terrorist attacks. To identify and respond to both naturally occurring disease outbreak and biological and chemical weapon attacks, we must establish an information network linking laboratories, first responders, health care providers, governmental agencies, and other facilities.

Now that terrorism is a clearer threat, it's all the more critical that states be prepared to recognize an outbreak of disease, circulate information to health-care providers, coordinate local response with federal and military systems, and allocate scarce medical resources such as antibiotics and vaccines.

> State and local leaders should take heart that the best way to **prevent** and **prepare for terrorism** is already available in the techniques and technologies now strengthening communities and protecting our neighborhoods.

A good first step is the Lightweight Epidemiology Advanced Detection & Emergency Response System deployed by hospitals and state medical offices in New York and Phoenix during the World Series. Building on this

Web-based system, medical personnel will have the ability to track outbreaks as they are reported by hospitals, map geographic regions where outbreaks are occurring, and determine response capabilities of various medical facilities.

Finally, it is important to connect everyone with 211 and 311. To provide information and services to everyone, we must establish statewide toll-free numbers for non-emergency information and referral services for health care and social services. At the time of the terrorist attacks and the anthrax scare, people called a non-emergency number for information and referral to health and social services when one was available. When a non-emergency number wasn't available, they called 911. But relying on 911 systems is potentially catastrophic, because the system could become inundated with non-emergency calls that clog out emergency calls. We need to expand the use of 211 and 311 as non-emergency information numbers. Connecticut's statewide 211 telephone system for information and referral is a model to follow.

These innovations would be key first steps toward fully integrating America's domestic defenses. State and local leaders should take heart that the best way to prevent and prepare for terrorism is already available in the techniques and technologies now strengthening communities and protecting our neighborhoods. Building on those methods will not only improve homeland security, it will also improve health care, policing, and other government services.

John D. Cohen is president of PSComm LLC and directs the Progressive Policy Institute's Community Crime Fighting Project.
John A. Hurson is a member of the Maryland House of Delegates, where he serves as chairman of the Environmental Matters Committee.

HOMELAND SECURITY & DEFENSE

Aerospace Giants Repackage Military Technology for Home

JOHN CROFT
WASHINGTON

Communications interoperability is more than a buzzword to Hugo B. Poza, Raytheon's vice president for homeland security—it's a sport utility vehicle.

Not just any sport-utility vehicle, Raytheon's First Responder Vehicle is unique: A four-wheel-drive self-contained computer-controlled command and control center with wireless, cell and satellite communications that permit emergency workers at "ground zero" to talk to one another, even with incompatible radios. Poza said the idea was conceived after the New York and Washington terror attacks and solidified in June when he and Raytheon Chairman and CEO Daniel P. Burnham met with U.S. Office of Homeland Security Director Tom Ridge.

Carrier said Northrop Grumman is involved in a widespread ongoing effort to evaluate classified program technologies that could be transferred to the civil side.

Burnham to Ridge: "Governor, is there anything that comes to mind as the No. 1 thing that keeps you awake at night?"

Ridge: "Communications interoperability."

Ridge was alluding to problems experienced by first responders both in New York and the Pentagon last year. At the Pentagon, emergency workers from 10 jurisdictions couldn't communicate initially because their radios were mismatched, a difficulty that sparked the First Responder idea at Raytheon.

Raytheon's effort to package off-the-shelf components military-style in a suburban family van is but one example of the technological solutions ginned up by defense-savvy aerospace companies in response to the Bush administration's calls for enhanced homeland security. Bush is asking for new biometric technologies, systems for detecting hostile intent and widespread, but secure, sharing of information between federal agencies and emergency responders.

It helps too that there's the potential for a massive cash infusion, pegged at more than $5 billion in Fiscal 2003 alone. It's a market that major aerospace players appear to be well-positioned to capture, given their experience with military and covert agency products and the ability to integrate large, complex information and data systems.

"IT and communications are the big markets," said Jenny Benavidez, an industry analyst for Frost & Sullivan's Aerospace & Defense Group, "and they're moving from the defense world to civilian side." Poza agreed, saying the "view from 60,000 ft. is that we're squeezing the technologies coming out of the defense world."

> **…Raytheon is proposing facial and fingerprint recognition technologies that are combined with an information engine called Genesis… a tool that is a "product of the new cooperation" between the classified and civil worlds.**

Northrop Grumman's Steve Carrier, vice president of business development and head of the company's homeland security integrated product team, said communications systems in the military and intelligence community are far superior to what's available in the civil sector. Carrier said first responders like police and fire fighters would benefit from a "common operating picture" of the situation, much like what is provided to planners and soldiers on the battlefield. He questioned however whether state and local authorities will be able to afford the price. "They don't have the money that a [Defense Dept.] agency has."

Carrier said Northrop Grumman is involved in a widespread ongoing effort to evaluate classified program technologies that could be transferred to the civil side. As a result, the company has included some classified technologies in more than 100 homeland security proposals and add-on contracts it has presented to the government. Once appropriate classified technologies are identified, Carrier said, Northrop Grumman will have to go through a process to get them released "out of that world." Transferring non-sensitive military technologies to public uses should not pose the same barriers.

One upcoming project that may showcase the technological acumen of both Northrop Grumman and Raytheon is the proposed Immigration and Naturalization Service (INS) entry/exit visa management system. Congress mandated that an automated system to record the 500–600-million annual alien arrivals and departures in the U.S. be operational by Dec. 31, 2003, for airports and seaports and 1–2 years later, for land ports of entry. Raytheon is teamed with AT&T on the project. The INS is expected to down-select to two competitors in December, with each receiving about $380 million for the next and final phase of the competition. The winner of the $3–4 billion, decade-long project will be selected next summer.

> **Lockheed Martin is assessing how technologies used for its military contracts could benefit the civil market.**

While Northrop Grumman would not comment, Poza said Raytheon is proposing facial and fingerprint recognition technologies that are combined with an information engine called Genesis, a tool Poza said is a "product of the new cooperation" between the classified and civil worlds. Developed for the intelligence community, it snoops through public and non-public databases to establish behavior patterns of an individual as a way to flag deviations that could indicate links to terrorism. "Genesis looks at your past and tells a government analyst, 'These are the things you have to watch out for,'" Poza said, adding that the program could also be used to evaluate behavior of cargo container shippers, adding a layer of protection in a transportation segment that receives scant scrutiny.

Northrop Grumman is competing with Raytheon in the communications interoperability arena as well. The company announced in August that it had partnered with Flarion Technologies, a spin-off company from Bell Labs, to produce a wireless network. The system would "overlay" existing communications networks, like phone systems, and could act as a unifying command and control network at a disaster scene, much as the First Responder Vehicle's hardware was designed to do.

Like Raytheon, Boeing has integrated an emergency communications system into a first-responder vehicle—called Mobile Broadband—but the company has yet to sell one of the vans (with pull-along trailer), said Randy Harrison, Boeing's director of communications for homeland security. That's not a problem, however, as Harrison said Boeing is positioning itself as a large-system integrator rather than a vendor of platforms and products. The tack appeared to be working: Boeing recently won a $508-million government contract to integrate explosives detection systems in hundreds of U.S. commercial airports by year-end—the largest homeland security contract issued to date.

Harrison said solving communications problems faced by first responders will require techniques similar to those Boeing is developing as part of a contract to restructure the U.S. Army: Network-centric warfare and integrated battlespace, or more simply put, using intelligence and information, including satellite communications and imagery, as efficiently as technologically possible so responders can maximize available resources. The key benefit of this system, he said, is that it's "very responsive" to "asymmetric" threats posed by terrorists.

Other technologies the company is considering bringing from the battlefield or government facility to supermarket or mall include a chemical and biological protection system developed for the C-17 Globemaster transport and a visual surveillance system that alerts operators to security breaches in and around buildings. Modifications to satellite observation systems used in the agricultural industry to help prevent agro-terrorism are in review and a program to track hazardous material shipments on the roads is in development.

Lockheed Martin is assessing how technologies used for its military contracts could benefit the civil market. Jane Rudolf, vice president of homeland security systems for Lockheed Martin's Mission Systems, said an Army program to deploy intrusion detection systems around secure development areas and weapons storage depots is promising. The company is working with the Port Authority of New York and New Jersey and the Metropolitan Transportation Authority in New York on a system that could monitor bridges and tunnels using the Army technology, Rudolf said.

Overall, many technologies on the horizon should help Ridge sleep soundly; Poza's $100,000–250,000 SUV appeared to be one of the first purchased by state or local authorities. Los Angeles County brought the first of eight vehicles sold so far. Poza said the Federal Emergency Management Agency and National Guard would like to buy hundreds if funding becomes available.

All four companies lamented that funding for homeland security projects is slower than anticipated. Northrop Grumman's Carrier put it the most succinctly: "There's a high percentage of PR [public relations] and a low percentage of doing something."

From *Aviation Week & Space Technology*, October 21, 2002, pp. 67-68. © 2002 by The McGraw-Hill Companies.

UNIT 7
Vulnerabilities and Threats

Unit Selections

Key Points to Consider

- Has the use of biological agents by terrorists become more likely? Is the public health system in the United States prepared to handle such an emergency? Explain.

- Is the United States prepared for nuclear or radiological terrorism? What are the political implications of a successful nuclear or radiological attack against the United States?

- Is the United States particularly vulnerable to cyberterrorism? What are the potential consequences of attacks against critical infrastructure?

- Will terrorism increase in the twenty-first century? What factors suggest the continued development of more destructive forms of terrorism?

 **Links: www.dushkin.com/online/**
These sites are annotated in the World Wide Web pages.

CDC Public Health Emergency Preparedness & Response Site
http://www.bt.cdc.gov
Emergency Preparedness Information for Terrorism
http://www.tnema.org/EP/EP_DomPrep.htm
The Myth of Cyberterrorism
http://www.washingtonmonthly.com/features/2001/0211.green.html
Nuclear Terrorism
http://www.nci.org/nuketerror.htm

The purpose of this unit is to give the reader a sense of existing threats. The attacks on the World Trade Center and the Pentagon spawned wild speculation and apocalyptic predictions concerning the future of U.S. security. These tragedies and the subsequent anthrax attacks have fueled fears and have led to exaggerations of terrorist capabilities. While the existing threats cannot and should not be ignored, the U.S. government and the media often project unrealistic images of terrorists, endowing them with capabilities far beyond their actual reach. These articles, rather than further perpetuating myths and fears, seek to provide insights into what some believe the future of terrorist threats may look like. Because terrorism is to be a top priority for homeland security, difficult choices must be made. As policymakers attempt to find ways to reassure a concerned public, choices between spending for security today and preparing for the threats of the future are becoming increasingly difficult.

Terrorism will undoubtedly remain a major policy issue for the United States well into the 21-first century. Opinions vary as to what future perpetrators will look like and what methods they will pursue. While some argue that the traditional methods of terrorism, such as bombing, kidnapping, and hostage-taking, will continue to dominate the new millennium, others warn that weapons of mass destruction or weapons of mass disruption, such as biological and chemical weapons or even nuclear or radiological weapons, will be the weapons of choice for terrorists in the future.

"Waiting for Bioterror" examines the U.S. government's preparedness for and response capability to biological attacks. Katherine Eban argues that there are problems with the public health system that, if left uncorrected, will leave the United States vulnerable.

"Not if, but when?" is Bill Keller's prediction in "Nuclear Nightmares." Arguing that the collapse of the former Soviet Union left nuclear weapons and radioactive materials vulnerable, he speculates as to how these materials might reach terrorists or potential state sponsors and pose a future threat for Western governments. Barton Gellman's article addresses the possibilities that our nation's critical infrastructure may be open to new forms of terrorism. He argues that a combination of cyberterrorism and traditional physical attacks poses a new and grave risk to U.S. security. Finally, Virginia Gewin in "Agriculture Shock" highlights the potential economic and physical consequences of an attack on plants and animals. She argues that potential threats to plant and animal health are often overlooked in discussions of homeland security.

WAITING FOR BIOTERROR

IS OUR PUBLIC HEALTH SYSTEM READY?

By KATHERINE EBAN

Just before the July 4 holiday this past summer, as National Guardsmen with sniffer dogs monitored the nation's bridges and airports, Jerome Hauer, an assistant secretary at the Health and Human Services Department, dispatched a technician to Atlanta to set up a satellite phone for the new director of the Centers for Disease Control.

If smallpox broke out, if phones failed, if the federal government had to oversee mass vaccination of an urban center, Hauer would have a way to communicate with the CDC director, who since last fall has worked with him on health crises, particularly bioterror. It was one of many precautions that might make the difference between a manageable event and full-scale disaster.

But at the same time, an attempt at crisis management of a more immediate kind was unfolding 2,500 miles to the west. As the FBI chased reports of potential new threats, including a possible attack on Las Vegas, Dr. John Fildes, the medical director of Nevada's only top-level trauma center, watched helplessly as a real medical disaster developed, one that had nothing and everything to do with the problems that Hauer was working to solve.

Faced with a dramatic spike in the cost of their malpractice insurance, fifty-seven of the fifty-eight orthopedic surgeons at University Medical Center in Las Vegas resigned, forcing the state's only trauma center that could treat it all—from car crash, burn and gunshot victims to potential bioterror casualties—to close for ten days.

With Las Vegas a potential target, a quarter-million tourists at the gaming tables and the closest high-level trauma center 300 miles away, the crisis barely registered in the federal government. Nevada's Office of Emergency Management called to inquire about a backup plan, which, as Dr. Fildes later recounted, was to dissolve the county's trauma system, send patients to less prepared hospitals and take the critically injured to Los Angeles or Salt Lake City, both about eighty minutes by helicopter.

During that anxious week Hauer's satellite phone and Fildes's resignation letters formed two bookends of the nation's disaster planning. Hauer—whose Office of the Assistant Secretary for Public Health Emergency Preparedness (ASPHEP) was created by the department Secretary, Tommy Thompson, after the anthrax attacks—can get a last-minute satellite phone, a crack staff and even the ear of President Bush on public health concerns.

The recent flurry of concern has not begun to address our greatest vulnerability: the decrepit state of our healthcare system.

But Fildes, whose trauma center is the third-busiest in the nation and serves a 10,000-square-mile area, struggles to keep his staff intact and the doors of his center open. And this is in a state with no appointed health director, few mental health facilities, no extra room in its hospitals and the nation's only metropolitan area, Las Vegas, without a public health laboratory within 100 miles. In the event of a public health disaster, like the bioterror attack, Fildes says, "we're prepared to do our best. And I hope our best is good enough."

A Public Health 'Train Wreck'

On taking office, President Bush eliminated the health position from the National Security Council, arguing that health, while in the national interest, was not a national security concern. In the wake of the anthrax attacks last year, he changed his tune, declaring, "We have fought the causes and consequences of disease throughout history and must continue to do so with every available means." Next year's budget for biodefense is up 319 percent, to $5.9 billion. States, newly flush with $1.1 billion in biodefense funds, have gone on shopping sprees for emergency equipment like gas masks, hazmat suits and Geiger counters. Newly drafted to fight the war on bioterror, doctors and public health officials are now deemed vital to national security, and their hospitals are even under threat, according to an alert released in mid-November by the FBI.

And yet this flurry of interest and concern has not begun to address America's greatest public health vulnerability: the decrepit and deteriorating state of our healthcare system. In states from Nevada to Georgia, dozens of health officials and doctors told *The Nation* that anemic state funding, overcrowding and staff shortages may be greater problems in responding to bioterror than lack of equipment or specific training. "We don't have enough ER capacity in this country to get through tonight's 911 calls," said Dr. Arthur Kellerman, chairman of the emergency medicine department at the Emory University School of Medicine in Atlanta. Two decades of managed care and government cuts have left a depleted system with too few hospitals, overburdened staff, declining access for patients, rising emergency-room visits and an increasing number of uninsured. The resulting strain is practically Kafkaesque: How do you find enough nurses to staff enough hospital beds to move enough emergency-room patients upstairs so that ambulances with new patients can stop circling the block?

The infusion of cash for bioterror defense without consideration of these fundamental problems is like "building walls in a bog," where they are sure to sink, said Dr. Jeffrey Koplan, the recently departed head of the CDC.

Between 1980 and 2000, the number of hospitals declined by 900 because of declining payments and increased demands for efficiency, according to the American Hospital Association, leaving almost four-fifths of urban hospitals experiencing serious emergency-room overcrowding. Burnout and low pay have left 15 percent of the nation's nursing jobs unfilled, and the staffing shortage has led to a drop in the number of hospital beds by one-fifth; in Boston by one-third, according to the Center for Studying Health System Change in Washington.

Meanwhile, emergency room visits increased by 5 million last year, according to the American College of Emergency Physicians. One in eight urban hospitals diverts or turns away new emergency patients one-fifth of the time because of overcrowding, the American Hospital Association reports. And the costs of health insurance and medical malpractice premiums continue to soar.

In public health, chronic underfunding has closed training programs and depleted expertise. According to a recent CDC report, 78 percent of the nation's public health officials lack advanced training and more than half have no basic health training at all. During the anthrax crisis inexperienced technicians in the New York City public health laboratory failed to turn on an exhaust fan while testing anthrax samples and accidentally contaminated the laboratory.

A government study of rural preparedness this past April found that only 20 percent of the nation's 3,000 local public health departments have a plan in place to respond to bioterror. Thirteen states have had no epidemiologists on payroll, said Dr. Elin Gursky, senior fellow for biodefense and public health programs at the ANSER Institute for Homeland Security. Meanwhile, 18 percent of jobs in the nation's public health labs are open, and the salaries create little hope of filling them. One state posted the starting salary for the director of its public health laboratory program—a PhD position—at $38,500, said Scott Becker, executive director of the Association of Public Health Laboratories. Becker calls the combination of state cuts and workforce shortages a "train wreck."

Amid this crisis, clinicians have a new mandate: to be able to fight a war on two fronts simultaneously. They must care for the normal volume of patients and track the usual infectious diseases while being able to treat mass casualties of a terrorist event. They now have some money for the high-concept disaster, but with many states in dire financial straits, there is less money than ever for the slow-motion meltdown of the healthcare system, in which 41 million Americans lack health insurance. In the event of a smallpox attack, the tendency of the uninsured to delay seeking treatment could be catastrophic.

Hauer hopes that the "dual use" of federal resources could herald a golden age in public health, with tools for tracking anthrax or smallpox being used also to combat West Nile virus or outbreaks from contaminated food. But politicians of all stripes continue to propose beefing up biodefense in isolation from more systemic problems. In October, Al Gore argued in a speech that the problem of the uninsured should take "a back seat" temporarily to the more urgent matter of biodefense. And Bush has proposed shifting key public health and biodefense functions into his proposed Department of Homeland Security, a move likely to weaken daily public health work like disease surveillance and prevention, according to the General Accounting Office. A bipartisan report recently issued by the Council on Foreign Relations warned that America remains dangerously unprepared for a terrorist attack, with its emergency responders untrained and its public health systems depleted.

The solution, say doctors, is to tackle the systemic and not just the boutique problems. "If you have a health system that is chaotic and has no leadership and is not worried about tuberculosis and West Nile and just worried about these rare entities, you'll never be prepared," said Dr. Lewis Goldfrank, director of emergency medicine at Bellevue Hospital Center in New York City. "To be useful, money has to be earmarked for public health generally, so that it will prepare you for terrorism or naturally occurring events."

President Bush strongly resisted federalizing airport security until it became clear as day that private security companies and their minimum-wage workers would continue to let a flow of box cutters, knives and handguns through the metal detectors. Some clinicians now say that the specter of bioterror raises a similar question, which almost nobody in Washington has yet begun to address: Has healthcare become so vital to national security that it must be centralized, with the federal government guaranteeing basic healthcare for everyone?

"Forget about paying for the smallpox vaccine," said Dr. Carlos del Rio, chief of medicine at Atlanta's Grady Memorial Hospital. "Who's going to pay for the complications of the vaccine? With what money? We haven't even addressed that. As you look at bioterror issues, it's forcing us to look at our healthcare delivery."

Crisis Management in Crisis

Hauer spends much of his time in a windowless set of offices within the vast Health and Human Services Department, trouble-shooting the medical consequences of a hypothetical dirty bomb or intentional smallpox outbreak. He must also navigate the knotted bureaucracy of forty federal agencies that respond to terrorism, twenty of which play some role in bioterror response, and guide the states through infrastructure problems so severe they boggle the mind. His tactic at a meeting in Washington this August with state emergency managers was to put the fear of God into them. In the event of mass vaccinations for smallpox, the logistics are "very daunting," he told the small and sleepy group in a conference room at the Mayflower Hotel. "They will fall on emergency management, and the health departments will turn to you and say, 'You need to open 200 vaccination centers.'"

This seemed to focus the group. Before Hauer got up, these local and regional representatives had been talking about lessons learned from managing hurricanes and the best kinds of handheld chemical-weapons detectors.

Tommy Thompson created Hauer's office after the CDC, then his lead agency on bioterror, appeared to bungle the anthrax response and the Administration found itself in a scientific and logistical quagmire. Some officials claimed the White House muzzled the CDC. Others accused the CDC of sloth and bad science for failing to realize quickly that anthrax spores can leak from taped envelopes. Hauer seemed like a good choice to find a way out of this mess: He had developed the nation's first bioterrorism response plan as director of New York City's Office of Emergency Management under Mayor Rudolph Giuliani.

Hauer told the group that his office had moved $1.1 billion to the states in ninety days and was now doing audits, offering technical assistance and helping to stage drills.

But it was the nitty-gritty of mass vaccination that really quieted the room. Training a vaccinator usually takes two hours, though it can be done in fifteen minutes; for every million people vaccinated, about two will die; the vaccinators need to be federally insured because of liability; and all those vaccinated must keep the vaccination site unexposed to others for up to twenty-one days. Who would pay the salaries of contract workers on their days off?

Few emergency managers seemed to have considered such problems. Most were still immersed in competing disaster plans and state budget battles, coping with teetering local health departments and venders hawking "equipment that will detect the landing of Martians ten miles away in a windstorm," as James O'Brien, emergency manager for Clark County, Nevada, put it.

Hauer returned that afternoon to just such a morass: figuring out how to create a unified command for the national capital area, encompassing Maryland, Virginia and the District of Columbia, seventeen jurisdictions over 3,000 square miles, with embassies, consulates, the World Bank and the International Monetary Fund. He had assigned this problem to a team from the Office of Emergency Response (OER), the federal office under ASPHEP that coordinates medical resources during disasters, who arrived at his office to report their progress.

Each state, unsurprisingly, wanted to be the lead responder, and the team recommended that Hauer try to break the logjam and give direction. He poured over the list of those invited to a coordinating committee meeting—twenty-nine people from twenty-nine different agencies—and concluded, "We need to come away with plans, not some loosie-goosie love fest where everyone pats each other on the back and jerks each other off."

The OER team trooped out with its marching orders and the next meeting began. The CEO of the New York Blood Center, Dr. Robert Jones, with a DC consultant in tow, came to ask for money to expand the center's program of making umbilical cord (placental) blood, used for patients exposed to massive radiation. Jones said the center already had about 18,000 units of cord blood stored in "bioarchive freezers" on First Avenue in Manhattan.

"You might want to think about storing it away from Manhattan," said Hauer, suggesting the obvious, as he got out a little booklet and looked up a one-kiloton nuclear bomb. "You'd need 20,000 to 40,000 units" to begin treating a city of people, said Hauer. "What's the lead time for getting it into a patient?"

Jones, who had never met Hauer before, seemed surprised to be taken so seriously and to be crunching numbers about three minutes into the conversation. Hauer, wanting to stockpile cord blood, seemed surprised that Jones had not brought a written proposal with a dollar amount. This was no time to be coy about asking for money.

Suddenly Hauer's secure phone rang and the room fell silent. "This is Jerry Hauer," he said. "You have the wrong number."

Leaving Las Vegas—in the Lurch

In Las Vegas, a gaming town with an appetite for risk, little by way of a medical infrastructure ever developed. With the population exploding and 6,000 families a month moving into the Las Vegas area in Clark County, population 1.4 million, it is also dramatically short on hospitals. By a thumbnail calculation—for every 100,000 people you need 200 beds—the county, which has eleven hospitals, is 600 beds short, said Dr. John Ellerton, chief of staff at University Medical Center, where the trauma center closed.

Even if you build more hospitals, how would you staff them? The state ranks fiftieth in its nurse-to-patient ratio, and because of the malpractice crisis, ninety of the state's 2,000 doctors have closed their practices and another eighty-three said they have considered leaving, according to Lawrence Matheis, executive director of the Nevada State Medical Association. The overcrowded emergency rooms are closed to new patients 40 percent of the time. Paramedics often drive and drive, waiting for an open emergency room. In turn, patients can wait four hours for an X-ray, three for a lab test. "There is no surge capacity, minimal staffing, minimal equipment," said Dr. Donald Kwalick, chief health officer of Clark County. "Every hospital bed in this county is full every day."

> *Last year Nevadans began to lose their cool as the medical system disintegrated. Then came the anthrax crisis.*

At times, the populace and even the doctors have seemed strangely indifferent. One night this summer an ambulance crew from the private company American Medical Response got called to a casino, and as they wheeled a stretcher amid the gaming tables, not a single patron looked up. Their patient: a man with a possible heart attack slumped over a slot machine. "The purity of our devotion to individual liberties tends to diminish our security and humane concern," said Matheis.

The September 11 attacks did not entirely transform this mindset. Since 1998 the city had been included on a federal government list of 120 cities that should prepare for possible attack. Eleven of the world's thirteen largest hotels, one with more than 5,000 rooms, are here. But this August, even the president of the state's medical association, Dr. Robert Schreck, said he worried little about terrorism. Al Qaeda's intent is "to kill capitalism," he said, sipping wine in the lobby of the elaborate Venetian Hotel, home to a massive casino and dozens of stores. "Why would they hit us?"

But last year Nevadans began to lose their cool as the medical system disintegrated. As malpractice insurance premiums skyrocketed, about thirty of Clark County's ninety-three obstetricians closed down their practices. Insurers, trying to reduce risk by limiting the remaining obstetricians to 125 deliveries a year, left thousands of pregnant women to hunt for doctors, some by desperately rifling through the Yellow Pages under "D." This year, the last pediatric cardiac surgery practice packed up and left the state.

Not surprisingly, Nevada was also unprepared for the anthrax crisis. Last October, when Microsoft's Reno office got suspicious powder in the mail that initially tested positive, an "outbreak of hysteria" ensued, said Matheis. The Clark County health district got 1,200 phone calls reporting everything from sugar to chalk dust, and investigated 500 of them with its skeletal staff. The state had no stockpiled antibiotics, and without a lab in Clark County, samples were shipped 500 miles north to Reno for testing.

The new federal money for bioterror preparedness, $10.5 million for Nevada alone, will help enormously. Of that, more than $2 million will go to building a public health laboratory in Las Vegas. But the money will do nothing to solve the problems of staff shortages and soaring medical malpractice premiums that forced the trauma center to close in July.

By July 4, the city of Las Vegas awoke to maximum fear of terror and a minimal medical system, with the trauma center closed for a second day. Governor Kenny Guinn had called an emergency session of the legislature and vowed to make sure that doctors did not abandon the state. An official at the nearby Nellis Air Force Base called the chief of orthopedics, Dr. Anthony Serfustini, asking what to do in the event of injuries. The lanky surgeon said that he reminded the man, You're the Air Force. You can fly your pilots to San Bernardino.

The community's medical infrastructure had declined to a level not seen in twenty-five years, said Dr. Fildes. And on July 4, the inevitable happened. Jim Lawson, 59, a grandfather of nine, was extracted from his mangled car and rushed to a nearby hospital—one with a nervous staff and little up-to-date trauma training—and died about an hour later. His daughter, Mary Rasar, said that she believes the trauma center, had it been open, could have saved him.

Atlanta's Health Emergency

On September 11, 2001, Dr. Arthur Kellerman was in Washington waiting to testify before Congress about the consequences of uninsurance when a plane struck the Pentagon, across the street from his hotel room. He immediately called back to Grady Memorial Hospital in Atlanta, where he oversees the emergency room residents, and got a disturbing report.

While Atlanta appeared to be safe from terrorism, the emergency room had twenty-five admitted patients waiting for hospital beds, the intensive-care area was packed and the staff had shut the emergency room to new patients. Worse, every emergency room in central Atlanta had declared saturation at the same time. None were taking new patients, and loaded ambulances were circling the block. If attacks had occurred in Atlanta that morning, "there was no way on God's earth we could have absorbed more patients," said Kellerman. Since then, all the Atlanta-area hospitals have gone on simultaneous diversion numerous times, leaving "nowhere to put casualties."

Despite all the effort to gear up for biological terror, the problem of overcrowded and understaffed emergency rooms—where terror's victims would be treated—has received only spotty attention. *U.S. News & World Report* featured the problem as a cover story, "Code Blue: Crisis in the E.R.," but it ran on September 10, 2001. A month after the attacks, Representative Henry Waxman prepared a report on ambulance diversions and their effect on disaster preparedness, finding a problem in thirty-two states. In at least nine states, every hospital in a local area had diverted ambulances simultaneously on a number of occasions, causing harm or even death to some patients. In Atlanta, one diverted patient was admitted only after he slipped into respiratory arrest while in the idling ambulance. The report quoted an editorial from the *St. Louis Post-Dispatch* last year:

> A word to the wise: Try not to get sick between 5 p.m. and midnight, when hospitals are most likely to go on diversion. Try not to get sick or injured at all in St. Louis or Kansas City, where diversions are most frequent. And if you're unlucky enough to end up in the back of an ambulance diverted from one E.R. to another, use the extra time to pray.

In Washington, Hauer has directed each region to identify 500 extra beds that can be "surged" or put into use quickly, which has led a number of states to identify armories, school auditoriums, stadiums and hotels that can be used as MASH hospitals. But no bubble tent can replace a hospital bed, with a full complement of services readily available within the "golden hour" so crucial to treating trauma patients, said Kellerman. And no proposal exists to address the problem as a systemic one, in which a shortage of nurses and cutbacks in reimbursement have made it impossible for hospitals to staff enough beds.

Without a solution in sight, Grady Memorial uses a makeshift system, parking admitted patients on stretchers in the hallways beneath handwritten numbers that run from 1 to 30. With the crisis deepening, more numbers—1a, 1b, 1c, for example, seventeen additional spaces in all—have been squeezed between the initial numbers up and down the hall. The other night Kellerman had fifty patients lined up waiting for rooms. "These are not disaster scenarios," he said. "This is Friday night. Wednesday afternoon."

September 11's Hard Lessons

New York City, with sixty-four hospitals, more than any other in the country, was probably the best prepared for a mass-casualty incident. Except that on September 11, most of the victims were dead. Within minutes, the Bellevue emergency room was crowded with hundreds of doctors, each bed with its own team of specialists, from surgeons and psychiatrists to gynecologists. "The entire physician and nursing force of the hospital just came down at once," said Dr. Brian Wexler, a third-year emergency medicine resident. At Long Island College Hospital in Brooklyn, Dr. Lewis Kohl, chairman of emergency medicine, said that by noon, he had a doctor and a nurse for each available bed and could have tripled that number. Doctors from all over the country at a defibrillation conference in downtown Brooklyn were begging to work, "I spent most of the day sending volunteers away," he recalled.

Tragically, so many people died that doctors had little to do. But the people who answered phones, counseled the distraught or drew blood from volunteers were overrun. A web-based patient locator system cobbled together by the Greater New York Hospital Association got 2 million hits within days from frantic relatives. Beth Israel Medical Center ran out of social workers, psychologists and psychiatrists to answer calls. "I answered the phone for half an hour and said, 'I'm not qualified to do this,'" said Lisa Hogarty, vice president of facility management for Continuum Health Partners, which runs Beth Israel.

If anything, New York learned that targeted improvements, such as the creation of regional bioterror treatment centers, will not work. Susan Waltman, senior vice president of the Greater New York Hospital Association, told a CDC advisory committee in June that on September 11, 7,200 people, many covered in debris, wound up at 100 different hospitals, jumping on trains, boats and subways, or walking, to get away from downtown Manhattan. Now imagine if the debris had been tainted with some infectious biological agent. "You can't put the concentration of knowledge or staffing or supplies in regional centers," she said, "because you can't control where patients go."

The anthrax attacks, when they came, were a wake-up call of the worst kind. Baffled government officials with minimal scientific knowledge attributed the outbreak initially to farm visits, then contaminated water and finally to a fine, weaponized anthrax that had been sent through the mail. With no clear chain of communication or command for testing the samples, reporting the results, advising the medical community or informing the public, samples vanished into dozens of laboratories. Conference calls between officials from different local, state and federal agencies were required to track them down, said those involved with the investigation. Testing methods were not standardized, with the Environmental Protection Agency, the postal service, the CDC, the FBI and the Defense Department all swabbing desktops and mailrooms using different methods and different kits, some of which had never been evaluated before. "A lot of those specimens that were said to be positive were not," said

Dr. Philip Brachman, an anthrax expert and professor at the Rollins School of Public Health at Emory University.

For three weeks, from the initial outbreak on October 4, 2001, Americans seeking clear information from the CDC were out of luck. Until October 20, the agency's website still featured diabetes awareness month instead of the anthrax attacks. Dr. David Fleming, the CDC's deputy director for science and public health, said that while the CDC did respond quickly and accurately, "we were too focused on getting the public health job done, and we were not proactive in getting our message out."

But it wasn't just the CDC. Few officials nationwide knew what to do. In New York, police were marching into the city's public health laboratory carrying furniture and computers they suspected of being tainted, recalled Dr. David Perlin, scientific director of the Public Health Research Institute, an advanced microbiology center then located a few floors above the city lab. Since those terrible days, the CDC under new director Dr. Julie Gerberding has made a great effort to establish its leadership and develop emergency response systems. "We have the people, we have the plans and now we have the practice," Gerberding, a microbiologist and veteran of the anthrax investigation, declared this September 11. "We're building our knowledge and capacity every day to assure that CDC and our partners are ready to respond to any terrorist event."

After September 11, however, such confident talk rings a little hollow. This past September the CDC laid out a radical plan for vaccinating much of the country within a week in the event of a smallpox attack. Medical experts greeted the plan as unrealistic and almost impossible to execute, given that disasters inevitably depart from plans to address them. They are pressing for the pre-vaccination of critical healthcare workers, and a decision on this is soon to be announced.

Preparing for the Worst

Past a strip mall outside Washington, and down a nondescript road, the federal OEP keeps a warehouse of equipment that can all but navigate the end of civilization. It has the world's most sophisticated portable morgue units, each one able to support numerous autopsies. Another pile of boxes unfolds to become a full operating theater that can support open-heart surgery, if need be.

All this equipment can function during "catastrophic infrastructure failure," said Gary Moore, deputy director of the agency. And all of it can be loaded onto a C-5 trans-

port plane and flown anywhere in the world. The federal government has massive resources—twelve fifty-ton pallets of drugs called the National Pharmaceutical Stockpile, which can get anywhere in the country in seven to twelve hours. After the New York City laboratory became contaminated, the Defense Department flew in six tons of laboratory equipment and turned a two-person testing operation into ten laboratories with three evidence rooms, a command center and seventy-five lab technicians operating around the clock.

This monumental surge capacity is crucial to preparedness. So are supplies. Dr. Kohl at Long Island College Hospital, who describes himself as a "paranoid of very long standing," feels ready. He's got a padlocked room full of gas masks, Geiger counters and Tyvek suits of varying thicknesses, most purchased after the anthrax attacks. Pulling one off the shelf, he declared confidently, "You could put this on and hang out in a bucket of Sarin."

But none of this can replace the simple stuff: hospital beds, trained people, fax machines, an infrastructure adequate for everyday use. Indeed, as states slash their public health and medical budgets, the opposite may be happening: We are building high-tech defenses on an ever-weakening infrastructure. In Colorado, for example, Governor Bill Owens cut all state funding for local public health departments in part because the federal government was supplying new funds. Public health officials there suddenly have federal money to hire bioterror experts but not enough state money to keep their offices open. While the Larimer County health department got $100,000 in targeted federal money, it lost $700,000 in state funds and fifteen staff positions. A spokesman for Governor Owens did not return calls seeking comment. States across the country are making similar cuts, said Dr. Gursky of the ANSER Institute, their weakened staffs left to prepare for bioterror while everyday health threats continue unchecked.

From her office window, Dr. Ruth Berkelman, director of Emory's Center for Public Health Preparedness, can see the new, $193 million infectious-disease laboratory rising on the CDC's forty-six-acre campus. While the new laboratory and information systems are needed, she says, if we detect smallpox, it's going to be because some doctor in an emergency room gets worried and "picks up the telephone."

Katherine Eban, an investigative journalist who covers medicine and public health for national magazines, lives in Brooklyn. Research support was provided by the Investigative Fund of the Nation Institute.

Nuclear Nightmares

Experts on terrorism and proliferation agree on one thing:
Sooner or later, an attack will happen here. When and how is what robs them of sleep.

By Bill Keller

The panic that would result from contaminating the Magic Kingdom with a modest amount of cesium would probably shut the place down for good and constitute a staggering strike at Americans' sense of innocence.

Not If But When Everybody who spends much time thinking about nuclear terrorism can give you a scenario, something diabolical and, theoretically, doable. Michael A. Levi, a researcher at the Federation of American Scientists, imagines a homemade nuclear explosive device detonated inside a truck passing through one of the tunnels into Manhattan. The blast would crater portions of the New York skyline, barbecue thousands of people instantly, condemn thousands more to a horrible death from radiation sickness and—by virtue of being underground—would vaporize many tons of concrete and dirt and river water into an enduring cloud of lethal fall-

out. Vladimir Shikalov, a Russian nuclear physicist who helped clean up after the 1986 Chernobyl accident, envisioned for me an attack involving highly radioactive cesium-137 loaded into some kind of homemade spraying device, and a target that sounded particularly unsettling when proposed across a Moscow kitchen table—Disneyland. In this case, the human toll would be much less ghastly, but the panic that would result from contaminating the Magic Kingdom with a modest amount of cesium—Shikalov held up his teacup to illustrate how much—would probably shut the place down for good and constitute a staggering strike at Americans' sense of innocence. Shikalov, a nuclear enthusiast who thinks most people are ridiculously squeamish about radiation, added that personally he would still be happy to visit Disneyland after the terrorists struck, although he would pack his own food and drink and destroy his clothing afterward.

Another Russian, Dmitry Borisov, a former official of his country's atomic energy ministry, conjured a suicidal pilot. (Suicidal pilots, for obvious reasons, figure frequently in these fantasies.) In Borisov's scenario, the hijacker dive-bombs an Aeroflot jetliner into the Kurchatov

Institute, an atomic research center in a gentrifying neighborhood of Moscow, which I had just visited the day before our conversation. The facility contains 26 nuclear reactors of various sizes and a huge accumulation of radioactive material. The effect would probably be measured more in property values than in body bags, but some people say the same about Chernobyl. Maybe it is a way to tame a fearsome subject by Hollywoodizing it, or maybe it is a way to drive home the dreadful stakes in the arid-sounding business of nonproliferation, but in several weeks of talking to specialists here and in Russia about the threats an amateur evildoer might pose to the homeland, I found an unnerving abundance of such morbid creativity. I heard a physicist wonder whether a suicide bomber with a pacemaker would constitute an effective radiation weapon. (I'm a little ashamed to say I checked that one, and the answer is no, since pacemakers powered by plutonium have not been implanted for the past 20 years.) I have had people theorize about whether hijackers who took over a nuclear research laboratory could improvise an actual nuclear explosion on the spot. (Expert opinions differ, but it's very unlikely.) I've been instructed how to disperse plutonium into the ventilation system of an office building.

The realistic threats settle into two broad categories. The less likely but far more devastating is an actual nuclear explosion, a great hole blown in the heart of New York or Washington, followed by a toxic fog of radiation. This could be produced by a black-market nuclear warhead procured from an existing arsenal. Russia is the favorite hypothetical source, although Pakistan, which has a program built on shady middlemen and covert operations, should not be overlooked. Or the explosive could be a homemade device, lower in yield than a factory nuke but still creating great carnage.

The second category is a radiological attack, contaminating a public place with radioactive material by packing it with conventional explosives in a "dirty bomb" by dispersing it into the air or water or by sabotaging a nuclear facility. By comparison with the task of creating nuclear fission, some of these schemes would be almost childishly simple, although the consequences would be less horrifying: a panicky evacuation, a gradual increase in cancer rates, a staggeringly expensive cleanup, possibly the need to demolish whole neighborhoods. Al Qaeda has claimed to have access to dirty bombs, which is unverified but entirely plausible, given that the makings are easily gettable.

Nothing is really new about these perils. The means to inflict nuclear harm on America have been available to rogues for a long time. Serious studies of the threat of nuclear terror date back to the 1970's. American programs to keep Russian nuclear ingredients from falling into murderous hands—one of the subjects high on the agenda in President Bush's meetings in Moscow this weekend—were hatched soon after the Soviet Union disintegrated a decade ago. When terrorists get around to trying their first nuclear assault, as you can be sure they will, there will be plenty of people entitled to say I told you so.

All Sept. 11 did was turn a theoretical possibility into a felt danger. All it did was supply a credible cast of characters who hate us so much they would thrill to the prospect of actually doing it—and, most important in rethinking the probabilities, would be happy to die in the effort. All it did was give our nightmares legs.

Tom Ridge cupped his hands prayerfully and pressed his fingertips to his lips. "Nuclear," he said simply.

And of the many nightmares animated by the attacks, this is the one with pride of place in our experience and literature—and, we know from his own lips, in Osama bin Laden's aspirations. In February, Tom Ridge, the Bush administration's homeland security chief, visited The Times for a conversation, and at the end someone asked, given all the things he had to worry about—hijacked airliners, anthrax in the mail, smallpox, germs in crop-dusters—what did he worry about most? He cupped his hands prayerfully and pressed his fingertips to his lips. "Nuclear," he said simply.

My assignment here was to stare at that fear and inventory the possibilities. How afraid should we be, and what of, exactly? I'll tell you at the outset, this was not one of those exercises in which weighing the fears and assigning them probabilities laid them to rest. I'm not evacuating Manhattan, but neither am I sleeping quite as soundly. As I was writing this early one Saturday in April, the floor began to rumble and my desk lamp wobbled precariously. Although I grew up on the San Andreas Fault, the fact that New York was experiencing an earthquake was only my second thought.

The best reason for thinking it won't happen is that it hasn't happened yet, and that is terrible logic. The problem is not so much that we are not doing enough to prevent a terrorist from turning our atomic knowledge against us (although we are not). The problem is that there may be no such thing as "enough."

25,000 Warheads, and It Only Takes One My few actual encounters with the Russian nuclear arsenal are all associated with Thomas Cochran. Cochran, a physicist with a Tennessee lilt and a sense of showmanship, is the director of nuclear issues for the Natural Resources Defense Council, which promotes environmental protection and arms control. In 1989, when glasnost was in flower, Cochran persuaded the Soviet Union to open some of its most secret nuclear venues to a road-show of American scientists and congressmen and invited along a couple of reporters. We visited a Soviet missile cruiser bobbing in the Black Sea and drank vodka with physicists and engineers in the secret city where the Soviets first produced plutonium for weapons.

Not long ago Cochran took me cruising through the Russian nuclear stockpile again, this time digitally. The days of glasnost theatrics are past, and this is now the only way an outsider can get close to the places where Russians store and deploy their nuclear weapons. On his office computer in Washington, Cochran has installed a detailed United States military map of Russia and superimposed upon it high-resolution satellite photographs. We spent part of a morning mouse-clicking from missile-launch site to submarine base, zooming in like voyeurs and contemplating the possibility that a terrorist could figure out how to steal a nuclear warhead from one of these places.

"Here are the bunkers," Cochran said, enlarging an area the size of a football stadium holding a half-dozen elongated igloos. We were hovering over a site called Zhukovka, in western Russia. We were pleased to see it did not look ripe for a hijacking.

"You see the bunkers are fenced, and then the whole thing is fenced again," Cochran said. "Just outside you can see barracks and a rifle range for the guards. These would be troops of the 12th Main Directorate. Somebody's not going to walk off the street and get a Russian weapon out of this particular storage area."

In the popular culture, nuclear terror begins with the theft of a nuclear weapon. Why build one when so many are lying around for the taking? And stealing tends to make better drama than engineering. Thus the stolen nuke has been a staple in the literature at least since 1961, when Ian Fleming published "Thunderball," in which the malevolent Spectre (the Special Executive for Counterintelligence, Terrorism, Revenge and Extortion, a strictly mercenary and more technologically sophisticated precursor to al Qaeda) pilfers a pair of atom bombs from a crashed NATO aircraft. In the movie version of Tom Clancy's thriller "The Sum of All Fears," due in theaters this week, neo-Nazis get their hands on a mislaid Israeli nuke, and viewers will get to see Baltimore blasted to oblivion.

Eight countries are known to have nuclear weapons—the United States, Russia, China, Great Britain, France, India, Pakistan and Israel. David Albright, a nuclear-weapons expert and president of the Institute for Science and International Security, points out that Pakistan's program in particular was built almost entirely through black markets and industrial espionage, aimed at circumventing Western export controls. Defeating the discipline of nuclear nonproliferation is ingrained in the culture. Disaffected individuals in Pakistan (which, remember, was intimate with the Taliban) would have no trouble finding the illicit channels or the rationalization for diverting materials, expertise—even, conceivably, a warhead.

But the mall of horrors is Russia, because it currently maintains something like 15,000 of the world's (very roughly) 25,000 nuclear warheads, ranging in destructive power from about 500 kilotons, which could kill a million people, down to the one-kiloton land mines that would be enough to make much of Manhattan uninhabitable. Russia is a country with sloppy accounting, a disgruntled military, an audacious black market and indigenous terrorists.

It's easier to take the fuel and build an entire weapon from scratch than it is to make one of these things go off.

There is anecdotal reason to worry. Gen. Igor Valynkin, commander of the 12th Main Directorate of the Russian Ministry of Defense, the Russian military sector in charge of all nuclear weapons outside the Navy, said recently that twice in the past year terrorist groups were caught casing Russian weapons-storage facilities. But it's hard to know how seriously to take this. When I made the rounds of nuclear experts in Russia earlier this year, many were skeptical of these near-miss anecdotes, saying the security forces tend to exaggerate such incidents to dramatize their own prowess (the culprits are always caught) and enhance their budgets. On the whole, Russian and American military experts sound not very alarmed about the vulnerability of Russia's nuclear warheads. They say Russia takes these weapons quite seriously, accounts for them rigorously and guards them carefully. There is no confirmed case of a warhead being lost. Strategic warheads, including the 4,000 or so that President Bush and President Vladimir Putin have agreed to retire from service, tend to be stored in hard-to-reach places, fenced and heavily guarded, and their whereabouts are not advertised. The people who guard them are better paid and more closely vetted than most Russian soldiers.

Eugene E. Habiger, the four-star general who was in charge of American strategic weapons until 1998 and then ran nuclear antiterror programs for the Energy Department, visited several Russian weapons facilities in 1996 and 1997. He may be the only American who has actually entered a Russian bunker and inspected a warhead in situ. Habiger said he found the overall level of security comparable to American sites, although the Russians depend more on people than on technology to protect their nukes.

The image of armed terrorist commandos storming a nuclear bunker is cinematic, but it's far more plausible to think of an inside job. No observer of the unraveling Russian military has much trouble imagining that a group of military officers, disenchanted by the humiliation of serving a spent superpower, embittered by the wretched conditions in which they spend much of their military lives or merely greedy, might find a way to divert a warhead to a terrorist for the right price. (The Chechen warlord Shamil Basayev, infamous for such ruthless exploits as taking an entire hospital hostage, once hinted that he had an opportunity to buy a nuclear warhead from the stockpile.) The anecdotal evidence of desperation in the military is plentiful and disquieting. Every year the Russian press provides stories like that of the 19-year-old sailor who went on a rampage aboard an Akula-class nuclear submarine, killing eight people and threatening to blow up the boat and its nuclear reactor; or the five soldiers at Russia's nuclear-weapons test site who killed a guard, took a hostage and tried to hijack an aircraft, or the officers who reportedly stole five assault helicopters, with their weapons pods, and tried to sell them to North Korea.

The Clinton administration found the danger of disgruntled nuclear caretakers worrisome enough that it considered building better housing for some officers in the nuclear rocket corps. Congress, noting that the United States does not build housing for its own officers, rejected the idea out of hand.

If a terrorist did get his hands on a nuclear warhead, he would still face the problem of setting it off. American warheads are rigged with multiple PAL's ("permissive action links")—codes and self-disabling devices designed to frustrate an unauthorized person from triggering the explosion. General Habiger says that when he examined Russian strategic weapons he found the level of protection comparable to our own. "You'd have to literally break the weapon apart to get into the gut," he told me. "I would submit that a more likely scenario is that there'd be an attempt to get hold of a warhead and not explode the warhead but extract the plutonium or highly enriched uranium." In other words, it's easier to take the fuel and build an entire weapon from scratch than it is to make one of these things go off.

Then again, Habiger is not an expert in physics or weapons design. Then again, the Russians would seem to have no obvious reason for misleading him about something that important. Then again, how many times have computer hackers hacked their way into encrypted computers we were assured were impregnable? Then again, how many computer hackers does al Qaeda have? This subject drives you in circles.

The most troublesome gap in the generally reassuring assessment of Russian weapons security is those tactical nuclear warheads—smaller, short-range weapons like torpedoes, depth charges, artillery shells, mines. Although their smaller size and greater number makes them ideal candidates for theft, they have gotten far less attention simply because, unlike all of our long-range weapons, they happen not to be the subject of any formal treaty. The first President Bush reached an informal understanding with President Gorbachev and then with President Yeltsin that both sides would gather and destroy thousands of tactical nukes. But the agreement included no inventories of the stockpiles, no outside monitoring, no verification of any kind. It was one of those trust-me deals that, in the hindsight of Sept. 11, amount to an enormous black hole in our security.

Did I say earlier there are about 15,000 Russian warheads? That number includes, alongside the scrupulously counted strategic warheads in bombers, missiles and submarines, the commonly used estimate of 8,000 tactical warheads. But that figure is at best an educated guess. Other educated guesses of the tactical nukes in Russia go as low as 4,000 and as high as 30,000. We just don't know. We don't even know if the Russians know, since they are famous for doing things off the books. "They'll tell you they've never lost a weapon," said Kenneth Luongo, director of a private antiproliferation group called the Russian-American Nuclear Security Advisory Council. "The fact is, they don't know. And when you're talking about warhead counting, you don't want to miss even one."

And where are they? Some are stored in reinforced concrete bunkers like the one at Zhukovka. Others are deployed. (When the submarine Kursk sank with its 118 crewmen in August 2000, the Americans' immediate fear was for its nuclear armaments. The standard load out for a submarine of that class includes a couple of nuclear torpedoes and possibly some nuclear depth charges.) Still others are supposed to be in the process of being dismantled under terms of various formal and informal arms-control agreements. Some are in transit. In short, we don't really know.

The other worrying thing about tactical nukes is that their anti-use devices are believed to be less sophisticated, because the weapons were designed to be employed in the battlefield. Some of the older systems are thought to have no permissive action links at all, so that setting one off would be about as complicated as hot-wiring a car.

Efforts to learn more about the state of tactical stockpiles have been frustrated by reluctance on both sides to let visitors in. Viktor Mikhailov, who ran the Russian Ministry of Atomic Energy until 1998 with a famous scorn for America's nonproliferation concerns, still insists that the United States programs to protect Russian nuclear weapons and material mask a secret agenda of intelligence-gathering. Americans, in turn, sometimes balk at reciprocal access, on the grounds that we are the ones paying the bills for all these safety upgrades, said the former Senator Sam Nunn, co-author of the main American program for securing Russian nukes, called Nunn-Lugar.

People in the field talk of a nuclear 'conex' bomb, using the name of those shack-size steel containers—2,000 of which enter America every hour on trains, trucks and ships. Fewer than 2 percent are cracked open for inspection.

"We have to decide if we want the Russians to be transparent—I'd call it cradle-to-grave transparency with nuclear material and inventories and so forth," Nunn told me. "Then we have to open up more ourselves. This is a big psychological breakthrough we're talking about here, both for them and for us."

The Garage Bomb One of the more interesting facts about the atom bomb dropped on Hiroshima is that it had never been tested. All of those spectral images of nuclear coronas brightening the desert of New Mexico— those were to perfect the more complicated plutonium device that was dropped on Nagasaki. "Little Boy," the Hiroshima bomb, was a rudimentary gunlike device that shot one projectile of highly enriched uranium into another, creating a critical mass that exploded. The mechanics were so simple that few doubted it would work, so the first experiment was in the sky over Japan.

The closest thing to a consensus I heard among those who study nuclear terror was this: building a nuclear bomb is easier than you think, probably easier than stealing one. In the rejuvenated effort to prevent a terrorist from striking a nuclear blow, this is where most of the attention and money are focused.

A nuclear explosion of any kind "is not a sort of high-probability thing," said a White House official who follows the subject closely. "But getting your hands on enough fissile material to build an improvised nuclear device, to my mind, is the least improbable of them all, and particularly if that material is highly enriched uranium in metallic form. Then I'm really worried. That's the one."

To build a nuclear explosive you need material capable of explosive nuclear fission, you need expertise, you need some equipment, and you need a way to deliver it.

Delivering it to the target is, by most reckoning, the simplest part. People in the field generally scoff at the mythologized suitcase bomb; instead they talk of a "conex bomb," using the name of those shack-size steel containers that bring most cargo into the United States. Two thousand containers enter America every hour, on trucks and trains and especially on ships sailing into more than 300 American ports. Fewer than 2 percent are cracked open for inspection, and the great majority never pass through an X-ray machine. Containers delivered to upriver ports like St. Louis or Chicago pass many miles of potential targets before they even reach customs.

"How do you protect against that?" mused Habiger, the former chief of our nuclear arsenal. "You can't. That's scary. That's very, very scary. You set one of those off in Philadelphia, in New York City, San Francisco, Los Angeles, and you're going to kill tens of thousands of

people, if not more." Habiger's view is "It's not a matter of *if*; it's a matter of *when*"—which may explain why he now lives in San Antonio.

The Homeland Security office has installed a plan to refocus inspections, making sure the 2 percent of containers that get inspected are those without a clear, verified itinerary. Detectors will be put into place at ports and other checkpoints. This is good, but it hardly represents an ironclad defense. The detection devices are a long way from being reliable. (Inconveniently, the most feared bomb component, uranium, is one of the hardest radioactive substances to detect because it does not emit a lot of radiation prior to fission.) The best way to stop nuclear terror, therefore, is to keep the weapons out of terrorist hands in the first place.

Fabricating a nuclear weapon is not something a lone madman—even a lone genius—is likely to pull off in his hobby room.

The basic know-how of atom-bomb-building is half a century old, and adequate recipes have cropped up in physics term papers and high school science projects. The simplest design entails taking a lump of highly enriched uranium, about the size of a cantaloupe, and firing it down a big gun barrel into a second lump. Theodore Taylor, the nuclear physicist who designed both the smallest and the largest American nuclear-fission warheads before becoming a remorseful opponent of all things nuclear, told me he recently looked up "atomic bomb" in the World Book Encyclopedia in the upstate New York nursing home where he now lives, and he found enough basic information to get a careful reader started. "It's accessible all over the place," he said. "I don't

mean just the basic principles. The sizes, specifications, things that work."

Most of the people who talk about the ease of assembling a nuclear weapon, of course, have never actually built one. The most authoritative assessment I found was a paper, "Can Terrorists Build Nuclear Weapons?" written in 1986 by five experienced nuke-makers from the Los Alamos weapons laboratory. I was relieved to learn that fabricating a nuclear weapon is not something a lone madman—even a lone genius—is likely to pull off in his hobby room. The paper explained that it would require a team with knowledge of "the physical, chemical and metallurgical properties of the various materials to be used, as well as characteristics affecting their fabrication; neutronic properties; radiation effects, both nuclear and biological; technology concerning high explosives and/or chemical propellants; some hydrodynamics; electrical circuitry; and others." Many of these skills are more difficult to acquire than, say, the ability to aim a jumbo jet.

The schemers would also need specialized equipment to form the uranium, which is usually in powdered form, into metal, to cast it and machine it to fit the device. That effort would entail months of preparation, increasing the risk of detection, and it would require elaborate safeguards to prevent a mishap that, as the paper dryly put it, would "bring the operation to a close."

Still, the experts concluded, the answer to the question posed in the title, while qualified, was "Yes, they can."

David Albright, who worked as a United Nations weapons inspector in Iraq, says Saddam Hussein's unsuccessful crash program to build a nuclear weapon in 1990 illustrates how a single bad decision can mean a huge setback. Iraq had extracted highly enriched uranium from research-reactor fuel and had, maybe, barely enough for a bomb. But the manager in charge of casting the metal was so afraid the stuff would spill or get contaminated that he decided to melt it in tiny batches. As a result, so much of the uranium was wasted that he ended up with too little for a bomb.

"You need good managers and organizational people to put the elements together," Albright said. "If you do a straight-line extrapolation, terrorists will all get nuclear weapons. But they make mistakes."

On the other hand, many experts underestimate the prospect of a do-it-yourself bomb because they are thinking too professionally. All of our experience with these weapons is that the people who make them (states, in other words) want them to be safe, reliable, predictable and efficient. Weapons for the American arsenal are designed to survive a trip around the globe in a missile, to be accident-proof, to produce a precisely specified blast.

But there are many corners you can cut if you are content with a big, ugly, inefficient device that would make a spectacular impression. If your bomb doesn't need to fit in a suitcase (and why should it?) or to endure the stress of a missile launch; if you don't care whether the explosive power realizes its full potential; if you're willing to accept some risk that the thing might go off at the wrong time or might not go off at all, then the job of building it is immeasurably simplified.

"As you get smarter, you realize you can get by with less," Albright said. "You can do it in facilities that look like barns, garages, with simple machine tools. You can do it with 10 to 15 people, not all Ph.D.'s, but some engineers, technicians. Our judgment is that a gun-type device is well within the capability of a terrorist organization."

All the technological challenges are greatly simplified if terrorists are in league with a country—a place with an infrastructure. A state is much better suited to hire expertise (like dispirited scientists from decommissioned nuclear installations

in the old Soviet Union) or to send its own scientists for M.I.T. degrees.

Thus Tom Cochran said his greatest fear is what you might call a bespoke nuke—terrorists stealing a quantity of weapons-grade uranium and taking it to Iraq or Iran or Libya, letting the scientists and engineers there fashion it into an elementary weapon and then taking it away for a delivery that would have no return address.

That leaves one big obstacle to the terrorist nuke-maker: the fissile material itself.

To be reasonably sure of a nuclear explosion, allowing for some material being lost in the manufacturing process, you need roughly 50 kilograms—110 pounds—of highly enriched uranium. (For a weapon, more than 90 percent of the material should consist of the very unstable uranium-235 isotope.) Tom Cochran, the master of visual aids, has 15 pounds of depleted uranium that he keeps in a Coke can; an eight-pack would be plenty to build a bomb.

Only 41 percent of Russia's weapon-usable material has been secured... So the barn door is still pretty seriously ajar. We don't know whether any horses have gotten out.

The world is awash in the stuff. Frank von Hippel, a Princeton physicist and arms-control advocate, has calculated that between 1,300 and 2,100 metric tons of weapons-grade uranium exists—at the low end, enough for 26,000 rough-hewed bombs. The largest stockpile is in Russia, which Senator Joseph Biden calls "the candy store of candy stores."

Until a decade ago, Russian officials say, no one worried much about the safety of this material. Vik-

tor Mikhailov, who ran the atomic energy ministry and now presides over an affiliated research institute, concedes there were glaring lapses.

"The safety of nuclear materials was always on our minds, but the focus was on intruders," he said. "The system had never taken account of the possibility that these carefully screened people in the nuclear sphere could themselves represent a danger. The system was not designed to prevent a danger from within."

Then came the collapse of the Soviet Union and, in the early 90's, a few frightening cases of nuclear materials popping up on the black market.

If you add up all the reported attempts to sell highly enriched uranium or plutonium, even including those that have the scent of security-agency hype and those where the material was of uncertain quality, the total amount of material still falls short of what a bomb-maker would need to construct a single explosive.

But Yuri G. Volodin, the chief of safeguards at Gosatomnadzor, the Russian nuclear regulatory agency, told me his inspectors still discover one or two instances of attempted theft a year, along with dozens of violations of the regulations for storing and securing nuclear material. And as he readily concedes: "These are the detected cases. We can't talk about the cases we don't know." Alexander Pikayev, a former aide to the Defense Committee of the Russian Duma, said: "The vast majority of installations now have fences. But you know Russians. If you walk along the perimeter, you can see a hole in the fence, because the employees want to come and go freely."

The bulk of American investment in nuclear safety goes to lock the stuff up at the source. That is clearly the right priority. Other programs are devoted to blending down the highly enriched uranium to a diluted product unsuitable for weapons but good as reactor fuel. The Nuclear Threat Initiative, financed by Ted Turner and led by Nunn, is studying ways to double the rate of this diluting process.

Still, after 10 years of American subsidies, only 41 percent of Russia's weapon-usable material has been secured, according to the United States Department of Energy. Russian officials said they can't even be sure how much exists, in part because the managers of nuclear facilities, like everyone else in the Soviet industrial complex, learned to cook their books. So the barn door is still pretty seriously ajar. We don't know whether any horses have gotten out.

And it is not the only barn. William C. Potter, director of the Center for Nonproliferation Studies at the Monterey Institute of International Studies and an expert in nuclear security in the former Soviet states, said the American focus on Russia has neglected other locations that could be tempting targets for a terrorist seeking bomb-making material. There is, for example, a bomb's worth of weapons-grade uranium at a site in Belarus, a country with an erratic president and an anti-American orientation. There is enough weapons-grade uranium for a bomb or two in Kharkiv, in Ukraine. Outside of Belgrade, in a research reactor at Vinca, sits sufficient material for a bomb—and there it sat while NATO was bombarding the area.

"We need to avoid the notion that because the most material is in Russia, that's where we should direct all of our effort," Potter said. "It's like assuming the bank robber will target Fort Knox because that's where the most gold is. The bank robber goes where the gold is most accessible."

Weapons of Mass Disruption The first and, so far, only consummated act of nuclear terrorism took place in Moscow in 1995, and it was scarcely memorable. Chechen rebels obtained a canister of cesium, possibly from a hospital they had commandeered a few months before. They hid it in a Moscow park famed for its weekend flea market and called the press. No one was hurt. Authorities treated the incident discreetly, and a surge of panic quickly passed.

The story came up in virtually every conversation I had in Russia about nuclear terror, usually to illustrate that even without splitting atoms and making mushroom clouds a terrorist could use radioactivity—and the fear of it—as a potent weapon.

The idea that you could make a fantastic weapon out of radioactive material without actually producing a nuclear bang has been around since the infancy of nuclear weaponry. During World War II, American scientists in the Manhattan Project worried that the Germans would rain radioactive material on our troops storming the beaches on D-Day. Robert S. Norris, the biographer of the Manhattan Project director, Gen. Leslie R. Groves, told me that the United States took this threat seriously enough to outfit some of the D-Day soldiers with Geiger counters.

No country today includes radiological weapons in its armories. But radiation's limitations as a military tool—its tendency to drift afield with unplanned consequences, its long-term rather than short-term lethality—would not necessarily count against it in the mind of a terrorist. If your aim is to instill fear, radiation is anthrax-plus. And unlike the fabrication of a nuclear explosive, this is terror within the means of a soloist.

If your aim is to instill fear, radiation is anthrax-plus. And unlike the fabrication of a nuclear explosive, this is terror within the means of a soloist.

That is why, if you polled the universe of people paid to worry about weapons of mass destruction (W.M.D., in the jargon), you would find a general agreement that this is probably the first thing we'll see. "If there is a W.M.D. attack in the next year, it's likely to be a radiological attack," said Rose Gottemoeller, who handled Russian nuclear safety in the Clinton administration and now follows the subject for the Carnegie Endowment. The radioactive heart of a dirty bomb could be spent fuel from a nuclear reactor or isotopes separated out in the process of refining nuclear fuel. These materials are many times more abundant and much, much less protected than the high-grade stuff suitable for bombs. Since Sept.11, Russian officials have begun lobbying hard to expand the program of American aid to include protection of these lower-grade materials, and the Bush administration has earmarked a few million dollars to study the problem. But the fact is that radioactive material suitable for terrorist attacks is so widely available that there is little hope of controlling it all.

The guts of a dirty bomb could be cobalt-60, which is readily available in hospitals for use in radiation therapy and in food processing to kill the bacteria in fruits and vegetables. It could be cesium-137, commonly used in medical gauges and radio-therapy machines. It could be americium, an isotope that behaves a lot like plutonium and is used in smoke detectors and in oil prospecting. It could be plutonium, which exists in many research laboratories in America. If you trust the security of those American labs, pause and reflect that the investigation into the great anthrax scare seems to be focused on disaffected American scientists.

Back in 1974, Theodore Taylor and Mason Willrich, in a book on the dangers of nuclear theft, examined things a terrorist might do if he got his hands on 100 grams of plutonium—a thimble-size amount. They calculated that a killer who dissolved it, made an aerosol and introduced it into the ventilation system of an office building could deliver a lethal dose to the entire floor area of a large skyscraper. But plutonium dispersed outdoors in the open air, they estimated, would be far less effective. It would blow away in a gentle wind.

The Federation of American Scientists recently mapped out for a Congressional hearing the consequences of various homemade dirty bombs detonated in New York or Washington. For example, a bomb made with a single footlong pencil of cobalt from a food irradiation plant and just 10 pounds of TNT and detonated at Union Square in a light wind would send a plume of radiation drifting across three states. Much of Manhattan would be as contaminated as the permanently closed area around the Chernobyl nuclear plant. Anyone living in Manhattan would have at least a 1-in-100 chance of dying from cancer caused by the radiation. An area reaching deep into the Hudson Valley would, under current Environmental Protection Agency standards, have to be decontaminated or destroyed.

Frank von Hippel, the Princeton physicist, has reviewed the data, and he pointed out that this is a bit less alarming than it sounds. "Your probability of dying of cancer in your lifetime is already about 20 percent," he said. "This would increase it to 20.1 percent. Would you abandon a city for that? I doubt it."

Indeed, some large portion of our fear of radiation is irrational. And yet the fact that it's all in your mind is little consolation if it's also in the minds of a large, panicky population. If the actual effect of a radiation bomb is that people clog the bridges out of town, swarm the hospitals and refuse to return to live and work in a contaminated place, then the impact is a good deal more than psychological. To this day, there is bitter debate about the actual health toll from the Chernobyl nuclear accident. There are researchers who claim that the people who evacuated are actually in worse health over all from the trauma of relocation, than those who stayed put and marinated in the residual radiation. But the fact is, large swaths of developed land around the Chernobyl site still lie abandoned,

much of it bulldozed down to the subsoil. The Hart Senate Office Building was closed for three months by what was, in hindsight, our society's inclination to err on the side of alarm.

There are measures the government can take to diminish the dangers of a radiological weapon, and many of them are getting more serious consideration. The Bush administration has taken a lively new interest in radiation-detection devices that might catch dirty-bomb materials in transit. A White House official told me the administration's judgment is that protecting the raw materials of radiological terror is worth doing, but not at the expense of more catastrophic threats.

"It's all over," he said. "It's not a winning proposition to say you can just lock all that up. And then, a bomb is pretty darn easy to make. You don't have to be a rocket scientist to figure about fertilizer and diesel fuel." A big fertilizer bomb of the type Timothy McVeigh used to kill 168 people in Oklahoma City, spiced with a dose of cobalt or cesium, would not tax the skills of a determined terrorist.

"It's likely to happen, I think, in our lifetime," the official said. "And it'll be like Oklahoma City plus the Hart Office Building. Which is real bad, but it ain't the World Trade Center."

The Peril of Power Plants Every eight years or so the security guards at each of the country's 103 nuclear power stations and at national weapons labs can expect to be attacked by federal agents armed with laser-tag rifles. These mock terror exercises are played according to elaborate rules, called the "design basis threat," that in the view of skeptics favor the defense. The attack teams can include no more than three commandos. The largest vehicle they are permitted is an S.U.V. They are allowed to have an accomplice inside the plant, but only one. They are not allowed to improvise. (The mock assailants at one Department of Energy

lab were ruled out of order because they commandeered a wheelbarrow to cart off a load of dummy plutonium.) The mock attacks are actually announced in advance. Even playing by these rules, the attackers manage with some regularity to penetrate to the heart of a nuclear plant and damage the core. Representative Edward J. Markey, a Massachusetts Democrat and something of a scourge of the nuclear power industry, has recently identified a number of shortcomings in the safeguards, including, apparently, lax standards for clearing workers hired at power plants.

One of the most glaring lapses, which nuclear regulators concede and have promised to fix, is that the design basis threat does not contemplate the possibility of a hijacker commandeering an airplane and diving it into a reactor. In fact, the protections currently in place don't consider the possibility that the terrorist might be willing, even eager, to die in the act. The government assumes the culprits would be caught while trying to get away.

A nuclear power plant is essentially a great inferno of decaying radioactive material, kept under control by coolant. Turning this device into a terrorist weapon would require cutting off the coolant so the atomic furnace rages out of control and, equally important, getting the radioactive matter to disperse by an explosion or fire. (At Three Mile Island, the coolant was cut off and the reactor core melted down, generating vast quantities of radiation. But the thick walls of the containment building kept the contaminant from being released, so no one died.)

One way to accomplish both goals might be to fly a large jetliner into the fortified building that holds the reactor. Some experts say a jet engine would stand a good chance of bursting the containment vessel, and the sheer force of the crash might disable the cooling system—rupturing the pipes and cutting off electricity that pumps the water through the core. Before nearby residents had begun to evacuate, you could have a meltdown that would spew a volcano of radioactive isotopes into the air, causing fatal radiation sickness for those exposed to high doses and raising lifetime cancer rates for miles around.

This sort of attack is not as easy, by a long shot, as hitting the World Trade Center. The reactor is a small, low-lying target, often nestled near the conspicuous cooling towers, which could be destroyed without great harm. The reactor is encased in reinforced concrete several feet thick, probably enough, the industry contends, to withstand a crash. The pilot would have to be quite a marksman, and somewhat lucky. A high wind would disperse the fumes before they did great damage.

Invading a plant to produce a meltdown, even given the record of those mock attacks, would be more complicated, because law enforcement from many miles around would be on the place quickly, and because breaching the containment vessel is harder from within. Either invaders or a kamikaze attacker could instead target the more poorly protected cooling ponds, where used plutonium sits, encased in great rods of zirconium alloy. This kind of sabotage would take longer to generate radiation and would be far less lethal.

Discussion of this kind of potential radiological terrorism is colored by passionate disagreements over nuclear power itself. Thus the nuclear industry and its rather tame regulators sometimes sound dismissive about the vulnerability of the plants (although less so since Sept.11), while those who regard nuclear power as inherently evil tend to overstate the risks. It is hard to sort fact from fear-mongering.

Nuclear regulators and the industry grumpily concede that Sept. 11 requires a new estimate of their defenses, and under prodding from Congress they are redrafting the so-called design basis threat, the one plants are required to defend against. A few members of Congress have proposed installing ground-to-air missiles at nuclear plants, which most experts think is a recipe for a disastrous mishap.

"Probably the only way to protect against someone flying an aircraft into a nuclear power plant," said Steve Fetter of the University of Maryland, "is to keep hijackers out of cockpits."

Being Afraid For those who were absorbed by the subject of nuclear terror before it became fashionable, the months since the terror attacks have been, paradoxically, a time of vindication. President Bush, whose first budget cut $100 million from the programs to protect Russian weapons and material (never a popular program among conservative Republicans), has become a convert. The administration has made nuclear terror a priority, and it is getting plenty of goading to keep it one. You can argue with their priorities and their budgets, but it's hard to accuse anyone of indifference. And resistance—from scientists who don't want security measures to impede their access to nuclear research materials, from generals and counterintelligence officials uneasy about having their bunkers inspected, from nuclear regulators who worry about the cost of nuclear power, from conservatives who don't want to subsidize the Russians to do much of anything—has become harder to sustain. Intelligence gathering on nuclear material has been abysmal, but it is now being upgraded; it is a hot topic at meetings between American and foreign intelligence services, and we can expect more numerous and more sophisticated sting operations aimed at disrupting the black market for nuclear materials. Putin, too, has taken notice. Just before leaving to meet Bush in Crawford, Tex., in November, he summoned the head of the atomic energy ministry to the Kremlin on a Saturday to discuss nuclear security. The subject is now on the regular agenda when Bush and Putin talk.

These efforts can reduce the danger but they cannot neutralize the fear, particularly after we have been so vividly reminded of the hostility some of the world feels for us, and of our vulnerability.

Fear is personal. My own—in part, because it's the one I grew up with, the one that made me shiver through the Cuban missile crisis and "On the Beach"—is the horrible magic of nuclear fission. A dirty bomb or an assault on a nuclear power station, ghastly as that would be, feels to me within the range of what we have survived. As the White House official I spoke with said, it's basically Oklahoma City plus the Hart Office Building. A nuclear explosion is in a different realm of fears and would test the country in ways we can scarcely imagine.

A mushroom cloud of irradiated debris would blossom more than two miles into the air. Then highly lethal fallout would begin drifting back to earth, riding the winds into the Bronx or Queens or New Jersey.

As I neared the end of this assignment, I asked Matthew McKinzie, a staff scientist at the Natural Resources Defense Council, to run a computer model of a one-kiloton nuclear explosion in Times Square, half a block from my office, on a nice spring workday. By the standards of serious nuclear weaponry, one kiloton is a junk bomb, hardly worthy of respect, a fifteenth the power of the bomb over Hiroshima.

A couple of days later he e-mailed me the results, which I combined with estimates of office workers and tourist traffic in the area. The blast and searing heat would gut buildings for a block in every direction, incinerating pedestrians and crushing people at their desks. Let's say 20,000 dead in a matter of seconds. Beyond this, to a distance of more than a quarter mile, anyone directly exposed to the fireball would die a gruesome death from radiation sickness within a day—anyone, that is, who survived the third-degree burns. This larger circle would be populated by about a quarter million people on a workday. Half a mile from the explosion, up at Rockefeller Center and down at Macy's, unshielded onlookers would expect a slower death from radiation. A mushroom cloud of irradiated de-bris would blossom more than two miles into the air, and then, 40 minutes later, highly lethal fallout would begin drifting back to earth, showering injured survivors and dooming rescue workers. The poison would ride for 5 or 10 miles on the prevailing winds, deep into the Bronx or Queens or New Jersey.

A terrorist who pulls off even such a small-bore nuclear explosion will take us to a whole different territory of dread from Sept. 11. It is the event that preoccupies those who think about this for a living, a category I seem to have joined.

"I think they're going to try," said the physicist David Albright. "I'm an optimist at heart. I think we can catch them in time. If one goes off, I think we will survive. But we won't be the same. It will affect us in a fundamental way. And not for the better."

Bill Keller is a Times columnist and a senior writer for the magazine.

From the *New York Times* Magazine, May 26, 2002, pp. 22, 24-29, 51, 54-55, 57. © 2002 by Bill Keller. Distributed by The New York Times Special Features. Reprinted by permission.

The Cyber-Terror Threat

Al Qaeda is working on computer-generated attacks, experts warn

By Barton Gellman
Washington Post Staff Writer

Late last fall, Detective Chris Hsiung of the Mountain View, Calif., police department began investigating a suspicious pattern of surveillance against Silicon Valley computers. From the Middle East and South Asia, unknown browsers were exploring the digital systems used to manage Bay Area utilities and government offices. Hsiung, a specialist in high-technology crime, alerted the FBI's San Francisco computer intrusion squad.

Working with experts at the Lawrence Livermore National Laboratory, the FBI traced trails of a broader reconnaissance. A forensic summary of the investigation, prepared in the Defense Department, said the bureau found "multiple casings of sites" nationwide. Routed through telecommunications switches in Saudi Arabia, Indonesia and Pakistan, the visitors studied emergency telephone systems, electrical generation and transmission, water storage and distribution, nuclear power plants and gas facilities.

Some of the problems suggested planning for a conventional attack, U.S. officials say. But others homed in on a class of digital devices that allow remote control of services such as fire dispatch and of equipment such as pipelines. More information about those devices—and how to program them—turned up on al Qaeda computers seized this year, according to law enforcement and national security officials.

Unsettling signs of al Qaeda's aims and skills in cyberspace have led some government experts to conclude that terrorists are at the threshold of using the Internet as a direct instrument of bloodshed. The new threat bears little resemblance to familiar financial disruptions by hackers responsible for viruses and worms. It comes instead at the meeting points of computers and the physical structures they control.

U.S. analysts believe that by disabling or taking command of the floodgates in a dam, for example, or of substations handling 300,000 volts of electric power, an intruder could use virtual tools to destroy real-world lives and property. They surmise, with limited evidence, that al Qaeda aims to employ those techniques in synchrony with "kinetic weapons" such as explosives.

"The event I fear most is a physical attack in conjunction with a successful cyber-attack on the responders' 911 system or on the power grid," Ronald Dick, director of the FBI's National Infrastructure Protection Center, told a closed gathering of corporate security executives hosted by Infraguard in Niagara Falls on June 12.

In an interview, Dick said those additions to a conventional al Qaeda attack might mean that "the first responders couldn't get there... and water didn't flow, hospitals didn't have power. Is that an unreasonable scenario? Not in this world. And that keeps me awake at night."

Regarded until recently as remote, the risks of cyberterrorism now command urgent White House attention. Discovery of one acute vulnerability—in a data transmission standard known as ASN.1, short for Abstract Syntax Notification—rushed government experts to the Oval Office on Feb. 7 to brief President Bush. The security flaw, according to a subsequent written assessment by the FBI, could have been exploited to bring down telephone networks and halt "all control information exchanged between ground and aircraft flight control systems."

Officials say Osama bin Laden's operatives have nothing like the proficiency in information war of the most sophisticated nations. But al Qaeda is now judged to be considerably more capable than analysts believed a year ago. And its intentions are unrelentingly aimed at inflicting catastrophic harm.

One al Qaeda laptop found in Afghanistan, sources say, had made multiple visits to a French site run by the Societe Anonyme, or Anonymous Society. The site offers a two-volume, online "Sabotage Handbook" with sections on tools of the trade, planning a hit, switch gear and instrumentation, anti-surveillance methods and advanced techniques. In Islamic chat rooms, other computers linked to al Qaeda had access to "cracking" tools used to search out networked computers, scan for security flaws and exploit them to gain entry—or full command.

Most significantly, perhaps, U.S. investigators have found evidence in the logs that mark a browser's path through the Internet that al Qaeda operators spent time on sites that offer software and programming instructions for the digital switches that run power, water, transport and communications grids. In some interrogations, the most recent of which was reported to policymakers two weeks ago, al Qaeda prisoners have described intentions, in general terms, to use those tools.

SPECIALIZED DIGITAL DEVICES ARE USED BY THE millions as the brains of American "critical infrastructure"—a term defined by federal directive to mean industrial sectors that are "essential to the minimum operations of the economy and government."

The devices are called distributed control systems, or DCS, and supervisory control and data acquisition, or SCADA, systems. The simplest ones collect measurements, throw railway switches, close circuit-breakers or adjust valves in the pipes that carry water, oil and gas. More complicated versions sift incoming data, govern multiple devices and cover a broader area.

What is new and dangerous is that most of these devices are now being connected to the Internet—some of them, according to classified "Red Team" intrusion exercises, in ways that their owners do not suspect.

Because the digital controls were not designed with public access in mind, they typically lack even rudimentary security, having fewer safeguards than the purchase of flowers online. Much of the technical information required to penetrate these systems is widely discussed in the public forums of the affected industries, and specialists say the security flaws are well known to potential attackers.

Until recently, says Director John Tritak of the Commerce Department's Critical Infrastructure Assurance Office, many government and corporate officials regarded hackers mainly as a menace to their e-mail.

"There's this view that the problems of cyberspace originate, reside and remain in cyberspace," Tritak says. "Bad ones and zeroes hurt good ones and zeros, and it sort of stays there.... The point we're making is that increasingly we are relying on 21st century technology and information networks to run physical assets." Digital controls are so pervasive, he says, that terrorists might use them to cause damage on a scale that otherwise would "not be available except through a very systematic and comprehensive physical attack."

The 13 agencies and offices of the U.S. intelligence community have not reached consensus on the scale or imminence of this threat, according to participants in and close observers of the discussion. The Defense Department, which concentrates on information war with nations, is most skeptical of al Qaeda's interest and prowess in cyberspace.

"DCS and SCADA systems might be accessible to bits and bytes," Assistant Security of Defense John P. Stenbit said in an interview. But al Qaeda prefers simple, reliable plans and would not allow the success of a large-scale attack "to be dependent on some sophisticated, tricky cyber thing to work."

"We're thinking more in physical terms—biological agents, isotopes in explosions, other analogies to the fully loaded airplane," he says. "That's more what I'm worried about. When I think of cyber, I think of it as ancillary to one of those."

WHITE HOUSE AND FBI ANALYSTS, AS WELL AS officials in the Energy and Commerce departments with more direct responsibility for the civilian infrastructure, describe the threat in more robust terms.

"We were underestimating the amount of attention [al Qaeda was] paying to the Internet," says Roger Cressey, a longtime counterterrorism official who became chief of staff of the President's Critical Infrastructure Protection Board in October. "Now we know they see it as a potential attack vehicle. Al Qaeda spent more time mapping our vulnerabilities in cyberspace than we previously thought. An attack is a question of when, not if."

Ron Ross, who heads a new "information assurance" partnership between the National Security Agency and the National Institute of Standards and Technology, reminded the Infraguard delegates in Niagara Falls that, after the Sept. 11 attacks, air traffic controllers brought down every commercial plane in the air. "If there had been a cyber-attack at the same time that prevented them from doing that," he said, "the magnitude of the event could have been much greater."

"It's not science fiction," Ross said in an interview. "A cyber-attack can be launched with fairly limited resources."

U.S. Intelligence agencies have upgraded their warnings about al Qaeda's use of cyberspace. Just over a year ago, a National Intelligence Estimate on the threat to U.S. information systems gave prominence to China, Russia and other nations. It judged al Qaeda operatives as "less developed in their network capabilities" than many individual hackers and "likely to pose only a limited cyber-threat," according to an authoritative description of its contents.

In February, the CIA issued a revised Directorate of Intelligence Memorandum. According to officials who read it, the new memo said al Qaeda had "far more interest" in cyber-terrorism than previously believed and contemplated the use of hackers for hire to speed the acquisition of capabilities.

"I don't think they are capable of bringing a major segment of this country to its knees using cyber-attack alone," says an official representing the current consensus, but "they would be able to conduct an integrated attack using a combination of physical and cyber resources and get an amplification of consequences."

Counterterrorism analysts have known for years that al Qaeda prepares for attacks with elaborate "targeting packages" of photographs and notes. But, in January, U.S. forces in Kabul, Afghanistan, found something new.

A computer seized at an al Qaeda office contained models of a dam, made with structural architecture and engineering software, that enabled the planners to simulate its catastrophic failure. Bush administration officials, who discussed the find, declined to say whether they had identified a specific dam as a target.

The FBI reported that the computer had been running Microstran, an advanced tool for analyzing steel and concrete structures; Autocad 2000, which manipulates technical drawings in two or three dimensions; and software "used to identify and classify soils," which would assist in predicting the course of a wall of water surging downstream.

To destroy a dam physically would require "tons of explosives," Assistant Attorney General Michael Chertoff said a year ago. To breach it from cyberspace is not out of the question. In 1998, a 12-year-old hacker, exploring on a lark, broke into the computer system that runs Arizona's Roosevelt Dam. He did not know or care, but federal authorities say he had complete command of the SCADA system controlling the dam's massive floodgates.

Roosevelt Dam holds back as much as 1.5 million acre-feet of water, or 489 trillion gallons. That volume could theoretically cover the city of Phoenix, down river, to a height of five feet. In practice, that could not happen. Before the water reached the Arizona capital, the rampant Salt River would spend most of itself in a flood plain encompassing the cities of Mesa and Tempe—with a combined population of nearly a million.

IN QUEENSLAND, AUSTRALIA, ON APRIL 23, 2000, police stopped a car on the road to Deception Bay and found a stolen computer and radio transmitter inside. Using commercially available technology, Vitek Boden, 48, had turned his vehicle into a pirate command center for sewage treatment along Australia's Sunshine coast.

Boden's arrest solved a mystery that had troubled the Maroochy Shire wastewater system for two months. Somehow the system was leaking hundreds of thousands of gallons of putrid sludge into parks, rivers and the manicured grounds of a Hyatt Regency hotel. Janelle Bryand of the Australian Environmental Protection Agency says "marine life died, the creek water turned black and the stench was unbearable for residents." Until Boden's cap-ture—during his 46th successful intrusion—the utility's managers did not know why.

Specialists in cyber-terrorism have studied Boden's case because it is the only one known in which someone used a digital control system deliberately to cause harm. Details of Boden's intrusion, not disclosed before, show how easily Boden broke in—and how restrained he was with his power.

Boden had quit his job at Hunter Watertech, the supplier of Maroochy Shire's remote control and telemetry equipment. Evidence at his trial suggested that he was angling for a consulting contract to solve the problems he had caused.

To sabotage the system, he set the software on his laptop to identify itself as "pumping station 4," then suppressed all alarms. Paul Chisholm, Hunter Watertech's chief executive, said in an interview two weeks ago that Boden "was the central control system" during his intrusions, with unlimited command of 300 SCADA nodes governing sewage and drinking water alike. "He could have done anything he liked to the fresh water," Chisholm says.

Like thousands of utilities around the world, Maroochy Shire allowed technicians operating remotely to manipulate its digital controls. Boden learned how to use those controls as an insider, but the software he used conforms to international standards and the manuals are available on the Web. He faced virtually no obstacles to breaking in.

Nearly identical systems run oil and gas utilities and many manufacturing plants. But their most dangerous use is in the generation, transmission and distribution of electrical power, because electricity has no substitute and every other key infrastructure depends on it.

Massoud Amin, a mathematician directing new security efforts in the industry, describes the North American power grid as "the most complex machine ever built." Commerce Department, participants say, government and industry scientists agreed that they have no idea how the grid would respond to a cyber-attack.

What they do know is that "Red Teams" of mock intruders from the Energy Department's four national laboratories have devised what one government document listed as "eight scenarios for SCADA attack on an electrical power grid"—and all of them work. Eighteen such exercises have been conducted to date against large regional utilities, and Richard A. Clarke, Bush's cyber-security adviser, says the intruders "have always, always succeeded."

Joseph M. Weiss of KEMA Consulting, a leading expert in control system security, reported at two recent industry conferences that intruders were "able to assemble a detailed map" of each system and "intercepted and changed" SCADA commands without detection.

"What the labs do is look at simple, easy things I can do to get in" with tools commonly available on the Internet, Weiss said in an interview. "In most of these cases, they are not using anything that a hacker couldn't have access to."

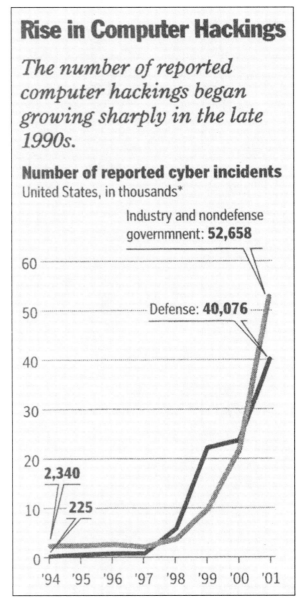

Rise in Computer Hackings

The number of reported computer hackings began growing sharply in the late 1990s.

Number of reported cyber incidents
United States, in thousands*

Industry and nondefense governmnent: **52,658**

Defense: **40,076**

2,340

225

'94 '95 '96 '97 '98 '99 '00 '01

* Includes probes, illicit entries and attacks aimed at causing damage or taking control.

SOURCE: Defense Department

THE WASHINGTON POST

Bush has launched a top-priority research program at the Livermore, Sandia and Los Alamos labs to improve safeguards in the estimated 3 million SCADA systems in use. But many of the systems rely on instantaneous responses and cannot tolerate authentication delays. And the devices deployed now lack the memory and bandwidth to use techniques such as "integrity checks" that are standard elsewhere.

In a book-length Electricity Infrastructure Security Assessment, the industry concluded on Jan. 7 that "it may not be possible to provide sufficient security when using the Internet for power system control." Power companies, it said, will probably have to build a parallel private network for themselves.

The U.S. government may never have fought a war with so little power in the battlefield. That became clear again on Feb. 7, when Clarke and his vice chairman at the critical infrastructure board, Howard A. Schmidt, arrived in the Oval Office.

They told the president that researchers in Finland had identified a serious security hole in the Internet's standard language for routing data through switches. A government threat team found implications—for air traffic control and civilian and military phone links among others—that were more serious still.

"We've got troops on the ground in Afghanistan and we've got communication systems that we all depend on that, at that time, were vulnerable," Schmidt recalls.

Bush ordered the Pentagon and key federal agencies to patch their systems. But most of the vulnerable networks were not government-owned. Since Feb. 12, "Those who have the fix in their power are in the private sector," Schmidt says. Asked about progress, he says: "I don't know that we'd ever get to 100 percent."

Frustrated at the pace of repairs, Clarke traveled to San Jose on Feb. 19 and accused industry leaders of spending more on coffee than on information security. "You will be hacked," he told them. "What's more, you deserve to be hacked."

Tritak, at the Commerce Department, appealed to patriotism. Speaking of al Qaeda, he said: "When you've got people who are saying, 'We're coming after your economy,' everyone has a responsibility to do their bit to safeguard against it."

New public-private partnerships are helping, but the government case remains a tough sell. Alan Paller, director of research at the SANS Institute in Bethesda, Md., says not even banks and brokerages, considered the most security-conscious businesses, tell the government when their systems are attacked. Sources say the government did not learn crucial details about September's Nimda worm, which caused an estimated $530 million in damage, until the stricken companies began firing their security executives.

Experts say public companies worry about the loss of customer confidence and the legal liability to shareholders or security vendors when they report flaws.

The FBI is having even less success with its "key asset initiative," an attempt to identify the most dangerous points of vulnerability in 5,700 companies deemed essential to national security.

"What we really want to drill down to, eventually, is not the companies but the actual things themselves, the actual switches... that are vital to [a firm's] continued operations," Dick says. He acknowledges a rocky start: "For them to tell us where their crown jewels are is not reasonable until you've built up trust."

Michehl R. Gent, president of the North American Electric Reliability Council, said in May that it will not happen. "We're not going to build such a list.... We have no confidence that the government can keep that a secret."

FOR FEAR OF TERRORIST INFILTRATION, CLARKE'S critical infrastructure board and Tom Ridge's homeland security office are now exploring whether private companies would consider telling the government the names of employees with access to sensitive sites.

"Obviously, the ability to check intelligence records from the terrorist standpoint would be the goal," Dick says.

There is no precedent for that. The FBI screens bank employees but has no statutory authority in other industries. Using classified intelligence databases, such as the Visa Viper list of suspected terrorists, would mean the results could not be shared with the employers. Bobby Gillham, manager of global security at oil giant Conoco Inc., says he doubts his industry would go along with that.

"You have Privacy Act concerns," he said in an interview. "And just to get feedback that there's nothing here, or there's something here but we can't share it with you, doesn't do us a lot of good. Most of our companies would not [remove an employee] in a frivolous way, on a wink."

Exasperated by companies seeking proof that they are targets, Clarke has stopped talking about threats at all.

"It doesn't matter whether it's al Qaeda or a nation-state or the teenage kid up the street," he says. "Who does the damage to you is far less important than the fact that damage can be done. You've got to focus on your vulnerability… and not wait for the FBI to tell you that al Qaeda has you in its sights."

Washington Post staff researcher Robert Thomason contributed to this report.

Agriculture shock

Fears about terrorism usually centre on nuclear or biological weapons.
But attackers could cause huge economic damage by spreading plant or animal diseases.
Virginia Gewin asks how this threat is being confronted.

The statistics on the 2001 outbreak of foot-and-mouth disease (FMD) in Britain make for disturbing reading. Four million cattle were culled to contain the disease, and estimates of the cost to the British economy—primarily to the agriculture and tourism industries—run as high as £30 billion (US$48 billion).

The outbreak was unintentional, probably the result of illegal imports of infected meat being fed to pigs. But it can also be seen as an expensive warning. Although smallpox and anthrax receive the bulk of government and media attention when it comes to assessing the risk of bioterrorism, a deliberate attack on agriculture could disrupt trade and cripple agricultural industries. The risk of human fatalities or a serious food shortage is low, but few events would cause more economic damage than attacking the food supply. "The British FMD epidemic has given a blueprint to any terrorist," says Martin Hugh-Jones, a veterinary epidemiologist at Louisiana State University in Baton Rouge.

If such an attack seems unlikely, it is worth noting that agricultural bioweapons have been used before. During the First World War, German agents infected Allied horses with the bacterium *Burkholderia mallei*, which causes glanders—a disease that can kill horses and can also infect humans. And Simon Whitby, a peace-studies researcher at the University of Bradford, UK, says that any country that has studied biological weapons, including the United States and Russia, will have looked at plant and animal diseases. Iraq, for example, is known to have weaponized wheat pathogens.

The main effects of any new attack are likely to be economic. The World Trade Organization lists few reasons for refusing to import crops and animals, but the presence of disease is one of them. Such bans can have rapid and severe consequences. When karnal bunt, a fungal disease of wheat, was found in northern Texas in 2001, over 25 countries banned wheat imports from the four infected counties within a single day. The estimated loss of revenue was $27 million.

Agriculture is also now more open to attack, as a result of large-scale methods such as the use of factory farms and monoculture cropping systems. "There is a vulnerability. It isn't anyone's fault, it's just how agriculture has evolved," says Jim Cook, a plant pathologist at Washington State University in Pullman. And although the ease with which a pathogen could be introduced is the root of the problem, weaknesses in the systems used to detect an outbreak could exacerbate any damage.

On the alert

Thankfully, the threat is now receiving attention. Funding in the United States has increased since the attacks on 11 September 2001—President George W. Bush's proposed budget for the 2003 financial year includes an extra $146 million to protect agriculture and the food supply, including money for monitoring animal health and for setting up a coordinated system to respond to disease outbreaks. And last September, the US National Academy of Sciences released *Countering Agricultural Bioterrorism,* a report detailing the problems that it says need to be addressed, from better diagnosis to improved communication between those who monitor potential outbreaks.

In Europe, defences are being boosted in response to an increase in the number of diseases that the continent's agriculture is expected to be exposed to, whether through increased trade or the possibility of climate change. "We have to be prepared to fight diseases that we didn't have to fight before," says Alex Thiermann of the Paris-based World Organization for Animal Health (OIE). Britain's FMD epidemic has also given a new urgency to research on diagnostic tools and vaccines, as well as encouraging countries to coordinate their plans for responding to future outbreaks.

Of all the lines of defence, rapid detection is considered most important. In many agricultural settings, surveillance systems usually rely on a farmer or local-government agent noticing something unusual. But the clinical symptoms of some diseases appear days after infection. With animals kept so closely confined, entire farms can rapidly become infected before anyone is aware of the problem. "Animals are kept in perfect environmental conditions for spread," says Larry Madden, a plant pathologist at Ohio State University in Columbus. It is not uncommon, for instance, to find

5,000 animals on 20 hectares of land in a typical US dairy operation. Rapid and extensive movement of animals between farms, slaughterhouses and markets also accentuates the problem. FMD, for example, had spread across Britain before it was detected.

The backbone of the global disease-detection system is the chain of 156 reference laboratories and collaborating centres run by the OIE, which analyse samples taken from animals that are thought to be infected. In the United States, the laboratory responsible for diagnosing exotic diseases is the Plum Island Animal Disease Center in New York, run by the US Department of Agriculture (USDA). It currently conducts fewer than 1,000 tests every year for FMD, each of which is sent to the lab. But an outbreak of FMD would require it to run tens of thousands of tests. And the quicker it could deliver the results, the sooner vets working in the field could decide what action to take.

'Pen-side' tests could help to speed up the process. Researchers at Britain's Institute for Animal Health in Pirbright, Surrey, for example, have adapted the laboratory procedure used to check for the presence of the FMD virus so that fieldworkers can perform the test by applying a treated paper to a tissue sample from a live animal. By monitoring the change in colour of the paper, the researcher can determine whether the antigens are present in about 10 minutes. The test has its drawbacks: false negatives can occur at rates of 10–20% when only small amounts of the FMD virus are present, and a cell-culture test is needed to confirm results that prove negative for the virus. But it could yet be a useful aid when time is short, and it is expected to undergo field trials in the next few months. "Those kits are extremely valuable if we have to make quick decisions," says Thiermann.

Another quick, but more sensitive, approach to FMD testing is being explored at Plum Island and Pirbright. Researchers have been evaluating field versions of a method for detecting viral RNA using the polymerase chain reaction (PCR), a common tool used to copy lengths of genetic material. Pirbright officials say they have a fully automated

version of the test that could readily be established in a mobile lab should the need arise.

Below the radar

Early detection of crop pathogens is also vital. The United States has more than four million square kilometres of farmland, much of it in remote areas where surveillance is virtually non-existent. Crop diseases can go unnoticed for a long time, during which they are continually spreading. It is estimated that the plum pox virus, discovered in Pennsylvania fields three years ago, was present for six to eight years before it was detected. In the past, a disease sample might have awaited identification until it eventually found its way to the often solitary plant clinician in the agricultural department of the local university.

The USDA is now attempting to improve this situation. Training modules are being developed for 'first responders', such as the farmers and crop consultants who are likely to be the first to notice a problem. And of the $43 million allocated to agricultural-bioterrorism preparedness in the 2002 budget, $20 million is earmarked to establish a network of diagnostic labs for plant and animal pathogens. Five new regional centres are currently being set up at universities around the country, with the goal of providing rapid and accurate diagnosis of disease threats. Many existing labs will also get much-needed improvements. For example, the Great Plains Diagnostic Network at Kansas State University in Manhattan couldn't even run tests involving PCR until the recent funding arrived.

Once diagnoses have been made at the regional centres, all of the relevant information will be transferred to the National Agricultural Pest Information System, a database maintained at Purdue University in West Lafayette, Indiana.

To treat an infection once it has been detected, better knowledge of the pathogen involved is often required. Gaps in our understanding are being filled by new genomic sequences of animal and plant pathogens. In September 2002, for example, scientists at The Institute for Genomic Research (TIGR) in Rockville, Maryland, sequenced the genome of

Brucella suis (V. G. DelVecchio *et al. Proc. Natl Acad. Sci. USA* **99,** 443–448; 2002), a pathogen that is considered a likely bioterrorism agent—the US military itself weaponized the bug in the 1950s. *B. suis* primarily affects animals, but can cause a debilitating disease in humans that can be lethal to people with weakened immune systems.

Surprisingly, the genome of this bacterium suggests that animal and plant pathogens are not as different as was once thought (see I. T. Paulsen *et al. Proc. Natl Acad. Sci. USA* **99,** 13148–13153; 2002). Many of the genes that control the metabolism of *B. suis* are also found in the plant pathogen *Agrobacterium tumefaciens,* as well as in *Mesorhizobium loti,* a soil bacterium that forms a symbiotic relationship with plants. By investigating these links, TIGR researchers hope to reveal how *B. suis* survives outside its host, and thus generate new leads for tackling the pathogen.

Progress with plant diseases has been less impressive. As of September 2002, less than 6% of microbial genomes that had been sequenced and made publicly available belonged to plant-associated microbes. Animal pathogens are generally viruses or bacteria, but over three-quarters of plant pathogens are fungi, which have much larger genomes. "Compared to human and animal pathogens, plant pathogens are definitely behind," says Jacqueline Fletcher, president of the American Phytopathological Society.

Things are set to improve, albeit slowly. The US Department of Energy's Joint Genome Initiative announced in October that it will sequence two species of *Phytophthora,* a genus of fungus that is responsible for diseases as varied as sudden oak death syndrome and potato blight. What's more, a joint USDA and National Science Foundation programme has funded the sequencing of *Fusarium graminearum,* a fungus that causes disease in wheat and barley.

Forensic studies of deliberately caused outbreaks could also benefit from sequence data. Take the investigation of the US anthrax attacks, for example. Scientists had already sequenced the type of anthrax used—the Ames strain—and so were able to whittle down the number of possible places from which the bug could have been obtained. If sequences of different strains of other pathogens were available, investigators could eliminate many dead ends, as well as gaining incriminating evidence. "One of the differences is to be able to trace back and be able to get enough evidence to bring a case against the perpetrator," says Cook.

Take the strain

But realizing these ambitions will take hard work. Fourteen more strains of anthrax are being sequenced, and for other pathogens, many strains will also have to be sequenced if genomic databases are to be of any forensic use. Several researchers have called for the creation of a database of pathogen genomes, which could be used to investigate outbreaks of animal diseases, but it will take many years to gather enough information to respond to the range of possible bioterrorism agents.

More immediate improvements to our defences could come from new vaccines that are currently under development. Vaccines are an important means for dealing with animal disease, but existing versions are plagued with problems. FMD vaccines, for example, struggle to cope with different strains of the pathogen. "No single vaccine can bring immunity to more than a few of strains," says Mark Wheelis, a bioterrorism expert at the University of California, Davis. Immunity is also often short-lived, and vac-cinated animals cannot be distinguished from infected ones—and so are impossible to sell—because a weakened version of the live virus is used in the vaccine.

A new class of vaccines could counter some of these problems. Rather than using a version of the live virus, researchers are creating deleted, or 'subunit', vaccines, in which some genes have been removed. Proteins that are not crucial for antibody production, for example, can be removed from the vaccine. The treatment still prompts the production of the antibodies that protect against the virus, but vaccinated animals do not produce antibodies against the missing protein, and so can be distinguished from infected animals. Subunit vaccines have already been developed for Aujeszky's disease in pigs and bovine respiratory disease in cattle, and several groups are working on one for FMD.

Prepare for the worst

Like most recent developments, the vaccine work is driven by the need to contain an accidental outbreak of disease. But should countries be preparing specifically for a deliberate pathogen release? An intentional release could cause even more damage than an accident. The perpetrator could choose to release several highly virulent pathogens simultaneously in remote areas, for example. Authorities in the United States and Europe say that they are considering specific anti-terrorism measures, but many of the steps, taken so far, such as the development of better diagnostic networks, tie in with conventional strategies for tackling plant and animal disease.

Given the scale of damage that a deliberate pathogen release could cause, some researchers say that stronger measures are needed. But others question this argument. In the bag of terrorist tricks, agricultural bioterrorism is the wild card, and some experts feel that is unlikely to appeal to terrorists. "People attracted to terrorism wouldn't be as attracted to this," says Rocco Casagrande, who studies biological-agent detectors at Surface Logix in Brighton, Massachusetts. "Most terrorists are urban. They want a big bang. Killing cows or pigs is not a big bang," agrees Hugh-Jones.

But others warn that different approaches are likely to be used in future terrorist attacks. Whitby, for example, says that he and his colleagues consider an attack on agriculture to be the most likely form of biological terrorism that we're going to see. Predicting the behaviour of terrorists is, of course, notoriously difficult. But if economic damage is the aim, agricultural bioterrorism is certainly a viable threat. The size of that threat may be hard to define, but the financial scars left by Britain's FMD outbreak show just how serious it could be.

Virginia Gewin is a freelance writer in Corvallis, Oregon.

UNIT 8

Civil Liberties and Civil Rights

Unit Selections

29. **Civil Liberties and Homeland Security**, Valerie L. Demmer
30. **Homeland Security and the Lessons of Waco**, Mary Zeiss Stange
31. **Fears Mount Over 'Total' Spy System**, J. Michael Waller
32. **Access Denied**, Brian Costner
33. **Heading in the Wrong Direction**, *The Economist*

Key Points to Consider

- Have legislative initiatives like the U.S. Patriot Act led to an erosion of fundamental rights in America? Discuss.

- According to Mary Zeiss Stange, what lessons should we have learned from the U.S. government's treatment of the Branch Davidians?

- Do U.S. government attempts to develop a Total Information Awareness program constitute an invasion of privacy? Why or why not?

- How can democratic governments maintain public access and openness while protecting themselves from those who would destroy them?

 **Links: www.dushkin.com/online/**
These sites are annotated in the World Wide Web pages.

EFF Analysis of USA Patriot Act
  http://www.eff.org/Privacy/Surveillance/Terrorism_militias/20011031_eff_usa_patriot_analysis.html
EPIC USA Patriot Act Page
  http://www.epic.org/privacy/terrorism/usapatriot
Human Rights Watch
  http://www.hrwatch.org/press/2002/11/homeland1121.htm

There is an inherent tension between the need for security and the need to ensure the protection of our civil liberties. Terrorism exploits this tension. While terrorism may have different objectives, one of its main purposes is to provoke government overreaction. As the government indiscriminately targets communities and groups that may pose, or are perceived to pose, a potential threat, the rights of innocent people are violated. Terrorists gain support. Violence escalates.

Democratic governments are in a difficult position. If governments fail to protect themselves and their citizens from terrorist attacks, they fail to fulfill one of their fundamental obligations and lose public support. If governments, in order to prevent terrorism, violate the civil rights of their citizens and threaten civil liberties, they undermine the very principles upon which they were founded. There is little room to maneuver between the two. There is little room for error.

Critics of the Bush administration and its legislative initiatives after 9/11 claim that the U.S. government is violating civil rights and jeopardizing civil liberties in its war on terrorism. They accuse Attorney General John Ashcroft and the government of using "McCarthy-like" tactics in the persecution of minorities. They fear that new powers, derived from legislation like the U.S. Patriot Act, will be used against U.S. citizens. They are concerned about the increased access of government agencies to personal information. They argue that the indefinite detention of terrorist suspects without charges, justified by the creation of special categories of prisoner, undermines basic constitutional protections.

Supporters of the administration argue that the U.S. Patriot Act has been instrumental in creating better cooperation and more effective information exchange between the CIA and the FBI. They argue

that terrorists hide behind and seek to abuse the inherent protections offered by democratic societies in order to destroy them. They believe that in order to weed out those who would abuse our system, they need greater access to public records and personal information. They argue that in order to protect our national security and prevent the occurrence of another 9/11, they must have greater flexibility in the treatment and interrogation of terrorist suspects. They see the creation of special categories of

prisoners and the use of prison camps outside of the United States as vital because they allow for the extraction of valuable information from terrorist suspects without interference from the constraints of the American legal system. Our right to be free from terror, they claim, is more important than a terrorist suspect's right to due process and legal representation. They believe that the use of special military tribunals is essential, as it will allow for the use of classified information by the prosecution while being able to limit the access of the accused.

The five articles in this unit reflect the tenor of the ongoing civil rights debate in homeland security. While most are concerned about the administration's policies, few offer credible alternatives. In the first article, Valerie Demmer highlights the potential conflicts between homeland security and civil rights. She fears that the new powers provided to intelligence and law enforcement agencies may be used to constrain freedom of speech and stifle political dissent. The second article attempts to draw a parallel between the 1993 incident in Waco and the present situation. It warns that the tactics used by the U.S. government against the Branch Davidians are similar to those used against Muslims in America. The third article focuses on the Total Information Awareness (TIA) program. It provides a perspective of both sides of the issue. Then, the fourth article explores the implications of government efforts to protect potentially sensitive information. It highlights the delicate balance between the need for increased security and the need for public access and oversight. Finally, the fifth article questions the creation of special categories of prisoners in the war against terrorism. Focusing on the detention of Jose Padilla (an alleged "dirty bomber"), it questions whether U.S. policy is "heading in the wrong direction."

"The Land of the Controlled and the Home of the Secure"

Civil Liberties
AND HOMELAND SECURITY

by VALERIE L. DEMMER

In response to the terrorist attacks of September 11, 2001, the Bush administration reacted swiftly and boldly, implementing programs it claimed would strengthen the security of the United States. President George W. Bush, Secretary of Defense Donald Rumsfeld, and Attorney General John Ashcroft have all adopted a firm and unyielding stance in executing their focused reply to the menace of global terrorism. An unfortunate byproduct of these aggressive moves, however, is the erosion of civil liberties. The administration has gone beyond the legitimate needs of national security and is infringing on constitutional freedoms in the name of patriotism and security.

The Patriot Act (Provide Appropriate Tools Required to Intercept and Obstruct Terrorism Act) was signed into law by Bush on October 26, 2001, after being rushed through Congress without giving members time to properly read or interpret its provisions. According to Representative Ron Paul of Texas (one of only three Republicans in the House to vote against the bill), "The bill wasn't printed before the vote—at least I couldn't get it.… It was a very complicated bill. Maybe a handful of staffers actually read it, but the bill definitely was not available to members before the vote."

In an interview given to *Insight,* Paul further said, "The insult is to call this a 'patriot bill' and suggest I'm not patriotic because I insisted upon finding out what is in it and voting no. I thought it was undermining the Constitution, so I didn't vote for it—and therefore I'm somehow not a patriot. That's insulting."

Ostensibly an anti-terrorist bill, the Patriot Act makes changes to over fifteen different statutes. Of particular concern, the legislation permits the government to arbitrarily detain or deport suspects; to eavesdrop on Internet communications, monitor financial transactions, and obtain individuals' electronic records; and to clandestinely survey records of religious and political organizations, whose privacy rights have usually been upheld in the courts. Critics of the act contend that these McCarthy-like tactics strip citizens of their fundamental rights while not being effective in—and often not having anything to do with—stopping terrorism.

The act even allows increased surveillance of church finances and bookstore records. For example, instead of being able to ask a court to quash a subpoena for customer information, booksellers may be required to turn records over immediately. The act allows surveillance through all types of electronic communications and affects telecommunications companies, Internet providers, cable companies—indeed anyone using this technology. Jim Dempsey, deputy director of the Center for Democracy and Technology, worries that investigators "will collect more information on innocent people and be distracted from the task of actually identifying those who may be planning future attacks."

Russ Feingold (Democrat–Wisconsin), the only dissenting voice in the Senate, addressed his colleagues in the Senate before the bill's passage, pointing out that the framers of the U.S. Constitution, even though they'd just been through a war with Britain, "wrote a Constitution of limited powers and an explicit Bill of Rights to protect liberty in times of war, as well as in times of peace." Feingold added:

> Of course there is no doubt that, if we lived in a police state, it would be easier to catch terrorists. If we lived in a country that allowed the police to search your home at any time for any reason; if we lived in a country that allowed the government to open your mail, eavesdrop on your phone conversations, or intercept your email communications; if we lived in a county that allowed the government to hold people in jail indefinitely based on what they write or think, or based on mere suspicion that they are up to no good, then the government would no doubt discover and arrest more terrorists.

> But that probably would not be a country in which we would want to live. And that would not be a country for which we could, in good conscience, ask our young people to fight and die. In short, that would not be America.

> Preserving our freedom is one of the main reasons that we are now engaged in this new war on terrorism. We will lose that war without firing a shot if we sacrifice the liberties of the American people.

And sacrificing liberties is just what the Bush administration would do. It announced last fall that 5,000 men between the ages of eighteen and thirty-three were being rounded up by the FBI for questioning. The young men have been in the country for two years and are from "suspect" countries. The list was provided by Ashcroft, who emphasized that "the objective is to collect any information that the individuals on this list may have regarding terrorist elements in this country and abroad. These individuals were selected for interviews because they fit the criteria of persons who might have knowledge of foreign-based terrorists." This action was denounced by the Center for Constitutional Rights in a press release which stated: "Questioning individuals without any evidence of wrongdoing amounts to the very definitions of racial profiling.... Since September 11, we have already seen thousands of people who have been harassed by local authorities over immigration matters totally unrelated to the attacks."

In another disturbing development, Ashcroft approved a rule that permits eavesdropping by the Justice Department on the confidential conversations of inmates and uncharged detainees with their lawyers—communication that is supposed to be inviolate. Robert Hirshon, president of the American Bar Association stated: "Prior judicial approval and the establishment of probable cause… are required if the government's surveillance is to be consistent with the Constitution and is to avoid ab-

rogating the rights of innocent people." Ashcroft's rule, however, was pushed through as an emergency measure without a waiting period. Senator Patrick J. Leahy (Democrat–Vermont), in a letter to Congress said, "I am deeply troubled at what appears to be an executive effort to exercise new powers without judicial scrutiny or statutory authorization."

Indeed, unilateral executive action is becoming a trend of this administration. For instance, on November 13, Bush issued a military order directing Rumsfeld to be responsible for military tribunals to try noncitizens charged with terrorism. Secret trials without benefit of a jury or the requirement of a unanimous verdict, as well as nondisclosure of evidence for "national security reasons," would be authorized by the use of these tribunals. Representative John Conyers (Democrat–Michigan, and the ranking member of the House Judiciary Committee) called Bush's order "a civil liberties calamity in this country" that puts the "executive branch in the unattainable role of legislator, prosecutor, judge and jury." At a press conference, Conyers, other Democratic legislators, and Representative Bob Barr (Republican–Georgia) described the military tribunals as an abuse of executive power jeopardizing the nation's civil liberties. Immediate hearings were called for by Barr. Representative Dennis Kucinich (Democrat–Ohio) said, "We should never be so fearful as to think somehow we can gain a great measure of security by being willing to set aside the Bill of Rights or any other hallowed legal principle that forms the bedrock of our society."

On December 6, Ashcroft appeared before the Senate Judiciary Committee for a lengthy hearing on Bush's order to use military tribunals, the Justice Department's monitoring of phone conversations between suspects and their lawyers, and the questioning of thousands of people of Middle Eastern heritage. Ashcroft was defiant, denied these actions undermine civil liberties, and charged that accusations promoting fear of lost freedom aid terrorists. The next day, the American Humanist Association commented, "Our nation is built on diversity, not unanimity, and is not bolstered by governmental attempts to suppress dissent. We appeal to Congress and the president to halt Ashcroft's assault on America's civil liberties."

With this wave of patriotism has come a zeal that affects all areas of our lives and threatens the very ideals the United States stands for.

Unfortunately, the current crackdown on civil liberties is nothing new, and the Bush administration is using earlier infringements on freedoms to justify its new policies. In World War I there was press censorship. During World War II, Japanese-Americans and other foreign-born citizens were interned. The Cold War era had its McCarthyism with black-listing of suspected communist sympathizers. During the Vietnam War, anti-war protest groups were infiltrated, harassed, and spied on. The Gulf War saw media coverage controlled through "pool reporting." As Feingold put it: "Wartime has sometimes brought us the greatest tests of our Bill of Rights."

In the first days and weeks immediately following the September 11 tragedies, a wave of nationalism swept across the United States the likes of which hadn't been seen since World War II. But with this wave of patriotism came a zeal threatening the very ideals the United States stands for.

In particular, the right to freedom of expression has been compromised. In one incident, the cartoon *Boondocks* was pulled from some newspapers in New York because it was deemed either "un-American" or too political. Rick Stromoski, cartoonist of *Soup to Nutz* and spokesperson for the National Cartoonists Society said, "I find that a little scary, that just because someone can take another point of view they're seen as unpatriotic or sympathetic to the terrorists…. Papers are afraid of offending their communities and losing even more readers."

The same could be said about television programs. Bill Maher's *Politically Incorrect* was dropped by fifteen stations after remarks he made after September 11 were deemed inappropriate—and most likely his contract won't be renewed in 2002.

Airport security has understandably been a prime concern since the terrorist attacks. But in the name of "national security" some passengers' civil liberties have been violated. Green Party USA coordinator Nancy Oden was stopped by government agents while trying to board an American Airlines flight in Bangor, Maine, in October. She wasn't arrested for anything—merely prevented from flying. Oden had been scheduled to speak at the Greens' national committee meeting in Chicago to work on details of a campaign against biochemical warfare and the party's peace agenda. According to Oden, "An official told me that my name had been flagged in the computer. … I was targeted because the Green Party USA opposes the bombing of innocent civilians in Afghanistan." Chicago Green activist Lionel Trepanier commented, "The attack on the right of association of an opposition political party is chilling. The harassment of peace activists is reprehensible."

On November 1 Circuit Court Judge James Stucky upheld the three-day suspension handed down by Sissonville High School officials against Charleston, West Virginia, student Katie Sierra for promoting an "Anarchy Club" and wearing anti-war T-shirts in school. In October, high-school student Aaron Pettit of Fairview Park, Ohio, was suspended for ten days for displaying anti-war posters on his locker—one depicting an eagle with a tear drop and others with bombers drawn on them with mes-

sages like "May God have mercy, because we will not." Pettit sued the school in federal court and was reinstated. Even teachers have been suspended for merely voicing their views about the military action and policies now enacted.

Websites have also been shut down. Hypervine, an Internet service provider, forced Cosmic Entertainment to pull three radio show sites on the Internet, among them *Al Lewis Live,* because they allegedly contained pro-terrorist materials. The sites were reportedly forced from the Net when Hypervine received calls from someone identifying himself as a federal agent and threatening seizure of Hypervine's assets if the sites weren't shut down. Al Lewis, who played Grandpa in the 1960s television show *The Munsters,* said, "I lived through the McCarthy period. It will get worse."

Apparently intimidated by developments immediately following the terrorist attacks, the Sierra Club and the Natural Resources Defense Council began *voluntarily* removing ad material that criticized Bush's environmental policies. The Sierra Club went so far as to remove material critical of Bush *prior* to September 11.

An October 4 article by Brook Shelby Biggs, contributing editor of MotherJones.com aptly sums up the clamp down on civil liberties:

> Far more surprising than government attempts to stifle criticism is the seeming willingness of the media, politicians, and activist groups—particularly those on the left—to censor themselves. Some may be backing off to avoid the kind of public crucifixion endured by *Politically Incorrect*'s Bill Maher. Others, however, apparently truly believe that frank and vibrant discourse is damaging to the country's moral fiber.

The trauma of the terrorist attacks has caused many people to seek solace in religion—and religionists are taking advantage of it. The phrase "God Bless America" is everywhere these days. Besides the endless renditions of the song at sporting and other public events, there is a movement afoot in Congress to have the song declared a national hymn and to have the slogan "God Bless America" displayed in schools and public buildings. Moreover, a minister of the United Church of Christ has observed that the message implied by "God Bless America" is: "to be genuinely patriotic you must be conventionally religious."

Stefan Presser, legal director of the Pennsylvania American Civil Liberties Union, referring to a lawsuit that challenges the constitutionality of displaying the Ten Commandments in a public courthouse in West Chester, Pennsylvania, eloquently summarized this issue by saying, "Even if 99 out of 100 people are in favor of keeping the plaque, the point of the Bill of Rights is that the majority does not rule when it comes to religious issues. Each person, in their own privacy, gets to make religious decisions." In our zeal to protect the country from the terrorist threat let us not forget the menace posed by religious excess.

Some of these encroachments on our civil liberties—those with sunset provisions—will expire automatically unless renewed by Congress. Others will be challenged in the courts as violations of the Constitution. Still others seem destined to become permanent encroachments—what Bush and his cronies believe are "necessary accommodations" to a changing world.

We would do well to remember the words of Supreme Court Justice Oliver Wendell Holmes Jr., who said many years ago, "The life of the law has not been logic: it has been experience. The felt necessities of the time... have had a good deal more to do than the syllogism in determining the rules by which men should be governed."

The question we must now ask ourselves is: how do we *feel* about the necessities of our time? You can be sure our laws are following close behind. If you don't agree with the laws curtailing your rights and the actions of your officials, this is the time to tell your legislators and your neighbors how you feel. It's the patriotic thing to do.

Valerie L. Demmer holds a degree in management from the University of Phoenix. She is an editorial consultant at the Humanist *and lives in Middleport, New York.*

From *The Humanist*, January/February 2002, pp. 7-9. © 2002 by Valerie L. Demmer.

Homeland Security and the Lessons of Waco

By Mary Zeiss Stange

IT DID NOT HAVE TO HAPPEN. We know this now. The 51-day siege at Mount Carmel, the Branch Davidian complex near Waco, Tex., cost 84 lives: four federal agents of the Bureau of Alcohol, Tobacco and Firearms and six Branch Davidians who died in the initial assault on February 28, 1993; and 74 Davidians who perished in the April 19th conflagration that bought the standoff to its disastrous close.

Why did it happen the way it did? Why did it happen at all? Those questions take on a special urgency now, 18 years later, given the current war against Iraq and the more amorphous homeland "war on terror." The USA Patriot Act, and its sequel-in-progress, the Domestic Security Enhancement Act, give federal agents unprecedented power to violate the religious and other rights of individuals and groups. Unchecked, an administration that feels as firmly as the current one does that God is on its side can be counted on to use those weapons against "dangerously divergent" groups—today, more likely to be Islamic than Christian. The more the political universe arranges itself into oppositions between "patriotic" Americans and "evildoers," the more nervous

Americans become, to the point of willingly abrogating the rights of "divergent" individuals and groups. Thus the events in Waco demand revisiting.

As far as most Americans knew in 1993, the Branch Davidians were a sinister "doomsday cult" founded by an unsavory character named David Koresh. In fact, however, the Davidian sect had been in existence in the Waco area since the 1920s, an offshoot of Seventh-Day Adventism. Indeed, the apocalyptic worldview that united the Mount Carmel community, Koresh's role there, and the content of his preaching are all incomprehensible without some understanding of Adventist millennialism.

Yet federal agents steadfastly spurned such understanding. FBI negotiators, some purportedly so clueless as to think that the seven seals Koresh referred to were aquatic mammals, dismissed his scriptural interpretation as "Bible babble." Religious-studies scholars tried in vain to convince them that in Koresh they were dealing with a religious leader, not a madman surrounded by weak-willed lunatics. But the FBI preferred its fiction of cultic crazies, which the

national news media obligingly reinforced.

Koresh was hardly blameless. Although allegations of child abuse now appear to have been baseless, he probably would have been found guilty of statutory rape under Texas law. Yet that charge was never brought; had it been, it would have been a matter for local rather than federal authorities.

The feds were there because of the Davidians' guns. Since most evidence was destroyed either in the fire or shortly thereafter by FBI bulldozers, it will never be clear whether the Davidians had, as the Bureau of Alcohol, Tobacco and Firearms had claimed, illegally converted semiautomatic to fully automatic firearms. But even if true, as one Texan quipped at the time, "down here in the 50-Caliber Belt" that crime was as serious as "spitting on the sidewalk."

Even when the FBI unwittingly stepped into the role that Davidian apocalypticism assigned it, Koresh and company were at best an unwilling Army of the Lord. One survivor, Livingstone Fagan, explained afterward that "it was not inevitable that events had to end the way they did. The final outcome was contingent on our adversaries' response to our efforts to communicate our position of faith.... All our efforts were ignored. Evidently the government wanted its deception, both for itself and its people."

THE QUESTION, as pertinent now as then, is: Why the deception? Why did the FBI prefer the advice of anticult "experts" over the more reliable information available from religious-studies scholars? Why did it persist in creating its cult fiction? Why the government wanted to exterminate members of an offbeat religious group that had never indicated the slightest intention of doing harm remains a largely unanswered question. What made Koresh and his followers such targets of government hostility?

It may be that what makes religious groups like the Branch Davidians especially threatening from a more "mainstream" point of view is their sheer devotion to a life-altering, and explicitly countercultural, message. Most Americans balk at that much commitment, and will tolerate only certain familiar forms of religious (or quasi-religious) zeal—the anti-abortion movement, animal rights, environmental activism. Beyond that, we as a people cannot, in T. S. Eliot's words, "bear very much reality."

Two days after the Mount Carmel conflagration, in an op-ed piece for the *Los Angeles Times*, I made essentially this case, arguing that applying the "crazy" label to the Branch Davidians effectively allowed the government, and the media-consuming public, not to see the Branch Davidians as a religious group at all. Another religious-studies scholar, in no less a venue than the *Journal of the American Academy of Religion,* insisted that I was undermining "the reputation of our profession" by lending the Branch Davidians the merest hint of credibility. He argued that spurious figures like Koresh did not deserve to be understood, lest

the attempt lend their viewpoints some degree of plausibility.

Today, a kindred argument against religious understanding has reasserted itself with special ferocity.

I've experienced this firsthand. Within days after 9/11, I wrote an op-ed essay for *USA Today* in which I argued, countering those who claimed there was "nothing religious" about the terrorists' point of view, that religion can sometimes drive people to do terrible things. (This was after Muhammad Atta's "last night" letter had come to light, clearly illustrating that for Atta, his was a religious act.) While I received some positive responses, I also received some truly vicious hate mail, including a disturbingly suspicious package that I turned over unopened to our postal inspector. My institution received angry letters from alumni, threatening to withhold contributions.

What was especially interesting about the hostile responses is that they continued 10-year-old themes: That I should not suggest that we try to understand how Muslim radicals construct their worldview. That to grant Al Qaeda's position even a whiff of comprehensibility is to commit a mortal sin against not only religion, but democracy. That, whatever coherence the study of religion might discern in radical or divergent points of view, those findings are better left unspoken.

ONE OF THE MOST ALARMING ASPECTS of the 51-day assault on Mount Carmel is that it passed without significant protest. It was as if, as one commentator remarked, the American people were watching a miniseries. Today, the readier analogy might be to reality television, a depressingly accurate assessment of what mainstream journalism has become.

The stars of *Waco: the Miniseries* were Koresh, in the role of mad prophet, squared off against heroic FBI agents, there to avenge the deaths of their fallen comrades. Janet

Reno also starred, in her debut as attorney general. The 130 Mount Carmel residents were simply extras. The government kept it that way: Videotapes made by the Davidians—which demonstrate that as a group they were educated, articulate, and anything but brainwashed—were withheld from the news media and the public by the FBI. The media failed to obtain their release. In any case, it was easier, and more ratings-friendly, to promote the image of the "wacko from Waco" and his anonymous, zombified flock.

The Branch Davidians' civil rights were violated in a number of ways the USA Patriot Act has actually rendered legal.

Of course, in situations of war and law enforcement, the authorities can exert considerable control over information. But that does not excuse the extent to which the news media served as government spokespersons at Waco. The FBI, praised for their nonaggression, subjected the Branch Davidians to harassment akin to torture. Federal agents were lauded for their "restraint" in withholding fire when an unarmed Davidian left the complex. When the final assault came on April 19, agents used armored vehicles to block exists, lobbed incapacitating, cyanide-producing gas and incendiary tear gas into the tinder-dry complex in high-wind conditions, and detained rescue workers and firefighters a mile from the scene. The news media called the result mass suicide. And the American public eagerly believed.

Rarely has there been a more blatant case of victim blaming. But in the popular imagination, the Branch Davidians barely qualified as victims. To the extent that they existed at all, they were not merely faceless, they were unworthy of public sympathy. They were child abusers.

They practiced polygamy. They owned all those weapons. They were zealots, probably crazy. They brought it on themselves, and they deserved whatever they got. So even if they were to some extent victims, they weren't innocent ones. Twenty-one children died, some argued, because they had bad mothers.

The discourse, like the death count, belongs to the winning side. As the FBI's tanks were battering down the walls, a voice on the loudspeaker kept intoning: "This is not an assault. This is not an assault." If victims are by definition guilty, then the aggressor must perforce be righteous. Which is what we are seeing today in Iraq: The way to achieve peace is through war, which is defined as a "humanitarian" action. Closer to home, the war on terror demands the suppression of rights, in the name of freedom.

Waco is thus eerily relevant. Ultimately, the federal authorities employed the same arguments for their "pre-emptive" strike against Mount Carmel as the Bush administration has for war against Iraq. The federal authorities prohibited news-media access to the Davidians in much the same way, and for essentially the same reasons, that journalists today are kept from learning the precise number, let alone the names, of detainees at Guantánamo Bay and elsewhere. Then as now, the mainstream media colluded in the process of demonizing the "other." The Branch Davidians' civil rights were violated in a number of ways the USA Patriot Act has actually rendered legal, although their former illegality neither stopped the federal agents nor led to any sanctions against them.

It is easier, and alarmingly more acceptable, to violate the rights of a broader spectrum of individuals and groups today than ever before. Recently, Supreme Court Justice Antonin Scalia underscored that point when he commented that the Constitution "just sets minimums" and that, especially during wartime, the government has considerable room to scale back people's rights.

David Thibodeau, one of a handful of Davidian survivors, has lamented that in the aftermath of Waco he came to see himself "as an outcast from an America that had always been mine." The steps being taken in the name of homeland security and the war on terror may leave untold numbers of Americans in a similar position, for religious or other reasons of conscience. The current assaults on civil and human rights in the United States demonstrate that too few Americans read the message in the flames that flared on that windswept plain 10 years ago.

Mary Zeiss Stange is an associate professor of women's studies and religion at Skidmore College and, most recently, the co-author of Gun Women: Firearms and Feminism in Contemporary America (*New York University Press, 2000*).

From *The Chronicle of Higher Education*, April 11, 2003, pp. B10-B11. © 2003 by Mary Zeiss Stange.

NATION: Homeland Security

Fears Mount Over 'Total' Spy System

Civil libertarians and privacy-rights advocates are fearful of a new federal database aimed at sorting vast quantities of personal data to identify terrorist threats.

By J. Michael Waller

The Pentagon has blundered into another self-made public-relations disaster, allowing critics for the second time in a year to fan flames of hysteria over development of high-tech means to wage the war on terrorism. Called Total Information Awareness (TIA), it is a small experimental program in its infancy deep within the Pentagon research unit that developed the Internet. TIA is designed to test whether terrorist attacks can be detected and stopped before they occur by combining massive amounts of electronic data already available on commercial and government databases.

Critics leaked, apparently falsely, that TIA would build electronic dossiers on the personal lives of all Americans. And while few would argue that it raises powerful concerns about civil liberties and the abuse of government power, the most inflammatory and paranoid allegations took on a life of their own when critics pointed to the official running TIA: retired Rear Adm. John Poindexter.

Law enforcement continues to suffer from the 1970s campaigns against the federal security and intelligence agencies, and the since-abolished intelligence units of state and local police.

As national-security adviser to President Ronald Reagan, Poindexter took responsibility for the so-called Iran-Contra scandal, in which the White House had planned to rescue American hostages in the Middle East in exchange for selling weapons to Iran. The proceeds would be used to circumvent congressional restrictions—imposed by lawmakers sympathetic to Marxist-Leninist revolutionaries in Central America—and fund the military needs of the anticommunist Nicaraguan resistance fighters, known as "contras."

Poindexter took the political and legal bullet for President Reagan, and was convicted on five felony counts of lying to Congress and related charges. A higher court overturned the convictions. While legally exonerated, Poindexter remained a political hot potato with plenty of political enemies in Congress and the media. Even some of his fans agree off-the-record that it was unwise to place a political lightning rod in charge of a program that raised so many civil-liberties questions.

And so, the real purpose of TIA was lost amid the controversy. *INSIGHT* has put together the pieces to explain what TIA is all about.

The Bush administration is building a layered defense against terrorists: First, destroy terrorist cells and capture or kill individual terrorists and their sponsors abroad. Second, neutralize their bases of operation in other countries. Third, erect a security barrier to prevent their entry into the United States. Fourth, deny sanctuary to those who either have entered the United States or have been recruited here. Fifth, monitor, infiltrate and disrupt their domestic-support networks. Finally, move in on the terrorists themselves before they strike.

Federal antiterrorist investigators tell *INSIGHT* that they severely lack the human resources—agents, officers and citizen volunteers—to make a dent in the terrorist-support infrastructure in the United States. While making some headway in such hot areas as Dearborn, Mich.—where a large, ethnic-Arab/ Muslim community serves as a proverbial sea in which the terrorist fish swim—the FBI and other agencies say they have a long way to go to shut down terrorist networks already on U.S. soil.

Law enforcement continues to suffer from the 1970s campaigns against the federal security and intelligence agencies, and the since-abolished intelligence units of state and local police. With the loss of literally thousands of trained personnel and their painstakingly built support networks, authorities at all levels sometimes are waging the domestic antiterrorism war without eyes or ears. They say they need to use new information technologies to help close the gap.

The federal government, to say nothing of the legal system and political culture, is only starting to get used to the idea that it is responsible for defending the American people against terrorist attacks before they occur. This post-9/11 perspective throws previous custom and practice out of the window. FBI Director Robert Mueller is battling the bureau to change from a reactive investigative force that busts bad guys only after they maim and kill to a proactive force that stops the terrorists before they attack. That's a huge cultural shift for the by-the-book G-men, and it means changing the very essence of what the FBI has been since its inception, to say nothing of the mind-set and legal practice of federal prosecutors, defense lawyers and the judges who issue warrants and hear criminal cases. With revolutionary information technologies offering a possible solution to the human-intelligence shortage, new controversies have arisen.

Someone to watch over you: Civil-rights advocates fear that TIA will allow the government to pry into minute details of Americans' private lives.

Now, a combination of left-wing activists, Islamist sympathizers of terrorist groups, civil libertarians, gun-rights advocates and mainline conservatives are up in arms about the latest proposals to prevent terrorists from killing more Americans. They fear, for different reasons, that the Bush administration and Congress are vastly increasing and centralizing the power of the federal government over the American population in the name of fighting terrorism.

The existence of TIA became public information when the Defense Advanced Research Projects Agency (DARPA), the Pentagon's central research-and-development organization, solicited proposals last March for private companies to bid on developing the program. But it received little attention until Congress was passing the Homeland Security bill in November and conservative *New York Times* columnist William Safire attacked it as George Orwell's *1984* come to life. "To this computerized dossier on your private life from commercial sources, add every piece of information that government has about you—passport application, driver's license and bridge-toll records, judicial and divorce records, complaints from nosy neighbors to the FBI, your lifetime paper trail plus the latest hidden-camera surveillance—and you have the supersnoop's dream: 'Total Information Awareness' about every U.S. citizen," Safire wrote.

Framed in terms of the government keeping dossiers on every citizen, press commentary on TIA since has wobbled between paranoia and prudence. For once *The Nation*, long the keeper of the party line of the pro-Soviet left, and the happily unreconstructed McCarthyites of *National Review* sounded the same alarm: Big Brother is here. "Fighting terror by terrifying U.S. citizens," the panicked *San Francisco Chronicle* called it. "Orwellian," editorialized the *Washington Post*. A screaming page-one banner

headline in the *Washington Times* cribbed Safire's line: "A supersnoop's dream." Popular Washington news-talk host Chris Core of WMAL radio likened TIA to the Soviet KGB and the Nazi Gestapo.

TIA was all the more dangerous, critics said, because the man running the alleged program was Poindexter. *National Review* called him a "pipe-smoking Reagan capo." Sen. Charles Schumer (D-N.Y.) grandstanded on television, demanding that Defense Secretary Donald Rumsfeld fire the scholarly admiral. Rumsfeld ignored him.

"Take a nice deep, deep breath," Rumsfeld chided reporters. "It's a case of 'Ready. Shoot. Aim.' The hyped and alarmed approach [in the media] is a disservice to the public," he said. "Nothing terrible is going to happen."

Oddly, some of the most reasoned commentary came from foreign news organizations—and not all of them friendly to the United States. *Khilafah.com*, an Islamic revolutionary news organization devoted to promoting the re-establishment of the caliphate, tagged TIA not as a spy system to snoop on U.S. citizens but an "information matrix to track movements of America's enemies."

The American Civil Liberties Union (ACLU), which led the successful fight in the 1970s to cripple the FBI and CIA and abolish local police-intelligence units that monitored terrorist and subversive groups, launched a new campaign against TIA. The DARPA project, it says, is "a computer system that would provide government officials with the ability to snoop into all aspects of our private lives without a search warrant or proof of criminal wrongdoing." According to the ACLU, "Under this program, our entire lives would be catalogued and available to government officials." Poindexter, the ACLU alleges, "has been quietly promoting the idea of creating 'a virtual centralized database' that would have the 'data-mining' power to pry into the most minute and intimate details of our private lives."

The Pentagon says TIA is simply "an experimental protótype in the works that will determine the feasibility of searching vast quantities of data to determine links and patterns indicating terrorist activity." DARPA conceived of the terrorist-prediction data-crunching system with the benefit of the 20/20 hindsight from studies of past major terrorist attacks. "In all cases, terrorists have left detectable clues that are generally found after an attack," according to a DARPA fact sheet on the issue. If in the course of investigation federal authorities could identify and act upon clues that would let them wrap up terrorist cells, TIA developers reasoned, they could pre-empt the terrorism and save lives.

Critics have cited the lack of communication between U.S. agencies as one of the main reasons several of the September 11 terrorists were able to enter the country.

Administration officials working on TIA and related initiatives agree that a domestic-security matter should not be under the purview of the Pentagon. "If DARPA didn't support it when we needed to give it a try, what other agency would have?" asks a counterterrorism official. "The fact is, there was no one else. We're in a war, Poindexter had an idea worth testing and DARPA stepped up to the plate."

Given those considerations, the Bush administration planned from the beginning to move such projects from out of the purview of the Pentagon and DARPA and designed a new Security Advanced Research Projects Agency (SARPA) under the new Department of Homeland Security.

Undersecretary of Defense Pete Aldridge, under whose authority DARPA falls, says that TIA's mission consists of three parts: to research technologies that would allow rapid language translation, to discover connections between current activities and future events, and to develop "collaborative reasoning and decisionmaking tools to allow interagency communications and analysis"—just the tools needed to keep one agency informed of the intelligence produced by another agency.

Critics have cited the lack of communication between U.S. agencies as one of the main reasons several of the Sept. 11

terrorists were able to enter the country. The CIA reportedly tracked some of the future hijackers from the Philippines and Malaysia as they entered the United States, but the FBI apparently neither received nor followed up on the reports, thus allowing the terrorists to organize and launch their attacks undetected. Recent investigative reports have found that the State Department issued visas to several of the 9/11 hijackers even though the applications contained unacceptably incomplete and even demonstrably false information, and that alleged Washington Beltway sniper John Muhammad actually procured a U.S. passport with a birth certificate that a U.S. consular official suspected was forged, but which her superior apparently instructed her to ignore.

Some of those problems could be solved with bureaucratic restructuring, improved training and discipline, and changes of mission—all problems being addressed. Others require vastly improved information technologies to collect, analyze and synthesize ever-increasing quantities of data for human analysts and policymakers who already are overloaded with information.

"Even if we could find these clues faster and more easily, our counterterrorism defenses are spread throughout many different agencies and organizations at the national, state and local levels," notes DARPA's Information Awareness Office (IAO), which supervises TIA development. "To fight terrorism, we need to create a new intelligence infrastructure to allow these agencies to share information and collaborate effectively, and new information technology aimed at exposing terrorists and their activities and support systems. This is a tremendously difficult problem because terrorists understand how vulnerable they are and seek to hide their specific plans and capabilities. The key to fighting terrorism is information. Elements of the solution include gathering a much broader array of data than we do currently, discovering information from elements of the data, creating models of hypotheses and analyzing these models in a collaborative environment to determine the most probable current or future scenario."

According to the IAO, "The goal of the TIA program is to revolutionize the ability of the United States to detect, classify and identify foreign terrorists and decipher their plans—and thereby enable the U.S. to take timely action to successfully pre-empt and defeat terrorist acts. To that end, the TIA objective is to create a counterterrorism information system that: (1) increases information coverage by an order of magnitude and affords easy future scaling; (2) provides focused warnings within an hour after a triggering event occurs or an evidence threshold is passed; (3) can automatically queue analysts based on partial pattern matches and has patterns that cover 90 percent of all previously known foreign terrorist attacks; and (4) supports collaboration, analytical reasoning and information-sharing so that analysts can hypothesize, test and propose theories and mitigating strategies about possible futures so decisionmakers can effectively evaluate the impact of current or future policies and prospective courses of action."

"We can develop the best technology in the world and, unless there is public acceptance and understanding of the necessity, it will never be implemented."

The $10 million program is only an "experiment," explains Aldridge. "In order to preserve the sanctity of individual privacy, we're designing this system to ensure complete anonymity of uninvolved citizens, thus focusing the efforts of law-enforcement officials on terrorist investigations." By collecting applications for passports, visas, driver's licenses, airline-ticket purchases and rental-car reservations, as well as purchases of firearms and precursor chemicals for explosives, medical data and credit- and debit-card purchases, flying lessons, arrests and reports of suspicious activities, proponents say they hope TIA will develop a product able to single out factors indicating preparations for a possible terrorist attack. But the idea is for the information to be anonymous until such time that a warrant is needed for surveillance, arrest or detention.

And given the nature of so slippery an invasion of privacy, how can Americans be sure of that? "The data are subject to the same Privacy Act restrictions that currently govern law enforcement and government," says Aldridge. To investigate further requires government agencies to go through the same processes of procuring judge-issued warrants and other legal hoops to protect individual rights, he says.

Civil libertarians, privacy advocates, gun-rights groups and others worry that even experimenting with such a system risks transfer of unprecedented power to an unaccountable—and often incompetent—central government. Poindexter says that the TIA system is being built with safeguards embedded in the software, with audit trails and the protection of individual identities, and that his shop is only creating the experimental technology. How that technology would be used, he states, would be up to the executive branch, Congress and the courts, with all the necessary safeguards. He recognizes that the project will go nowhere without public support. Though his office now says he is not taking press interviews, he told the *Washington Post*, "We can develop the best technology in the world and, unless there is public acceptance and understanding of the necessity, it will never be implemented."

J. MICHAEL WALLER IS A SENIOR WRITER FOR Insight MAGAZINE.

Access DENIED

To forestall potential terrorist actions, the Energy Department
closed Web sites and removed documents from the Internet.
In the process, the public got shut out.

by Brian Costner

FOLLOWING THE SEPTEMBER 11 attacks on the World
Trade Center and the Pentagon, the Energy Department
not only enhanced physical security at its national laboratories and sites, it began questioning the information
available on its Web sites. In October, Energy Department
managers, concerned about the breadth and the ease of
availability of information on the Internet, began pulling
thousands of files to see if they contained anything that
could be used by terrorists. The search extended to documents in public reading rooms. Citizens living near the
Pantex Plant outside Amarillo, Texas, found the shelves
of their public reading rooms cleared. Even documents
on groundwater pollution and other environmental impacts of plant operations had been replaced by a sign ex-
pressing an apology for the inconvenience.

On October 26, Deputy Energy Secretary Frank Blake
formalized the removals by issuing a department-wide
directive to "review the operational information accessible to members of the public and remove or restrict access, as appropriate, to information that may be used to
target the Department of Energy." Blake identified a
number of areas as potential threats to security, including
emergency planning hazard assessments, safety analysis
reports, environmental impact statements, detailed site
and facility maps, photographs of facilities, and personal
data on employees.

Once pulled, documents were put in line for security
reviews, very much like reviews they passed years, or in
some cases months, ago. Blake gave the Security and
Emergency Operations Office some responsibility for coordinating the review plans, but the reviews themselves
were assigned to managers responsible for discrete activities, such as a single Web site. By late January, while
some documents had been returned to the public domain,
hundreds were still being examined.

At headquarters

The Energy Department's home page and its directly
linked pages show no obvious signs that anything has
changed. Dig a little deeper, though, and the absence of
documents becomes apparent.

As of January 29, the link to the Security and Emergency Operations Web site in Energy's directory of office
headquarters automatically redirected visitors back to the
department's home page. Web sites for the offices of Defense Nuclear Nonproliferation, Fissile Materials Disposition, and Defense Programs had been taken off-line
"until further notice."

Although Web sites of other Energy offices still allowed access, they too displayed large holes where data
used to be. The Office of Civilian Radioactive Waste Management is responsible for the controversial Yucca Mountain project in Nevada. Energy Secretary Spencer
Abraham has recommended that President Bush give the
project a green light, and both supporters and opponents
are preparing for a tough legal and public opinion battle.
But a number of Yucca Mountain documents were removed from the Web site, including the draft environmental impact statement; the site viability assessment;
lists of once-available technical documents; online databases; elements of a virtual tour of the Yucca Mountain
site and surrounding Nye County; a video showing a 360-
degree view from the top of Yucca Mountain; and maps.

The Web Site explained that, "The Office of Civilian Radioactive Waste Management promotes the open review of
documents by the public during the Yucca Mountain site
recommendation consideration process. However, following the attacks of September 11, 2001, we have removed
certain content from our Internet site to minimize the risk

Where has all the data gone?

The Energy Department's Web site wasn't the only one purged of electronic documents after the September 11 attacks. At least a dozen other federal and state agencies reportedly pulled information off the Internet because they deemed it a potential security risk.

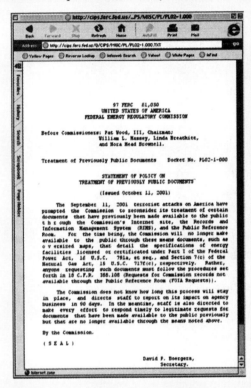

Some posted messages similar to the one at the Environmental Protection Agency's chemical accident prevention and risk management plan site. The site had contained information about emergency plans and chemicals used at 15,000 locations nationwide, but explained, "Risk management plan files that do not contain off-site consequence analysis information have been temporarily removed by EPA from its Web site in light of September 11. EPA is reviewing the information we make available over the Internet and assessing how best to make the information publicly available. We hope to complete that effort as soon as possible."

Similar worst-case scenario (off-site consequence analysis) information about potential chemical accidents has been kept off-line in limited-access reading rooms since 1999 due to legislation promulgated after the Oklahoma City bombing.

The Federal Aviation Administration barred access to enforcement information due to "security concerns." Transportation Department officials restricted pipeline mapping information, pipeline data, and data on unusually sensitive drinking water areas to approved pipeline operators and community officials. The Nuclear Regulatory Commission disabled a number of links, including those to the reactor oversight process, the nuclear reactor research program, regulatory initiatives for high-level waste disposal, and locations of reactors, whether operating or decommissioned. The Federal Energy Regulatory Commission barred online access to its records, including oversized maps detailing specifications of energy facilities. NASA's Glenn Research Center limited public access to technical data, such as instrumentation, control, and sensors information and ground and flight projects.

At the state level, the New York State Emergency Management Office removed driving directions to New York's two stockpiles of emergency supplies; New York's Public Service Commission removed a map of all existing and planned power plants in the state; and the State of New Jersey was withholding chemical information on 30,000 private sector facilities collected through its Community Right-to-Know program.

How quickly this information will be returned to the Internet, if at all, is unknown, and more may be removed before long. The National Infrastructure Protection Center, after receiving reports that U.S. infrastructure-related information was being accessed over the Internet from locations around the world, issued an advisory January 17 urging all content providers to review Web sites for "details on critical infrastructure, emergency response plans, and other data of potential use to persons with criminal intent."

Paul Rogers

Paul Rogers is a freelance writer in Chicago, Illinois.

of providing potentially sensitive information that could result in adverse impacts to national security."

Parties interested in the information could still obtain it off-line by calling 1-800-225-6972. But the site noted, "A name and street address will be required."

In some cases, a lucky or determined researcher might find documents that appear to have been removed in other areas. For example, reports on life-cycle costs and funding adequacy were no longer available from the technical documents section of the Yucca Mountain Web site but were obtainable at the Radioactive Waste office's publications page.

The Environmental Management office targeted any document with photographs or detailed maps of facilities, even though budget data, life-cycle cost estimates, and information about waste, pollutants, and program activities made up the bulk of each document. The office offered no explanation of what had been removed or why.

Among the missing documents: five reports on long-term stewardship (Energy's name for efforts to manage

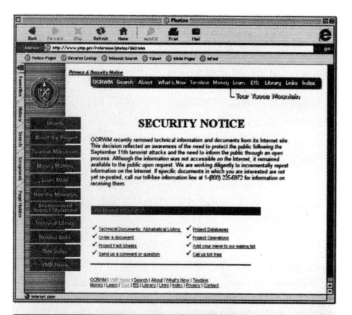

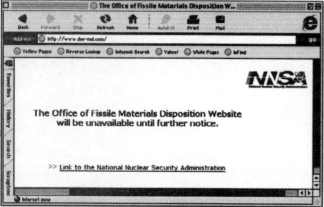

environmental hazards that will persist for generations); and historical documents, including the popular "Closing the Circle on Splitting the Atom" and "Linking Legacies." Slated for removal but still available at the end of January were summaries of environmental science and technology activities at seven Energy sites and case studies describing the successful use of new technologies to deal with environmental hazards.

"It is frustrating that certain documents with no possible security value have been swept up in this dragnet," said Jim Werner, an Energy official during the Clinton administration who was responsible for the preparation of many of the recently removed Environmental Management documents. "Broad, timely, and detailed environmental management information made the program more efficient, more effective, and more reliable and is a core reason for the program improvements during the 1990s. For example, if states and the public had not been given broad access to waste shipment and budget information, it is likely that the mixed waste and foreign spent fuel programs would have failed."

The Office of Environment, Safety, and Health develops policies for and provides semi-independent oversight of the department's efforts to protect workers, the public, and the environment. The office restricted public access to reports of its oversight and accident investigations, with the explanation, "In support of our mission to protect national security, and the health and safety of our workers, the public, and the environment, [the Energy Department] is performing a review of information on our Web sites. Some information may be temporarily removed during this review. We appreciate your patience and understanding as we perform our critical work."

The same explanation appeared on a non-functional search page for the Environment, Safety, and Health Web site and on the index page for the office's online document collection.

Environment, Safety, and Health is also responsible for Energy's compliance with the National Environmental Policy Act (NEPA)—the law requiring preparation of environmental impact statements and environmental assessments. Over the past five years, the department made most of its NEPA documents available without restrictions through a central Web site, along with guidance for implementing the law. After September 11, everything was briefly removed. Then the guidance was made available, but the NEPA documents remained unavailable. In January, internal access for department employees and some contractors was restored, but public access was still denied.

In the field

Meanwhile in New Mexico, as of January 29, people living near the Los Alamos National Laboratory were still waiting for access to hundreds of documents, including local NEPA guidance. The link to an electronic version of the "Environmental Justice Guide for LANL NEPA Analysis" produced only the message: "Electronic reports are unavailable. We regret the inconvenience."

Requests for most Los Alamos publications in its online research library were denied. The Energy Department blocked access to documents on such wide-ranging subjects as the evaluation of habitat use by elk, environmental remediation technologies, pollution prevention, bat population studies, science education programs, physics, and the laboratory's history. What had been the only publicly available, complete copy of the Resource Conservation and Recovery Act permit for the lab, along with an index of supporting documents, was also gone.

Removal of the documents in the midst of the permit review process has especially frustrated activists.

"Our ability to ensure that the permitting process for [Los Alamos] adequately addresses and prioritizes the environmental management requirements at [the lab] for past, current, and future operations has been put to a halt for the time being," said Colin King, research director for Nuclear Watch of New Mexico in Santa Fe.

Across the country in South Carolina, managers at the Savannah River Site pulled their entire Web site on October 25 and returned a greatly slimmed down version nearly a month later.

"Information had been rigorously reviewed prior to September 11, and the re-review has validated the strength of the original review," explained Kevin Hall, director of the Safeguards, Security, and Cyberspace Office for the Savannah River Site. "Not all content has been restored as the additional review process, while not necessarily identifying information of concern, is time consuming."

By January 29, none of the site's publications, environmental information, records about tritium operations, or information about science and technology activities had been restored. And while the shelves of the local public reading room remained full, the database allowing searches of available documents was taken off-line while the documents themselves were reviewed.

At the rest of Energy's facilities, the degree of change varied widely. The Hanford Site barely revised its Web content at all. Substantive documents, including many environmental impact statements and environmental assessments, remained publicly available. And the Fernald Environmental Management Project Web site continued to provide information about waste and contamination that was denied elsewhere.

In the end

The Energy Department is far from having resolved how it will control information access, especially via the Web, in light of September 11. Deputy Secretary Blake's directive reflected the desire of many within the department to act quickly, and that in itself limits options.

"The system works not with a scalpel, but with dull, blunt instruments," said former Energy official Werner. Since many people examining security are unfamiliar with the details of the thousands of documents available on the Web, they had little choice but to pull them and undertake a detailed review, he said.

To ensure that the public at least knows what material was pulled by Energy, the Natural Resources Defense Council (NRDC) filed a request in January under the Freedom of Information Act to find out which documents were recalled. Energy's response came quickly but did not include a list of documents. Instead, it challenged the council's request for a fee waiver.

"Since the advent of the Bush administration, various federal agencies have initially challenged appropriate requests for fee waivers then granted the waiver before the situation escalated," said NRDC attorney Geoffrey Fettus. The council has since addressed the Energy challenge and expects the department to begin cataloguing the missing documents.

"So far, [the Energy Department] has indicated that the information is being removed pending review. I would like to take them at their word, and I suspect that we will eventually get back to more or less where we were with document availability, though there will be a struggle to get there, with a lot of gnashing of teeth," said Werner. "Legitimate security concerns will ultimately get sifted out, assuming there is a continuing public demand and interest."

Brian Costner is an independent consultant based in Washington, D.C., and former senior policy adviser for Environment, Safety, and Health under Energy Secretary Bill Richardson.

Missing links

Many government agencies pulled documents off-line or shut down Web sites for document review. As of January 29, the URLs listed below either redirected viewers to other sites, contained disabled links, led to shuttered sites, or offered some rationale for removing data.

Energy Department sites

Environment, Safety, and Health Office of Oversight: tis.eh.doe.gov/oversight

Los Alamos National Laboratory Research Library: lib-www.lanl.gov/pubs/la-pubs.htm

Civilian Radioactive Waste Management Office: www.rw.doe.gov

Defense Programs Office: www.dp.doe.gov

Environmental Management Office: www.em.doe.gov

Fissile Materials Disposition Office: www.doe-md.com

Defense Nuclear Nonproliferation: www.nn.doe.gov

Security and Emergency Operations Office: www.so.doe.gov

Savannah River Site: www.srs.gov

Yucca Mountain Project: www.ymp.gov

Other sites

Department of Transportation Office of Pipeline Safety: www.npms.rspa.dot.gov/data/npms_data_down.htm

Environmental Protection Agency: www.epa.gov/ceppo/review.htm#rmpreview

Federal Aviation Administration: av-info.faa.gov/dd_sublevel.asp?Folder=%5Ceis

Federal Energy Regulatory Commission: cips.ferc.fed.us/Q/CIPS/MISC/PL/PLO2-1.000.TXT

NASA Glenn Research Center: www.grc.nasa.gov/Doc/grcweb.htm

New Jersey Department of Environmental Protection: www.state.nj.us/NASApp/pCRTK/jsp/ecrtkview.jsp

Nuclear Regulatory Commission: www.nrc.gov/reactors.html and www.nrc.gov/waste.html

Terrorism and civil liberties

Heading in the wrong direction

The Bush administration is making a dangerous hash of its terrorism laws

IN 1962 the apartheid regime in South Africa, no re-specter of civil liberties, picked up a suspected terrorist leader who had just returned from training in bomb-making and guerrilla warfare in Ethiopia. It marked the start of 27 years in jail, but Nelson Mandela was given access to lawyers and his prosecutors had to follow rules of due process. Last year, the world's foremost democracy, the United States, detained one of its own citizens, Jose Padilla, at Chicago airport as a witness to a grand-jury probe and then categorised the so-called dirty bomber as an "enemy combatant"—which, according to the government, gives it the right to hold him indefinitely, with no access to a lawyer and minimal judicial review.

Though Mr Padilla is unlikely to become a Mandela, his treatment is but one cause for concern about the Bush administration's approach to civil liberties. Of course, September 11th prompted America to reconsider the balance between liberty and security, and to favour the latter; America's freedoms seemed to have helped 19 hijackers to live and train in the country for up to two years. And given the relative lack of a legal structure to deal with terrorism, the American government has often had to think on its feet. Yet even allowing for all this, George Bush is heading in the wrong direction.

The importance of due process

If you accept, as most do, that the war on terrorism justifies wider powers of surveillance and detention, then two principles still need to be applied. First, the government's new powers should, where possible, be enacted in clearly-worded terrorism laws, passed by Congress. Second, wider powers should be balanced by wider review. Spies, now less constrained, should be more answerable for their actions; suspects, deprived of their lawyers for longer periods, should eventually have more opportunity to present their case to a judge and, where possible, a jury; and the whole process should be subject to political and judicial review.

Precisely the opposite has happened. Far from establishing new checks and balances, the government has moved repeatedly to quash those that exist. It whistled one new terrorism law, the USA Patriot Act, through Congress soon after September 11th; now a draconian new "Patriot II" may be pushed through during a war with Iraq. But the government has also claimed new powers by executive fiat, citing precedent from tangentially related cases. Mr Padilla's strange status is justified by an obscure second world war ruling, putting him in a legal limbo similar to that of the "enemy combatants" in Guantanamo Bay. In practice, the government's main legal defence has been delay: it could take ages for the challenges to its behaviour to reach the Supreme Court.

The irony is that, particularly when it comes to surveillance, there is a good case for stronger powers. Despite fiddling with the FBI, America lacks a proper domestic intelligence-gathering service equivalent to Britain's MI5. Similarly, many of the ideas that so exercise American civil libertarians—such as the notion of government agents snooping on places of worship—seem reasonable precautions. But Mr Bush could make his case much more easily if he could also show that the use of these new snooping powers was itself being watched, and questioned, by judges and politicians.

The most disturbing aspect of America's approach comes once terrorist suspects have been arrested. Again, proper terrorism laws should allow a government to treat such people differently from normal criminals, as they are potentially more dangerous than humdrum law-breakers. But the differences should be of degree. By all means hold a terrorist suspect longer before he has access to a lawyer or before specific charges need to be made; but let the lawyer appear in due course. As for claims to be able to hold people indefinitely, powers like these smack of third-world dictatorship.

This week, John Ashcroft, Mr Bush's attorney-general, boasted that the government's tougher methods are yielding results. Recent arrests strengthen his argument. But would his immediate anti-terrorism battles have been so much less effective if he had paid more attention to the basic rules of due process? The public-relations cost has been frightful—particularly among groups such as immigrants and Muslims, whose help is most needed in battling terrorism.

Achieving a balance between security and liberty was never going to be easy. "For a vast and free nation, there is no such thing as perfect security," Mr Bush reflected last week. But America has jumped too far in one direction. A reassessment is called for, if it wants to avoid rude comparisons with South Africa four decades since.

UNIT 9

Intelligence and Homeland Security

Unit Selections

Key Points to Consider

- Could the U.S. Intelligence Community have prevented the attacks on September 11, 2001? Defend your answer.

- What role does new information technology play in the intelligence process?

- What changes need to be made to reform the U.S. Intelligence Community?

 **Links: www.dushkin.com/online/**
These sites are annotated in the World Wide Web pages.

Domestic Security: The Homefront and the War on Terrorism
http://www.pbs.org/newshour/bb/terrorism/homeland/intelligence.html

FAS Intelligence Resource Program
http://www.fas.org/irp/congress/2002_hr/index.html

Statement of DCI Tenet on Homeland Security and Intelligence
http://www.fas.org/irp/congress/2002_hr/062702tenet.html

Much of the criticisms of security failures after 9/11 have been addressed to the U.S. Intelligence Community (IC). Critics argue that the Intelligence Community failed in its primary task: to protect the United States from foreign threats. As investigations of the intelligence failures of 9/11 continue, little has apparently changed. While the FBI and CIA directors are talking about increased cooperation, the turf wars continue. Behind the scenes, intelligence officials appear more concerned with protecting their own fiefdoms and budgets from the potential encroachment of the new Department of Homeland Security than in pursuing the significant reforms needed to address future threats.

The U.S. Intelligence Community was established by the National Security Act of 1947. It currently consists of 14 government agencies, with an annual intelligence budget of around $35 billion. The most recent change to the structure of the community occurred in December 2001, when the U.S. Coast Guard was officially added to the roll of the Intelligence Community. Other members currently include the Central Intelligence Agency, the Defense Intelligence Agency, the National Security Agency, Army Intelligence, Navy Intelligence, Air Force Intelligence, Marine Corps Intelligence, the National Imagery and Mapping Agency, the National Reconnaissance Office, the Federal Bureau of Investigation, the Department of the Treasury, the Department of Energy, and intelligence components of the Department of State.

The Intelligence Community was created in 1947 to cope with the rapidly growing Soviet threat. For more than 40 years, most of its resources were targeted at the Soviet Union. Organizational structures and collection systems were developed specifically to gather intelligence from state actors. The dominant role of the military agencies in the community reflects cold war priorities. After the fall of the Soviets in 1990, despite significant debate and calls for reform, no significant structural reforms were made.

In the mid 1990s, in response to changing priorities and emerging threats, the Intelligence Community began to shift its focus increasingly to international terrorism and nonstate actors. Rather than designing new systems to deal with these threats, the Intelligence Community attempted to modify and use the systems and tools that it had used to spy on states to deal with nonstate actors. Little effort was made to reform its huge bureaucracies, eliminate the duplication of effort, address the lack of interoperability, and improve interagency communications. Rather than rethinking its approach to intelligence collection and analysis, state-centric models of threat assessment continued to prevail. The fundamental flaw of this approach was reflected in the belief that the best way to protect the homeland and prevent terrorism was to attack or invade a country.

The three articles in this unit examine the role of the Intelligence Community in homeland security. In the first article, Michael Scardaville argues that "… the greatest failing on September 11 was the inability of our intelligence and law enforcement agencies to prevent the attack." He offers a series of recommendations to improve intelligence and homeland security. The second article provides information about software currently being developed to help the intelligence community. New software capable of transactional analysis and data integration offer a glimpse into the future of the Intelligence Community. Lastly, "Time for a Rethink" examines the problems facing the Intelligence Community. It argues that the time has come to "rethink" and reform the Intelligence Community.

Filling the Gaps in Security

The greatest failing on September 11 was the inability of our intelligence and law enforcement agencies to prevent the attacks.

MICHAEL SCARDAVILLE

The September 11 terrorist attacks made it abundantly clear that U.S. national security policy in the post–Cold War era had not paid enough attention to a vital area—the American homeland.

Over the last decade, numerous nebulous issues have been deemed vital to national security. For example, in 2000, President Bill Clinton identified the AIDS epidemic in Africa as a threat to national security, and in 1995 and '99 the United States found itself fighting in the Balkans to restore "humanity" to the Yugoslav civil war. Meanwhile, the American people were left vulnerable to the threat of terrorism, contrary to the recommendations of numerous national commissions.

Osama bin Laden taught the American people and their leadership a hard lesson on September 11. The immediate reaction by many was disbelief, followed by anger, and, finally, a rush to correct a decade's worth of neglect.

The result was a new focus in government offices, boardrooms, and community centers around the nation. But where does one begin such a monumental task? Indeed, while the United States maintained a civil defense capability during the 1950s and 1960s, today's homeland security mission is much broader. It requires a new way of thinking, one that applies national security strategizing to a diversity of domestic policy decisions

that occur in both the public and private sectors.

During the swearing in of Gov. Tom Ridge as assistant to the president for homeland security, President George W. Bush noted, "We face a united, determined enemy. We must have a united and determined response."

To develop that response, the president established the Office of Homeland Security (OHS), assigning Ridge, its director, responsibility for coordinating emerging policies across the government and developing a long-term national strategy for protecting Americans from terrorism. To see the importance of this often-criticized office, one need only look at how federal support for first responders, a vital element of homeland security policy, developed in its absence.

Need for a systematic strategy

Large-scale terrorism during the first half of the 1990s (that is, the 1993 World Trade Center bombing, the 1995 Oklahoma City bombing, and the sarin gas attack on the Tokyo subway) motivated both Congress and the Clinton administration to enact policies to better prepare for the threat of biological or chemical terrorism in the United States. These policies were created ad hoc instead of as part of a strategy. In 2000 the General Accounting Office criticized the lack of

coordination in the federal government's efforts to prepare state and local first responders for terrorism with weapons of mass destruction. It noted, for example, that the Department of Defense and Department of Justice have targeted the same cities while others were ignored and criticized.

As a result, only 2,680 of the nation's approximately nine million first responders received hands-on training with chemical agents between 1996 and 1999, and only 134,000 received any form of federal training. More recently, Bruce Baughman, director of the Office of National Preparedness, testified before Congress that "even the best prepared states and localities do not possess adequate resources to respond to the full range of terrorist threats."

The federal government should first address any remaining problems in the nation's transportation systems.

The status quo cannot be the model for the future. Further, while consolidating programs or reorganizing federal agencies can reduce disorganization, neither approach will ever combine everyone under one roof. A coordinating body in the White House, similar to the National Security Council and with the backing of the president, will prove vital to implementing a long-term strategy for homeland security, regardless of the final form of the federal government.

Opportunities Missed in the 1990s

- During the first half of the 1990s, large-scale terrorism motivated Congress and the Clinton administration to enact policies to counter the threat of biological or chemical terrorism in the United States.

- These policies were created ad hoc instead of as part of a strategy. In 2000 the GAO criticized the lack of coordination in the federal government's efforts to prepare for terrorism.

- Only 2,680 of the nation's approximately nine million first responders received hands-on training with chemical agents between 1996 and '99, and only 134,000 received any federal training.

- More recently, Bruce Baughman, director of the Office of National Preparedness, testified that "even the best prepared states and localities do not possess adequate resources to respond to the full range of terrorist threats."

- The status quo cannot be the model for the future.

Today, our top priority is filling in the gaps in security that allowed al Qaeda to attack the United States on September 11. The Heritage Foundation's Homeland Security Task Force, commissioned shortly after the attacks, recommended four key areas in which action must be taken immediately: infrastructure protection, civil defense, intelligence and law enforcement, and use of the military. Over the long term, the lessons learned in fixing existing shortcomings in these areas should form the basis of an all-en-compassing national strategy for securing the American homeland.

Protecting America's infrastructure

The hijackers took advantage of weaknesses in aviation security, but attacks on other kinds of national infrastructure could have devastating consequences. For example, an attack on parts of the nation's energy grid could kill hundreds or thousands during the winter or summer months and cause mass panic. Biological or chemical contamination of a city's water supply is an ancient technique of warfare that terrorists could use with deadly consequences. An assault on a train carrying toxic chemicals could potentially kill more Americans than a small nuclear bomb.

To address these weaknesses, the federal government should first address any remaining problems in the nation's transportation systems. While the Aviation Security Act (P.L. 107-71) will likely help improve security in some ways (and possibly limit it in others), it does not do enough. One provision of the act requires all aircraft originating abroad to use the Advanced Passenger Information System (APIS).

Keeping ahead of the storm: An important part of America's infrastructure, the trucking industry needs continual surveillance and upgrading.

A program run jointly by the Customs Service, the Immigration and Naturalization Service (INS), and the Animal Plant Health Inspection Service, APIS requires participating airlines to submit their passenger manifests to the office after each flight leaves a foreign airport. While APIS would likely not have prevented the September 11 hijackings, the concept behind it is solid.

The program should be expanded and brought into the twenty-first century in order to fulfil its potential. First, the system should be used for all flights servicing the United States, regardless of whether they originate domestically or internationally. Also, it should use advanced Internet technologies to cross-reference federal terrorist watch lists with passenger manifests as tickets are being sold. That way the airline could be notified to delay the passenger, and airport security could be alerted to take appropriate action.

Our current regime of maritime trade also presents a ripe target for terrorists. Each year, 46 percent of the merchandise that enters the American economy from overseas does so through cargo container ships. Less than 3 percent of these ships are inspected, however. As Robert Bonner, director of the Customs Service, noted during a presentation at the Center for Strategic and International Studies, "The prescreening we do is not enough, nor is it done early enough."

As a result, terrorists could easily transport weapons (or other terrorists) into the United States undetected. Unfortunately, inspecting all the cargo containers that enter this country would bring international shipping to its knees and, with it, the American economy. Instead, the United States should experiment with a point-of-origin inspection regime. Like an expanded APIS, a point-of-origin inspection program would focus on detecting threats in advance.

Civil defense

Shortly after September 11, Congress and American media outlets were attacked by anthrax sent by an as yet undetermined terrorist. Americans should not be surprised by this occurrence. Biological warfare has been part of military tactics since at least 1346, and it has been used by foreign militaries and terrorists on U.S. soil before.

With the discovery of plans and laboratories for producing chemical, biological, radiological, and nuclear weapons at al Qaeda facilities in Afghanistan, the next catastrophic attack may very well employ a weapon of mass destruction (WMD). According to Sen. Bill Frist (R-Tennessee), the only doctor in Congress, "The consequences of such an attack, whether it is with anthrax, smallpox, tularemia, pneumonic plague, nerve agents or blister agents, are huge."

Courtesy of the Department of Defense

On duty in Montana: Members of the Army and Air National Guard dig a firebreak during training exercises near Helena. The guard is America's first line of defense at home.

As we learned last October, the key to mitigating the consequences of a WMD attack, particularly one with a biological or chemical weapon, is early detection. At present, we know an attack has occurred only when numerous people start to get sick. If future terrorists decide to strike with a contagious agent, such as smallpox, every hour will be vital, as each sick person will be spreading the disease.

> **Federal agencies do not adequately share information they have on suspected terrorists; nor do they share such information with state and local law enforcement.**

The most effective way to accelerate America's ability to recognize such attacks is to develop a national health surveillance network. This system should be built from the ground up and should incorporate existing technologies while remaining flexible to fit the unique needs of America's communities. A number of communities have already instituted their own systems. They should be linked to their state's health department and further connected to the federal government through an expansion of National Health Alert Network (NHAN).

After studying the compatibility of existing community networks with the NHAN, the OHS should issue a set of guidelines that communities and states can implement. As a nationwide network becomes available, public health officials will gain a broader perspective, allowing them to see unusual trends on the local, state, and national levels. A certain percentage of those initially exposed will still become sick and possibly die, but with earlier detection that number can be limited.

Intelligence and law enforcement

Perhaps the greatest failing on September 11 was the inability of our intelligence and law enforcement agencies to prevent the attacks. All of the 19 terrorists responsible had entered the United States on legal visas, but 3 had stayed on expired visas and another 5 were on federal watch lists. Two had even been pulled over for speeding shortly before the attack and were let off with a warning and a traffic ticket.

Federal agencies do not adequately share information they have on sus-

pected terrorists; nor do they share such information with state and local law enforcement. Clearly, no single resource can provide the police officers or intelligence agents with all the information they need quickly.

According to Sen. Orrin Hatch, "One of the first lessons we have learned from the September 11 attacks is that we must do a better job of encouraging information sharing between and among our law enforcement institutions." One way to break the information-sharing logjam is to create a national law enforcement information "fusion center," potentially building off of the FBI's Strategic Information and Operations Center.

The center should take in information on suspected and known terrorists from all federal, state, and local law enforcement agencies and disseminate it throughout the community. Participants in the fusion center should include the FBI, INS, Customs, Secret Service, consular affairs, state and local police departments, and the OHS.

Though the participants will not receive the same information, a general sense of awareness must be the end result. The center should take advantage of electronic data-mining technology, as applicable, to facilitate this process, and more effective data sharing must begin immediately by what ever means possible. In the long run, correcting this deficiency is the most important thing the federal government can do to improve homeland security.

The armed forces must be equipped to conduct traditional military operations abroad and contribute to homeland security domestically. Al Qaeda's speedy removal from its base in Afghanistan shows how important traditional military capabilities will continue to be in the war on terrorism. Further, the 2001 Quadrennial Defense Review maintains an appropriate balance between planning and capability for counterterrorist operations, traditional warfare, and other low-intensity conflicts.

Use of military for homeland security

The U.S. National Guard (USNG) is the primary component of the Department of Defense contributing to homeland security. As President Bush noted on February 14, 2001, "The National Guard will be more involved in homeland security, confronting acts of terror and the disorder our enemies may try to create."

Taking part in international peacekeeping operations and providing support services for the active forces encumber the USNG. It should be relieved of these duties, and additional personnel should be added to the active forces to conduct these missions. Further, the secretary of defense, in consultation with governors, the adjutant general, and the National Guard Bureau, should ensure that all National Guard units are integrated into the state and community incident-response plans in a support role.

The steps outlined above represent just a few of the immediate policy changes the United States should enact to improve domestic security. While none of these recommendations will guarantee that another attack does not occur, fixing these gaps in security will decrease its likelihood and increase the nation's ability to respond.

Further, these recommendations are merely the beginning of an effective homeland security policy. They should evolve into a national strategy, which should be adjusted annually as lessons are learned and priorities change. Other issues, such as how the federal government organizes for homeland security, should only be addressed after the most important immediate concerns are met and the nation has an effective national strategy.

Michael Scardaville is a policy analyst for the Heritage Foundation. He focuses on homeland security issues.

can sense-making keep us safe?

NEW INTELLIGENCE SOFTWARE HELPS INVESTIGATORS SEE PATTERNS AND WRING MEANING FROM A CHAOS OF CLUES— HELPING TO FIND TERRORISTS BEFORE ATTACKS TAKE PLACE.

by m. mitchell waldrop

A few years ago, says Jeff Jonas, a friend arranged for him to give a talk at the secretive National Security Agency, widely renowned as the most technology-savvy spy shop in the world. He wasn't quite sure what to expect. "I had never even set foot in Washington," says Jonas, founder and chief scientist of Systems Research and Development, a Las Vegas maker of custom software that was being used by casinos and other companies to screen employees and prevent theft. True, Jonas was proud of NORA, his company's Non-Obvious Relationships Awareness analytic software. The system can cross-correlate millions of transactions per day, extracting such items of interest as the info nugget that a particular applicant for a casino job has a sister who shares a telephone number with a known underworld figure. But Jonas reckoned that this would seem like routine stuff to the wizards of the NSA.

Wrong. "I was shocked," Jonas says. After his talk, several members of the audience told him that his technology was more sophisticated than anything the NSA had. And now Systems Research and Development has several government customers. Indeed, he says, "since September 11, the urgency has really peaked."

But maybe Jonas shouldn't have been shocked. There are many explanations for the failure of the U.S. Central Intelligence Agency, the Federal Bureau of Investigation, and their fellow intelligence agencies to "connect the dots" in time to stop the terrorist attacks. The list of reasons could start with the well-known inability of these organizations to communicate. But their analysts' out-of-date tool kit surely didn't help. Over the past decade, the business market has seen extraordinary advances in data mining, information visualization, and many other tools

for "sensemaking," a broad-brush term that covers all the ways people bring meaning to the huge volumes of data that flood the modern world. And yet, in a major study released last October, the Markle Foundation's Task Force on National Security in the Information Age emphasized that "we have not yet begun to mobilize our society's strengths in information, intelligence, and technology."

SEPTEMBER 11 BROUGHT A TECHNOLOGICAL IMPERATIVE: PUT THE PIECES OF DATA GATHERING AND ANALYSIS MACHINERY TOGETHER.

That's not quite fair. The mobilization has begun, albeit in piecemeal, internecine fashion. Individual agencies have been eager customers for the new technologies for several years. And since 1999 the CIA has been funding some of the most promising sensemaking companies (including Jonas's) through In-Q-Tel—the agency's own Arlington, VA-based venture capital firm. What's more, in early 2002 the U.S. Defense Advanced Research Projects Agency upped the ante by systematically developing sensemaking technology through its controversial new Information Awareness Office. But the problem, says the Markle task force, is that because each of the agencies is so intent on obtaining its own intelligence and buying its own technology, there has been no overall planning or coordination. Nor has a significant fraction of the annual $38 billion budgeted for homeland defense been devoted to building a capacity for sharing information or integrating its analysis.

That won't do. The era inaugurated with such fury by the assault of September 11 imposes a technological imperative: put the pieces of the data gathering and analysis machinery together. We must mobilize the nation's strengths in networking and analytical technology to create what the Markle task force calls a virtual analytic community: a 21st-century intelligence apparatus that would encompass not just the agencies in Washington, but also private-sector experts, local officials, and even ordinary citizens. The cold war was a mainframe-versus-mainframe confrontation, but the war against terrorism pits the United States against a network. It's time to take intelligence gathering and interpretation into the network age.

collecting the dots

"We're entering a new era of knowledge management," declares In-Q-Tel CEO Gilman Louie. "Call it the era of chaos or complexity or whatever trendy term you want. We're looking at a level of integration that has never been contemplated before in govermnent."

It's too soon to know how (or whether) officials in Washington will approach this challenge. Any effort will most likely be spearheaded by the U.S. Department of Homeland Security, which is still in the process of organizing itself. Nevertheless, it certainly is not too soon to take a look at how such a virtual intelligence system might work and how it might use technology most effectively.

Before we can connect the dots, we first have to *collect* the dots. And in the war on terrorism, notes the Markle report, "most of the people, information, and action will be in the field." Critical clues can come from unexpected places: "a cop hearing a complaint from a landlord, an airport official who hears about a plane some pilot trainee left on a runway, an FBI agent puzzled by an odd flight-school student in Arizona, or an emergency room resident trying to treat patients stricken by an unusual illness."

Likewise, in most cases, most of the expertise required to interpret particular pieces of intelligence or to devise responses will reside with local officials and other agencies outside the centralized-intelligence community. If, for example, a town is facing a threat to its water system, an appropriate response team might include state officials and local hospitals, as well as public utility commissioners, building inspectors, and watershed conservationists. So the virtual community's most basic requirement will be an online meeting space that's open to any and all such officials. Such a system could be implemented as a virtual private network running on top of the Internet, with standard encryption techniques providing the security. Many companies have been operating virtual private networks for several years.

But simple communication is only part of what's needed. Investigators from myriad federal, state, and lo-

cal agencies will also have to share data quite freely, if only because there's no way to know in advance what information will be relevant to whom. This commonsensical notion is *not* the norm in conventional intelligence agencies, where to protect sources and methods, information is kept tightly compartmentalized. Yet information sharing among employees is increasingly common in the corporate world; open communication helps companies become much more flexible, innovative, and responsive to customers. And it is even taking root in the Pentagon, where information sharing is known as network centric warfare. A prime example: the Afghanistan war, during which everyone involved—imagery analysts, fighter pilots, and experts on Afghanistan itself—had access to the same data and could interact in real time.

a time to share

It's one thing to advocate widespread data sharing; achieving it is another. Even with access to a secure network, for example, local police officials and other municipal officials may not have enough storage capacity or processing power to make good use of the data. But maybe such investigators could tap into the network itself for the resources they need. During the past few years, researchers have made rapid progress in "distributed computing," which uses high-speed Internet connections to link many computers so they work together as one machine. Grid computing, for instance, links mainframes together, and peer-to-peer systems similarly unite personal computers. But for all users, even if their own computers are terribly underpowered, the bottom line is much the same: so long as they can plug into the network, they will be able to access data files, analytical tools, and raw computational power as easily as if they were sitting at the world's greatest supercomputer. In a sense, they will be.

Provision of ample processing power will not completely alleviate the problems of information sharing, however. First, there's a technical issue: old databases (and even many new ones) store information in myriad incompatible formats. Then there's a policy issue: a long list of organizations control critical databases, and the overseers of many of them believe that their files contain information too sensitive to release to outsiders.

The trick is to share the information anyway. Techniques to make this feasible are under development. Innovation is especially active on systems for "structured" data: the kind in which names and numbers fit neatly in rows and columns, as in a spreadsheet or airline reservations database. One approach, advocated most notably by database giant Oracle, is to convert everything into a standard format and store it all in a common data warehouse. This approach has the virtue of simplicity, and because it allows for efficient searching, it is widely used for commercial data mining—the systematic processing of data to find useful pieces of information. Indeed, it is the approach Systems Research and Development uses for its

A Sampling of Sensemakers

COMPANY	LOCATION	ACTIVITY
Entrieva	Reston, VA	Management of unstructured data such as text files, Web pages, and audio and video
i2	Cambridge, England	Information visualization software
IBM	Armonk, NY	"Federated" management of structured data such as an airline reservations database, as well as unstructured data
In-Q-Tel	Arlington, VA	CIA's venture fund for companies with technologies that show promise for intelligence work
Intelliseek	Cincinnati, OH	Integration of information search and analysis tools
Stratify	Mountain View, CA	Management of unstructured data
Systems Research and Development	Las Vegas, NV	Software that finds subtle patterns in complex webs of relationships and transactions

system, which can monitor thousands of data sources in real time.

"Our largest installation to date was for a large corporation that wanted to aggregate data on customers and has 4,200 daily feeds," Jonas says. That's about nine million transactions per day. As each transaction occurs, the data it generates are translated into a standard format—typically one based on extensible markup language, an information-rich variant of the hypertext markup language used to code most Web pages. The proprietary software further refines the data using a process that tries to determine whether records for, say, "Bob Smith," "Rob Smith," and "Robert Smith" represent three people, two, or one. "Often the differences are unintentional," says Jonas. "But sometimes it's people trying to obfuscate who they are." Finally, he says, the algorithm looks for correlations that might relate one person to someone on a terrorist watch list. Results are generated in about three seconds. "Imagine that you have this ocean of data," he says. "When each new drop comes in, we can see all the ripples."

For one client, a large U.S. retailer facing nearly $40 million per year in fraud-related losses, Jonas's software examined the records of the company's thousands of employees and identified 564 who had relationships with either a company vendor—a possible source of illegal collusion—or a person the retailer previously had had arrested. And in a trial conducted for a retail association in Washington, the system turned up evidence of a ring of underage thieves who had been shoplifting a popular brand of jeans.

The company now has installations running at the FBI and several other government agencies, Jonas says. Most of that deployment is new since September 11. But if one of these had been monitoring the appropriate data feeds in late August 2001, he says, it might have noticed that using their real names and addresses, two men on the terrorist watch list of the U.S. Department of State had purchased airline tickets for American Airlines flight 77, which hijackers would crash into the Pentagon. Noting that coincidence, the system might have checked to see whether anyone else was using the addresses, frequent-flier information, and phone numbers provided by the two men.

Continuing in this way, the system might have created a chain of associations leading to many of the other 19 hijackers, including ringleader Mohammad Atta. Without the advantage of hindsight, of course, such a chain would not necessarily have screamed, Terrorists! But it might have put analysts on alert. And, with several days remaining before the scheduled flight, they might have turned up other links to such puzzling information not available online as a common interest in flight schools. Maybe—just maybe—agents might have stopped the conspirators at the gate on the morning of September 11.

database babel

We can never know what might have been. In the meantime, however, we must still contend with the problem of very sensitive data. The owners of certain data don't want to let their information anywhere near a common data warehouse. In such cases, the notion of "federated" information suggests an approach that may be more applicable.

DERIVING MEANING FROM FRAGMENTARY CLUES IS AN ESSENTIALLY HUMAN PROCESS. BUT TECHNOLOGY CAN HELP.

"It's a way to have integration without centralization," explains Nelson Mattos, director of information integration at IBM, which is forcefully developing this approach. The idea is to leave each data repository where it is—forget the warehouse—and instead provide it with a "wrapper": a piece of software that knows how to translate the inner workings of that particular database to and from a standardized query language. This way, says Mattos, "a single query can be sent out to access all forms of information, wherever it's stored." The answers that come back are arrayed on the user's screen in neat rows and columns, as if, he explains, they had been "all stored in a single database."

This architecture solves the compatibility problem automatically, Mattos says. It also helps to ensure that sensitive information goes only to the right people. In a federated system, he says, "I continue to own my data. But I can write a wrapper that allows outsiders to access parts of my data, without giving away the whole thing." The wrapper around a medical database might answer queries from public health officials about statistical information while denying access to information about specific patients. Likewise, the wrapper around an intelligence database might protect sources and methods. Such a system might be augmented by digital rights management, which could make it impossible to copy a digitally shared document.

start making sense

As powerful as they are, such tools as data mining help only to collect and refine the dots. Federated systems, for their part, help only to share these clues. And neither approach helps connect the dots—or piece together an understanding of what a cadre of terrorists or another criminal group is up to. This is perhaps the most difficult aspect of sensemaking. Working from fragmentary clues to develop an understanding of the how and why of a crime is what detectives do. It's also what scientists do, as they consider experimental evidence and develop a hypothesis that explains a phenomenon. In many ways, sensemaking is an essentially human process—one that's not going to be automated anytime soon, if ever. "You need good human judgment," emphasizes In-Q-Tel's Louie, "and an ability to draw sensible conclusions," qualities that must be built on knowledge of history, religion, culture, and current events.

Still, technology can help. For example, consider how many clues (and indeed, how many of the insights needed to make sense of them) have their origins not in structured information, but in the vast realm of so-called unstructured data, which range from text files and e-mail to CNN feeds and Web pages. And "vast" is the word for it; when fully digitized, CNN's video archives alone will require some four *petabytes* of storage, according to IBM, which is performing the conversion. That's the equivalent of about a million PC disk drives. No human being can hope to read, view, or listen to more than the tiniest fraction of the world's unstructured information. Even the best search engines are blunt tools. Do a Google search on "bonds," for instance: you'll get about five million hits on

pages related to municipal bonds, chemical bonds, Barry Bonds, and a slew of other concepts.

What you really want is to have only the documents that interest you automatically find their way to you, says Ramana Venkata, founder and chief technical officer of Stratify, a Mountain View, CA, company funded by In-Q-Tel. Ideally, the documents would do more than just announce their existence. "They should put themselves into the context of other documents or of key historical trends," Venkata asserts. And, of course, they should prioritize themselves, identifying which are most important, so that you don't drown in information. For now, that's still a pipe dream. But in the past few years, Stratify and a number of other companies have taken steps in that direction with their development of information classification software.

Even before September 11, Stratify's Discovery System had been in use by the CIA and other intelligence agencies, Venkata says. To understand how it works, he suggests, imagine that somebody hands you a 30-gigabyte disk drive that is discovered in a cave in Afghanistan and asks you to figure out what's on it. Or maybe you've downloaded a big collection of documents from a Web search. However you get them, he says, "the idea is to understand and organize the documents in terms of the topics and ideas they refer to, not just the specific words they contain."

The first step, says Venkata, is to develop a taxonomy for the collection—a kind of card catalog that assigns each document to one or more categories. A taxonomy for information about aircraft, for example, might have subcategories for "helicopters" and "fixed wing," with the latter subdivided into "fighters," "bombers," "transports," and so on. Stratify's software is set up to use or modify a standard taxonomy, says Venkata. Some organizations already have them. (Over the years, librarians have developed elaborate schemes for classifying information about biology, engineering, and countless other fields.)

But the software also can generate taxonomies automatically. Using proprietary algorithms, it scans through all the documents to extract their underlying concepts. On the basis of their conceptual similarity, it groups the documents into clusters, then links these clusters into larger clusters defined by broader concepts, continuing until every cluster is linked into a single taxonomy.

Furthermore, notes Venkata, the system assigns each document (and every new document that is added) to its appropriate place within the taxonomy. To ensure accuracy, Stratify's software pools the results of multiple sorting procedures and algorithms, which range from manual sorting and supervised machine learning ("*This* document is a good example of *that* category; look for others like it") to matching the statistical distribution of words. When appropriate, the system assigns documents to more than one category.

Of course, the user can edit the machine's results at any time. But the machine-generated taxonomy provides an

Cracking a Case

A dirty bomb is set to go off in Times Square on New Year's Eve. Plotters leave clues scattered around the world.

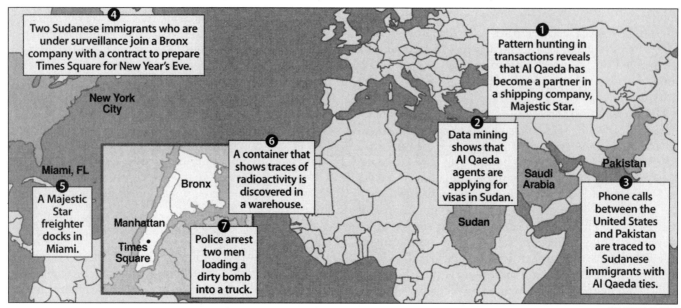

JOHN MACNEILL

efficient and effective way to understand what a collection of documents is *about*. After all, Venkata says, "taxonomies are not an end to themselves. They're tools to help you deal with huge amounts of information in a much more intuitive, natural way—to see patterns when you don't know what you're looking for."

seeing is believing

Once a system or framework is in place, other technologies can help keep track of the multitude of clues, not to mention the enormous array of possible interpretations. A good example is Analyst's Notebook, a set of visualization tools developed over the past decade by a Cambridge, England-based company called i2. Originally created for police and insurance investigators, Analyst's Notebook has recently attracted a following among U.S. intelligence agencies. Indeed, the company claims that President Bush is regularly briefed with charts from i2.

Right after September 11, says Todd Drake, i2's U.S. sales manager, "we were asked to come help out at FBI headquarters," where a hurriedly convened interagency intelligence group was struggling to get up and running. "Our software was already heavily deployed inside both the FBI and the Defense Intelligence Agency. So we saw cases where a DIA guy would walk past the cube where an FBI guy was sitting and say, 'Hey, I know this program!' And suddenly they'd be working together. If the bureaucratic barriers fall, technology can help cooperation happen."

Analyst's Notebook provides timelines that illustrate related events unfolding over days, weeks, or even years, as well as transaction analysis charts that reveal patterns

in, say, the flow of cash among bank accounts. But most dramatic of all are its link analysis charts. These look a bit like the route maps published in airline magazines, with crisscrossing lines connecting cities around the world. But the "cities" in these charts are symbols that represent people, organizations, bank accounts, and other points of interaction. (An i2 demonstration chart that traces only publicly available information shows the links that tie the September 11 hijackers to Osama bin Laden.)

Each element in a chart is hyper-linked to the evidence that supports it; that evidence, in turn, is tagged with such additional information as sources, estimated reliability, and security levels. If it later becomes apparent that information from a particular source is in fact *disinformation*—that is, lies—a single keystroke can purge from the chart all of that source's contributions. It is similarly straightforward to eliminate elements that are related to classified information. The "sanitized" chart, still quite useful, may be freely shared with collaborators who lack the requisite security clearances. "Why," Drake asks, "should the Drug Enforcement Administration have to redo something the Defense Intelligence Agency already did?"

thinking straight

Yet another way technology can enhance sensemaking is by providing tools that help steer analysts clear of certain mental pitfalls. That's the goal of the Structured Evidential Argumentation System, which was developed by SRI International under Project Genoa, a recently completed DARPA program. (Genoa II, a follow-on project, is now under way at DARPA's Information Awareness Office.)

According to SRI team leader John Lowrance, the argumentation system "helps you organize your thinking and keeps you from jumping to conclusions too soon." Too often, he says, when people are struggling to make sense of fragmentary clues, they succumb to the subconscious temptation to focus on one likely interpretation, neglecting to give other possibilities the attention they merit.

To help analysts avoid such blinkered thinking, SRI's system uses "structured argumentation," which marshals evidence according to a specified template. Depending on the task at hand, Lowrance says, the template might take the form of a flow chart, say, or a legal argument. The tool Lowrance's team developed appears as a hierarchy of yes-or-no questions. Someone monitoring country X might start an analysis with a high-level question: Is country X headed for a political crisis? Answering that question requires the analyst to get answers to several more specific queries, such as, Is political instability increasing? Is there a government power struggle with potentially destabilizing consequences? Each of those questions, in turn, might find its answers in terms of still more specific queries: Is there evidence of growing factionalism?

This drilling-down process continues until it generates questions that can be answered with specific pieces of intelligence, such as field reports, Internet downloads, or the output of data-mining systems. On the basis of those results, the analyst refers to a five-color scale and selects the color that conveys the degree of the answer's certainty: red, for "almost certainly yes"; orange, for "likely"; and so on, down to green, meaning "almost certainly no." The system automatically aggregates these conclusions into color-coded assessments of the higher-level questions. And it provides a number of displays—including a color-coded overview of the entire hierarchy—that starkly outline the areas of greatest concern in red and orange.

SRI's tool gives "a very quick sense of what's driving the conclusion," says Lowrance. Perhaps its most important benefit, he says, is that because the tool communicates results specifically, rapidly, and graphically to people who are not familiar with a situation, it offers an effective alternative to writing memos. SRI is exploring the possibility of developing a commercial version.

open secrets

Software companies have come up with a host of other analytical tools. In fact, with so many already available or under development, analysts are challenged to get everything to work together seamlessly. That's why In-Q-Tel is funding Cincinnati-based Intelliseek, one of the few companies that specialize in such integration.

"There is no silver bullet," says Intelliseek CEO Mahendra Vora. "And no one company has the complete solution to solve all our homeland security problems." What's needed, Vora says, is an open architecture that can incorporate new applications as they come along. For this reason, the company's systems use open standards, such as extensible markup language, that make it easy for different pieces of sensemaking software to work in harmony. This open technical approach is, perhaps, a metaphor for the new age of homeland security itself.

For many people, mere technical protections against governmental infringement on privacy provide little reassurance. Witness last fall's uproar in response to the news that John Poindexter, notorious for his involvement in the Iran-Contra affair, would head DARPA's Information Awareness Office. (William Safire fulminated in the *New York Times* about "this master of deceit" and his "20-year dream" to snoop on every U.S. resident.) Many Americans have a visceral aversion to domestic-intelligence gathering in any form, notes Lee Tien, an attorney with the Electronic Frontier Foundation, and, he adds, they have good reason. Whenever he hears a bright new idea for high tech intelligence, he says, "My question is, 'What would J. Edgar Hoover do with such a system?'"

If anything can improve the level of trust, says Tien, it is even greater openness. "Skepticism grows from secrecy," he says. "If officials are going to hide, not give any details, and just tell us they're protecting privacy, that's not a strategy that will reassure people." Conversely, he says, by being as forthcoming as possible, the Department of Homeland Security and any other agency that coordinates the intelligence-gathering effort could reap big dividends in the form of public cooperation and political support.

We can only savor the irony. It is our openness as a society that makes us so vulnerable to terrorism. Yet our openness—on both the technological and the human levels—may very well be our strongest defense.

From *Technology Review*, March 2003, pp. 43-48 by M. Mitchell Waldrop. © 2003 by MIT Technology Review. Reprinted by permission.

America's intelligence services

Time for a rethink

Just when they are most needed, America's spies are in a mess. But reform will happen only if George Bush wants it

WASHINGTON, DC

IMAGINE a huge $30-billion conglomerate. It operates in one of the few businesses that might genuinely be described as cutthroat. Its competitors have changed dramatically, and so have its products and technologies. But its structure is the same as when it was founded, in 1947. Nobody leads this colossus (there is just an honorary chairman) and everyone exploits it. Demoralised and bureaucratic, it has just endured its biggest-ever loss. The response: the firm has been given even more money, and nobody has been sacked.

Soon, the intelligence committees from the two houses of Congress will begin a special joint review of America's spies. The joint chairmen, Congressman Porter Goss and Senator Bob Graham, both insist that reform is possible. But structural change depends on the administration, and George Bush has already backed George Tenet, the Director of Central Intelligence (DCI), who staggeringly refuses to admit that September 11th was a failure. "Failure", says Mr Tenet, "means no focus, no attention, no discipline—and those were not present in what either we or the FBI did here and around the world."

The best protection for the intelligence services is that so few people understand what they do. Most Americans associate espionage with the Central Intelligence Agency and the DCI, the most conspicuous creations of the 1947 National Security Act. In fact, the "intelligence community" contains 13 federal organisations, and the CIA accounts for only around a tenth of the intelligence budget of $30 billion. Most of the real money goes to high-tech military

agencies, such as the National Reconnaissance Office (NRO), which runs the satellites, and the National Imagery and Mapping Agency (NIMA). The biggest, the National Security Agency (NSA), once so secret that it was referred to as No Such Agency, employs 30,000 eavesdroppers. By contrast, the CIA's Directorate of Operations—its human spying bit—has only around 4,000 people.

Some critics argue that the true cost of intelligence-gathering is closer to $50 billion, and the number of agencies dealing with the subject is closer to 45 (or even 100). They count in various bits of the FBI (which oversees counter-intelligence at home), parts of the new Office of Homeland Security, and sundry military and diplomatic organisations. Generally speaking, the system gets more convoluted the lower down you go, eventually becoming a blur of incompatible computer systems, different chains of command and an obtuse budgeting system.

Above all, there is the question of responsibility. Mr Tenet, as DCI, is both boss of the CIA and also director of all America's intelligence-gathering. He has a "community management staff" to assist him, but his real clout is small. Most of the intelligence budget is controlled by proper departments, whose bosses sit in the cabinet. Jim Woolsey, a former DCI, recalls that his predecessor, Bob Gates, warned him that his position was like the king's in medieval France: the nobles all swear fealty to you, but do not fear you.

Blown to pieces

Many people think this tangled structure (see chart) caused the failures around September 11th. Others point to mismanage-

ment, culture and even the American way of life. Who is right?

The mismanagement school of critics, which wants Mr Tenet's head, can only be buttressed by the pig-headed refusal of the seventh floor at Langley to admit to any failure. The excuses proffered vary. Some pass the buck around the labyrinth: CIA people point out that it was the FBI's job to trail terrorists at home. Others point to the list of atrocities that have been averted, which is fair enough, though at least one of the examples, the capture of a bomber with Los Angeles airport as his target, owed more to an observant customs official than to good intelligence.

Al-Qaeda, America's spymasters tried to claim, was peculiarly difficult to infiltrate, since it was open only to kinsmen of members. That notion was blown apart by the appearance of John Walker Lindh, a Californian airhead, in Osama bin Laden's trenches. As one former CIA boss puts it, "Al-Qaeda was an evangelical organisation: it wanted members. We never suggested any."

Enough. By any reasonable definition, the fact that 19 terrorists could slaughter 3,000 people should count as a monumental failure of intelligence—the worst since Pearl Harbour. Besides, as one senior Bush adviser argues, "it is not as if there were not enough clues to be picked up for our $30 billion a year." The World Trade Centre was a known target; al-Qaeda people had plotted to fly aircraft into buildings before; a suspect had been picked up having flying lessons; and so on.

Those who point to gross mismanagement are, however, currently less influential than the "culture" critics. According to these, Mr Tenet is less culpable than symp-

Simplicity itself
America's intelligence apparatus

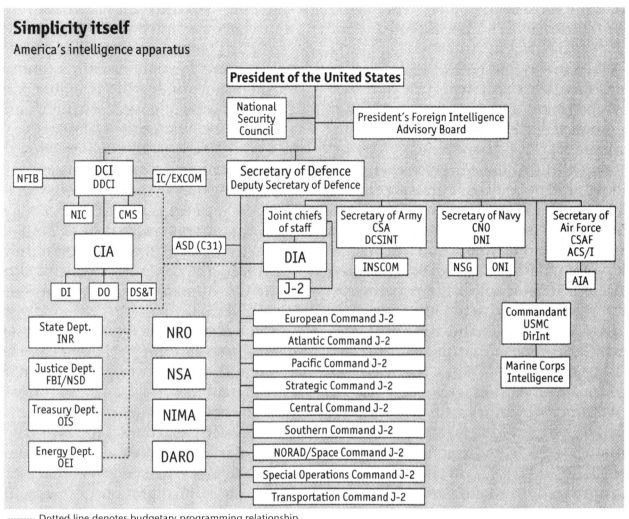

```
-------- Dotted line denotes budgetary programming relationship
```

ACS/I	Assistant Chief of staff/Intelligence	FBI	Federal Bureau of Investigation
AIA	Air Intelligence Agency	IC/EXCOM	Intelligence Community Executive Committee
CIA	Central Intelligence Agency		
CMS	Community Management Staff	INSCOM	Intelligence and Security Command
CNO	Chief of Naval Operations	INR	Bureau of Intelligence and Research
CSA	Chief of Staff, US Army	J–2	Joint Staff Intelligence
DARO	Defence Airborne Reconnaissance Office	NIC	National Intelligence Council
DCI	Director Central Intelligence	NIMA	National Imagery and Mapping Agency
DDCI	Deputy Director Central Intelligence	NRO	National Reconnaissance Office
DI	Directorate of Intelligence	NSD	National Security Division
DIA	Defence Intelligence Agency	NSG	Naval Security Group
DNI	Director of Naval Intelligence	OEI	Office of Energy Intelligence
DO	Directorate of Operations	OIS	Office of Intelligence Support
DS&T	Directorate of Science and Technology	USMC	United States Marine Corps

Source: William Oden, "Modernising Intelligence", National Institute for Public Policy, Jan 2002

tomatic of an intelligence community that has been in steady decline, held back by political correctness and an over-reliance on technology. Crucially, this explanation fits the political agenda of both the spies and the Bush administration.

Reined-in and risk-averse

Some trace the decline to the 1970s, when, after a series of scandals, the CIA was reined in by Congress. Many Republicans prefer to start with Bill Clinton, who, they claim, was

unwilling to wage war on terrorism. In 1996, in the wake of the murder of a Guatemalan by a CIA informant, officers were told to contact Langley before "establishing a relationship with an individual who has committed serious crimes or human-rights abuses or other repugnant acts." Nobody has been turned down under these guidelines. But they cannot have encouraged CIA people to make friends with, say, drug-smugglers.

The idea that the Directorate of Operations became risk-averse has been widely

promoted by frustrated ex-case-officers. In "See No Evil" (Crown, 2002), Robert Baer recalls how in Tajikistan in the early 1990s he asked for Dari and Pushtu speakers to interrogate Afghan refugees. He was first told that the CIA no longer collected data on Afghanistan, then offered a four-person sexual-harassment briefing team. Even defenders of the spy system admit it has a job-for-life mentality. John Gannon, a CIA analyst who has just moved to the private sector, says that he has fired more people in the past eight months than during his entire career in the service.

Yet daredevilry has never been more needed. During the cold war, an intelligence system that relied on intercepting Soviet military signals and picking up diplomatic gossip made sense. Now there are no ponderous tank divisions to track; and you are unlikely to meet your opposite number from al-Qaeda at the Brazilian ambassador's cocktail party.

In last July's *Atlantic Monthly*, Reuel Marc Gerecht, who worked for the agency in the Middle East, labelled America's counter-terrorism effort in the Arab world "a myth". An active spy describes coverage of Iran as "embarrassing" (America has not had an embassy there since 1979). A Bush adviser furiously says that "the White House has discovered more about *madrassas* [fundamentalist Islamic schools] in the papers during the past three months than we got from the intelligence system in the previous six years."

The sheer lack of American knowledge about some areas of the world has led to a form of poker game between its allies. For instance, European intelligence services that know the Arab world have been keen to balance information that Israel "spoonfeeds" to America. (All the spies, however, grudgingly admire Israel's masterly exposure of an Iranian-financed attempt to smuggle weapons to the Palestinians, which ensured Iran's insertion in the "axis of evil" speech and Mr Arafat's temporary excommunication by Mr Bush.)

There are "cultural" problems at home, too. America has no equivalent of MI5, Britain's domestic intelligence agency. The FBI is a law-enforcement agency: it looks for people breaking the law and arrests them. Intelligence-gathering is based on watching people, regardless of whether they break the law, and arresting them is often counter-productive.

Needless to say, there is not much love lost between the FBI and the CIA. Indeed, turf-consciousness spreads throughout the many domestic agencies that should play some part in intelligence-collection: witness the lousy sharing of information about the September 11th hijackers between the FBI, the Immigration and Naturalisation Service and local cops. The coordinating Office of Homeland Security has had little impact.

No James Bonds
Many spooks think the most important cultural barrier is a startlingly simple one: Americans do not like spying. There is no local equivalent of James Bond; in fiction, spies are mostly portrayed as right-wing lunatics or bungling fools. Americans are less interested in going overseas than other people are, and they stick out more when they do. Even during the CIA's mythical heyday during the cold war, nearly all its best agents were freedom- or cash-loving traitors who offered their services without prompting. And the agency has never been that good on the Islamic world.

More important, at home Americans value privacy more than most other people. They hate the security cameras that Europeans tolerate. They have opposed attempts to share knowledge about, say, suspicious movements of foreigners. One former CIA chief speculates that you could call September 11th "the failure of the ideology of the open society".

Some of these cultural shortcomings are now being addressed. Rules about recruiting dubious people have been relaxed. Some of the language gaps are being closed. The CIA alone has received more than 60,000 job applications. Many spies think that this will be enough.

That seems wrong in at least two fundamental ways. First, the current obsession with human intelligence downplays the importance of its technological equivalent. Here, though America unquestionably leads the world, a variety of technical problems still need to be fixed.

The NSA, for instance, has far too many old, incompatible computer systems, and finds it difficult to eavesdrop on fibre-optic cables. There is a row about whether the NRO should buy ever bigger, ever more expensive satellites, as the defence industry wants, or whether surveillance could be better achieved by smaller systems, not all of them space-based. At NIMA, there is the challenge of making imagery systems three-dimensional.

General William Odom, a former head of the NSA, says the intelligence community has received as much new technology as big companies like IBM, but has undergone none of the structural reforms of the sort seen in the private sector. The technical agencies are also struggling to deal with the huge amount of "open-source" information now available. At present, the technology often works best as a retrospective tool rather than a forward-looking one. After September 11th, all sorts of details were tracked down in America's digital vaults, but only once people knew the names to look for.

Telling the satellites and phone-taps where to look is also getting ever harder. Mr Gannon points back to 1998. Before the year began, he allocated the CIA's analytic resources to the priorities that had been established with the White House. In fact, more than 50% of the actual crises that year occurred in "lower-priority areas", and many of the biggest ones, such as the global financial crisis, the Kosovo war and India's nuclear test, were unanticipated.

Technology aside, the view that more manpower will make up the intelligence deficit is wrong for another reason. Structural problems often underlie the cultural ones. At the micro level, analysts are moved around too quickly. Mr Gerecht suggests that the best way to improve human intelligence rapidly would be to move spies out of the embassies. Above all, there is the question of who controls what. When the CIA's spy satellites missed India's nuclear test, this was surely because the satellites were run by generals interested in tanks.

The chief spook and his enemies
"Reforming" America's intelligence services is not simply a matter of getting better people and giving them more money and a slightly freer hand. The structure needs modernising from top to bottom.

Like anybody who has been copiously rewarded for doing bad work, America's intelligence services seem strangely caught between paranoia and arrogance. Staff at the CIA's Counter-Terrorist Centre joke that the only way they can spend the hundreds of millions of dollars they now have is to upgrade themselves on trips from business class to first class. Mr Tenet seems to have ridden the storm, and has even collected the odd plaudit for the spies' current work in Afghanistan.

His supporters point out that the former Senate intelligence staffer is more than just a political hack. His five-year reign has brought stability, and he has both the president's ear and political *nous* (he named the CIA's headquarters after Mr Bush's father). Moreover, Mr Tenet, who is said even by his detractors to be adept at covering his back, warned the Bush administration several times during the summer about the possibility of a bin Laden attack. Cynical spies point out that, had he been sacked, Mr Tenet might have contradicted the Bush administration's claim that it has always been more vigilant than its predecessor—something that does not seem to have been true before September 11th.

Recently, a commission chaired by Brent Scowcroft, a former national security adviser, came up with a proposal to put the three main technical agencies (NSA, NRO and NIMA) under Mr Tenet's control. The first reaction of the defence secretary, Donald Rumsfeld, was to squash this. It was not just a matter of turf-protection: military men point out that the vast majority of signals intercepts and imaging will always be for the Pentagon. On the other hand, the current system plainly puts the intelligence services second.

Few in Washington expect radicalism from the new joint congressional committee. Congressman Goss is a former CIA man; so is the staff director of the inquiry, who also used to work for Mr Tenet in his Senate committee days. More generally, Senator Graham talks gloomily about intelligence reform running into an iron triangle of the executive agency, its departmental backer and outside interests.

The idea of a cumbersome bureaucracy limping on simply because nobody can face reforming it is depressingly unAmerican. The grounds for hope begin with some of the people involved. Messrs Graham and Goss are generally respected by their peers. Ask either man how he might redesign the intelligence system, if he had a free hand, and both come up with radical solutions. Others whisper that Mr Rumsfeld, who is known to be appalled by the chaos, might be willing to support dramatic reform providing there was a comprehensive plan. Even Mr Tenet has a vested interest in reform: at present, he risks a place in history as the captain who did not go down with his sinking ship.

Wholesale reform would be relatively easy to enforce. Most changes could be brought about by an executive order from the president. Mr Tenet also has far more room to be brutal: spies' jobs are theoretically less well protected than those of other bureaucrats.

Out of Langley

What should be done? Given the fact that nothing has really changed for 50 years, the list is long. Two big jobs, however, stick out. The first is that the intelligence community needs a proper chief executive—not another token tsar, but one with real budgetary power over the technical military agencies (and with far more power over who runs them). As a corollary, this new *über*-DCI should be taken out of Langley, and a separate person should run the CIA. One reason why reform has always failed is that it has usually been seen in the Defence Department as a power-grab by the CIA.

One difficult question is how much of the actual analysis needs to be centred around this new DCI. Some duplication is inevitable—every general wants to have his own intelligence analysis. And the sheer number of agencies may be less of a problem than the fact that most of them act as vertical "stovepipes"—an insane idea for a community that is supposed to be collecting information. Congress should be less interested in how much money is being spent at NIMA than in how much is being spent fighting bioterrorism.

The other priority is to break down the artificial barrier between intelligence-gathering at home and abroad. Any thought of increased surveillance at home will annoy Americans and increase their worries about civil liberties. That is why it will need political bravery from Mr Bush. But September 11th illustrated the shortcomings of a 50-year-old intelligence system. Senator Graham argues that it is basic Darwinism: "If you don't understand changes in your habitat, you will die."

UNIT 10
The Future of Homeland Security

Unit Selections

37. **The State of Homeland Security**, Alex Salkever
38. **Government, Business, and the Response to Terrorism**, Murray Weidenbaum
39. **Principles the Department of Homeland Security Must Follow for an Effective Transition**, Michael Scardaville
40. **Defusing Dangers to U.S. Security**, Harlan Ullman

Key Points to Consider

- Is America safer now than before September 11, 2001? Explain. How has security been improved?

- What effect has homeland security had on private enterprise? What are the economic ramifications of the increased need for security?

- What role does information technology play in the future of homeland security?

- What are the most important elements to consider when developing an effective policy framework to ensure future security?

 **Links: www.dushkin.com/online/**
These sites are annotated in the World Wide Web pages.

Homeland Security Act of 2002
   http://www.outsourcing-law.com/homeland_security_critical_infrastructures.htm

It seems premature to speculate about the future of the new Department of Homeland Security while the ink on the plans for the transition and the merger of the various agencies involved has yet to dry. With DHS still in its infancy, many questions about the future of the department remain unanswered. What we do know is that it faces a monumental challenge—to protect the United States from future terrorist attacks. How well it will be able to accomplish this task remains to be seen. The future of homeland security depends on three main factors: the relative success of the new Department of Homeland Security, future developments in international terrorism, and continued public support of homeland security policies.

The future of DHS depends on the ability of the new department to manage the transition. In what may be a multiyear process, Tom Ridge and his newly appointed undersecretaries must reform, restructure, and integrate 22 different agencies into a cohesive unit capable of protecting the homeland. Organizational cultures, past interagency rivalries, and turf wars with other government agencies must be overcome in order for DHS to be effective.

The success of DHS also depends on future developments in international terrorism. While the total number of international terrorist incidents declined significantly in 2002, largely due to a decrease in the number of oil pipeline bombings in Latin America, authorities are increasingly concerned about the use of weapons of mass destruction (WMD) by international terrorists. For the DHS, changes in international terrorism pose a two-fold problem. If terrorists choose to limit their activities and focus on attacks against U.S. resources abroad, political and economic support for domestic security may eventually wane. If terrorists manage to repeatedly attack targets in the United States, the competence and utility of the new department will soon be questioned.

Finally, the success of homeland security is dependent on public support. Since the attacks on 9/11, there has been a tremendous amount of support for homeland security policy. While some individuals have voiced concerns about specific actions taken by the Bush administration, most accept the fact that the administration's primary motive is to protect the American people. Most Americans trust the U.S. government to act in their best interest. History, however, teaches us that public trust in government can quickly erode. Watergate, the Church Committee hearings, and the Iran-Contra affair offer stark warnings to those who would abuse the public trust. Homeland security will only be successful if it has the support and trust of the American people.

The four articles in this unit examine the prospects for the future of homeland security. The first article focuses on the changes that have been made in homeland security since 9/11. It offers an assessment of ongoing efforts. The second article focuses on the role of private enterprise in homeland security. It argues that the government must take into consideration the long-term economic effects on businesses in the United States as it develops its plans for homeland defense. The third article addresses the difficult problem of transition. It suggests five basic principles that the new DHS should follow in accomplishing this complex task. Lastly, Harlan Ullman outlines major outstanding issues that the Bush administration must resolve in order to ensure the nation's security.

The State of Homeland Security

While observers are sharply divided over how much real progress is being made, the political will and technology now exists—and that's a huge improvement

On May 12, a simulated explosion in Seattle and the revelation of dangerous germ-warfare toxins in Chicago kicked off a $16 million exercise to test America's first responders and emergency personnel. Thousands of firefighters, police, hospital workers, and others from dozens of federal, state, and local agencies took part. Going under the code name TOPOFF2, the exercise was the largest of its kind to date. Officials hope lessons learned from the event will help all levels of government better understand how to deflect a terrorist attack using weapons of mass destruction.

Announced a week before it took place, TOPOFF2 has become a magnet for both criticism and praise of the vast efforts to shore up homeland security. The glass-half-empty crowd wondered why first responders were told well in advance not only that an exercise would occur but also about the nature of the danger they would face and even the precise location of the different parts of the exercise. The glass-half-full crowd noted that these types of government drills, which have rarely occurred in the past, are becoming a routine part of running the country.

The juxtaposition of those viewpoints reflects the state of homeland security some 18 months after the September 11, 2001, terrorist attacks on New York and Washington: The U.S. is somewhat safer than it was in those innocent days, but the quest for true security has only just begun.

LITTLE LEFT UNTOUCHED. The search for greater security certainly has had long tentacles. At some level it has reached into every nook and cranny of the U.S. Homeland security efforts have touched small-town water systems and big-time telecom companies, chemical plants in New Jersey, and nuclear reactors in North Carolina. This reaction to the World Trade Center attacks has also engendered the largest modern-era federal reorganization, a massive consolidation of various functions previously conducted by 169,000 employees in 22 separate federal agencies representing $37 billion in government funding into the newly formed Homeland Security Dept. headed by former Pennsylvania Governor Tom Ridge.

The push to shore up homeland security has spurred a dizzying array of research efforts into bioterrorism, chemical weapons, and transportation security, among others. Across broad industries, companies have added guards with guns and have plotted survival strategies in case of physical attack. Many companies have chosen to more widely disperse their employees to prevent the type of catastrophic business interruption Wall Street suffered after the Twin Towers fell.

And yet the questions remain: Is America safer now than before? And if so, has the improvement been commensurate with the level of effort and expenditures so far—including the U.S. invasion of Iraq? To a large degree, the answers depend in part on whom you talk to. Witness the diverging views of two expert observers—Kathleen Sarten and Steve Flynn.

SAFER PORT.   Sarten is the Seattle service port director for the Customs & Border Protection (CBP) bureau of the Homeland Security Dept. Her job prior to 9/11 was to chase narcotics traffickers, counterfitters, and software pirates who exploit the 100,000 or so tractor-trailer size shipping containers that pass through the Port of Seattle each month. Now, Sarten's job is all terrorism, all the time—"anything connected with anti-terrorism," she says.

> # A collaborative program with other governments allows U.S. Customs inspectors to examine loads coming in from other ports before the ships even set sail.

She sees Seattle as a far safer port today. Within the past year, Sarten say she has gotten enough funding—she won't say how much—to double the number of staff dedicated to seaport cargo processing and maritime security over the last year. Seattle has also received its own VACIS (Vehicle & Cargo Inspection System), one of 20 such devices ordered by U.S. Customs since September 11. This truck-mounted machine uses gamma rays to peer inside containers to help customs inspectors spot anomalies that might indicate dangerous cargo. A complete scan of a 40-foot container using a VACIS machine takes less than a minute.

As a result, Sarten's forces can scan suspect containers rather than having to fully unload and manually search them. And today, all of Sarten's inspectors have personal radioactivity-detection badges—portable Geiger counters that until recently only a few U.S. Customs officials had.

SOUNDS GOOD, UNTIL...   New procedures have also helped Customs do its jobs more efficiently. As of March, 2003, ships arriving at the Port of Seattle must forward a list of their cargo to customs inspectors no less than 24 hours before docking. And a collaborative program with other governments allows U.S. Customs inspectors to examine loads coming in from foreign ports before the ships even set sail.

Also in the works is a new program called Operation Safe Commerce, a cooperative effort between Customs inspectors and large shippers to computerize and automate the tracking of containers throughout a company's supply chain. The ports of Seattle and Tacoma have re-

quested $36.5 million for the project from the Transportation Safety Administration and have lined up 18 private-sector participants.

All of which sounds encouraging until you speak with Steve Flynn, a senior fellow at the Council on Foreign Relations and former U.S. Coast Guard officer. Flynn remains far less sanguine about the prospect of protecting U.S. ports. While he appreciates the type of progress that Sarten claims, "most of what you have to date are unfunded mandates on the transportation industry," says Flynn. As for the government enforcement agencies, "you have very serious constraints on manpower, [info-tech] backbone, and things you need to maintain a serious presence."

OUTDATED SHIPS.   He also thinks Washington has been too parsimonious. While some money has been forthcoming, to date Congress and the Bush Administration haven't shown a huge interest in spending big bucks for transportation security, says Flynn. He points to a $1 billion bill floated by North Carolina Democratic Senator Fritz Hollings that lost by six votes. In the current Homeland Security budget, Flynn feels the increases have mainly covered ongoing operational costs and manpower with very little going toward capital improvements.

> # Critics of the nuclear industry say the Nuclear Regulatory Commission has failed to adequately police the sector, allowing lax security and avoiding any serious enforcement actions.

Take the U.S. Coast Guard. The White House significantly raised its budget to $3.5 billion in fiscal 2003. That included a $650 million request to upgrade the USCG's deepwater capabilities. However, Flynn points out that the Administration has stuck to a 30-year replacement cycle for the majority of the Coast Guard fleet. That means for the foreseeable future its seaborne interdiction capability will depend of outdated ships running older technology. In fact, observers are still trying to pick through the budget requests and the big consolidation at Homeland Security to discern whether some functions will actually receive less funding in 2004 than in 2003.

What also bothers Flynn is that some of the technology that could make it far easier for the U.S. to track ships is easily affordable. Equipping the 40,000 or so seagoing cargo vessels of significant size with a satellite beacon that would allow the U.S. or anyone else to track them anywhere on the globe would cost $1,500 per ship, he says. The total cost of equipping the world's fleet with the means to create a global seaborne traffic-control system would run less than $60 million in up-front costs with minimal upkeep. "That's chump change," says Flynn, who notes such a system could easily be international in nature and might improve safety for the global shipping trade.

REPEATING PATTERN. No doubt, it's easy to take either side of the argument, and both are correct in many respects. People inside the government often express a "can-do" attitude sorely lacking in the past. But at the same time detractors like Flynn question whether the priorities are correct, the progress is real, and the entire effort isn't paper-thin.

This pattern of raging optimism and gnawing skepticism appears across the homeland security spectrum. In matters of chemical-plant and storage security, critics claim that the chemical industry has resisted serious efforts to enforce more stringent security measures to safeguard the 15,000 facilities that hold what the Environmental Protection Agency considers to be dangerous substances. But EPA homeland security liason Robert Bostock points to legislation moving through Congress that would allow the EPA to levy $250,000 fines against plants that fail to meet safety standards.

Critics of the nuclear industry say the Nuclear Regulatory Commission has failed to adequately police the sector, allowing lax security and avoiding any serious enforcement actions. But Roy Zimmerman, NRC deputy director of nuclear regulatory research, says his agency is about to resume more stringent security-testing drills, also known as "force-on-force" drills, which pit inspection teams against plant guards in simulated combat designed to mimic terrorist assaults.

MIXED REVIEWS. The NRC is also in the process of updating its evaluations on how susceptible various plant structures are to airborne attacks or explosive devices. That's thanks to additional funding of $30 million, money the NRC could never have received in the pre 9/11 environment.

When it comes to the private sector, the reports are generally mixed. Telecoms have won accolades for sitting down together on the Network Reliability & Interoperability Council to lay out joint plans for weathering a terrorist attack. And many key infrastructure providers in the power, water, and utility sectors have put in place more guards, guns, and physical barriers to ward off attackers seeking low-hanging fruit.

At the same time, critics wonder why the airline industry, the recipient of so much federal largesse, refuses to match bags to individual passengers on domestic flights. This practice is mandatory in Europe and is considered by experts to be a key security provision.

And Flynn wonders why companies shipping goods across the globe at rates less than half what they were five years ago would resist small price increases levied by transportation companies. "To increase the cost of ship-

ping on a $120 pair of Nike's from 30 cents to 50 cents is not going to upset the free-market system," he says.

PRIVACY CONCERNS. Increasingly, though, homeland security initiatives have run afoul of civil libertarians. Screening procedures for immigration processes and air-travel passengers that involve deep background checks against large databases and, in the case of immigration, biometric identification, have raised particular ire. Critics say the powerful new databases add little to security since the authorities could easily have tracked the 9/11 terrorists with existing means but failed to do so for because of a stifling bureaucracy and poor police work.

> ## The Bush Administration has enhanced safety by boosting security staffing and taking basic but previously overlooked steps to ensure better coordination among agencies and between the private and public sectors.

"Efforts by federal agencies to incorporate computerized travel records into government dossiers have created an urgent need for comprehensive federal travel-data privacy legislation modeled on the data-privacy laws in Canada and Europe," says Edward Hasbrouck, author of a travel book series titled *The Practical Nomad* and a vocal critic of the Transportation Safety Administration's new iteration of the Computer Assisted Passenger Screening System, dubbed CAPPS II (see BW Online, 3/27/03, "Putting the Blinders Back on Big Brother"). Congress so far has expressed its own misgivings with the current balance between security and privacy by refusing to pass a new, more intrusive version of the U.S. Patriot Act, key parts of which are scheduled to expire in 2005.

Meantime, the hype over the ability of technology to improve homeland security continues to outrun its achievements. Most projects using truly advanced technology remain in the pilot phase—even though they offer insights into a new era when much of the drudge work that now depends on humans—and that suffers from human error—will be automated. At North Island Naval Air Station in San Diego, the military has installed a computer-driven system from Atlanta company VistaScape that uses data culled from images grabbed by high-quality video cameras to create a virtual visual perimeter around ships.

JUST THE BEGINNING. This could ultimately replace sailors with binoculars scanning the horizon. Designed to prevent a repeat of the USS Cole attack where a small boat laden with explosives blew a hole in the side of a Navy destroyer anchored in Yemen, the VistaScape system can spot small craft as far as 4 kilometers out and relay their exact coordinates to officers on watch. "The software doesn't blink," claims Glenn McGonnigle, VistaScape's CEO.

Both critics and boosters of homeland security efforts to date agree that the journey toward better security is just beginning. Seattle's Sarten recalls a conversation she had recently with a Chinese shipping official. He explained that in many parts of the Middle Kingdom, the first stage of logistics involves bringing products to a small truck on a horse-drawn cart. That small truck is driven to meet a small train. The small train is then moved to meet a larger train carrying standard containers that, finally, make it onto the ship.

Sarten's point? Even if U.S. inspectors look at the final step of the delivery process, they'll miss the previous four. "You can put a good seal on a bad cargo, and all that means is that you have put a good seal on something you don't want to allow into the U.S., anyway," she says.

SIMPLE STEPS. In other words, basic intelligence and legwork still remain the key factors driving enhanced security. "What has worked well is good old-fashioned police work. Investigating terrorist networks has resulted in arrests. Interdicting terrorist funding has worked. Rolling up terrorist networks, both at home and abroad, has made us all safe," says Bruce Schneier, a security expert and publisher of the *Crypto-Gram* cyber-security newsletter.

In that respect, despite big failings and perhaps a lack of vision, the Bush Administration has enhanced safety by boosting security staffing and taking basic but previously overlooked steps to ensure better coordination among agencies and between the private and public sectors. The TOPOFF2 exercise running the week of May 12 is an example of that. Sure, it's a bit of a cakewalk. But it'll help get homeland security responders and planners ready for more rigorous tests later. After all, getting in the right frame of mind is half the security battle.

By Alex Salkever, Technology editor for BusinessWeek Online

Government, Business, and the Response to
TERRORISM

"… The ongoing activities of international terrorist groups will continue to levy a hidden tax on American business in the form of added costs of operation."

BY MURRAY WEIDENBAUM

THE MULTIFACETED national response to the Sept. 11 terrorist attacks are altering the balance between the public and private sectors in the U.S. Threats to national security are always present. At the end of the Cold War in the late 1980s, defense planners knew that the nature of those threats were changing, particularly toward "unconventional" forms of warfare such as terrorism. Nevertheless, the rise of audacious international terrorism networks was not widely appreciated until the assaults on the Pentagon and the twin towers of the World Trade Center in lower Manhattan.

The struggle against international terrorism has become the mega priority among Federal government programs and activities. Issues closely related to terrorism have been elevated in terms of the attention and financial support given. International terrorism is an enduring phenomenon, and the issue is likely to remain an important spur to government activity.

The larger role for government is taking many forms: increased military spending, unprecedented emphasis on homeland security, special assistance to companies heavily affected, and a rapid expansion in the form and extent of government regulation of private activity, especially business. An impressive array of new or expanded government activities is designed to respond to terrorist threats.

The Office of Homeland Security has overall responsibility for developing government-wide policies on enhancing the nation's domestic safety. Operating responsibilities are assigned to a variety of departments and agencies, which deal with businesses on an individual basis.

Department of the Treasury. The first major antiterrorist action on the part of the Federal government in response to the Sept. 11 attack was a presidential executive order issued on Sept. 24, providing for a freeze on the bank accounts and other assets of specific terrorists and terrorist groups. The Department of the Treasury was given the basic assignment to carry out the order.

The impacts of the freeze on terrorists' funds were widespread, extending beyond banks to cover brokers, mutual funds, insurance companies, commodity traders, casinos, and money transferrers such as American Express and Western Union. The Treasury Department directed these private companies to do many things (at their own expense):

- To conduct more "due diligence" investigations of account holders, especially private banking clients, to make sure they were not terrorist groups

FEMA News photo by Andrea Booher

A health club in a building adjoining the World Trade Center shows the devastation wreaked on a number of nearby businesses by the Sept. 11 terrorists attack.

- To set up anti-money-laundering programs—or to expand their existing efforts—in order to prevent the conversion of illegal funds into legitimate financial accounts, with special focus to be given to private banking accounts, particularly those owned by foreign political figures
- To report "suspicious" activities to the Treasury Department
- To cease transactions with "shell banks" that have no physical presence in any country
- To gain more information about the foreign banks they do business with
- In the case of hedge funds, not to accept money from anonymous sources.

These new functions underscore the role of the Treasury Department as the second-largest law enforcement agency of the Federal government, after the Department of Justice. In addition to the activities of the Comptroller of the Currency and the Office of the Secretary of the Treasury, which are directly involved in dealing with financial institutions, the increased emphasis on antiterrorism work is expanding the role of the department's Bureau of Customs, which inspects goods coming into the U.S. from foreign sources.

Department of Transportation. The largest terrorist-induced expansion in civilian agencies is occurring in the Department of Transportation with the passage of the Aviation and Transportation Security Act of Nov. 19, 2001. That law established a new Transportation Security Agency and requires the Federal government to overhaul its security policies on all modes of transportation. With a target workforce exceeding 30,000, this new bureau has taken over from private companies the responsibility for examining baggage and dealing with security matters at airports and other modes of transportation. Previously, airport security was not a Federal responsibility, but shared between public airport authorities and commercial airlines.

Other parts of the Transportation Department are involved in the straggle against terrorism. The Federal Aviation Administration regulates various aspects of aircraft operations, including setting new standards for guarding pilots and their cockpits, as well as training crews to deal with terrorist incidents. The Coast Guard has a broad mandate to patrol and protect the nation's long coastlines. It is working with commercial fishermen who provide "eyes and ears" to report suspicious vessels or incidents. The fishermen participating in this effort are required to register and undergo reviews of their backgrounds.

Department of Justice. The Immigration and Naturalization Service is expanding, especially to provide more-intensive inspection of people trying to come into the U.S. and deal with those who overstay their legal entry period. The USA Patriot Act of Oct. 26, 2001, gives the Justice Department greater expanded powers of investigation and surveillance, including authority for nationwide search warrants as part of terrorism investigations. Under the act, the Federal government can seize voice mail pursuant to a Warrant and require consumer credit agencies to furnish information to Federal agencies for use in combating international terrorism.

The new far-reaching powers of the Department of Justice include collecting information on alien students from flight and language schools, as well as other vocational institutions. Committing an act of terrorism against a mass transit system also becomes a Federal crime. It is now illegal for people or groups to possess substances that can be used as biological or chemical weapons unless their purpose for holding them is "peaceful."

Department of Health and Human Services has been assigned a variety of health-related antiterrorist responsibilities. The Public Health Service is heavily involved in such matters as dealing with biological and chemical terrorist threats. Related concerns include protecting the nation's water supply and responding to threats of anthrax, smallpox, and other biological sources.

In early 2002, the Food and Drug Administration issued voluntary guidelines designed to help prevent terrorist attacks on the nation's food supply. Separate guidelines cover importers and domestic food producers, processors, and retailers. For example, the FDA urges the food industry to check job applicants against a Federal list of known criminals, as well as to establish procedures for checking suspicious liquids or powders found on imported food.

The Century 21 department store, located nearby to the World Trade Center, was severely damaged on Sept. 11. It reopened for business in March, 2002, signifying the area's rebirth.

Many other government agencies are involved in the struggle against international terrorism. Enhanced infrastructure protection involves a host of those that deal with various private companies. The Nuclear Regulatory Commission focuses on the security of nuclear power plants, while the Federal Energy Regulatory Commission has a broader charter covering power plants generally, transmission lines, and natural gas pipelines. The Federal Communications Commission has an important responsibility for the integrity of the nation's telecommunications systems. Following the anthrax episodes of late 2001, the Postal Service, especially via its corps of postal inspectors, is alert to terrorist threats involving the processing and delivery of the mail.

State and local governments are also involved in the heightened security arrangements. Virginia's Preparedness and Security Panel has developed a comprehensive program, including construction of an emergency operations headquarters, improved terrorism response training programs for emergency personnel, and increased physical security at bridges and ports. To provide comprehensive security at the 2002 Winter Olympics held in Salt Lake City, approximately 60 Federal, state, and local agencies were involved. The Super Bowl and Olympics

fell under a new Federal government category of "National Security Special Events."

The private enterprise system, too, plays an important and varied role in the fight against terrorism. The first task of business in the straggle against terrorism is helping to cut off the money flows to terrorists. Numerous banks and other financial institutions are involved in a great many nations. The flow of money is vital to international terrorist groups, but they use relatively small amounts. The 1993 bombing of the World Trade Center killed six people and injured more than 1,000 others. The cost to the conspirators, however, has been estimated at less than $50,000 in bomb materials and other expenses. Estimates of the cost to the terrorists of the far-more-deadly Sept. 11 attacks range up to $2,000,000, compared to the tens of billions of damage they inflicted. Thus, the effort to curtail the flow of funds to terrorists and to inhibit their use of the money is akin to the proverbial search for a needle in a haystack. The global financial "haystack" is especially daunting, with more than one trillion dollars crossing borders each day.

The antilaundering and related antiterrorism efforts of financial institutions, although difficult to estimate in terms of additional expenses incurred, surely increase the overhead costs of these businesses. To the extent that they inconvenience their legitimate customers in the process, the new procedures may also reduce the amount of business they transact. More than banks are involved. The antiterrorist regulations extend to many other types of financial intermediaries, including brokerage firms, mutual funds, casinos, and wire transfer services.

Although the Federal government sets the basic policies on screening transfers at border crossings and airports, and determines many other internal security matters, on a day-today basis, the public interacts in large measure with corporate security people or otherwise encounters the security policies of businesses. Thus, private enterprises such as airlines, railroads, and private building managements increasingly screen customers, visitors, and their vehicles. Private employers more frequently do background reviews on new hires, while mall and other deliveries to private establishments are checked more carefully than prior to Sept. 11.

Business primarily designs and produces the antiterrorist equipment and systems used by the public and private sectors. This market is hardly stagnant these days. The demand for bomb-sniffing dogs is increasing dramatically. A man-and-dog team costs $100-250 an hour, with a typical daily minimum charge of $2,000. The desire for explosive-detecting gadgets is rising rapidly. Sales of gloves and other protective devices for people are booming, while guards and inspectors of all sorts are in demand, as are the metal detectors that they use. The construction of barriers to vehicles has become increasingly common, as is the use of identification cards and security keys and readers. The application of new technology is in high demand, notably stepped-up research and development and production of new electronic systems to locate and identify terrorists. Invariably, consultants with various specialties are heavily involved, especially those with experience relevant to terrorism and other forms of unconventional warfare.

In addition, business develops and produces the medicines and the related equipment used to respond to biological and chemical attacks. Unlike nuclear materials (which are almost all controlled by governments), chemical and biological agents are overwhelmingly in the possession of private industry. Thus, business bears the primary responsibility for devising ways to keep such material out of the hands of potential evildoers. Medicines to alleviate and vaccines to prevent such diseases as anthrax and smallpox have become an important category of health care budgets. A great variety of new items is being marketed. Current outlays and future budgets are rising for procurement of aircraft, bombs, missiles, ships, and related equipment, especially tracking and communications devices.

Business contributes in many indirect ways to the fight against terrorism. In its overseas activities, private enterprise helps bolster the economies of the nations who are America's allies in the struggle against terrorism. Many of those countries are poor and developing, and they are a fertile ground for recruitment of future terrorists. Their economic health as well as their national stability often depend in good measure on the income from exports.

At home, private enterprise contributes in many ways. Companies provide a variety of assistance to domestic victims of terrorism. Direct corporate financial contributions to them and their families have been substantial. Counseling services to employees are provided, especially in industries hit by terrorists or particularly subject to terrorist attacks. The most indirect role of business may be the most powerful—to maintain the flow of goods and services to consumers and, in the process, generate the jobs, incomes, and taxes that keep the economy moving ahead and the government adequately financed.

The role of economic policy is very different in these circumstances than in conventional wars. In previous conflicts, civilian spending had to be restrained in order to provide adequate resources for a military effort that quickly used up a great amount of them. Under current circumstances, though, the need is to maintain the strength of the national economy so it can support a long-term struggle against terrorism. There are few shortages of supplies for military operations. Most of the actual operations involve equipment already in the Pentagon's inventory or items that can readily be ordered for existing production lines. Thus, the main task of business is to continue "minding the store."

Perhaps, the most underappreciated role of business is the day-to-day interaction overseas with residents of other nations. In many foreign countries, more of the local people interact with American businesses than with U.S. government officials—either as employees of American companies or their suppliers, or as purchasers and users of U.S.-produced or designed products and services. The latter cover a wide terrain ranging from the food and refreshments marketed by well-known corporations such as McDonalds, Coca-Cola, and KFC to movies, music, and videos. A number of those doing business overseas are employers of local labor, and they often follow company standards that are higher than those prevailing in the country in which their factories are located.

Such a benign relationship is not always the case, however. Some products identified with the U.S. may violate prevailing local customs and mores. Local contractors and subcontractors of American firms do not always follow the highest standards in dealing with their employees. Business needs to be aware of the powerful, albeit indirect, impacts of its actions overseas, particularly in the vital worldwide battle for hearts and minds.

The negative side

From the viewpoint of the individual enterprise, heightened security measures are basically an expense. A bigger outlay for those overhead items raises the cost of production. For the economy as a whole, this means, in general, producing the same output with more input, which results in a decline in productivity and is a downward force on the national standard of living. These new costs include security services, personnel investigations, protective equipment, higher insurance premiums, more inventory to protect against delays in delivery, and the acquisition of teleconferencing equipment and services to replace travel.

Simultaneously, a slowdown in globalization is occurring, notably a review of international supply chains with a view toward their curtailment. There is also greater reluctance to travel by air, especially abroad. Fewer Americans want to work overseas, particularly in countries where terrorism is a major threat. Thus, the outlook is for reduced investments in developing nations due to higher perceived risks and increased costs of exports and imports due to delays resulting from heightened border security. In effect, terrorism has imposed a new tax on international business.

The continuing struggle against international terrorism, although it imposes significant costs on society in general and on business in particular, is a source of new or expanded market opportunities for some companies. The rise of terrorist threats influences business decision-making in other important ways, ranging from locational decisions and changes in procurement patterns to a far-more-fundamental shift in emphasis from enhancing productivity via new investments and toward controlling rapidly mounting overhead costs.

Many companies that have been producing for conventional markets are adapting their products to meet the rapidly rising demand for antiterrorist equipment. Thus, medical CAT scan technologies are being retooled into machines that scan luggage for explosives. Others find that their products are directly relevant to the new marketplace, notably traditional providers of security services.

Following the terrorist attacks of Sept. 11, many firms have altered the way they do business. The "second order" responses are far more important over the years. Domestically, some companies are decentralizing their operations to avoid excessive concentration of resources in one highly visible and vulnerable headquarters office. Specifically, several financial institutions that had centered their operations in or near the World Trade Center have been moving portions of their activities to nearby locations in Connecticut or New Jersey. Many individuals, in business and as consumers, are using the railroad with far-greater frequency than in the recent past, and phone calls and e-mail rather than conventional post office services. Overseas, some U.S. corporations are shifting activities from nations deemed to be unstable and thus risky locations for business to more-stable, albeit more-expensive, areas of operation.

The continuing concerns about future terrorist attacks are prompting companies to do more disaster planning.

For larger corporations, this often involves some form of "offsite" computer backup to supplement in-house records should they be destroyed. Some are developing contingency plans to deal with future terrorist attacks, particularly if they operate in a variety of countries.

The struggle against terrorism may be viewed as being waged on two fronts. The first is the most obvious: government forces, military and civilian, directly fight the terrorists and their networks. The second front is also vital, especially for a long struggle: to maintain—and utilize—the economic power of the U.S. The heart of that strength is the private enterprise system. (In World War II, it was called the Arsenal of Democracy.)

In time, business is likely to develop more-effective and less-costly ways of responding to the concerns generated by terrorist threats. Nevertheless, the ongoing activities of international terrorist groups will continue to levy a hidden tax on American business in the form of added costs of operation.

Murray Weidenbaum, Ecology Editor of USA Today, is the Mallinckrodt Distinguished University Professor, Washington University in St. Louis (Mo.).

From *USA Today* magazine (Society for the Advancement of Education), May 2002, pp. 26-28. © 2002 by the Society for the Advancement of Education.

PRINCIPLES THE DEPARTMENT OF HOMELAND SECURITY MUST FOLLOW FOR AN EFFECTIVE TRANSITION

MICHAEL SCARDAVILLE

On March 1, 2003, the recently established Department of Homeland Security (DHS) will begin to absorb the federal agencies currently responsible for the functions being transferred to the new department. The most difficult aspects of making the transition from a disorganized federal bureaucracy incapable of adequately defending the homeland to a streamlined and efficient program with a strategic focus will become evident in the coming months and years.

As Secretary of Homeland Security Tom Ridge begins this transition, a number of principles should be followed:

- **Develop** a multi-use culture for the DHS by building on the example of high-performing agencies that have successfully managed many diverse responsibilities.

- **Learn** from the best practices of the private sector to effect an efficient transition and promote maximum rationalization of redundant programs and processes.

- **Ensure** that traditional American civil liberties are advanced hand-in-hand with homeland security policies by empowering the Officer for Civil Rights and Civil Liberties and the Privacy Officer.

- **Begin** to rectify deficiencies in the Homeland Security Act of 2002,[1] beginning with restructuring the Border and Transportation Security Directorate and establishing an intelligence fusion center.

- **Provide** better assistance to state and local governments by creating a network of high-level regional offices and reforming the first responder grant program.

DEVELOPING A MULTI-USE CULTURE

The one challenge shared by all of the diverse agencies being transferred to the DHS is the need to balance security missions with non-security duties or concerns. Indeed, how the department would balance sometimes seemingly conflicting duties was a major focus of the congressional debate over whether or not to create it and continues to be an item of consideration today.

Fortunately, the DHS will include two federal agencies, the United States Coast Guard (USCG) and the Federal Emergency Management Agency (FEMA), that have excelled at meeting diverse needs in a cost-effective manner.[2] Secretary Ridge should promote the multi-mission focus of these agencies as a guiding ideology for the entire department.

At its core, a multi-use culture would develop programs to meet homeland security and non-homeland security challenges through shared resources and methods. In many incidents, such a flexible culture of operations will be a practical necessity as the cause—natural disaster, human error, or terrorist act—is not always immediately clear. In addition, this approach is also more cost-effective than the alternative of creating numerous, frequently redundant programs designed to respond to specific types of incidents.

FEMA and the Coast Guard offer clear examples of such a culture. FEMA's "all-hazards" approach to dealing with many different kinds of disasters has enabled it to develop strong relationships with the first-response community that has been central to its success. FEMA has recognized that local governments can afford only one set of first responders, so they must be equipped and trained to meet the variety of challenges they are likely to face. As a result, training programs and equipment are designed to work in many applications.

Similarly, the Coast Guard's focus on maritime operations has allowed it to develop tactics that are applicable to any situation that arises on America's waterways. To meet this challenge, the Coast Guard has focused on developing a program known as "Maritime Domain Awareness" that allows it to recognize what is occurring on America's waterways and quickly respond (usually within two hours). The process of surveillance, detection, classification, and interception is generally the same for each mission. Similarly, the assets used to observe, evaluate, and respond are typically the same.

A multiple-use approach to homeland security assets is the best strategy to enable the department to meet its important mission efficiently and effectively. Organizationally, such an approach also would be cost-effective. Thus, this is an issue not only of good governance, but also of practical necessity if the federal government is to interact efficiently with local agencies involved in its various missions.

LEARNING FROM THE PRIVATE SECTOR TO EFFECT AN EFFICIENT TRANSITION

The construction of the DHS is a merger on a nearly unprecedented scale: 22 federal agencies with approximately 177,000 employees will be brought together under new leadership. In addition, several entirely new offices have been created. Success, however, is by no means preordained. Fortunately, the experience of private-sector business mergers provides a model upon which a smooth, efficient, and cost-effective transition can be built.

Mergers that emphasize reducing redundancy and overlapping functions are more likely to achieve productivity gains and savings by emphasizing economies of scale. Many businesses are measurably successful, in budgetary and managerial terms, because of the sound principles they use to guide mergers and acquisitions.

One of the most important principles is maintaining an adaptable and versatile leadership that can make decisions with the shared goal of improving the effectiveness and efficiency of the ever-changing company.[3] This flexibility allows business leaders to make necessary adjustments to meet the needs of a consolidated, restructured, and larger company; it is especially significant in personnel practices, as the changing needs of the company can include a redefinition of job descriptions, new policies and procedures, and cultural and attitudinal adjustments for every employee. Upholding the important principle of flexible and versatile leadership helps ensure that the merger is a success and that the separate companies are combined smoothly into one.

Flexibility is also an important factor in determining the financial success of the merger. The consolidation process of companies involved in a merger presents a timely opportunity to reduce inefficiencies and achieve cost savings with a more streamlined process of doing business. Historically, business mergers can result in substantial administrative savings by eliminating redundant functions.[4]

Thus, the process of mergers and acquisitions in the business sector, when using sound guiding principles, presents ample scope for generating profit. Indeed, an estimated 34 percent of companies enjoy such profits as a result of a well-planned process.[5] The consulting firm of Booz Allen Hamilton has cited procurement savings of 3 percent to 25 percent.[6] If the consolidation of federal homeland security programs into the DHS achieves similar overhead savings with the President's proposed homeland security budget for FY 2004 of $36.2 billion,[7] this would mean budgetary savings in the hundreds of millions of dollars.

While cost reduction is not considered to be the sole goal of mergers and acquisitions, it is often the fortunate result of a flexible and well-managed business deal. The same is true of the creation of the Department of Homeland Security, which is intended to make the disjointed federal homeland security effort more effective. By bringing together federal programs and agencies from a myriad of departments, the creation of this new department is similar to a large-scale business merger. The consolidation effort will require flexibility and principled management decisions so that the federal government's many existing redundant functions can be coordinated and streamlined effectively.

ADVANCING CIVIL LIBERTIES AND SECURITY

The infusion of security practices into everyday domestic operations is relatively unprecedented in American history. For the nation's first century, two great oceans provided a degree of security from external threats, and while that has not been the case for decades, the mythology that America's foes will be fought overseas, not on U.S. soil, has lingered.

Homeland security policy necessarily challenges that illusion. The terrorist attacks on September 11, 2001, illustrated that vulnerabilities in domestic operations—whether simple aircraft boarding procedures or immigration and customs programs that emphasized economics and drug interdiction—present opportunities for America's enemies to attack. This new area of national security planning has rightfully led supporters and skeptics alike to question the effect that new policies will have on traditional American freedoms. In fact, both civil liberties and homeland security must be advanced together and in a mutually reinforcing manner.

To ensure that the privacy and civil liberties of all Americans are upheld with the increased level of security provided by the new department, the DHS will include two new positions: an Officer for Civil Rights and Civil Liberties and a Privacy Officer. The Officer for Civil

Rights and Civil Liberties will be responsible for reviewing and assessing all information claiming an abuse of civil rights, civil liberties, or racial and ethnic profiling by DHS employees or officials. Implicit in this role is the public communication and promotion of this office's functions and responsibilities, as well as readily available contact information for filing a claim. The Secretary of Homeland Security will be required to review this information and report annually to Congress on the implementation of this office and the funds used toward its goal, as well as details of all allegations of abuse and the response by the department.

The Privacy Officer will be responsible for assuring that all technologies used by the DHS uphold and do not erode the privacy protections relating to use, collection, and disclosure of personal information as granted in the Privacy Act of 1974. In this capacity, it will be vital that the Privacy Officer quickly forge close relationships with the Director of the Office for Science and Technology in the Directorate for Information Analysis and Infrastructure Protection as well as the Undersecretary for Science and Technology. Similarly, it will be crucial for this officer to be aware of technologies being developed by other members of the homeland security community that may have applications for the DHS, such as the Defense Advanced Research Projects Agency's Total Information Awareness program.[8] This officer will also be tasked with reviewing legislative and regulatory proposals involving the collection, use, and disclosure of personal information by the federal government. Additionally, the officer will assess the department's privacy rules and report annually to Congress on its activities, including reports of privacy violations.

The establishment of these positions is consistent with the DHS's fundamental responsibility to improve security while protecting the civil liberties of all Americans. As the DHS develops ways to prepare for and predict terrorist threats, it is also important that it not overreach and either infringe on civil liberties or lay the groundwork on which a future administration might restrict freedom.

Establishing offices to fulfill this responsibility is certainly a step in the right direction. While their oversight of such concerns seems appropriate at present, it must be flexible in the long term. The new department will be constantly researching and developing improved methods for homeland security, as technology continues to offer many solutions in this area. Such growth, however, will inevitably raise new concerns regarding privacy and civil liberties issues.[9] Therefore, these two positions must be adaptable for proper oversight of the DHS's expanding capabilities in the future.

Both the Officer for Civil Rights and Civil Liberties and the Privacy Officer should be individuals who are thoroughly experienced and familiar with these issues, particularly within the federal government. A candidate with a background in national security issues, intelligence practices, and national security, criminal, constitutional, and

privacy law would be well prepared to assess the true risk that is facing our country while also measuring it against the sensitive personal information that is needed to counter that risk. The delicate balance between increased security and upholding the civil liberties granted by the Constitution of the United States may indeed be one of the toughest challenges facing the new department, but it is also one of the most critical.

RECTIFYING THE DEFICIENCIES OF THE HOMELAND SECURITY ACT

From the day President Bush proposed the creation of the Department of Homeland Security, the reorganization was compared to the establishment of the Department of Defense (DOD) in 1947. Likewise, the Homeland Security Act of 2002 was frequently compared to the National Security Act of 1947.[10]

No commentator at the time could have known how true this analogy would be. Like the National Security Act, the Homeland Security Act failed to fully implement the vision behind it. For DOD, full reform did not come until 1986 with passage of the Goldwater-Nichols Act.[11] Similar reform will be necessary in the DHS and the rest of the federal bureaucracy involved with homeland security, although this time Congress will share responsibility with the President because of the significant reorganization authority the Act grants the executive.

The two most glaring shortcomings of the Homeland Security Act were failure to effect the dramatic reform of America's border security agencies and failure to establish an intelligence fusion center that would solve the communication failures that prevented unraveling al-Qaeda's plot before the September 11 attack. In recent weeks, the Bush Administration has offered two proposals to rectify these imperfections: restructuring of the Border and Transportation Security Directorate and establishment of the Terrorist Threat Integration Center (TTIC).

Restructuring America's Border Security Agencies

On January 30, 2003, Secretary of Homeland Security Tom Ridge announced a restructuring of the DHS's Border and Transportation Security Directorate. Ridge's proposal would take the elements of the Immigration and Naturalization Service (including the Border Patrol), the Customs Service, the Animal and Plant Health Inspection Service, and the Federal Protective Service and consolidate their functions into two new entities:[12]

- **The Bureau of Customs and Border Protection** would be responsible for securing points of entry into the United States and conducting physical inspections of people and conveyances at these points.

- **The Bureau of Immigration and Customs Enforcement**, on the other hand, would be responsible for enforcing customs and immigration laws within the United States and securing federal property.

This reform, although overdue, may face opposition from Congress, which fought hard to keep these functions separate in the Homeland Security Act. Congress transferred all of the federal government's critical border security functions to the DHS, but it did so in a fragmented fashion. The Homeland Security Act was written in a way that separated customs and immigration enforcement.[13] While placing both functions under one Undersecretary for Border and Transportation Security was a step in the right direction, it will do little to reduce redundancy at points of entry. Secretary Ridge's proposal would rectify this oversight.

Effective Information Sharing Through Intelligence Fusion

During his State of the Union Address, President Bush also announced the creation of a Terrorist Threat Integration Center to fuse and analyze terrorism-related information from all sources. The TTIC will report to the Director of Central Intelligence (DCI) and will consist of members of the DHS, the Federal Bureau of Investigation's Counterterrorism Division, the DCI's Counterterrorist Center, and the DOD.

Most important, the TTIC not only will have access to the full scope of intelligence and law enforcement information collected by the United States for analysis, but also will be responsible for ensuring that this information is shared with other agencies and state and local authorities. The center will be responsible for completing this mission through the use of shared databases and by maintaining an up-to-date database of known and suspected terrorists.

The findings of the joint inquiry of the Senate Select Committee on Intelligence and the House Permanent Select Committee on Intelligence into the September 11, 2001, terrorist attacks,[14] as well as other aspects of the investigation into 9/11 and the analysis and recommendations of nearly every report on homeland security since then, have all demonstrated the need for such a center. In the months and years before September 11, 2001, for example, two FBI offices and the CIA were conducting independent investigations related to the attacks, but none of these offices knew about the other's investigations; the names of the suspects being investigated were not even added to existing terrorist watch lists. Although legal impediments prevented the FBI and CIA from sharing this crucial information, the biggest obstacle was bureaucratic and human.

To deal effectively with this dangerous state of affairs, a solution that crosses agency lines and removes the human quotient from data transfers is necessary to ensure that all federal, state, and local entities with a counter-terrorism role have access to the information they need to prevent future attacks. To be successful, the TTIC must:

- **Include** access to and the ability to explore all government databases, including those maintained by the intelligence, regulatory, and law enforcement communities;
- **Integrate** the information found in those databases for use by individual analysts;
- **Make** automated independent judgments about that information; and
- **Allow** analysts to provide more complete and accurate warning.[15]

In addition, an intelligence fusion center is a better solution to the intelligence failures that preceded 9/11 than is the recommendation of some—including the Gilmore Commission, Senator Joseph Lieberman (D-CT), and others—that a new domestic intelligence agency be established. Such an agency would merely add another stovepiped agency to the collection of departments and offices that already do not adequately share information while also presenting serious challenges to American civil liberties.[16]

PROVIDING BETTER ASSISTANCE TO THE STATES

Creation of the Department of Homeland Security in no way reduces the crucial role of state and local government in providing homeland security. Local agencies are the most likely to respond first in a crisis.

For example, the approximately 17,000 state and local police departments may be the first to identify evidence of a possible terrorist threat. State and local health care communities will likely be the first to recognize the symptoms of a chemical or biological attack. Local fire, Emergency Medical Service (EMS), and police departments will nearly always arrive first at the scene of a terrorist attack. The September 11, 2001, attack on the Pentagon demonstrated this clearly: The local Arlington County fire department managed the response through the early days.

However, with the recent focus on federal efforts for the new DHS, many of the needs of state and local communities have been neglected.

Establishing a System of Regional Offices

Communication between local, state, and federal authorities is vital. The DHS will include an Office for State and Local Government Coordination (OSLGC) in the Office of the Secretary to coordinate DHS policy related to state and local programs, assess state and local resources, and manage communication between the DHS and these agencies. The department's authorizing bill, however, provides no guidance on how the OSLGC should conduct these responsibilities, and merely establishing an office in Washington that is required to answer calls from state and local officials would be insufficient. To be fully effective, the office must have a presence outside of Washington, where it can closely interact with governors and mayors.

The DHS will inherit a variety of field offices from many of the 22 federal agencies it is absorbing, which the President has proposed consolidating as part of his FY 2004 budget request.[17] Their functions would be bolstered by the appointment of a highly visible non-career appointee who would represent the DHS Secretary in a given geographic region and report to him through the Office of State and Local Government Coordination. This person should be the primary contact for officials in the region seeking advice or voicing concerns.

Similarly, regional liaison officers should be the primary link for transmitting federal objectives and priorities to states and localities. The regional liaison officer should supervise an operations center to communicate the federal response to a local incident in a coordinated, interagency manner.

The regional offices, however, should focus on managing the DHS's relationship with state and local governments and on providing them the resources they need. They should not have operational authority over the existing regional federal offices, which fulfill specific federal missions and should continue to answer to the appropriate undersecretary.

Reforming First Responder Grants

Well-prepared first responders at the state and local level are crucial to an effective homeland security policy because they will always be the first to arrive on the scene of an attack. In 2003, to provide for these crucial assets more effectively, President Bush offered his First Responder Initiative, which included a dramatic increase in federal grants from $300 million to $3.5 billion, and a proposal to consolidate all federal, homeland security-related grants to first responders into one program that would be managed by the Federal Emergency Management Agency and designed to meet the different needs of recipient states.

In his FY 2004 budget request, President Bush asked Congress for $3.5 billion in grants for the Department of Homeland Security to deliver to state and local responders. This was the same amount he had requested as part of his First Responder Initiative in FY 2003. However, when Congress passed the omnibus appropriations bill (H.J. Res. 2) on February 13, 2003, the $3.5 billion was divided between $2 billion for domestic preparedness and $1.5 billion to law enforcement as part of established but underperforming grants managed by the Department of Justice for traditional policing purposes.[18]

In addition, Congress micromanaged how half of the domestic preparedness funds could be spent instead of providing Secretary of Homeland Security Ridge the flexibility to meet the varying needs of America's states and cities. This rigidity will dramatically reduce the usefulness of the funds.

All federal grants designed to assist first responders in preparing for disasters—whether terrorist, natural, or man-made—should be consolidated into a single, flexible program in the Department of Homeland Security,[19] which should initially be funded at the President's requested level of $3.5 billion. The Secretary of Homeland Security should manage this consolidated grant program through the Office of State and Local Government Coordination, which will have the most direct interaction with the local governments that need support. Existing specialized domestic preparedness grants, whether under the DHS or another federal agency, should be eliminated.

The consolidated domestic preparedness grant program should provide assistance to first responders for planning, procuring equipment, training, and exercising. However, Congress should not micromanage how much the DHS can spend in each area. Instead, the OSLGC should be free to provide funds based on a state's needs.

In order to receive funds, states should be required to submit an application to the DHS that includes an all-hazards response plan featuring mutual assistance agreements among local communities and promotes interoperability of equipment and procedures. Funds should then be distributed through the state governors' offices consistent with such plans. The federal government should require that the majority of funds be transferred to the local level expeditiously. Finally, the grant level should be reassessed six months after the consolidation occurs, and annually afterwards, to ensure that the needs of America's first responders are being met.

CONCLUSION

The establishment of the Department of Homeland Security can dramatically improve domestic security in the United States. However, the efficiency of the transition from the previous sclerotic bureaucracy to the new department is crucial. Secretary Ridge should ensure that the department adopts a multi-use culture to balance its security and non-security missions, promote maximum consolidation as a best business practice, ensure that civil liberties and homeland security are advanced simultaneously, address the deficiencies of the Homeland Security Act of 2002, and take additional measures to assist state and local governments as effectively as possible.

NOTES

1. Public Law 107–296.
2. For more on the example provided by the USCG and FEMA, see Michael Scardaville, "Why a Multi-Use Approach Is Necessary to the Success of the DHS," Heritage Foundation *Backgrounder* No. 1571, July 18, 2002.
3. "Lessons from Master Acquirers: A CEO Roundtable on Making Mergers Succeed," *Harvard Business Review*, June 2000.
4. "Merger Integration: Delivering on the Promise," Booz Allen Hamilton, 2001.
5. "Making Acquisitions Work: Capturing Value After the Deal," Booz Allen Hamilton, 1999.
6. *Ibid.*
7. For details, see White House, "Securing the Homeland, Strengthening the Nation," February 2002, at *http://www.whitehouse.gov/omb/budget/fy2004/homeland.html.*
8. For more on this program, see Paul Rosenzweig and Michael Scardaville, "The Need to Protect Civil Liberties While Combating Terrorism: Legal Principles and the Total Information Awareness Program," Heritage Foundation *Legal Memorandum* No. 6, February 6, 2003.
9. For more on the principles that should be applied to these issues, see Paul Rosenzweig, "Principles for Safeguarding Civil Liberties in an Age of Terrorism," Heritage Foundation *Executive Memorandum* No. 854, January 31, 2003.
10. Public Law 80–253.
11. Public Law 99–433.
12. U.S. Department of Homeland Security, *Border Reorganization Fact Sheet*, January 30, 2003.
13. Public Law 107–296, Title 4, Subtitles B and D.
14. See, for example, the final report of the Joint Inquiry, at *www.fas.org/irp/congress/2002_rpt/findings.html.*
15. For a more complete discussion of how an intelligence fusion center should operate, see Larry M. Wortzel, Ph.D., "Creating an Intelligent Department of Homeland Security," Heritage Foundation *Executive Memorandum* No. 828, August 23, 2002.
16. For a more complete discussion of why a domestic intelligence agency is not a good policy prescription, see Larry M. Wortzel, Ph.D., "Americans Do Not Need a New Domestic Spy Agency to Improve Intelligence and Homeland Security," Heritage Foundation *Executive Memorandum* No. 848, January 10, 2003.
17. U.S. Department of Homeland Security, "Budget in Brief," p. 4, at *www.dhs.gov/interweb/assetlibrary/FY_2004_BUDGET_IN_BRIEF.pdf.*
18. David Muhlhausen, "How Congress Can Improve Its Financial Support for Law Enforcement," Heritage Foundation *Executive Memorandum* No. 827, August 12, 2002.
19. Programs to assist local law enforcement's prevention and investigative responsibilities, post-incident recovery programs, and other homeland security-related grants unrelated to first responders and domestic preparedness should remain separate from this consolidated grant program.

Michael Scardaville is Policy Analyst for Homeland Security in the Kathryn and Shelby Cullom Davis Institute for International Studies at The Heritage Foundation.

From *The Heritage Foundation Backgrounder*, February 28, 2003, pp. 1-8. © 2003 by The Heritage Foundation.

Defusing Dangers to U.S. Security

by Harlan Ullman

September 11 is a date that "changed America forever," or so goes conventional wisdom. In fact, the horror of that day really showed how the world had changed. The consequence was that the United States was no longer safe, secure, and insulated from the violence and terror that were commonplace around the world.

On that day, 19 men armed with box cutters and loyal to a cause, not a country, turned commercial airliners into flying bombs and in a matter of moments did far more physical, psychic, and economic damage to the United States than did the tens of thousands of Soviet nuclear weapons aimed at us during the Cold War.

Sadly, in the year and a half since, despite much rhetoric and breast-beating, the United States has still not faced up to the realities of this changed world. Indeed, it is very possible that the danger is the most serious the country has faced since the Civil War. Understanding how we arrived at this point is critical to seeing the way ahead and the means of defusing the dangers that threaten our security.

Every major war creates legacies, or pieces of "unfinished business," often with profound consequences. From World War I came fascism, communism, and World War II. From that war emerged the Cold War and the Gulf War in 1991. It is from them that five major pieces of business remain unfinished. Unless or until we deal with each, the safety of the United States is in grave jeopardy. President George W. Bush must confront these legacies, ironically inherited from the days when his father, George H.W. Bush, was president.

FREEDOM AND SECURITY

The first piece of unfinished business is the most serious. The attacks of September 11 were directed against the basic nature of American society—its openness, freedom, and complete accessibility. As security becomes more important, its needs inherently conflict with freedom. By exploiting that tension, those wishing this nation

harm can do fundamental damage even without killing a single American. It is the basis of our political system that is the target. How we deal with this potential weakness and vulnerability may prove the most difficult challenge the nation has faced since 1861.

The second piece is the inherent vulnerability to disruption of the U.S. infrastructure; that is, our networks for commerce, communications, banking, power, food, emergency services, and the rest of the sinews upon which our way of life depend. There are no means for protecting all or even much of this infrastructure for an extended period.

Third, the country's national security organization was designed for an era that no longer exists—the Cold War. The Commission on National Security Strategy/Twenty-first Century, cochaired by former Senators Gary Hart and Warren Rudman, called this structure "dysfunctional." The commission study, released in February 2001, predicted that a major terrorist attack, possibly with weapons of mass destruction, would occur within 25 years. Unfortunately, these events took place less than eight months later. Both senators went on to serve on another commission, reporting in October 2002 that America was "still unprepared… and still in danger."

Fourth, the chief danger to the United States emanates from the "crescent of crisis," the region bounded in the west by the Arab-Israeli-Palestinian conflict, extending through the Middle East and Persian Gulf to the Bay of Bengal and east to the Straits of Malacca. Egypt, Saudi Arabia, Iraq, Iran, India, Pakistan, and Indonesia are key states in which extremism abounds. Osama bin Laden and al Qaeda are the current enemies. However, as long as the causes that breed this extremism exist, then the United States will be at great risk.

The final piece of unfinished business is the need to construct a strategic framework to replace that of the Cold War. The United States has not yet been able to weave together NATO, the European Union, Russia, China, and other key states in some form of partnership or relationship to deal with these new dangers.

What Needs Updating

⊃ The attacks of September 11 were directed against the basic nature of American society—its openness, freedom, and complete accessibility.

⊃ The terrorist attacks revealed the inherent vulnerability of the U.S. infrastructure.

⊃ Our national security organization is designed for an era that no longer exists—the Cold War.

⊃ The chief danger to the United States emanates from the "crescent of crisis," stretching from Israel to Indonesia.

⊃ The most important piece of unfinished business is the need to reconstruct a strategic framework.

President Bush has defined the danger as terrorism and declared a global war against it, in the form of al Qaeda. But what motivates al Qaeda and bin Laden, arousing in his followers a commitment to die in the process? The answer is not unique to today: it is the basis for extremism, whether manifested in the Crusades or the extremist movements of the late nineteenth and twentieth centuries. The danger is the intent to foment political change by using terror.

Bin Laden has done that with ruthless cunning. Drawing on a psychotic interpretation of Islam, he believes Western and American infidels have violated holy Saudi soil by their presence. Seizing on Israel, bin Laden has added the plight of the Palestinians to his list of grievances. His aim is to achieve some form of fundamentalist Islamic regime throughout the crescent of crisis, buttressed with Saudi oil money and made powerful by Pakistan's nuclear weapons.

This scheme need not involve one large or several integrated states but rather a loose collection of countries with fundamentalist regimes all loyal to an extremist interpretation of Islam. Terror is the tactic and tool. Saudi Arabia and Pakistan are the long-term prizes, and the United States is the immediate target. Hence, attacks such as September 11 must be expected. Sadly, bin Laden and his followers discovered that the target in America, to use Bill Clinton's favorite phrase, "is the economy, stupid!" Disruption of our economy will be a principal aim.

WHAT CAN BE DONE?

As this goes to press, the United States may well be at war against Iraq. However odious Saddam Hussein may be, Iraq is incidental to the larger danger of extremism. Hence, another Gulf War will dilute our attention from the main event.

Here is what we must do to deal with the five pieces of unfinished business. The crucial test is that in the process of protecting ourselves, we do not do grave damage to our freedom. We need to work within the framework of the Constitution, our laws, and the fundamental constraints imposed by checks and balances. Only by reestablishing trust and confidence is that possible. This is not something that can be done through laws, campaign promises, or fancy slogans.

Three domestic deficits arising from this unfinished business must be corrected: deficits in the rationality of the political process, in our security structure, and in our ability to attract the best and brightest to public service.

To attack the first deficit, Congress and the executive branch must be able to function with little or no partisanship when it comes to defending and protecting the nation. This was the case during World War II and the Cold War. It is not today.

Congress should create a committee for national security and defense that directly relates with the president's National Security Council. This committee would have the authority to set policy for Congress in conjunction with the NSC, thereby removing many of the current bureaucratic logjams.

Next, the National Security Act of 1947 must be revised to restructure the country's organization in line with the twenty-first century—not the Cold War. The old structure is vertical, with responsibilities neatly divided among diplomacy (State Department), military force (Defense Department), intelligence (CIA), and other agencies. This was fine when there was a seemingly monolithic, single threat such as the Soviet Union.

Today, the dangers of terror and extremism are horizontal, cutting across many government agencies and branches. For example, law enforcement and intelligence are no longer separable when it comes to terror. The consular service, responsible for granting visas to foreign nationals, is as much the first line of defense as were U.S. forces stationed in Germany and Japan during the Cold War. The National Security Act does not recognize these realities.

DEFUSING EXTREMISM

The revised act should take into account homeland security and break down these bureaucratic barriers. One model is Great Britain, where MI-5 is responsible for domestic intelligence, MI-6 takes care of foreign intelligence, and Scotland Yard performs the principal law enforcement tasks. Given the extraordinary difficulty in establishing a new cabinet position for homeland security, changing the law will be harder. But if it is not done, we will never be secure.

Regarding personnel, tens if not hundreds of thousands will be needed as homeland security becomes a higher priority. Incentives are crucial. One means of attracting good people would be to expand the four military service academies to national security schools and double their enrollment. Not all graduates would have to serve on active duty, though they would have a period of mandatory government service in national security billets.

Without closing these domestic deficits, the nation cannot possibly hope to become safer or more secure. Internationally, the challenge is at least as great. To deal with the crescent of crisis, a new and expanded form of the Marshall Plan, which rebuilt Europe and Japan after World War II, is crucial. A newer version should focus on reducing or eliminating the causes of extremism, which vary greatly from state to state.

For example, until the Arab-Israeli Palestinian conflict is resolved, the roots of extremism will flourish. The only workable solution is extraordinarily difficult. We need some form of international force on the ground to keep the peace. It would have to start small, perhaps in Gaza or a tiny slice of the West Bank. However, unless such a force is put in place and underwritten with economic resources, there will never be peace.

In Pakistan, such a plan would have to cope with the poverty that forces thousands of youth to enter *madrassas* for food, clothing, and shelter. These schools, virulently anti-Western and anti-American, teach the most extreme forms of Islam.

Finally, a new strategic framework is essential. A starting point is preventing the use and spread of weapons of mass destruction, nuclear weapons in particular. The United States should convene a series of strategic stability talks among the known nuclear states (United States, United Kingdom, France, Russia, China, India, and Pakistan) and include Israel and North Korea. We need to ensure these weapons will never be used and reduce them to the lowest possible number. From this framework, other vital issues can be added and membership shaped accordingly.

September 11 and what it means will require a fundamental change in how the nation goes about protecting and defending itself. If we fail to face up to these challenges and complete these pieces of unfinished business, neither we nor our children will be safe and secure.

Harlan Ullman is a senior associate in the International Security Program at the Center for Strategic and International Studies in Washington, D.C.

Index

Index

Test Your Knowledge Form

We encourage you to photocopy and use this page as a tool to assess how the articles in *Annual Editions* expand on the information in your textbook. By reflecting on the articles you will gain enhanced text information. You can also access this useful form on a product's book support Web site at *http://www.dushkin.com/online/*.

NAME:

DATE:

TITLE AND NUMBER OF ARTICLE:

BRIEFLY STATE THE MAIN IDEA OF THIS ARTICLE:

LIST THREE IMPORTANT FACTS THAT THE AUTHOR USES TO SUPPORT THE MAIN IDEA:

WHAT INFORMATION OR IDEAS DISCUSSED IN THIS ARTICLE ARE ALSO DISCUSSED IN YOUR TEXTBOOK OR OTHER READINGS THAT YOU HAVE DONE? LIST THE TEXTBOOK CHAPTERS AND PAGE NUMBERS:

LIST ANY EXAMPLES OF BIAS OR FAULTY REASONING THAT YOU FOUND IN THE ARTICLE:

LIST ANY NEW TERMS/CONCEPTS THAT WERE DISCUSSED IN THE ARTICLE, AND WRITE A SHORT DEFINITION:

We Want Your Advice

ANNUAL EDITIONS revisions depend on two major opinion sources: one is our Advisory Board, listed in the front of this volume, which works with us in scanning the thousands of articles published in the public press each year; the other is you—the person actually using the book. Please help us and the users of the next edition by completing the prepaid article rating form on this page and returning it to us. Thank you for your help!

ANNUAL EDITIONS: Homeland Security 04/05

ARTICLE RATING FORM

Here is an opportunity for you to have direct input into the next revision of this volume.
We would like you to rate each of the articles listed below, using the following scale:

1. **Excellent: should definitely be retained**
2. **Above average: should probably be retained**
3. **Below average: should probably be deleted**
4. **Poor: should definitely be deleted**

Your ratings will play a vital part in the next revision.
Please mail this prepaid form to us as soon as possible.
Thanks for your help!

RATING	ARTICLE
	1. America the Vulnerable
	2. The Experiment Begins
	3. A Watchful Eye
	4. The State of Our Defense
	5. Organizing the War on Terrorism
	6. The Ultimate Turf War
	7. Requirements for a New Agency
	8. Homeland Security Funding Primer: Where We've Been, Where We're Headed
	9. The NRC: What Me Worry?
	10. Transportation Security Administration Faces Huge Challenges
	11. Total Information Awareness: Down, but Not Out
	12. Catastrophic Terrorism—Local Response to a National Threat
	13. Governing After September 11th: A New Normalcy
	14. Bush Meets With N.Y. Mayor and Promises More Aid for Cities
	15. States, Cities Step Up Security and Squabble Over Costs
	16. A Burnt-Orange Nation
	17. Man With a Plan
	18. All Citizens Now First Responders
	19. Community Policing and Terrorism
	20. Smallpox, Big Worries
	21. Managing the Response to a Major Terrorist Event
	22. Guarding Against Missiles
	23. Modernizing Homeland Security
	24. Aerospace Giants Repackage Military Technology for Home
	25. Waiting for Bioterror
	26. Nuclear Nightmares
	27. The Cyber-Terror Threat
	28. Agriculture Shock
	29. Civil Liberties and Homeland Security
	30. Homeland Security and the Lessons of Waco
	31. Fears Mount Over 'Total' Spy System
	32. Access Denied
	33. Heading in the Wrong Direction

RATING	ARTICLE
	34. Filling the Gaps in Security
	35. Can Sense-Making Keep Us Safe?
	36. Time for a Rethink
	37. The State of Homeland Security
	38. Government, Business, and the Response to Terrorism
	39. Principles the Department of Homeland Security Must Follow for an Effective Transition
	40. Defusing Dangers to U.S. Security

(Continued on next page)

ABOUT YOU

Name

Date

Are you a teacher? ☐   A student? ☐
Your school's name

Department

Address   City   State   Zip

School telephone #

YOUR COMMENTS ARE IMPORTANT TO US!

Please fill in the following information:
For which course did you use this book?

Did you use a text with this ANNUAL EDITION?   ☐ yes ☐ no
What was the title of the text?

What are your general reactions to the *Annual Editions* concept?

Have you read any pertinent articles recently that you think should be included in the next edition? Explain.

Are there any articles that you feel should be replaced in the next edition? Why?

Are there any World Wide Web sites that you feel should be included in the next edition? Please annotate.

May we contact you for editorial input?   ☐ yes ☐ no
May we quote your comments?   ☐ yes ☐ no